ALCOHOL AND DRUG ABUSE

BINGE EATING AND BINGE DRINKING

PSYCHOLOGICAL, SOCIAL AND MEDICAL IMPLICATIONS

ALCOHOL AND DRUG ABUSE

Additional books in this series can be found on Nova's website under the Series tab.

Additional e-books in this series can be found on Nova's website under the e-book tab.

ALCOHOL AND DRUG ABUSE

BINGE EATING AND BINGE DRINKING

PSYCHOLOGICAL, SOCIAL AND MEDICAL IMPLICATIONS

SIMON B. HARRIS
EDITOR

Copyright © 2013 by Nova Science Publishers, Inc.

All rights reserved. No part of this book may be reproduced, stored in a retrieval system or transmitted in any form or by any means: electronic, electrostatic, magnetic, tape, mechanical photocopying, recording or otherwise without the written permission of the Publisher.

For permission to use material from this book please contact us:
Telephone 631-231-7269; Fax 631-231-8175
Web Site: http://www.novapublishers.com

NOTICE TO THE READER

The Publisher has taken reasonable care in the preparation of this book, but makes no expressed or implied warranty of any kind and assumes no responsibility for any errors or omissions. No liability is assumed for incidental or consequential damages in connection with or arising out of information contained in this book. The Publisher shall not be liable for any special, consequential, or exemplary damages resulting, in whole or in part, from the readers' use of, or reliance upon, this material. Any parts of this book based on government reports are so indicated and copyright is claimed for those parts to the extent applicable to compilations of such works.

Independent verification should be sought for any data, advice or recommendations contained in this book. In addition, no responsibility is assumed by the publisher for any injury and/or damage to persons or property arising from any methods, products, instructions, ideas or otherwise contained in this publication.

This publication is designed to provide accurate and authoritative information with regard to the subject matter covered herein. It is sold with the clear understanding that the Publisher is not engaged in rendering legal or any other professional services. If legal or any other expert assistance is required, the services of a competent person should be sought. FROM A DECLARATION OF PARTICIPANTS JOINTLY ADOPTED BY A COMMITTEE OF THE AMERICAN BAR ASSOCIATION AND A COMMITTEE OF PUBLISHERS.

Additional color graphics may be available in the e-book version of this book.

Library of Congress Cataloging-in-Publication Data
Binge eating and binge drinking : psychological, social and medical implications / editor, Simon B. Harris.
       pages cm
  Includes index.
  ISBN: 978-1-62618-580-7 (hardcover)
 1. Compulsive eating. 2. Compulsive eating--Treatment. 3. Binge drinking. 4. Binge drinking--Treatment. I. Harris, Simon B., editor of compilation.
   RC552.C65B528 2013
   616.85'26--dc23
                                      2013010956

Published by Nova Science Publishers, Inc. † New York

Contents

Preface		vii
Chapter 1	Next Stop Dependence - Binge Drinking on the Road to Alcoholism: Preclinical Findings on Its Neurobiology from Rat Animal Models *Richard L. Bell, Kelle M. Franklin, Sheketha Hauser and Eric A. Engleman*	1
Chapter 2	Binge Eating Disorder: Causes, Cofactors and Complications *Summar Reslan, Karen K. Saules and Valentina Ivezaj*	61
Chapter 3	Understanding the High Co-Prevalence of Problematic Eating and Drinking *Kenny A. Karyadi, Ayca Coskunpinar, Andree Entezari, Conner Long and Melissa A. Cyders*	97
Chapter 4	Binge Drinking: A Neurocognitive Profile *Eduardo López-Caneda, Nayara Mota, Teresa Velasquez and Alberto Crego*	127
Chapter 5	Binge Eating Disorder: An Overview on Neural, Biological and Genetic Factors *Deniz Atalayer, Nerys M. Astbury and Christopher N. Ochner*	151
Chapter 6	Cultural Variations in the Pursuit of Attractiveness and Associated Harms *Carolyn M. Pearson, Tamika C. B. Zapolski, Cheri A. Levinson, Amanda Woods and Gregory T. Smith*	169
Chapter 7	Revision of the Measures to Detect Childhood Binge Eating Disorder and Other Related Disordered Eating *Ausiàs Cebolla, Conxa Perpiñá and Cristina Botella*	187
Chapter 8	Binge Drinking: Pathophysiological and Psychological Aspects *Tatjana Radosavljević and Danijela Vučević*	201

Chapter 9	Borderline Personality Disorder Mediates the Effect of Childhood Abuse on Substance Dependence *Jessica L. Combs, Leila Guller, Stacey B. Daughters, Gregory T. Smith and Carl Lejuez*	**217**
Index		**231**

PREFACE

In this book, the authors present current research in the study of the psychological, social and medical implications of binge eating and drinking. Topics discussed in this compilation include the preclinical findings on the neurobiology of binge drinking from rat animal models; the causes and co-factors of binge eating disorders; understanding the high co-prevalence of problematic eating and drinking; a neurocognitive profile of binge drinking; the neural, biological and genetic factors associated with binge eating disorders; cultural variations in the pursuit of attractiveness and associated harms; measures to detect childhood binge eating disorders; the pathophysiological and psychological aspects of binge drinking; and borderline personality disorder mediating the effect of childhood abuse on substance dependence.

Chapter 1 – Binge alcohol drinking continues to be a major public health concern worldwide. Thus, continued clinical and preclinical research is needed to understand the neurobiology of this behavior. Substantial progress has been made in defining binge drinking for clinical research. However, the definition of binge-like drinking for preclinical research is still evolving. It has been shown that binge drinkers often manifest many of the same cognitive and emotional deficits seen in individuals that have experienced multiple detoxifications. These findings suggest that neuroadaptations associated with cycles of high blood alcohol concentrations followed by a period of abstinence are common to both binge alcohol drinking and alcohol dependence. This supports a role for binge drinking in the initial stages of alcohol dependence when impulsive drinking and the positive reinforcing properties of alcohol predominate. Moreover, it coincides with clinical evidence that binge alcohol drinking is a developmental phenomenon occurring predominantly in adolescents and young adults. Here the authors present pre-clinical approaches to examine binge alcohol drinking using selectively bred rats. The selectively bred alcohol-preferring P and the high alcohol drinking HAD1 and HAD2 rat lines display behaviors that in many respects parallel that of humans with alcohol use disorders. This includes differences in binge-like alcohol drinking between peri-adolescent rats and their adult counterparts. Findings obtained from research with these rat lines support clinical findings that the mesocorticolimbic dopamine "reward" system is crucial in mediating binge-like drinking and alcohol use disorders in general. Similarly, this research indicates that activity of the glutamate, GABA, dopamine, serotonin, acetylcholine, and multiple peptide systems is crucial in mediating binge drinking, alcohol use disorders and addiction in general. It is clear that substantial progress has been made in understanding the neurobiology of these behaviors. However, the translation of these important findings into the clinical setting will require more research using models that bear some face validity with clinical populations. Towards this end, selectively bred rat lines, such as the P, HAD1 and HAD2 lines will continue to facilitate this endeavor.

Chapter 2 – Rates of obesity and overweight have been rising steadily for nearly three decades, and the associated psychosocial and medical complications are creating a public health crisis. Although obesity rates have no doubt been impacted by a host of environmental, behavioral, and genetic variables, a very important contributor has been Binge Eating Disorder (BED). BED is associated with myriad mental and physical health problems, many of which can be both causes and consequences of disordered eating behavior, resulting in a complex interplay of etiologic and associated features. In particular, a lifetime history of BED is associated with obesity in its most severe form, and BED is also highly comorbid with other documented mortality risk factors (e.g., tobacco use and alcohol abuse).

This chapter provides an overview of BED, with an emphasis on the authors' current understanding of the disorder. First, historical changes in the conceptualization of BED are covered, including the changes to the BED diagnosis in the Diagnostic and Statistical Manual of Mental Disorders (DSM-5). Next, the authors review BED's psychosocial cofactors (e.g., sex, ethnicity, body image) and comorbid conditions. Finally, they conclude by drawing parallels between BED, binge eating (BE), and addictive behavior, suggesting related directions for future research.

Chapter 3 – Prior studies have indicated a high prevalence of comorbidity between problematic levels of eating and drinking. This high co-prevalence has been partly attributed to the disinhibiting effects of alcohol on eating behaviors. Specifically, alcohol consumption has been shown to increase food intake by disinhibiting eating behaviors. Alternately, it is also possible that food and alcohol consumption might become associated through repeated pairings. Through these repeated pairings, food cues and food consumption might elicit alcohol cravings and subsequent alcohol use. Similarly, alcohol cues and alcohol consumption might elicit food cravings and subsequent food intake. Finally, other common factors might explain both eating and drinking behaviors. In particular, the tendency to cope with distress through food and alcohol consumption has been shown to increase the risk for problematic levels of eating and drinking. The current chapter will review evidence supporting and theories underlying these pathways in order to better understand the high co-prevalence of problematic eating and drinking.

Chapter 4 – Binge Drinking (BD) is a highlighted topic on current research, possibly due to its intrinsic integration of biological and social health concerning vulnerabilities. Especially prevalent during adolescence, a neurodevelopmental period marked by accentuated social relevance on decisions, BD has an underestimated financial, social and health cost. Described as the consumption of high quantity of alcohol in a short period of time, BD has shown to be related to differential brain activity and neuropsychological performance. Thus, there is growing scientific evidence reporting a wide range of neurocognitive impairments in adolescents and young people with a BD pattern, involving especially cognitive processes such as attention, executive functions, and learning and memory. However, the potential mid and long-term effects of BD remain unclear, so further studies should be conducted to elucidate the evolution of this neurocognitive profile, as well as to provide a more precise estimation of its reflection on the social functionality of binge drinkers. Therefore, the aim of the proposed chapter is to provide an updated scientific comprehension of BD neurocognitive profile, complemented by a discussion of some aspects related to it. Firstly, a definition and description of the binge drinking phenomena will be conducted. Secondly, it will be presented a review about neurodevelopment on adolescence and youth, period in which BD episodes are more common, followed by the principal outcomes about BD observed in animal studies. Then, a comprehension of neurostructural impact of BD, as well as a description of neurocognitive profile associated to BD will be offered, mentioning neurofunctional and neuropsychological consequences of this alcohol consumption pattern. Finally, future perspectives will be proposed, considering the evolution of BD neurocognitive profile and its related aspects.

Chapter 5 – Given the obesity epidemic and the comorbidity between obesity and binge eating disorder (BED), it is important to understand the pathophysiology of BED which causes significant distress for many overweight and obese individuals. BED has been traditionally viewed as a behavioral disorder and, as a result, its genetic and biological bases are not yet fully understood. As with most psychological disorders, both genetic and environmental factors are involved in the development of BED; however it is unclear how much they each contribute to its etiology. This chapter will review the current literature on the underlying genetic and biological factors of BED, as well as the neural mechanisms associate with the etiology of BED and binge-like eating by using evidence from both animal models and human studies. Evidence from heritability and its interaction with environment as well as hormonal and neural dysregulation involved in eating disorders will be presented to elucidate the possible predictors and diagnostic biomarkers that predispose an individual towards binge eating and BED.

Chapter 6 – The authors tested the following hypotheses concerning appearance standards in women from three different cultural groups (European American, African American, and Japanese): Women in each group (a) have appearance concerns related to their culture's specific standards of beauty; (b) invest more in pursuit of their culturally defined form of beauty; and (c) experience varying harms of different severity from pursuing culturally congruent forms of beauty. European American, African American, and Japanese women completed questionnaires measuring the importance, investment, and harms of pursuing thinness, straight hair, and tall appearance. Results from this study support the above hypotheses and suggest that women in different cultural groups tend to be exposed to different risks for harms as they pursue specific cultural markers of a positive appearance. These findings are important in the context of eating disorders and the growing influence of western culture.

Chapter 7 – Binge eating disorder (BED) is characterized by the presence of recurrent overeating episodes, accompanied by loss of control in a short period of time. BED may manifest itself differently in children than in adults. Recently, researchers have proposed provisional criteria for measuring BED in children, the most frequent of all eating disorders in obese children. Research has shown that children who report episodes of loss of control have more severe obesity and increased symptoms of depression and anxiety. Furthermore, these children have been found to have greater difficulties and need longer weight loss treatments than children who only have overeating episodes. In order to make a differential diagnosis and detect the early signs of binge eating disorder, and thus improve treatment, it is essential to have sensitive and psychometrically valid instruments. The aim of this chapter is to review the most useful psychological instruments for the detection of BED and its associated symptoms. The present review will include instruments that directly measure the presence of binge eating, such as the Questionnaire of eating and weight patterns, adolescent and parent version or the Children's binge eating disorder scale. It will also describe other instruments that measure traits or styles directly related to BED, such as emotional eating, restraint or diet, weight preoccupation, compensatory behaviors or risk factors. Finally, the latest research developed to treat BED will be reviewed, and future directions will be suggested.

Chapter 8 – Binging is a behavior with undesirable outcomes for drinkers and those around them. A debate over recent years has focused on how this harmful and potentially life threatening pattern of drinking should be defined and how many drinks make up a binge. From a clinician's stand-point, a binge refers to a pattern of drinking to intoxication, usually a solitary activity lasting up to several days and involving loss of control over consumption.

The National Institute of Alcohol Abuse and Alcoholism defines binge drinking episodes as consumption of five or more drinks (male) or four or more drinks (female) in the space of about 2 hours. However, this definition does not consider the amount of alcohol intake in one binge episode, nor the possibility that some individuals may go on several binges during the same day. Generally speaking, binge drinking implies "drinking too much too fast." Periods of binge drinking (several consecutive days, weeks or months) are typically followed by periods of abstinence or, in some cases, significantly lower levels of consumption.

Thus, the nature and severity of the problems that binge drinking causes depends on how frequently it occurs and over how long a period it is maintained. This pattern of drinking is extremely common, especially among young adults, and remains the leading cause of death among college-aged students in the US, with similar worldwide rates of problematic alcohol use across Europe, South America and Australia. Due to the physiological and psychological changes occurring in adolescence and youth, binge drinking may have lasting harmful consequences, including greater risk for the development of alcohol dependence. It is known that alcohol affects virtually every organ system in the body, and in high doses, can cause coma and death. Namely, in the brain it affects several neurotransmitter systems, including opiates, γ-aminobutyric acid (GABA), glutamate, serotonin and dopamine. Increased opiate levels help explain the euphoric effect of alcohol, while its effects on GABA cause anxiolytic and sedative effects. Additionally, binge drinking increases the risk of acute hemorrhagic and ischemic strokes by up to ten-fold.

It also leads to cardiovascular problems (atrial fibrillation, known as "holiday heart", sudden cardiac death, etc.). Repeated binge drinking can cause damage to the esophagus resulting in acute hemorrhage, gastritis, pancreatitis and myopathy. For pregnant women, binge drinking has been correlated with harm to the developing fetus, especially during the early stages of pregnancy. This pattern of drinking combined with smoking is responsible for a rise in oral cancer in men and women in their twenties and thirties. Additionally, it is feared that the increase in binge drinking among young women will lead to a significant increase in breast cancer in the next half century. It is well established that binge drinking causes a higher level of psychological morbidity, particularly anxiety and neurosis, than the same amount of alcohol consumed more steadily over a longer period. Interestingly, young binge drinkers are substantially more likely than non-binge drinkers to take illegal drugs.

Chapter 9 – To better understand the sequelae of childhood emotional, physical and sexual abuse, the authors provided the first test of a risk model in which borderline personality disorder (BPD) is differentiated from post-traumatic stress disorder (PTSD) in the mediation of the influence of childhood abuse on substance dependence. Among 311 adults in a substance abuse rehabilitation center, childhood abuse was associated with alcohol and cocaine dependence in adulthood and that relationship was significantly mediated by BPD but not PTSD. The additive influence of sexual abuse above physical and emotional abuse on alcohol and cocaine dependence was also mediated by BPD, and this relationship was significantly stronger than for experiencing non-sexual forms of abuse alone. Individuals with histories that include sexual abuse appear to be at increased risk for BPD and alcohol and cocaine dependence, even in a substance abuse population. Substance use dependence, including binge drinking is related to sexual trauma exposure in women.

In: Binge Eating and Binge Drinking
Editor: Simon B. Harris

ISBN: 978-1-62618-580-7
© 2013 Nova Science Publishers, Inc.

Chapter 1

NEXT STOP DEPENDENCE - BINGE DRINKING ON THE ROAD TO ALCOHOLISM: PRECLINICAL FINDINGS ON ITS NEUROBIOLOGY FROM RAT ANIMAL MODELS

Richard L. Bell[*], *Kelle M. Franklin, Sheketha Hauser and Eric A. Engleman*

Indiana University School of Medicine, Department of Psychiatry,
Institute of Psychiatric Research, Indianapolis, IN, US

ABSTRACT

Binge alcohol drinking continues to be a major public health concern worldwide. Thus, continued clinical and preclinical research is needed to understand the neurobiology of this behavior. Substantial progress has been made in defining binge drinking for clinical research. However, the definition of binge-like drinking for preclinical research is still evolving. It has been shown that binge drinkers often manifest many of the same cognitive and emotional deficits seen in individuals that have experienced multiple detoxifications. These findings suggest that neuroadaptations associated with cycles of high blood alcohol concentrations followed by a period of abstinence are common to both binge alcohol drinking and alcohol dependence. This supports a role for binge drinking in the initial stages of alcohol dependence when impulsive drinking and the positive reinforcing properties of alcohol predominate. Moreover, it coincides with clinical evidence that binge alcohol drinking is a developmental phenomenon occurring predominantly in adolescents and young adults. Here we present pre-clinical approaches to examine binge alcohol drinking using selectively bred rats. The selectively bred alcohol-preferring P and the high alcohol drinking HAD1 and HAD2 rat lines display behaviors that in many respects parallel that of humans with alcohol use disorders. This includes differences in binge-like alcohol

---

[*] Corresponding Author: Richard L. Bell, Ph.D., Associate Professor, Indiana University School of Medicine, Department of Psychiatry, Institute of Psychiatric Research, PR415, 791 Union Drive, Indianapolis, IN 46202, USA; TEL: 1-317-278-8407; FAX: 1-317-274-1365; e-mail: ribell@iupui.edu.

drinking between peri-adolescent rats and their adult counterparts. Findings obtained from research with these rat lines support clinical findings that the mesocorticolimbic dopamine "reward" system is crucial in mediating binge-like drinking and alcohol use disorders in general. Similarly, this research indicates that activity of the glutamate, GABA, dopamine, serotonin, acetylcholine, and multiple peptide systems is crucial in mediating binge drinking, alcohol use disorders and addiction in general. It is clear that substantial progress has been made in understanding the neurobiology of these behaviors. However, the translation of these important findings into the clinical setting will require more research using models that bear some face validity with clinical populations. Towards this end, selectively bred rat lines, such as the P, HAD1 and HAD2 lines will continue to facilitate this endeavor.

1. BACKGROUND ON CLINICAL RESEARCH

1.1. Prevalence and Impact of Alcohol Use Disorders on Society

Over half of adult Americans have a family history of alcoholism or alcohol (ethanol) abuse (Research Society on Alcoholism, 2009), although a smaller percentage of these individuals have this trait in multiple generations. Additionally, nearly half of all individuals meeting life-time diagnostic criteria for alcohol dependence do so by the age of 21, with this percentage increasing to approximately 65% by the age of 25 (Hingson et al., 2006). Previous estimates of the ratio of men to women who abuse alcohol have varied between 2:1 and 3:1 (Brienza and Stein, 2002), with this gender gap narrowing among youth and the elderly [Brienza and Stein, 2002; Nelson et al., 1998; Substance Abuse and Mental Health Services Administration (SAMHSA), 2012; Wilsnack et al., 1991). In the United States alone, the cost of alcoholism is at least $185 billion each year (e.g., Harwood et al., 2000), and the Centers for Disease Control and Prevention (CDC) ranks alcohol drinking as the third leading cause of preventable death (Mokdad et al., 2004). As one example, the mortality of women with substance use disorders is four times that of breast cancer (Blumenthal, 1997). Moreover, research indicates there is a causal relationship between alcohol use and at least 50 different medical conditions (Rehm et al., 2003; also see Reed et al., 1996 for a discussion on the role of genetics regarding this interaction).

Today's youth (Miller et al., 2001; Quine and Stephenson, 1990; Winters, 2001), whether they be men or women (Nelson et al., 1998; Kandel et al., 1997), are initiating alcohol use earlier and experiencing more alcohol-related problems than ever before (Bava and Tapert, 2010; Gore et al., 2011; Miller et al., 2007; Pitkanen et al., 2005). Approximately 80% of high school seniors in the United States have consumed alcohol and half of them initiated drinking before the eighth grade (Johnston et al., 1999). This is significant as early onset of alcohol use is a strong predictor of future alcohol dependence (Anthony and Petronis, 1995; Chou and Pickering, 1992; Grant and Dawson, 1997; Hawkins et al., 1997); although, in some populations, this effect is dependent upon the presence, vs. absence, of a conduct disorder (Rossow and Kuntsche, 2013; see also Capaldi et al., 2013). Moreover, adolescent onset of use is associated with a more rapid, compared with individuals who initiated use as adults, progression to dependence (Clark et al., 1998). In the United States, approximately 30% of high school seniors report binge drinking (Johnston et al., 1991, 1993), with more than 70% of college students reporting binge drinking during high school (Wechsler et al.,

2000). Therefore it is not surprising that, among college students, binge drinking is becoming more prevalent and is also a strong predictor of future alcohol-related problems in North America (Dawson et al., 2004; Johnston et al., 2008; Presley et al., 1994; Wechsler et al., 2000; White et al., 2006) and Europe (Kuntsche et al., 2004). It is estimated that greater than 1 out of 3 male college student engage in binge drinking in the United States and that a significant proportion of these consume at least 2 to 3 times the binge definition threshold (e.g., Wechsler et al., 2000; White et al., 2006). However, in some locales adolescent girls may actually engage in binge drinking more than adolescent boys (c.f., Plant and Plant, 2006). Regarding younger individuals, the seriousness of this problem is underscored by the fact that adolescents between 12 and 20 years of age drink 11 percent of all alcohol consumed in the United States, with more than 90 percent of it consumed in the form of binge drinking (NIAAA, 2012).

Pattern of drinking (e.g., social vs. binge vs. episodic vs. chronic) and total volume consumed are important characteristics for evaluating alcohol abuse and dependence as well as their antecedents and trajectory (Flory et al., 2004; Heather et al., 1993; Lancaster, 1994; Zucker, 1995). This characterization has led to the development of different typologies and/or drinking profiles for alcoholics (Babor et al., 1992; Cloninger, 1987; Conrod et al., 2000; Epstein et al., 1995; Lesch and Walter 1996; Moss et al., 2007; Prelipceanu and Mihailescu, 2005; Windle and Scheidt, 2004; Zucker, 1987). In addition, the pharmacological efficacy of some treatments for alcoholism appears to depend upon where an individual ranks within a particular typology (Cherpitel et al., 2004; Epstein et al., 1995; Dundon et al., 2004; Johnson et al., 2003). Therefore, age-of-onset and pattern of drinking have significant predictive validity for a life-time diagnosis of alcohol abuse or dependence and, in some cases, can predict the effectiveness of treatments targeting these disorders.

1.2. Alcohol Abuse, Dependence and the Addiction Process

In general, alcohol dependence is a chronic, progressive, relapsing disorder that advances in stages from experimentation to dependence (Heilig and Egli, 2006; Jupp and Lawrence, 2010; Koob, 2009; Koob and LeMoal, 2008; Koob and Volkow, 2010; Spanagel, 2009; Volkow and Li, 2005). Alcohol dependence progresses from rewarding, euphoric and positive-reinforcement aspects of alcohol intake, in the early stages, to the dysphoric and negative-reinforcement aspects that drive dependence in its later stages. Alcohol is positively reinforcing by producing a euphoria/high or a perceived positive sense of well-being (e.g., increases in perceived confidence). Alcohol is negatively reinforcing by removing dysphoria (e.g., anxiety) or a negative sense of well-being (e.g., hangover and physiological withdrawal). Once dependence is acquired, alcohol's negative-reinforcement aspects tend to overshadow alcohol's positive-reinforcement aspects. Progression from experimentation to dependence is not linear in nature, with individuals often returning to earlier stages of the disease process before advancing to the final stages of dependence. Similarly, as a chronic disorder, alcoholism is often associated with multiple detoxifications, periods of abstinence and subsequent relapse. Regarding this, many of the emotional (e.g., impaired processing of perceived facial expressions and anxiety), physiological [e.g., altered hypothalamic-pituitary-adrenal (HPA) axis activity] and cognitive deficits (e.g., impaired response inhibition) seen in individuals that have experienced multiple detoxifications (Duka et al., 2002, 2003, 2004;

Sinha et al., 2011; Townshend and Duka, 2003) are also seen in individuals that engage in regular binge drinking or binge drug intake (e.g., Townshend and Duka, 2005), with preclinical studies supporting these findings as well (Zorrilla et al., 2001; see Stephens and Duka, 2008 for a discussion of both). It is noteworthy that a very recent study (Gierski et al., 2013) reported that nonalcoholic family history positive (FHP) for alcohol dependence individuals displayed greater impulsivity and lower executive function relative to nonalcoholic family history negative (FHN) for alcohol dependence controls. This suggests that these two characteristics, associated with binge alcohol drinking, may predate the development of alcohol abuse and dependence in some genetically predisposed individuals. Forensically, it has been hypothesized that the alcohol elimination rate of binge drinkers and alcoholics are approximately the same, with both eliminating alcohol at a higher rate than that of moderate drinkers (Jones, 2010). The latter point suggests metabolic tolerance is seen in both binge drinkers and alcoholics.

The roles of positive-reinforcement and negative-reinforcement also have been characterized in terms of impulsive and compulsive alcohol drinking. Essentially, impulsive drinking leads to binge drinking and intoxication, which in turn leads to compulsive drinking to mitigate physical and behavioral withdrawal from alcohol; and, in the absence of alcohol, there is a preoccupation with, and anticipation of, future alcohol consumption (Koob and Le Moal, 2008). Thus, impulsive drinking and positive reinforcement predominate in the early stages of alcohol dependence, whereas compulsive drinking and negative reinforcement predominate in later stages of alcohol dependence (Koob and Le Moal, 2006, 2008). These cycles are repeated and become more exaggerated over time, such that when these repeated cycles are coupled with the development of tolerance, alcohol intake increases and signs/symptoms of alcohol withdrawal worsen. This conceptualization allows for the hypothesis that the impulsive stage(s) of alcohol abuse is mediated, at least in part, by the ventral striatum [the nucleus accumbens (NAc)] and the compulsive stage(s) of alcohol dependence/addiction is mediated, again at least in part, by the dorsal striatum (the caudate-putamen). Both preclinical (c.f., Everitt et al., 2008; Robison and Nestler, 2011) and clinical (e.g., Rominger et al., 2012; Weerts et al., 2011; also see Andrews et al., 2011; Yau et al., 2012 on findings with family history positive for alcoholism subjects) evidence support alterations in the NAc and caudate-putamen during the development of alcohol dependence/addiction. Regarding binge drinking, this type of drinking is directly associated with alterations in NAc function (e.g., George et al., 2012; Lallemand et al., 2011; Szumlinski et al., 2007).

1.3. Towards a Clinical Definition of Binge Alcohol-Drinking

In an extensive discussion on binge drinking in Britain, Plant and Plant (2006; also see Marczinski et al., 2009 as well as Martinic and Measham, 2008) note that until the last decade-and-a-half binge drinking often was defined as what many clinicians and laypeople would call a "bender." Binge/bender in this context refers to the act of consuming high amounts of alcohol in a sustained manner for at least two days that results in intoxication, gross impairment and possibly unconsciousness (e.g., Cloninger, 1987; Newburn and Shiner, 2001; Schuckit, 1998; Wechsler and Austin, 1998). More recently in seminal reviews (e.g., Courtney and Polich, 2009; Marczinski et al., 2009; Martinic and Measham, 2008) the history and development of a definition for binge alcohol-drinking have been discussed at length. Some key points are that prior to Wechsler and colleague's (1995) definition of binge-drinking as 4 drinks in a row for women and 5 drinks in a row for men during the past 2 weeks, the definition for binge-drinking was greater than the "4/5 rule" (Wechsler et al., 1994). A similar definition defined binge drinking as greater than 10 drinks consumed during no more than 2 days per week (Kokavec and Crowe, 1999). By modifying the definition to 4/5 drinks at one time with time of inclusion extended to at least 90 days, significantly more respondents were identified as binge-drinkers than would have been identified using the "in the past 2 weeks" rule (Cranford et al., 2006; Vik et al., 2000). An early study that incorporated blood alcohol concentrations/levels (BACs, 0.08 or greater) suggested the 4/5 rule was too low and should be changed to a 5/6 rule (Lange and Voas, 2000). Wechsler and Nelson (2006) discuss and provide a cogent argument (initially in 2001) for the at least 4/5 drinks in a row in the past 2 weeks definition of binge drinking. Subsequent research included the role of periodicity, defined by "heavy episodic" or "frequent" vs. "infrequent bingers", as to how often the individual engaged in binge drinking (Clapp et al., 2003; Knight et al., 2002; Miller et al., 2007; Okoro et al., 2004). These findings as well as the work of Duka and colleagues (Townshend and Duka, 2002, 2005; Weissenborn and Duka, 2003), who developed the "Binge Drinking Score," highlight the importance of pattern of drinking in identifying binge drinking behavior.

Noteworthy is the point made by Townshend and Duka (2002) that the characterization of binge drinking should include a behavioral/physiological component beyond the mere act of drinking (e.g., intoxication/drunkenness). This may stem, in part, from the Prime Minister's Strategy Unit's classification of individuals who "drink to get drunk" as binge drinkers (Prime Minister's Strategy Unit, 2004). Given the variance in how an individual might define drunk, it is clear this definition has its own difficulties (Marczinski et al., 2009). Nevertheless, it does have merit as a conceptual definition of binge drinking because recent definitions of binge drinking involve levels of intake and BACs that result in intoxication for individuals without dependence upon alcohol.

1.4. National Institute on Alcohol Abuse and Alcoholism's Definition of Binge Drinking

In 2004, the National Institute on Alcohol Abuse and Alcoholism (NIAAA) proposed a standardized definition of alcohol binge drinking as "…a pattern of drinking alcohol that brings BAC to 0.08 gram percent or above. For the typical adult, this pattern corresponds to consuming five or more drinks (male) or four or more drinks (female) in about two hours" (page 3: NIAAA, 2004). Moreover, NIAAA sought to place the definition within the context of alcohol-drinking as a continuum with the following caveats (a) "Binge drinking is distinct from 'risky' drinking (reaching a peak BAC between .05 gram percent and .08 gram percent) and a 'bender' (2 or more days of sustained drinking)" and (b) "People with risk factors for the development of alcoholism have increased risk with any level of alcohol consumption even that below a 'risky' level" (page 3: NIAAA, 2004). In general, this definition of binge drinking, or its modification to reflect a similar amount of alcohol in a country's standard unit of measure (c.f., Marczinski et al., 2009; Plant and Plant, 2006 for discussion), has been accepted by the clinical community. However, the preclinical research community has lagged in developing a standardized definition of binge drinking, a point which we return to later.

1.5. Binge-Drinking As a Developmental Phenomenon

To the best of the authors' knowledge, all recent studies indicate that binge drinking behavior is engaged by adolescents and young adults more often and to a greater magnitude than older (>24 years old) adults (c.f., Courtney and Polich, 2009; Marczinski et al., 2009; Martinic and Measham, 2008; Plant and Plant, 2006). Possible early studies reporting contrary findings may have been influenced by the changing definition of binge drinking over time. The fact that binge alcohol drinking occurs mostly in adolescents and young adults (ages associated with high school and college) is undoubtedly due in part to the observation that, for some behavioral measures, younger subjects are less affected by alcohol than older individuals. Most of the literature evaluating this observation has been done in rodent models (see discussion by Spear, 2010), with some evidence from clinical observations supporting this contention. The most obvious observation is that adolescents tend to drink substantially more alcohol per occasion than their adult counterparts (NIAAA, 2012; SAMHSA, 2012) even though younger adolescents can achieve the same BACs as adults with fewer drinks (Donovan, 2009; NIAAA, 2012; SAMHSA, 2012). Regarding insensitivity to alcohol's effects, Rohsenow and colleagues (2012) examined college seniors, with a 1 to 4 year follow-up, and found that hangover insensitivity was significantly correlated with intoxication insensitivity and future alcohol problems, even after controlling for demographic variables. Another recent study (Gilman et al., 2012) has examined the effects of alcohol in heavy and light social drinkers although not all subjects were in the adolescent to young adult age range (light drinkers average age ~29, heavy drinkers average age ~25). The study examined individual subjective and objective, as measured by fMRI to emotional stimuli, responses while BACs were clamped (via controlled intravenous infusion of 6% alcohol) at 80 mg% (0.08 in clinical terms). These authors reported that not only do heavy, relative to light, drinking individuals have reduced sensitivity to alcohol's subjective effects, but they also display reduced activation of the NAc and Amyg to emotional stimuli, relative to light drinkers.

In addition, there is some evidence suggesting that young heavy drinkers, although not necessarily restricted to binge drinking, experience greater stimulation on the rising limb of the BAC-curve and experience lower sedation on the descending limb of the BAC-curve than young light drinkers (e.g., Holdstock et al., 2000; King et al., 2002). In a follow-up study, King and colleagues (2011) replicated their previous findings that young heavy drinkers (defined as weekly binge drinkers) experience greater stimulation and less sedation following alcohol consumption than young light drinkers. Moreover, these authors reported that greater stimulation and lower sedation predicted escalated binge drinking behavior during quarterly follow-ups, which occurred for 2 years. In turn, escalated binge drinking behavior predicted an increased likelihood of meeting diagnostic criteria for alcohol abuse and dependence (King et al., 2011). These findings parallel research indicating that FHP individuals experience greater stimulation on the ascending limb of the BAC-curve and less sedation on the descending limb of the BAC-curve and a greater propensity to abuse alcohol compared with family history negative (FHN) for alcoholism controls (e.g., Brunelle et al., 2004, 2007; Newlin and Thomson, 1990, 1999).

A recent study, indicated that, in alcohol-dependent individuals, a polymorphism of the mu-opioid receptor (OPRM1) is also directly associated with the hedonic (those experienced during the rising limb of the BAC curve), but not anhedonic, effects of alcohol (Ray et al., 2013). The difficulty with evaluating whether adolescent and young adult binge drinkers experience greater reward (e.g., stimulation) and less aversion (e.g., sedation) than light drinkers or older drinkers is that it is illegal to provide alcohol to individuals less than 21 years old in the United States. Another problem is the role that expectancies play in describing a subjective response and that younger individuals that engage in binge-like drinking report positive outcome expectancies from drinking to intoxication, such as increased peer affiliation as well as feelings of high, excitation, etc. (c.f., Duka et al., 1998; Marczinski et al., 2009; Martinic and Measham, 2008; Plant and Plant, 2006).

Unfortunately, the rubric of binge drinking includes drinking behaviors that could be considered "extreme" drinking (see also White et al., 2006), although the term "extreme drinking" has been associated with a conceptual definition of binge drinking as well (e.g., Martinic and Meashem, 2008).

A noteworthy example of extreme drinking would be the common, and often socially accepted, excessive drinking associated with an individual's 21st birthday, at least in the United States where the legal purchase of alcohol commences at age 21. The population most commonly associated with this type of drinking is the college population, such that approximately 80% of college students engage in this "rite-of-passage" with an estimated average of 13 drinks consumed resulting in BACs approaching or greater than 200 mg% (0.20 in clinical terms) (Neighbors et al., 2006; Rutledge et al., 2008). The present authors believe alcohol-drinking that results in BACs approaching 200 mg% and greater should be considered extreme drinking and clearly falls within the framework of the addiction cycle and escalation of intake.

These levels of intake undoubtedly result in the development of tolerance to alcohol-associated effects, which is a significant diagnostic criterion for alcohol abuse and dependence [*Diagnostic and Statistical Manual of Mental Disorders, Fourth Edition, text revision* (DSM-IV-TR: American Psychiatric Association (APA), 2000)].

As part of the addictive process, binge alcohol drinking (or binge drug intake) has been defined as an escalation in self-administration (c.f., Covington and Miczek, 2011) seen in the development of alcohol and/or drug abuse as well as dependence. This, to some degree, is supported by the BAC requirement (greater than 0.08 gram percent) found in NIAAA's definition of binge-drinking (NIAAA, 2004). There is preclinical evidence (e.g., Bell et al., 2000, 2001) indicating that alcohol-exposure approximating these BAC levels can induce tolerance to alcohol-induced motor impairment (i.e., ataxia).

As noted in the discussion on the addiction process, escalation of intake is associated with tolerance to effects induced by alcohol which, in turn, leads to abuse and dependence. However, as noted by (Ahmed, 2011), escalation in alcohol drinking, or the intake of substances of abuse, does not necessarily stem from the development of neuronal tolerance in humans. Although, it also should be noted that these other possible explanations for the development of tolerance in humans (Ahmed, 2011), such as social and economic factors, are not easily amenable to examination using animal models.

Table 1. Approximate parallel ages between the rat, associated developmental stage, and the human equivalent

Rat Ages [Post-Natal Days (PNDs)]							
1—7	8—21	21	22—27	28—42	43—60	61—75	76—90
Neonate	Prejuvenile	Weaning	Juvenile	Adolescent	Peri-Adolescent	Early Young Adult	Young Adult
-3 to 0 Months	0—6	6	7—12	13—18	18—21	21—24	25—28
Human Ages (Years)							

Nevertheless, animal models have been used to evaluate the effects of alcohol, as well as drugs of abuse, exposure on a subject's behavior and neurobiology with an emphasis on the adolescent and young adult stages of development (see Table 1 for a comparison of rat and human ages; for reviews of peri-adolescent animal models examining alcohol and drug abuse see Adriani and Laviola, 2004; Andersen, 2003; Chambers et al., 2003; Smith, 2003; Spear, 2000, 2004a, 2004b, 2007, 2010; Spear and Varlinskaya, 2006; Witt, 1994, 2006, 2010; also see Cudd, 2005 for a discussion of early post-natal development as the third trimester equivalent in humans).

2. BACKGROUND ON PRECLINICAL RESEARCH

2.1. Peri-Adolescent Stages of Development in the Rat

When discussing developmental stages it must be kept in mind that there are individual differences regardless of the species examined. Therefore, the concept of "early bloomers" and "late bloomers" should not be restricted to the context of humans alone. In important reviews, Spear (2000, 2007; Spear and Brake, 1983) has indicated that the boundaries of the adolescent window of neurobehavioral development for rats often differ given the parameters (e.g., behavioral vs. neurochemical) examined. Nonetheless, neurochemical and neurobehavioral differences from post weanling through adulthood support a hypothesized adolescent developmental window of postnatal days (PNDs) 28 to 42 (Spear, 2000, 2007; Spear and Brake, 1983). When assessing the effects of pharmacological pretreatment, during adolescence, on adult behaviors in male and female rats, Spear (2000, 2004a, 2007) has suggested that this conservative window (PNDs 28 to 42) could be extended to PND 60. This extended window allows one to examine the earliest adolescent/pubertal changes in the female rat as well as the latest adolescent/pubertal changes in the male rat. As a caveat, the focus of this review will be on rat animal models because an examination of mouse animal models is beyond the scope of this chapter (c.f., Bennett et al., 2006; Crabbe, 2008, 2012; Crabbe et al., 2006, 2010a, 2010b, 2011, 2013; Ehlers et al., 2010; Milner and Buck, 2010).

These windows of development correspond with adolescent (a) changes in glutamatergic *N*-methyl-D-aspartate (NMDA) receptor binding of the prefrontal cortex (Insel et al., 1990); (b) decreased excitatory synaptic transmission in the NAc relative to juveniles (Kasanetz and Manzoni, 2009); (c) changes in central gamma-amino-butyric acid-A (GABA-A) receptor subunit levels and GABAergic activity (Hedner et al., 1984; Yu et al., 2006); (d) changes in GABAergic interneurons of the medial prefrontal cortex, during early peri-adolescence, and dopaminergic projections, as well as their modification by serotonin, to these interneurons during the peri-adolescent window (Benes et al., 2000); (e) modulation of early adolescent hyperactivity of central dopaminergic, noradrenergic and serotonergic systems by sex hormones (Knoll et al., 2000); (f) changes in accumbal dopaminergic activity (Philpot and Kirstein, 2004, also see Spear and Varlinskaya, 2006); (g) changes in central (primarily within later maturing regions such as the frontal cortex) serotonergic, dopaminergic, and noradrenergic transporter densities, which appear to be related to level of innervation (Moll et al., 2000); (h) changes in central cholinergic systems (Won et al., 2001); (i) greater cerebral metabolic activity relative to adults (Chugani et al., 1987; Spear 2000, 2007; Tyler and van Harreveld, 1942); (j) synaptic pruning/remodeling of subcortical regions, in early peri-adolescence, and cortical regions, in later peri-adolescence (Casey et al., 2000; Dumas, 2004; Schochet et al., 2008; Trommer et al., 1996); (k) timing of the growth spurt (Kennedy, 1967; Spear, 2000); (l) timing of emergence from the protected nest in the wild (Galef, 1981); and (m) maturation of genitalia in female (Döhler and Wuttke, 1975) and male (Clermont and Perry, 1957) rats. Neurogenesis is age-dependent (e.g., He and Crews, 2007), and male as well as female gonadal hormones can facilitate or interfere with certain stages of neurogenesis (c.f., Galea, 2008). Thus, it is important to remember that more gonadal hormones, as seen during peri-adolescence, is not necessarily better with level of gonadal hormones exerting an inverted U-shaped effect on neurogenesis (c.f., Galea, 2008; also see Nixon et al., 2010 for a discussion about neurogenesis and adolescent vulnerability to develop alcohol abuse and dependence). For discussions on possible roles for central glutamatergic and GABAergic activity in the development of adolescent alcohol abuse and the vulnerability to develop alcohol dependence see reviews by Chin and colleagues (2010), Ehlers and Criado (2010), Guerri and Pascual (2010; also Pascual et al., 2009), as well as Nixon and colleagues (2010). For a discussion of the mesocorticolimbic DA system and its alteration by adolescent alcohol exposure see a review by Maldonado-Devincci and colleagues (2010). For a discussion of genetic markers for a predisposition towards adolescent alcohol abuse and dependence see a review by Schwandt and colleagues (2010).

2.2. A Primer on Neurotransmitters and Neuromodulators Mediating Alcohol Abuse and Dependence

Several neurochemical systems are activated by exposure to rewarding stimuli. And, many of these neurotransmitter systems operate within the brain's mesocorticolimbic DA system (described in the next section). Increased activation of these systems promotes behaviors aimed at repeating prior hedonic/positive experiences. This activation of the mesocorticolimbic DA system reinforces behaviors that are necessary for an individual's survival, such as the procurement and ingestion of food and water as well as procreation. Evidence indicates that reinforcement from drug use as well as non-substance behavioral compulsions, such as binge eating and gambling, is processed by the same neurocircuitry that promotes behaviors oriented toward gaining natural rewards. However, these maladaptive behaviors are typified by a loss of control and escalation, reflective of dysregulations of these neural pathways. Repeated experience with alcohol and drugs of abuse leads to compensatory neuroadaptations, the brain's efforts to maintain homeostasis, that result in dampened reward and increased negative reinforcement processes which motivate addiction-related behaviors (see the previous section on the addictive process). Alcohol, as a small (two carbon chain) molecule, has widespread neurobiological effects. It is due to this diverse action, and the neuroadaptations associated with alcohol abuse and dependence that makes developing pharmacological treatments for these disorders difficult. Acute or repeated binge alcohol drinking alters the activity of a number of neurotransmitter and neuromodulatory systems, such as the glutamate, GABA, dopamine, serotonin, norepinephrine, acetylcholine, as well as peptides including the endogenous opioids, neuropeptide Y (NPY), corticotrophin releasing factor (CRF), and ghrelin.

2.2.1. Glutamate and GABA

The amino acid glutamate is the primary excitatory neurotransmitter in the central nervous system (CNS). It interacts with several receptor subtypes, including NMDA and Group I and II metabotropic glutamate receptors (mGluRs). Substantial evidence suggests that glutamatergic activity mediates natural reward as well as reward from drug and non-drug abuse through direct and indirect interactions with other neurotransmitter/neuromodulatory systems within the mesocorticolimbic DA system and associated brain regions (Carlezon and Wise, 1996, Grace et al., 2007, Kupila et al., 2012, Sun et al., 2008). One hypothesis that has received considerable attention is that sensitized mesocorticolimbic glutamate neurotransmission and the subsequent hypergluatmatergic state that it creates is a major contributor to alcohol abuse and dependence (Gass and Olive, 2008, Vengeliene et al., 2008). Regarding the addictive process, alcohol-associated positive and negative reinforcement are both mediated, in part, through glutamate neurotransmission (Kryger and Wilce, 2010). Pre-clinical evidence supports clinical findings that alcohol acutely inhibits, and chronically sensitizes and upregulates glutamate neurotransmission, in brain regions such as the NAc, mPFC, and CeA (Carlezon and Wise, 1996; Chandler et al., 1993; Ding et al., 2012a; Floyd et al., 2003; Gass and Olive, 2008; Kapasova and Szumlinski, 2008; Nevo and Hamon, 1995; Nie et al., 1993, 1994; Weitlauf and Woodward, 2008). The hyperglutamatergic state associated with alcohol abuse and dependence may be due, in part, to changes in glutamate clearance mechanisms (Ding et al., 2012b; Kapasova and Szumlinski, 2008; Parks et al., 2002; Sari et al., 2011; Smith, 1997; Smith and Zsigo, 1996; Thoma et al., 2011).

Changes in glutamatergic neurotransmission are also associated with binge alcohol drinking. Work with animal models of binge drinking indicate that binge-like exposure resulting in high BACs induces neuroadaptations in the glutamate system, including changes in glutamatergic-associated gene expression (Coleman et al., 2011; McBride et al., 2010) and alterations in downstream signaling cascades (Cozzoli et al., 2009), which result in enhanced glutamate neurotransmission and receptor activation in areas such as the mesocorticolimbic system (Li et al., 2010; Szumlinski et al., 2007). In support of these findings glutamate receptor antagonists such as acamprosate and MPEP reduce binge drinking dose-dependently (Grace et al., 2007; Gupta et al., 2008). Increases in excitatory neurotransmission may be greater during periods of acute ethanol withdrawal, such as those commonly associated with binge drinking, compared to more protracted withdrawal periods (Ward et al., 2009). Thus, it has been suggested that binge alcohol abuse could increase susceptibility to alcohol-induced excitotoxic brain damage, relative to on-going alcohol dependence (Hunt, 1993). Overall, it is likely that glutamatergic adaptations following repeated binge-drinking behavior leads to a glutamate-GABA functional imbalance (Enna, 1997; Fadda and Rossetti, 1998; Szumlinski et al., 2007), and are responsible, in part, for withdrawal symptomology. This withdrawal symptomology in turn increases the negative reinforcement-associated properties of continued binge drinking. These effects are consistent with a neural signaling-related transition from repeated binge alcohol drinking to dependence. Taken together, it is likely that glutamatergic adaptations contribute to the excitotoxic and oxidative events associated with the hyper-glutamatergic CNS state seen with chronic alcohol intake, as well as withdrawal anxiety. Moreover, these findings provide evidence that glutamate is involved in some of the cognitive and behavioral effects that promote alcohol drinking, as well as the escalation from the initial alcohol experience to binge drinking to dependence. As one neurochemical equilibrant to glutamate, GABA is the primary inhibitory neurotransmitter in the CNS. Several research groups have reported associated differences in GABA gene variants, expression levels, and activation in areas such as the mesocorticolimbic system and the extended amygdala (which includes substructures of the bed nucleus of the stria terminalis, amygdala and nucleus accumbens), with high alcohol-consuming phenotypes and risk for developing alcohol dependence in alcoholics as well as alcohol-preferring rats (Dick and Bierut, 2006; Enoch et al., 2012; Herman et al., 2012; Korpi and Sinkkonen, 2006; McBride et al., 2010; Tabakoff et al., 2009). Thus, differential GABA signaling could reflect one mechanism that predisposes individuals to consume alcohol. In addition, GABA receptor systems are functional modulators of the mesocorticolimbic system (Eiler and June, 2007; Melis et al., 2002; Rahman and McBride, 2002), supporting the role of GABA in DA-associated responses to reward.

Acute alcohol experience potentiates GABA signaling and facilitates its hyperpolarizing actions (Koob, 2004). GABA-A and GABA-B receptors are involved in some of the rewarding, reinforcing, and motivational effects of alcohol consumption and alcohol binge drinking (Eiler and June, 2007; Nowaket al., 1998; Tanchuck et al., 2011; also see Agabio et al., 2012). Although the GABAergic mechanisms affecting binge alcohol drinking are not fully known, there is evidence for its involvement. For instance, binge alcohol drinking alters GABA gene expression in the whole brain of C57BL6/J mice (Coleman et al., 2011), as well as in the NAc and CeA of alcohol-preferring P rats (McBride et al., 2010). Also, selective reductions of the GABA-Aalpha1 subunit in the ventral pallidum and GABA-Aalpha2-regulated toll-like receptor 4 in the CeA were found to reduce DID-MSA (described later) binge alcohol drinking in alcohol-preferring P rats (Liu et al., 2011). In addition, the partial inverse GABA-A receptor agonist Ro15-4513 reduces alcohol binge drinking (using the DID model) when administered systemically or directly into the posterior VTA of C57Bl/6J mice (Melon and Boehm, 2011). It is possible that a GABA system impaired by binge alcohol drinking exacerbates binge drinking-induced excesses in glutamate activity. This may lead to a general state of behavioral and neural disinhibition. By extension, neural disinhibition may lead to deficits in cognition and impulse control. Given these reasoning skills are still maturing during adolescence, binge drinking during this critical stage of development may compromise attainment of this developmental milestone. For example, acute withdrawal from chronic binge-like alcohol drinking interferes with working memory due, in part, to changes in mPFC GABA neurotransmission (George et al., 2012). In addition, chronic binge-like drinking induces long-lasting changes in tonic GABA-A-regulated neurotransmission in the dentate gyrus and CA1 region of the hippocampus (Fleming et al., 2012), areas associated with learning and memory. In line with the above findings, some current and potential medications for the treatment of alcoholism concomitantly affect glutamate and GABA neurotransmission. For a review of glutamate and GABA-associated ligands tested in five of the selectively bred high alcohol-consuming (AA, HAD1, HAD2, P and sP) international rat lines and CNS disturbances of the glutamatergic and GABAergic systems in these rat lines see Bell et al. (2012b). For reviews on patented treatments for alcohol abuse and dependence that target the glutamatergic and GABAergic systems see Agabio et al. (2012), Barron et al. (2012), and Bell et al. (2012a). Together, these findings implicate a glutamate-GABA imbalance in binge and excessive alcohol drinking (De Witte, 2004). In addition, they suggest a strong role for these amino acids in the loss of control and cognitive deficits associated with escalated alcohol consumption from initial exposure to binge drinking to dependence.

2.2.2. Dopamine

Substantial evidence indicates dopamine (DA) plays a large role in the processing of reward, reinforcement, and motivation to obtain reinforcing stimuli. DA release is increased in several brain regions associated with reward and motivation following the ingestion of alcohol and other drugs of abuse, or when an individual engages in other addictive activities. This increased DA activity serves to promote further use of these addictive stimuli through positive reinforcement processes. However, following prolonged alcohol abuse or addictive behavior, individuals display tolerance to their DA-releasing properties, which promotes further addiction through negative reinforcement processes. In addition, individuals (humans or animals possessing the requisite genotype) with a predisposition to develop alcoholism may display a reduction in basal DA tone that makes alcohol-stimulated DA overflow more reinforcing. In line with this suggestion, alcohol-naïve rats bred for high alcohol consumption exhibit reduced NAc tissue DA levels, compared to outbred rats or their alcohol non-preferring counterparts (Engleman et al., 2006; McBride et al., 1993a; Murphy et al., 1982, 1987; Quintanilla et al., 2007; Smith and Weiss, 1999; Strother et al., 2005; also see Bell et al., 2012b for a review of this effect in five international rat lines selectively bred for this phenotype). A prevailing hypothesis for the role of DA in alcohol dependence is that alcohol is consumed to compensate for this reduced DAergic activity.

Considerable evidence supports the involvement of the mesocorticolimbic DA system in the rewarding and reinforcing effects of alcohol (e.g., Di Chiara and Imperato, 1988; Melendez et al., 2002; Palmer et al., 2003) as well as alcohol preference (McBride and Li, 1998). Pharmacologically relevant alcohol levels increase VTA-DA neuronal firing (Brodie et al., 1990; Gessa et al., 1985). In addition, local or systemic alcohol treatment increases extracellular DA levels in the NAc (Franklin et al., 2009; Imperato and Di Chiara, 1986; Smith and Weiss, 1999; Yoshimoto et al., 1992). Evidence that systemic alcohol exposure increases extracellular mPFC DA levels is mixed (Engleman et al., 2006; Fadda et al., 1990; Hegarty and Vogel, 1993; Tu et al., 2007). Also, alcohol stimulation of VTA-DA neurons has been reported to increase DA levels in the mPFC of female Wistar rats (Ding et al., 2011). Behaviorally, mesocorticolimbic DA neurotransmission has been implicated in alcohol self-administration (Gonzales and Weiss, 1998; Hodge et al., 1996; Melendez et al., 2002; Samson and Chappell, 2003; Weiss et al., 1996). For a review of DAergic-associated ligands tested in five of the selectively bred high alcohol-consuming (AA, HAD1, HAD2, P and sP) international rat lines and CNS disturbances of the DA system in these rat lines see Bell et al.

(2012b). For a review on patented treatments for alcohol abuse and dependence that target the DAergic system see Bell et al. (2012a).

Alcohol also acts to disinhibit mPFC functioning and by extension interferes with some of the executive processes mediated by cortical brain regions (de Oliveira and Nakamura-Palacios, 2003; Kähkönen et al., 2003). This dysregulation could have extensive effects on an individual's situation-specific decision-making capacity, particularly in younger drinkers who exhibit the greatest incidence of binge drinking. Thus, it is not surprising that there is a growing literature indicating a role for DAergic activity in binge alcohol drinking. For example, the DA-D1-like receptor antagonist S33138 has been reported to reduce alcohol binge-like drinking in high alcohol-consuming rodents (Rice et al., 2012; Sabino et al., 2013). Sabino et al. (2013) reported that this suppressant effect was maintained longer in subjects receiving intermittent vs. continuous alcohol drinking access, and could be indicative of a sensitized state in DA-D1 receptors following binge-like alcohol drinking. Taken together, these results suggest that binge or chronic alcohol drinking/exposure interferes with DA regulatory mechanisms within the mesocorticolimbic system, and the CNS recruits adaptive mechanisms to compensate for these dysregulations in basal DA tone.

2.2.3. Serotonin

The neurotransmitter serotonin (5-HT) is associated with addictive behaviors, appetite regulation, behavioral inhibition, mood, and cognitive functions. A dysregulation in the 5-HT system has been implicated as a factor in alcohol addiction. There are seven families of 5-HT receptors (5-HT1–7) and at least 14 distinct 5-HT receptor subtypes (Barnes and Sharp, 1999), which makes the task of understanding which 5-HT receptor subtypes mediate addictive behaviors a complex one. The raphe nucleus, where 5-HT neurons originate, sends 5-HT projections to numerous regions including the VTA, NAc, and PFC and studies have shown that the 5-HT system regulates DA neuronal activity in these subregions of the mesocorticolimbic system (Azmitia and Segal 1978; Herve et al. 1987; Parent et al. 1981; Halliday and Tork, 1989; Van Bockstaele et al. 1994). For example, 5-HT activates VTA-DA neurons (Pessia et al. 1994), induces DA release in VTA slices (Beart and McDonald 1982), enhances DA release in NAc when locally applied to the VTA (Guan and McBride 1989), potentiates the excitatory actions of alcohol on VTA-DA neurons (Brodie et al. 1995), and increases extracellular DA release in the PFC (Iyer and Bradberry, 1996). In addition, there is evidence that activation of the dorsal raphe nucleus can increase extracellular levels of DA in the NAc (Yoshimoto and McBride, 1992).

Alterations in the 5-HT system are believed to mediate some of alcohol's effects in rat lines selectively bred for high alcohol consumption (c.f., Bell et al., 2012b) and alcoholic individuals with a polymorphism of the 5-HT transporter can respond favorable to certain medication combinations (Johnson, 2010). Acute alcohol exposure appears to increase 5-HT activity (McBride et al., 1993b; Smith and Weiss, 1999), whereas chronic exposure to alcohol may result in the development of tolerance to this effect (Smith and Weiss 1999). Clinical and/or pre-clinical studies have reported deficiencies of 5-HT and/or its major metabolite 5-HIAA in the brains of human alcoholics (Schmidt et al., 1997; Pivac et al., 2004) and genetically selected alcohol-preferring rats (Murphy et al., 1987; Zhou et al., 1991; McBride et al., 1993b). Moreover, treatments that reduce 5-HT neurotransmission can elevate self-administration of alcohol (Lyness and Smith 1992; Ciccocioppo et al. 1999). Drug treatments with antidepressants that affect 5-HT CNS activity have been shown to reduce craving and/or symptomatic behavior associated with alcohol dependence (c.f. Goodman 2008). Therefore, it has been proposed that modulation of the 5-HT system is a viable therapy for alcoholism in a sub-set of patients (Johnson 2004, 2010; Wrase et al., 2006). For a review of 5-HT-associated ligands tested in five of the selectively bred high alcohol-consuming (AA, HAD1, HAD2, P and sP) international rat lines see Bell et al. (2012b). For a review on patented treatments for alcohol abuse and dependence that target the 5-HT system see Bell et al. (2012a). Research on the involvement of 5-HT in binge alcohol drinking has been limited. Pre-clinical studies have shown that binge drinking induced a blunted 5-HT response in the Scheduled High Alcohol Consumption (SHAC) binge drinking model (Szumlinski et al., 2007). Additionally, acute withdrawal from alcohol after binge-like exposure lead to a wide-spread reduction in 5-HT and other neurotransmitters in several brain regions including those associated with the mesocorticolimbic system (Smith et al., 2008). In general, these findings indicate that serotonergic treatments may disrupt binge alcohol drinking and may interfere with the progression to alcohol dependence, in certain individuals, as well.

2.2.4. Acetylcholine (Cholinergic)

The cholinergic (ACh) system has been implicated in addiction. Nicotinic acetylcholine receptors (nAChRs) are widely distributed throughout the brain (Perry et al., 2002). There are 12 subunit-associated nAChRs (with combinations of alpha2 through alpha10 and beta2 through beta4 subunits) with neuronal nAChRs being pentameric in nature (Dani and Harris, 2005). The alpha4-beta2 nAChR combination is the most common in the CNS, it has the highest affinity for nicotine, and rapidly desensitizes (nonfunctional state in which associated ion channels are closed) to the effects of nicotine (Dani and Harris, 2005). The alpha7-associated nAChR has the lowest affinity for nicotine and are present on excitatory glutamatergic terminals within the mesocorticolimbic system (Albuquerque et al., 2009; Gotti and Clementi 2004; Nayak et al., 2000; Wonnacott 1997). Pidoplichko and colleagues (2004) have suggested that nicotine's prolonged effect on DA neurotransmission may be due to alpha7 nAChRs on these presynaptic glutamate terminals, because they do not desensitize to nicotine as rapidly as alpha4 and alpha6 associated receptors.

nAChRs are thought to mediate the reinforcing effects of alcohol as well. nAChRs receptors are present in the VTA and NAc where they are thought to mediate the rewarding/reinforcing effects of alcohol and nicotine (Blomqvist et al., 1996, 1997; Corrigall et al., 1994; Nisell et al., 1994; Soderpalm et al., 2000). Regarding this, alcohol appears to elevate DA levels within the mesocorticolimbic system via indirect activation of nAChRs (Ericson et al., 2003). Interestingly, it has been shown that alcohol can interfere with the desensitization of nAChRs caused by nicotine and this may be one of the contributing factors to the high prevalence of alcohol and nicotine co-abuse (Schlaepfer et al., 2008; Marszalec et al., 1999). As described below, selectively bred P rats are more sensitive to the reinforcing effects of alcohol (Rodd et al., 2004a) and nicotine (Hauser et al., 2013) when self-administered directly into the posterior VTA than outbred control Wistar rats. In addition, recent findings indicate that nicotine exposure can enhance alcohol-seeking and alcohol relapse drinking by P rats (Hauser et al., 2012a), which suggests continued use of nicotine during alcohol abstinence may increase the probability of relapse, at least in individuals genetically predisposed to abuse alcohol. In addition, P rats readily consume alcohol-nicotine solutions in sufficient amounts to achieve binge-like BAC's (> 80 mg%) while achieving nicotine blood levels found in 'heavy smokers' (~56 ng/ml; Hauser et al., 2012b).

Collectively, these findings provide support for the hypothesis that nicotine and alcohol addiction may share common genetic vulnerabilities.

There is some evidence implicating nAChRs in binge alcohol drinking. For instance, Hendrickson et al. (2009) found that nicotine, cytisine (nAChR agonist) and mecamylamine (non-selective nAChR antagonist) reduced binge-like alcohol drinking (Sprow and Thiele, 2012). Similarly, lobeline, a mixed agonist-antagonist of nAChRs, reduced binge alcohol drinking (using the DID model) without altering sucrose intake (Sajja and Rahman, 2011; Sprow and Thiele, 2012). For a review of acetylcholine-associated ligands tested in five of the selectively bred high alcohol-consuming (AA, HAD1, HAD2, P and sP) international rat lines and CNS disturbances of the cholinergic system in these rat lines see Bell et al. (2012b). For reviews on both promising and patented treatments for alcohol abuse and dependence that target the cholinergic system see Rahman and Prendergast (2012) and Rezvani et al. (2012). It is clear that the cholinergic system is involved in alcohol and drug abuse as well as addiction, however, more research needs to be done to develop pharmacological treatments targeting this system.

2.2.5. Opioids

There are several classes of endogenous opioids including enkephalins, endorphins, dynorphins, and endomorphins. These classes of ligands bind with some specificity to the delta, kappa and mu-receptors, respectively. One role of these peptides in the brain is to process information about rewarding stimuli, including alcohol (Oswald and Wand, 2004). These peptides have been shown to influence the development of alcohol abuse and dependence, including binge drinking behaviors. Opioid receptors are found pre-synaptically on DAergic neurons of the mesocorticolimbic system (e.g., within the NAc) where they control the release of DA. Thus, opioid activity like that of the glutamatergic and GABAergic systems modulates DA activity in this "reward" neurocircuit.

Variations in opioid-related gene expression and function may contribute to high levels of alcohol consumption as well (e.g., Marini et al., 2013). For example, high alcohol drinking rats exhibit a greater level of mu-opioid receptor (MOR)-associated and enkephalin mRNA, compared to low alcohol drinking rats (Morganstern et al., 2012). For a review of neurobiological differences in the opioid system between selectively bred high and low alcohol-consuming rats see Bell et al. (2012b). A great deal of existing evidence for the role of opioids in alcohol abuse and dependence comes from pharmacological experiments using the FDA-approved treatment for alcoholism, naltrexone (ReVia) and other non-specific opioid antagonists. Naltrexone blocks alcohol-induced changes in gene transcription in several receptor systems, including the mu-opioid system. Evidence from knock-out mice lacking MORs or dynorphin suggest that MORs and kappa-opioid receptors (KORs) are involved in the rewarding or reinforcing effects of alcohol (Blednov et al., 2006; Hall et al., 2001; Roberts et al., 2000).

In line with a role in alcohol reward and reinforcement, opioid ligands alter alcohol consumption, although the direction of alteration is receptor subtype- and CNS site-specific (Barson et al., 2010; Kemppainen et al., 2012; Margolis et al., 2008). For a review of opioid ligands tested in five of the selectively bred high alcohol-consuming (AA, HAD1, HAD2, P and sP) international rat lines see Bell et al. (2012b). For a review on patented treatments for alcohol abuse and dependence that target the opioid system see Bell et al. (2012a). There is a limited amount of pharmacological evidence that directly implicates opioids in binge drinking behavior. Naltrexone was found to reduce alcohol intake dose-dependently, using the DID (Kamdar et al., 2007), SHAC (Tanchuck et al., 2011), limited access (Ji et al., 2008), and intermittent alcohol access (Sabino et al., 2012) models of binge drinking. It is impossible from these reports to associate a particular opioid receptor system with binge drinking, as these studies did not utilize receptor-specific agents. However, recent evidence that binge drinking maintains an immature adolescent-like high distribution of mPFC DORs (Nielsen et al., 2012) suggests a role for these receptors in this behavior. In conjunction with reports that DOR blockade reduces alcohol drinking (June et al., 1999), this finding may suggest that overactive DORs are associated with impulsive binge alcohol drinking. The fact that naltrexone reduces (a) the risk of relapse in some alcoholic patients (Farren and O'Malley, 1997; Volpicelli et al., 1992), (b) alcohol cue-induced human brain activity (Dayas et al., 2007; Myrick et al., 2008), (c) alcohol-induced DA efflux in the NAc (Benjamin et al., 1993), and (d) alcohol reinstatement/relapse in rodents (Ciccocioppo et al., 2002; Le et al., 1999) indicates continued research will be conducted on the endogenous opioid system in order to produce more effective compounds to treat alcoholism.

2.2.6. Neuropeptide Y

Neuropeptide Y (NPY) is a 36-amino acid neuromodulator that is expressed throughout the brain in regions such as the cortex, hypothalamus, hippocampus, and Amyg (Allen et al., 1994; Gray and Morley, 1986; Heilig and Widerlov, 1990; Wettstein et al., 1995) and it acts on five receptor subtypes (Y1, Y2, Y4, Y5, and Y6) (Palmiter et al., 1998). It is involved in regulating a number of behaviors such as feeding (Clark et al., 1984), anxiety (Heilig et al., 1993; Heilig and Widerlov, 1995), and alcohol addiction (Pandey, 2003; Pandey et al., 2003). In the alcohol research field, a number of studies have focused on understanding NPY's actions in the Amyg. The Amyg is a focal brain region involved in the negative reinforcing properties of alcohol.

For example, it has been postulated that the P rats' high alcohol intake is due to higher anxiety levels than its low alcohol-consuming NP counterpart (Badia-Elder et al., 2007; Pandey et al., 2005; Suzuki et al., 2004). Support for this hypothesis comes from the observation that, depending upon the behavioral test used, P rats do express innate anxiety (Stewart et al., 1993) and alcohol acts as an anxiolytic for P rats (Gilpin and Roberto, 2012; Stewart et al., 1993; Zhang et al., 2010). Neurobiological support comes from the observation that P rats have lower basal levels of NPY in the central amygdala (CeA) and/or medial amygdala (MeA) compared to NP rats (Ehlers et al., 1998; Hwang et al., 1999, 2004; Pandey et al., 2005). In addition, NPY expression levels in the CeA and/or MeA can be increased in P rats following alcohol exposure (Pandey et al., 2005; Zhang et al., 2010). Also, quantitative trait locus (QTL) analyses have identified NPY as a candidate gene for the high alcohol drinking/preference phenotype in inbred P rats (Spence et al., 2005, 2009, 2013).

Currently, other than the observation that central treatment with NPY reduces the alcohol deprivation effect (ADE) in P rats (Bertholomey et al., 2011; Gilpin et al., 2008), there are no reports of the effects of NPY on binge alcohol drinking by P rats. However, there is some evidence that NPY mediates binge-like drinking using the drinking-in-the-dark (DID) mouse model. Central administration of NPY and a selective Y2 receptor antagonist reduces binge alcohol intake using this model (Sparrow et al., 2012; Sprow and Thiele, 2012). In contrast, activation or inhibition of the Y1 receptor appears to have reciprocal effects, such that a Y1 receptor agonist decreases whereas a Y1 receptor antagonist increases DID binge-like drinking (Sparrow et al., 2012; Sprow and Thiele, 2012). In addition, a history of binge-like drinking reduced NPY and Y1R expression levels in the CeA and removal of alcohol following three cycles of binge drinking increased the expression of both Y1 and Y2 receptors (Sparrow et al., 2012; Sprow and Thiele, 2012). Collectively, these findings indicate that NPY signaling is involved in regulating excessive alcohol intake during binge alcohol drinking and, by extension alterations in NPY function contribute to the development of alcohol dependence.

2.2.7. Ghrelin

The neuropeptide ghrelin is a 28-amino acid gut peptide that acts on the growth hormone secretagogue receptor (GHS-R1A). The GHS-R1A is located both peripherally (e.g., gut and stomach) and centrally (e.g., hypothalamic nuclei and the VTA) (Guan et al., 1997; Kageyama et al., 2008; Kojima et al., 1999; Zigman et al., 2006). Given the location of its receptor, it is not surprising that ghrelin promotes the consumption of palatable food, alcohol and drugs. Ghrelin is postulated to mediate reward through actions on VTA-DA neurons. A numbers of studies have shown that systemic and central administrations of ghrelin increases extracellular levels of DA in the NAc (Abizaid et al., 2006; Jerlhag et al., 2006, 2007, 2008, 2010a) and/or induces excitation of VTA neurons (Abizaid et al., 2006). In addition, systemic administration of ghrelin can reorganize VTA neurons, such that these neurons experience greater excitatory input and diminished inhibitory input (Abizaid et al., 2006).

It appears that ghrelin's mediation of rewarding stimuli includes interactions with both glutamatergic (NMDA) (Jerlhag et al., 2011) and nACh (containing alpha3beta2, beta3, and/or alpha6 subunits) (Jerlhag et al., 2006) receptors. A recent study reported that alcohol preferring AA rats have increased gene expression for the GHS-R1A in the VTA, NAc, PFC, hippocampus and the Amyg compared to low alcohol-consuming ANA rats (Landgren et al., 2011). Similar to some clinical studies (Addolorato et al., 2006; Badaoui et al., 2008) chronic alcohol consumption leads to a reduction in ghrelin in AA rats compared with ANA rats (Landgren et al., 2011). In general, central ghrelin signaling stimulates the mesocorticolimbic reward pathway and is necessary for the ingestion of rewarding stimuli including food, alcohol and drugs of abuse, and has been posited as a possible drugable target for addiction (c.f., Jerlhag et al., 2010, 2011; Jerlhag and Engel, 2011; Leggio et al., 2011; Perello and Zigman, 2012; Schellekens et al., 2012).

2.2.8. Other Neurotransmitter and Neuromodulatory Systems

While the neurotransmitter/neuromodulatory systems reviewed above play important roles in addiction to a number of rewarding stimuli, there are a number of other neurotransmitter/neuromodulatory systems that influence neurotransmission in the mesocorticolimbic reward system as well. Some of these other systems include the endocannabinoid system and its receptors in the VTA and NAc; glycine and its binding site on the NMDA receptor as well as its own receptor in the NAc; corticotrophin releasing factor (CRF) as well as orexin and their receptors in the VTA and NAc (particularly for orexin), along with projections from the hypothalamus and activity in the amygdala; the melanocortin system [adrenocorticotrophic hormone (ACTH) and its fragments including alpha-melanocyte stimulating hormone (alpha-MSH)] and its receptors in the VTA and NAc, as well as the hypothalamus; glucocorticoids [an end-product of hypothalamic-pituitary-adrenal (HPA) axis activity] and their receptors in the amygdala; and other sytems [e.g., leptin, orphanin, brain-derived neurotrphic factor (BDNF) and glial-derived neurotrophic factor (GDNF)]. For recent reviews on the neurobiology of alcohol use disorders see Bartlett and Heilig (2013), Charlet et al. (2013), Deehan et al. (2013), Filbey and DeWitt (2012), Kenna et al. (2012), Koob (2013), Mason and Higley (2013), Noori et al. (2012), Soderpalm and Ericson (2013), as well as Spanagel and Vengeliene (2013).

2.3. A Primer on Neurocircuitry Mediating Alcohol Abuse and Dependence

The mesocorticolimbic dopamine (DA) system has long been known to mediate various aspects of rewarding behavior in vertebrate animals (Koob et al., 1998; Ikemoto, 2007). The mesocorticolimbic DA system has been found to be involved in the orientation to, and procurement of rewards including food, sex, and drugs. Theorists suggest that addictive drugs may "hijack" this system to perpetuate and increase levels of self-administration (e.g., Schultz, 2011). Research with animals and humans has increased our understanding of some of the neurotransmitter systems and receptors involved in mediating the rewarding effects of alcohol and how the mesocorticolimbic DA system system is involved. Although many different brain sites have been found to play a role in addiction (Noori et al., 2012), the mesocorticolimbic DA system can be described as a core neurocircuit mediating most addictions, such that all addictive behaviors alter the mesocorticolimbic DA system. Key sites within the mesocorticolimbic DA system (see Figure 1) include the medial prefrontal cortex (mPFC), amygdala (Amyg), ventral tegmental area (VTA), and nucleus accumbens (NAc); and subnuclei within each of these sites have been shown to mediate various aspects of addictive behavior (Ikemoto, 2007; McBride, 2002; Noori et al., 2012).

2.3.1. Medial Prefrontal Cortex

The mPFC is a critical site for behavioral and cognitive regulation, and undergoes very active neuronal development (synaptic proliferation and subsequent pruning) during peri-adolescence. During this stage of development, it may be particularly vulnerable to the effects of alcohol and other drugs of abuse (Spear, 2000; Chambers et al., 2003; Clark et al., 2008). The mPFC receives glutamate, acetylcholine (Ach), and DA inputs and has glutamatergic projections to mesolimbic brain areas involved in drug and alcohol abuse (Kalivas, 2009; Kalivas et al., 2005; see Figure 1) and the prelimbic and infralimbic subregions of the mPFC are thought to mediate distinct functions of drug acquisition and intake (Peters et al., 2008). Cues associated with consumption of, or access to, natural rewards also elevate DA in the mPFC (Phillips et al., 2008). Data from our laboratory (author EAE) indicate that eight weeks of alcohol free-choice drinking increases the extracellular levels of DA in the mPFC, and microinjections of DA-D2, but not -D1, antagonists into the mPFC reduce scheduled-access alcohol drinking in P rats. In addition, microinjections of a CB1 anatagonist into the mPFC reduce operant responding for alcohol (Hansson et al., 2007). Other findings indicate a role for other neurotransmitter and peptide systems in regulating mPFC efferents and various aspects of reward behavior (e.g., Berglind et al., 2009; Corominas, et al., 2010; Giacchino and Henriksen, 1998; Van den Oever, et al., 2010a, 2010b). Together, these data indicate a role for the mPFC in reward processes and suggest that drugs of abuse (including alcohol) can produce a dysregulation in the glutamatergic outputs from the mPFC, which may impair the ability of an individual to evaluate the risks and rewards of engaging in drug-taking behavior.

2.3.2. Nucleus Accumbens

The nucleus accumbens (NAc) is a key brain structure supporting the self-administration of alcohol and other drugs of abuse (Koob et al., 1998; Engleman et al., 2009). It is a mesocorticolimbic site that receives DA input, mainly from the VTA, but also from the substantia nigra (Noori et al., 2012). It has glutamatergic input from the mPFC and Amyg and has GABAergic efferent projections to the VTA and Amyg as well (see Figure 1). Administration of drugs of abuse and natural rewards elevate DA levels in the NAc and these elevations are associated with the incentive/motivation properties of these compounds (Hernandez et al., 2011; Phillips et al., 2008). Moreover, several drugs of abuse (Katner et al., 2011; McBride et al., 1999) including alcohol (Engleman et al., 2009) are self-administered directly into the NAc. In at least some cases, this behavior is dependent on DA-D1 and -D2 receptor function (McBride et al., 1999). Repeated moderate alcohol exposure via systemic administration (Smith and Weiss, 1999) or voluntary oral intake (Melendez et al., 2002; Thielen et al., 2004), increases extracellular DA levels in the NAc. These effects are thought to be mediated, in part, through a reduction in DA-D2 autoreceptor function in the NAc (Engleman et al., 2000, 2003; Thielen et al., 2004). Glutamate release in the NAc is enhanced during alcohol self-administration, and the increases are directly associated with increased motivation to consume alcohol (Li, et al., 2010). Moreover, these enhanced levels of glutamate may be due to altered glutamate transport/uptake (Melendez et al., 2005; Sari et al., 2011) and continue into protracted abstinence (Melendez et al., 2005). Alcohol self-administration is blocked by microinjections of LY279268, an mGluR2/3 agonist which reduces glutamate release (Besheer et al., 2010). Similarly, microinjections of an mGluR5 antagonist into the NAc also reduced alcohol self-administration (Besheer et al., 2010) as did antagonism of opioid receptors (June et al., 2004). Similar to findings in the mPFC, a CB1 receptor antagonist microinjected into the NAc blocks alcohol drinking in selectively bred high alcohol-consuming AA rats (Malinen and Hyytia, 2008). There is evidence that alcohol drinking or self-administration is mediated by GABA-A receptor activity in the NAc as well (Liu et al., 2011; June et al., 1998).

2.3.3. Ventral Tegmental Area

The VTA contains DA cell bodies which are the main source of DA in the mesocorticolimbic DA system. Activity in these neurons and their projection fields is thought to mediate various aspects of reward and the reinforcing properties of drugs of abuse including alcohol (Koob et al., 1998; McBride et al., 1999). The DA efferents from the VTA innervate many forebrain areas including the mPFC, NAc and Amyg (see Figure 1). The VTA also receives glutamatergic input from the Amyg and mPFC as well as receiving GABAergic input from the NAc (Ikemoto, 2007; see Figure 1). The posterior portion of the VTA in selectively bred high alcohol-consuming P rats supports the self-administration of cocaine (Rodd et al., 2005a) and alcohol (Rodd-Henricks et al., 2000a; Rodd et al., 2005b, 2005c).

This effect is dependent upon the activation of DA neurons and is sensitized after cycles of forced abstinence and re-exposure (Rodd et al., 2005b, 2005c). Alcohol drinking or self-infusion into the VTA has been found to be dependent on the activity of VTA-DA neurons (Nowak et al., 2000; Rodd et al., 2004c; Hauser et al., 2011); serotonergic (5-HT) 5-HT2A (Ding et al., 2009) and 5-HT3 (McBride et al., 2004; Engleman et al., 2008; Rodd et al., 2010) receptors, as well as GABA-A (Nowak et al., 1998; Eiler and June, 2007), mGluR5 (Bäckström et al., 2004), muscarinic ACh (Katner et al., 1997) and nicotinic ACh (Söderpalm et al., 2009) neurotransmission in the VTA. Opioid (June et al., 2004) and cannabinoid-CB1 receptor antagonism in the VTA of selectively bred P and AA rats, respectively, also blocks alcohol intake (Malinen and Hyytia, 2008). A recent study from our laboratory suggests that chronic alcohol drinking may produce reduced extracellular DA levels in the VTA; which, in turn, may result in lower auto-feedback regulation of DA neurons and thus enhance DA output to mesocorticolimbic DA system projection areas (Engleman et al., 2011).

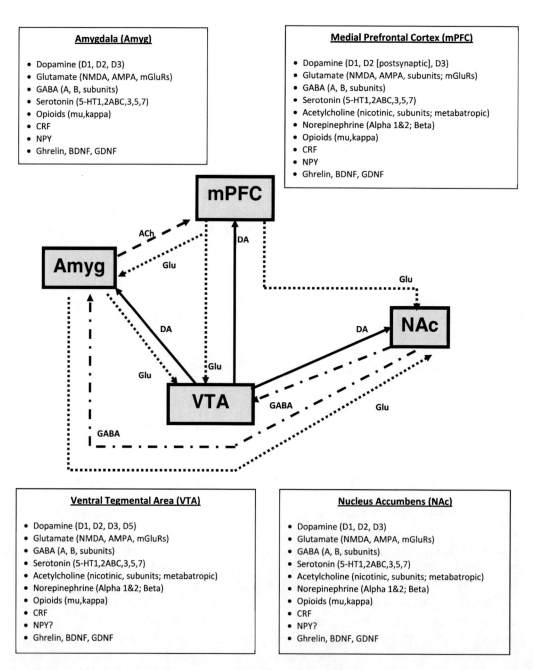

Figure 1. Key Subregions of the Mesocorticolimbic Dopamine System.

2.3.4. Amygdala

The Amyg is a brain structure that serves to integrate information regarding stress and emotional states, as well as modulate the anhedonic/aversive effects associated with drug dependence and withdrawal. Within the Amyg, the basolateral and central nuclei play major roles in addiction (McBride, 2002), in particular these nuclei promote the negative reinforcing properties of drugs during periods of withdrawal (Koob and Volkow, 2010). The Amyg is well connected with other structures in the mesocorticolimbic DA system and receives DA input from the VTA, GABA input from the NAc, and glutamate input from the mPFC (Ikemoto, 2007; Koob and Volkow, 2010; see Figure 1). Many neurotransmitter systems within the Amyg have been shown to play a role in addiction. For instance, glutamatergic receptors, in particular NMDA and AMPA, are thought to play key roles in the development of alcohol dependence (McCool et al., 2010). Similarly, activity of the GABA (Liu et al., 2011; Foster et al., 2004; Koob and Volkow 2010), corticotropin-releasing factor (CRF) (Koob and Volkow, 2010), neuropeptide Y (NPY) (Pandey et al., 2005; Gilpin et al., 2008; Zhang et al., 2010), substance P (SP) (Yang et al., 2009) and opioid (Foster et al., 2004) systems within the Amyg has been implicated in alcohol and drug dependence as well.

2.3.5. Other Brain Structures

Many brain structures outside the core mesocorticolimbic DA system structures also provide input and affect processing of reward-related stimuli. Some of these include: olfactory bulb, insula, caudate-putamen (striatum), septal region, bed nucleus of the stria terminalis, globus pallidus, hypothalamus, habenula, hippocampus, pedunculopontine nucleus, thalamus, subthalamic nucleus, substantia nigra, raphe nuclei, and the locus coeruleus (c.f., McBride, 2002; Noori et al., 2012; Spanagel, 2009).

3. USING SELECTIVELY BRED RATS TO INVESTIGATE THE NEUROBIOLOGY OF BINGE DRINKING

3.1. Usefulness of Selectively Bred Animal Models to Study Alcohol-Associated Effects

Animal models have been successfully used to investigate the treatment of psychiatric disorders and other medical conditions (e.g., Griffin, 2002; McKinney, 2001; Nestler and Hyman, 2010). An animal model has the advantage of allowing the experimenter to control characteristics of the animal's genetic background, environment and prior drug exposure. An animal model also permits the examination of neurobehavioral, neurochemical and neurophysiological correlates with the disorder being modeled. Despite reservations as to whether a valid animal model of alcoholism could be developed (Cicero, 1979), certain criteria for an animal model of alcoholism have been proposed (Cicero, 1979; Lester and Freed, 1973; McBride and Li, 1998). Briefly, these criteria are as follows: 1) the animal should orally self-administer alcohol; 2) the amount of alcohol consumed should result in pharmacologically relevant blood alcohol levels; 3) alcohol should be consumed for its post-ingestive pharmacological effects, and not strictly for its caloric value or taste; 4) alcohol should be positively reinforcing, in other words, the animals must be willing to work for alcohol; 5) chronic alcohol consumption should lead to the expression of metabolic and/or functional tolerance; 6) chronic consumption of alcohol should lead to dependence, as indicated by withdrawal symptoms after access to alcohol is terminated; and 7) an animal model of alcoholism should display characteristics associated with relapse as well.

Selective breeding is a powerful genetic tool for studying the genetics of many alcohol-associated phenotypes (Crabbe, 2008). Compared to pure association studies such as genome-wide association studies (GWAS) and recombinant inbred lines (RILs), selective breeding from a heterogeneous outbred stock can make low frequency/rare alleles (minor allele frequency <0.05) more common (i.e., these rare alleles are captured within the respective high- or low-expressing line for the trait). Thus, selective breeding will result in phenotypic expression levels in the high and low lines that will greatly exceed the range found in the foundation stock from which they were selectively bred. Additionally, selective breeding for any phenotype, such as alcohol preference, is hypothesis driven and genetically correlated traits of the primary selected phenotype (presumably due to pleiotropic actions of genes: Crabbe et al., 1990) can be identified and studied. The alcohol-preferring P and high alcohol-drinking HAD (replicate 1 and 2) rat lines were selectively bred to prefer a 10% alcohol solution over water and consume greater than 5 g of alcohol/kg body weight/day (Bell et al., 2005, 2006b, 2012b; McBride and Li, 1998; Murphy et al., 2002). A substantial literature (reviewed in Bell et al., 2005, 2006b, 2012b; McBride and Li, 1998; Murphy et al., 2002) indicates that the alcohol-preferring P rat meets all, and the high alcohol-drinking HAD1 and HAD2 replicate rat lines meet most, of the existing adult criteria proposed for a valid animal model of alcoholism (Cicero, 1979; Lester and Freed, 1973; McBride and Li, 1998). Because alcohol binge-drinking is such a serious public health issue and often is directly associated with the development of alcohol abuse and dependence, its inclusion as a criterion for an animal model of alcoholism appears to be paramount.

3.2. Towards a Pre-Clinical Definition of Binge-Like Drinking

For the most part, the NIAAA (2004) definition of binge drinking as determined by the amount consumed, length of time spent drinking per incident, and peak BACs achieved has been widely accepted in the human literature. However, a clear definition of binge-exposure/drinking for animal studies has evolved much more slowly; and, for that matter, remains elusive even now. For example, a quick online literature (2010-2012) search of [binge and (alcohol or ethanol) and rat] revealed 34 studies (see Table 2). From this literature search, only 7 "binge" studies examined free-choice alcohol drinking, where water and food were freely available; 3 studies examined forced-choice alcohol liquid diet, where water and food were not freely available; 20 studies examined intragastric administration of alcohol; 2 studies examined intraperitoneal administration; and 1 report was an in vitro study of a cell line. The alcohol exposure in the vast majority of these studies resulted in peak BACs approximating 300 mg% (0.30 in clinical terms) and greater, which almost quadruples the NIAAA (2004) definitional threshold (80 mg%) for binge drinking. With this in mind and depending upon the research question examined, each of these model systems has certain strengths and weaknesses. Simpler methodology (i.e., experimenter-administered alcohol) is important in evaluating questions on the effects of alcohol binge-exposure as it pertains to molecular biology and neuropathology.

Table 2. Pre-clinical conception of binge, from an Ovid MEDLINE® search (2010-2012) of [binge and (alcohol or ethanol) and rat]

No. Studies	Alcohol Exposure	Description (X% = concentration of alcohol)
1	Free-choice 24 hr/7 days/week	HAD1 and HAD2 rats (15%)
3	Free-Choice 24 hr/3 days/week (M, W, F)	Intermittent access in outbred rats (20%)
1	Free-Choice 24 hr/3 days/week (M, W, F)	Intermittent access in outbred rats (beer)
2	DID-MSA 3 hr/day/5 days/week (M—F)	P rats (15%)
1	Operant (90 min/day)/ 5 days/week (M—F)	P rats (15%)
2	Liquid diet 24 hr/7 days/week	>300 mg%
1	Lieber-DeCarli 24 hr/7 days/week	4 weeks then IG 5g/kg
20	Alcohol Intragastric (IG, ~3x/day for 4 days)	2.75—6 g/kg/infusion
2	Alcohol Intraperitoneal (IP)	3 g/kg/injection
1	Alcohol in vitro (cell culture)	50—200 mM

Effects of binge-like exposure on these parameters may not be apparent following more subtle alcohol treatments, such as free-choice drinking. Because alcohol abuse and addiction are mediated by complex neurobiological, environmental and behavioral interactions; findings from experimenter-administered studies should be confirmed with methods that have greater face-validity, such as free-choice drinking. However, even research conducted with selectively bred high alcohol-consuming rats, which naturally consume significant amounts of alcohol, has its own limitations. For instance, the clinical literature indicates that a majority of adolescents and young adults experiment with alcohol, and many of these individuals also binge drink; but (a) most of these individuals do not become dependent upon alcohol and (b) only a subset of these individuals have a genetic predisposition (i.e., are FHP for alcoholism) to abuse alcohol. Nevertheless, many and possibly a majority of FHP, especially if FHP across multiple generations, individuals do (a) have an early onset of alcohol use; (b) engage in alcohol abuse, including binge and extreme drinking; (c) experience more problems associated with alcohol; and (d) become dependent upon alcohol more often and quicker, compared with FHN individuals that don't have this genetic predisposition. Thus, our laboratory uses these selectively bred animal models to investigate alcohol binge-drinking across peri-adolescence and adulthood.

3.3. Modeling Binge-Like Drinking and Its Consequences Using Alcohol Deprivation Effect Protocols

The first model of binge-like drinking established in our laboratory was based on protocols resulting in an alcohol deprivation effect (ADE). The ADE is a transient increase in alcohol consumption, above basal levels, displayed by animals when given free-choice access to alcohol after a period of forced abstinence (Sinclair and Senter, 1967). Our laboratory's standard protocol for examining the effects of an ADE include an initial 6 week free-choice (alcohol, water and food are all freely available) continuous (24 hours/day, 7days/week) access stage followed by cycles of 2 weeks of deprivation from and 2 weeks of re-exposure to alcohol access.

The ADE model was chosen because, upon re-exposure to alcohol access, BACs exceeding 80 mg% are readily achieved. Regarding the ADE, the P rat line has been the best rat line characterized under both home-cage and operant access conditions thus far (Engleman et al., 2011; Guccione et al., 2012; Hargreaves et al., 2011; McKinzie et al., 1998; Rodd et al., 2003, 2006; Rodd-Henricks et al., 2000d, 2001; Schroeder et al., 2005; Thielen et al., 2004; Toalston et al., 2008; Vengeliene et al., 2003; also see Bell et al., 2012b for review). Behaviorally, the P rat will display an increase in alcohol consumption that escalates in magnitude and duration (across days of re-exposure to alcohol) over repeated deprivation cycles (Figure 2). This pattern of escalation, associated with the ADE, in rats has led to its characterization as a model of relapse-like alcohol drinking/self-administration (Martin-Fardon and Weiss, 2013; Rodd et al., 2004b; Spanagel and Holter, 1999). The high alcohol-drinking rat lines (replicates HAD1 and HAD2) also display a robust ADE when multiple concentrations of ethanol are made available and/or multiple deprivations are experienced (Oster et al., 2006; Rodd et al., 2008; Rodd-Henricks et al., 2000c).

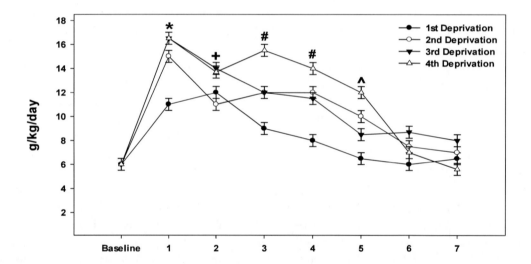

Figure 2. The mean (±SEM) alcohol consumed (g/kg/day) by P rats (n =9 per group) under 24-hr free-choice conditions. The rats had continuous access to multiple concentrations of alcohol (10%, 20%, 30%, vol/vol, available concurrently) for 6 weeks. Food and water were available ad libitum. The original 6-week access period was followed by 4 cycles of deprivation from and re-exposure to alcohol access. The data reflect a 3-day baseline (the 3 days before each deprivation period) and the first 7 days of re-exposure to alcohol access following each deprivation period. *, p<0.05, alcohol intake on the 1st day of re-exposure exceeded that of each baseline and 1st day alcohol intakes following the 2nd through 4th deprivation periods exceeded the 1st day alcohol intake following the 1st deprivation period. +, p < 0.05, 2nd day alcohol intakes exceeded that of their respective baselines, but did not differ from each other. #, p< 0.05, 3rd as well as 4th day alcohol intakes exceeded their respective baselines and 3rd as well as 4th day alcohol intakes following the 4th deprivation period exceeded 4th day alcohol intakes following the 1st through 3rd **deprivation periods**. ^, p < 0.05, 5th day alcohol intakes following the 2nd through 4th deprivation periods exceeded their respective baselines; although alcohol intakes following the 2nd and 3rd deprivation periods did not differ from each other, alcohol intake following the 4th deprivation period significantly exceeded alcohol intakes following the 2nd and 3rd deprivation periods (adapted from Rodd-Henricks et al., 2001).

It is noteworthy that even rat lines selectively bred to avoid alcohol (i.e., the alcohol-nonpreferring NP and low alcohol-drinking replicates LAD1 and LAD2) will display a significant escalation in alcohol intake across a multiple deprivation ADE protocol (Bell et al., 2004). Adaptive changes in DA neurotransmission are thought to be associated with the transition from heavy drinking to alcohol dependence (Koob et al., 1998). Previous work from our laboratory showed that adult P rats receiving 24 hours free-choice access to alcohol for eight weeks, with or without 2-weeks of alcohol deprivation (i.e., forced abstinence/detoxification), resulted in elevated extracellular levels of DA in the NAc (Thielen et al., 2004). This parallels findings of elevated DA levels in the NAc induced by daily scheduled alcohol access sessions (1 hr/day) in adult P rats (Engleman et al., 2000, 2003) or peripheral administration of alcohol in adult rats (Smith and Weiss, 1999; Franklin et al., 2009). These increased extracellular levels of DA in the NAc may be due to dysregulated auto-regulatory feedback from the NAc to the VTA, and/or functional or physiological down-regulation of presynaptic DA-D2 autoreceptors, which normally reduce the release of DA (Engleman et al., 2000, 2003; Thielen et al., 2004). Although these studies indicated that the observed elevations in DA were likely due to changes in release rather than clearance (Engleman et al., 2000, 2003; Thielen et al., 2004), other studies have shown that animal self-administration of alcohol can up-regulate DA transporter (DAT) activity in the NAc (Carroll et al., 2006; Sahr et al., 2004), whereas experimenter-administered alcohol does not appear to alter DAT function in the NAc (Badanich et al., 2007). The latter two studies were conducted in peri-adolescent animals (P and outbred albino rats) and the Carroll et al. (2006) study was conducted in adult animals (HAD1 rats).

In an early study, Engleman and colleagues (2002) examined the effects of alcohol deprivation length on DA efflux in the NAc. P rats had access to multiple concentrations of alcohol (18% and 44% available concurrently with water and food). A water control group received water as its only fluid throughout the study.

The other four groups received free-choice access to alcohol in their home cages according to the schedules illustrated in Table 3. Briefly, the groups were: Nondeprived (ND); one two-week deprivation (1DP2W); one eight-week deprivation 1DP8W; four two-week deprivations (4DP2W). At the end of the respective access periods, extracellular levels of DA were determined by no-net-flux microdialysis. The results (Figure 3) revealed that non-deprived rats displayed reduced extracellular DA levels in the NAc and the deprivation interval of 6 weeks resulted in an even greater reduction in DA levels than that seen after 2 weeks of deprivation. It is noteworthy that in other studies where elevations of DA in the NAc have been reported (Engleman et al., 2000, 2003; Thielen et al., 2004) peak alcohol intakes approximated 1 g/kg/1 hr session to 5g/kg/day and the studies lasted 4-6 weeks, and 8 weeks, respectively.

In the study by Engleman and colleagues (2002), the nondeprived group consumed approximately 8 g/kg/day, whereas the group experiencing four 2-week deprivation intervals displayed peak alcohol intakes approaching 15 g/kg/day. Therefore, one possibility for the disparate findings (decreased DA efflux in the NAc reported by Engleman et al., 2002 vs. increased DA efflux in the NAc reported by Engleman et al., 2000, 2003; Thielen et al., 2004) is due to greater levels of alcohol intake, longer periods of alcohol access and possibly greater dependence. Although dependence was not assessed in any of these studies, there is evidence that P rats display signs of alcohol dependence after chronic free-choice alcohol drinking (Kampov-Polevoy et al., 2000; Waller et al., 1982).

Table 3. Alcohol drinking protocol used in Engleman et al. (2002) for assessing adaptive changes in extracellular dopamine in the NAc using quantitative microdialysis.

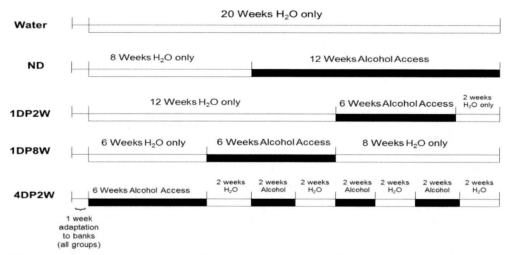

A Water group received water as its only fluid throughout the study. The other four groups always had water and received free-choice access in the home cage to 18 and 44% (v/v) alcohol according to the schedules illustrated in the timeline above. The groups were: Nondeprived (ND); one two-week deprivation (1DP2W); one eight-week deprivation 1DP8W; four two-week deprivations (4DP2W). At the end of the respective access periods, extracellular levels of dopamine (DA) were determined by no-net-flux microdialysis.

Regarding DAergic receptor changes, one study (Sari et al., 2006) examined the effects of continuous access to alcohol (15% and 30%) for 14 weeks vs. alcohol access for 6 weeks followed by 2 cycles of 2 weeks of deprivation from and 2 weeks of re-exposure to alcohol access (repeated ADE) vs. alcohol naïve adult male inbred P (iP) rats on DA-D1 and -D2 receptor expressions levels in the extended Amyg (NAc and Amyg nuclei). These authors found that D1 receptor expression levels were increased in the anterior NAc core in both the repeatedly deprived and continuous access animals along with increases in the lateral and intercalated Amyg in the repeatedly deprived animals only. D2 receptor expression levels were increased in both the anterior NAc core and shell in both repeatedly deprived and continuous access animals.

These findings indicate that there may be differential effects of alcohol which are dependent upon the presence or absence of deprivation intervals (i.e., repeated detoxifications). In addition, pharmacological evidence indicates that the serotonergic (5-HT) and glutamatergic systems also modulate the ADE. For instance, peripheral administration of antagonists, MDL 72222 and ICS 205-930, of the 5-HT3 receptor interfere with the ADE in P rats (Rodd-Henricks et al., 2000b). Regarding the glutamatergic system, peripheral administration of LY404039, an antagonist of the metabotropic glutamate 2/3 receptor (mGluR2/3) subtype, significantly reduces the operant ADE displayed by P rats (Rodd et al., 2006).

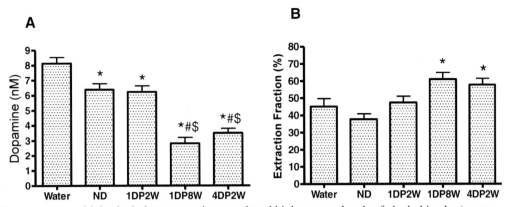

The access to multiple alcohol concentrations produced high average levels of alcohol intake (greater than 8 g/kg/day). Analysis showed that there were no differences in alcohol intake for any groups receiving alcohol access prior to any deprivation. A multiple regression analysis of the DA levels in the no-net-flux experiment (DAin plotted against DAout: DAout subtracted from DAin) provided regression lines for each treatment group. Panel A shows that extracellular DA levels significantly decreased in all of the treatment groups compared with the water only group [Overall DA concentration X group interaction effect: $F(4,404) = 19.60$; $p < 0.0001$]. The 1DP2W group that only received one 2 week period of alcohol deprivation was not significantly different from the ND group ($p = 0.63$). However, rats receiving 8 weeks total of alcohol deprivation, with or without periods of alcohol re-exposure (the 1DP8W and 4DP2W groups), showed further reductions in extracellular DA levels that were significantly lower than rats in the ND group ($p < 0.0001$). Panel B shows that the DA extraction fraction (which is an indication of clearance; i.e., DAT activity) was elevated in the 1DP8W and 4DP2W groups compared with the Water group. * = different from Water ($p < 0.05$); # = different from ND ($p < 0.05$); $ = different from 1DP2W ($p < 0.05$) (Adapted from Engleman et al., 2002).

Figure 3. Effects of excessive alcohol drinking and forced abstinence on extracellular levels of dopamine (DA) in the NAc.

In addition, a potent noncompetitive antagonist of the mGluR5 subtype, 2-methyl-6-(phenylethynyl)-pyridine (MPEP), reduces both alcohol-seeking behavior and the ADE in rats (Backstrom et al., 2004). The glutamatergic N-methyl-D-aspartate (NMDA) receptor has also been implicated with antagonists, including ifenprodil which has selectivity for the NMDA-2B subunit containing receptor (NR2B), disrupting the ADE in albino rats (Vengeliene et al., 2005). Multiple peptide systems have been pharmacologically implicated in the expression of the ADE as well.

The opioid system has been implicated, such that peripheral administrations of both naltrexone, a pan-opioid receptor antagonist, and LY255582, a selective mu-opioid receptor antagonist, disrupt the operant ADE displayed by P rats (Dhaher et al., 2012b). Similarly, there is evidence that the orexin system is involved in the expression of the ADE, since peripheral administration of SB-334867, an orexin-1 receptor antagonist, attenuates this behavior in P rats (Dhaher et al., 2010). In addition, neuropeptide Y (NPY) has been linked to the ADE since central [intracerebroventricular (ICV) and CeA] administration of this peptide interferes with the expression of an ADE by P rats (Bertholomey et al., 2011; Gilpin et al., 2008).

3.4. Modeling Binge-Like Drinking and Its Consequences Using Episodic Alcohol Access

A subsequent animal model of binge-like alcohol intake incorporated shorter periods, than that used for the ADE, of alcohol access and forced abstinence. In this intermittent alcohol access model, rats are given free-choice access to alcohol for an initial 8 days followed by cycles of 4 days of deprivation from and 4 days of re-exposure to alcohol access. One study examining this protocol in male and female, adult, high alcohol-consuming rats (P, HAD1 and HAD2) found an escalation in alcohol intake which peaked after the 3rd deprivation interval (Bell et al., 2008). These authors also reported that an ADE, relative to initial levels of intake, was expressed by both HAD lines but not by the P line of rats. In addition, the control group which had uninterrupted free-choice access to alcohol also escalated their alcohol intake, which matched intakes of rats, of all 3 lines, experiencing episodic access after the 4th deprivation interval.

This "episodic" protocol was modified slightly to examine changes in glutamatergic receptor-subunit-associated protein levels in the extended Amyg (NAc and Amyg nuclei) of adult P rats (Obara et al., 2009). Three groups of P rats were run: group (1) remained alcohol-naïve throughout the experiment, group (2) had uninterrupted free-choice access to alcohol for 6 months, and group (3) had free-choice access to alcohol 4 days/week for 6 months. After the 6 months of alcohol-drinking, half of the animals from each group were sacrificed after 24-hrs and half of the animals were sacrificed after 4 weeks. Overall, the findings (see Table 4, adapted from Obara et al., 2009) indicated that there are differential effects on glutamatergic receptor-associated proteins within the extended Amyg following either continuous or episodic alcohol access as well as following either a 24-hr or 4-week final deprivation period.

Table 4. Summary of the findings examining the effects of either episodic (EA: 4 days/week) or continuous (CA: 7 days/week) alcohol (15% and 30% concurrently with water and food) access on Homer and glutamate receptor-associated protein expression levels in the NAc shell (NACsh) and core (NACc) as well as expression levels in the central nucleus (CeA) of the Amyg of adult P rats following a final short-term (24 hr) withdrawal (SW) or long-term (4 weeks) withdrawal (LW) period

	Homer2a/b		mGluR1		mGluR5		NR2a		NR2b	
	EA	CA	EA	CA	EA	CA	EA	CA	EA	CA
NACsh	nc	nc	nc	nc	nc	nc	+sw, lw	nc	-sw, lw	-sw
NACc	+sw	+sw, lw	+sw	+sw	+sw, lw	+sw	+sw	+sw	+sw	+sw
CeA	+sw, lw	+sw, lw	+sw	+sw	+sw	nc	+sw	+sw	+sw, lw	+sw, lw

+, indicates significant (p < 0.05) increase in the level of protein relative to alcohol-naïve animals;
-, indicates a significant (p < 0.05) decrease in the level of protein relative to alcohol-naïve animals;
"nc" indicates no change relative to alcohol-naïve animals; "nd" indicates the protein was not detected;
sw, indicates significant (p < 0.05) changes detected after the short-term withdrawal (24 hrs) period;
lw, indicates significant (p < 0.05) changes detected after the long-term withdrawal (4 weeks) period.

3.5. Modeling Binge-Like Drinking and Its Consequences Using an Alcohol Drinking-in-the-Dark—Multiple-Scheduled-Access Procedure

The most recent model of binge-like drinking used by our laboratory is the drinking-in-the-dark—multiple-scheduled-access (DID-MSA) procedure (e.g., Bell et al., 2006a, 2006b, 2009, 2011; McBride et al., 2010). This procedure parallels the DID procedure used in mice to model alcohol binge drinking (e.g., Boehm et al., 2008; Crabbe et al., 2009; Lyons et al., 2008; Moore and Boehm, 2009; Navarro et al., 2009; Rhodes et al., 2005). Again, the focus of this review is on rat animal models because a discussion on mouse animal models is beyond the scope of this paper. The DID-MSA protocol used by our laboratory involves giving selectively bred (P and HAD) rats multiple scheduled 1-hr access sessions to two concentrations of alcohol (15% and 30%) during the animals' active period (the dark-/nocturnal-cycle/phase). As with all of our procedures, water and food are freely available ad libitum. The initial session is initiated at the beginning of the dark cycle, with each session (between 2 and 4 each day) being separated by 2 to 5 hours. Note that the initiation of the first session in the DID rat model differs from that used in the DID mouse model. Early work on the DID procedure in mice indicated that maximal ethanol intake required initiating the procedure 2 to 4 hours into the dark cycle (Rhodes et al., 2005), whereas, in P rats, maximal intake requires the first session to be initiated at the beginning of the dark cycle (Bell et al., 2006b). DID-MSA access is available 5 days a week, with the animals experiencing a 2 day deprivation interval each weekend.

Regarding validation of the model, our laboratory has shown that this model results in alcohol drinking behavior yielding BACs greater than 80 mg% [the threshold BAC in NIAAA's (2004) definition for binge drinking] and motor impairment as a measure of intoxication (Bell et al., 2006b, 2011). These benchmarks were achieved in both peri-adolescent and adult P rats of both sexes. Moreover, Bell and colleagues (2011) reported that whereas adult P rats, of both sexes, given continuous access consumed more alcohol than those given binge-like access; the reverse was true for peri-adolescent P rats, of both sexes, with binge-like access animals consuming significantly more than their continuous access counterparts each day. The latter finding provides some "face" validity for this developmental alcohol binge-drinking model, such that peri-adolescent rats consumed more alcohol than their adult counterparts both in terms of total consumption per day and consumption per one hr access period. It is noteworthy, that an examination of the 24-hr alcohol drinking behavior of P (Bell et al., 2006c) and HAD (Dhaher et al., 2012a) rats has revealed that both rat lines display repeated 6-min bouts of alcohol intake, across each 24-hr period, that exceed 1.0 g of alcohol/kg body weight/6-min bout. These levels of alcohol intake within this relatively short time span result in BACs approximating 80 mg% or greater. However, under 24-hr access conditions the timing of these bouts of alcohol drinking varies from day-to-day. Therefore, to repeatedly capture these levels of alcohol intake we use the DID-MSA procedure, with 60% of the alcohol drinking occurring within the first 6-min and over 95% of the alcohol drinking occurring within the first 12-min of each 1-hr session (Bell et al., 2006b).

An early study using the DID-MSA procedure examined protein expression changes in the NAc and Amyg after six-and-a-half weeks of DID-MSA (4 sessions/day) binge (rats consumed ~ 5 g of alcohol/kg body weight/day) vs. continuous alcohol (rats consumed ~ 5 g of alcohol/ kg body weight/day) drinking vs. alcohol-naïve adult male inbred P (iP) rats (Bell et al., 2006a). These authors reported three key findings: first, DID-MSA altered expression levels for 12 of the 14 identified proteins in the NAc, compared with controls; second, continuous access changed expression levels for 22 of the 27 identified proteins in the Amyg, compared with controls; and, third, 86% of the proteins that changed in the NAc showed greater expression levels vs. controls, whereas 58% of the proteins that changed in the Amyg displayed reduced levels of expression vs. controls. These results indicate brain-region specific effects contingent upon the presence or absence of multiple deprivation (i.e., detoxification) intervals. The identified proteins could be grouped into biological categories associated with intracellular chaperones, cytoskeleton/synaptic plasticity, intracellular communication, membrane transport, metabolism, energy production and neurotransmission. Of the neurotransmitter systems mediating alcohol abuse and dependence within the mesocorticolimbic DA system, the protein expression changes observed in this study implicated the neurosteroid/GABAergic system to the greatest degree.

A second study using the DID-MSA procedure examined gene expression changes in the NAc after 8 weeks of DID-MSA (3 sessions/day) binge (rats consumed ~ 6.5 g of alcohol/kg body weight/day) vs. continuous alcohol (rats consumed ~ 9.5 g of alcohol/kg body weight/day) drinking vs. alcohol-naïve adult male P rats (Bell et al., 2009). Unexpectedly, when the whole NAc (see McBride et al., 2010) was examined the only group that displayed significant differences from the controls was the continuous access group (i.e., the gene expression levels in the NAc of the binge-drinking group did not differ significantly from that observed in the control group). Gene Ontology (GO) analyses revealed over representation of significantly changed genes in 20 GO categories of biological function. These GO categories included negative regulation of protein kinase activity, anti-apoptosis, and regulation of G-protein-coupled receptor signaling.

Ingenuity® pathway analyses indicated a network of transcription factors including the *Fos, Jun, Junb* oncogenes, which suggests chronic alcohol drinking increased neuronal activity in the NAc. Several neurotransmitter-associated genes implicated in alcohol abuse and dependence were also altered within the NAc, including activity regulated cytoskeletal-associated protein [ARC which is associated with brain derived neurotrophic factor (BDNF) and neuropeptide Y (NPY) activity]; cholinergic receptor, nicotinic, alpha polypeptide 7 (*Chrna7*), which modulates glutamatergic and DAergic activity within the mesocorticolimbic DA system; corticotrophin releasing hormone (CRF), which is implicated in the negative reinforcing properties of alcohol during withdrawal, craving and relapse; and Homer homolog 1 (*Homer1*), which serves as a glutamatergic receptor-associated scaffolding/membrane-docking protein.

A third study using the DID-MSA procedure examined gene expression changes in the NAc shell and central nucleus of the Amyg after 8 weeks of DID-MSA (3 sessions/day) binge (rats consumed ~ 5 g of alcohol/kg body weight/day) drinking vs. alcohol-naïve adult male P rats (McBride et al., 2010). These authors reported that there were significantly more genes up-regulated than down-regulated by alcohol binge drinking. Ingenuity Pathway Analysis of gene changes in the NAc shell revealed one biological pathway that included cytoskeletal-, calmodulin- and glutamate receptor-associated genes. The findings indicated that binge-like alcohol drinking by P rats produced region-specific changes in gene expression levels, with biological functions associated with transcription, synaptic function and neuronal plasticity implicated. Moreover, similar to the findings in the proteomics study (Bell et al., 2006a), different mechanisms may underlie alterations in these biological functions, because very few genes that displayed significant changes in expression were common to both the NAc shell and the central nucleus of the Amyg. Combined, these studies indicate that binge-like alcohol drinking by P rats alters neuronal activity within brain structures of the mesocorticolimbic DA system and the associated extended Amyg. These changes involve physiological alterations in the glutamatergic, DAergic and GABAergic neurotransmitter systems corroborating other research implicating these neurotransmitter systems in the development of alcohol abuse and dependence as well as binge drinking. These neurobiological findings as well as the pharmacological treatments discussed above, and elsewhere (e.g., Bell et al., 2012b) parallel other reports in the alcohol abuse and dependence literature using mice and nonhuman primates as well as human subjects. Overall, the results support the conceptualization that binge alcohol drinking (or drug intake) is part of the addiction process and is mediated by similar neurocircuitry as that seen in alcohol (or drug) abuse and dependence.

CONCLUSION

Alcohol abuse, especially binge drinking, and dependence continue to be serious public health concerns. Adolescents and young adults are particularly vulnerable to the cognitive as well as emotional disruptive effects of alcohol and are prone to engage in binge drinking. Binge alcohol drinking appears to be a developmental phenomenon with the majority of this type of drinking occurring during adolescence and young adulthood. Early onset of alcohol use, usually in the form of binge drinking, markedly increases the probability of developing alcohol dependence during one's life-time.

Within the context of addiction, the progression from casual alcohol drinking to dependence is incremental and cyclical in nature. Early in the addiction cycle alcohol drinking is impulsive and binge-like, with the positive reinforcing/hedonic properties of alcohol driving the process. During the later stages of addiction alcohol drinking is compulsive and appears to be driven by the negative reinforcing/anhedonia and anxiety reducing effects of alcohol. The addiction cycle is marked by escalation of intake overtime, which is exacerbated by repeated cycles of abstinence and relapse. However, progress through the addiction cycle is not linear, with many individuals returning to earlier stages of the cycle before progressing to full-blown dependence.

Definitionally, escalation of alcohol or, for that matter, any drug or reinforcer, intake is a primary characteristic of binge drinking or self-administration. The present clinical definition of binge alcohol drinking identifies individuals who consume at least 4 or 5, for women and men respectively, standard alcoholic drinks within 2-hrs, and this drinking results in BACs of 80 mg% (0.08 in clinical terms) or greater as well as the expression of overt intoxication at least once in a set period of time (usually 2 weeks). A preclinical definition of binge alcohol exposure is still evolving. At this point, the primary preclinical characteristic is alcohol exposure that results in BACs greater than 80 mg%. Most preclinical models of binge alcohol exposure result in BACs that approximate 300 mg% or greater. In humans, BACs of 200 mg% or greater are readily achieved during extreme drinking (which is, perhaps unfortunately, often characterized as binge drinking in the clinical literature), such as celebrating ones 21st birthday in the United States. This type of drinking clearly results in the development of tolerance to alcohol's effects, which is a diagnostic criterion for alcohol abuse and dependence.

Findings from the existing clinical research on the effects of binge alcohol drinking indicate that many of the cognitive and emotional disruptive effects of alcohol seen in binge drinkers are also seen in alcoholics who have experienced multiple detoxifications. Therefore, many of the preclinical (and clinical) findings on the neurobiology of alcohol abuse and dependence appear to be relevant for research on the antecedents and consequences of binge drinking. Neurobiological evidence indicates that alcohol, and drug, abuse is mediated by the mesocorticolimbic DA system, which includes the VTA, NAc, mPFC and Amyg. These key brain regions are highly interconnected and are essential in the acquisition and valuation of rewards, including natural reinforcers such as food and sex. Within these brain regions, a number of neurotransmitter systems including glutamate, GABA, DA, serotonin, acetylcholine, opioids, NPY and ghrelin mediate (a) the acquisition of, (b) the maintenance of, and (c) relapse to alcohol drinking and abuse. Moreover, these neurotransmitter systems and their associated neurocircuitry are altered by both acute and chronic exposure to alcohol.

From the preclinical perspective, animal models have been essential in determining the neurobiological antecedents and consequences of alcohol abuse and dependence. In particular, selectively bred rat lines have been shown to be valid animal model systems for studying this neurobiology. In general, the selectively bred alcohol-preferring P and high alcohol-drinking HAD1 and HAD2 meet all or most, respectively, of the criteria proposed for valid animal models of alcoholism. These lines of rats display binge-like alcohol drinking under (a) free-choice, 24-hr access; (b) ADE/relapse-like access; (c) both home-cage and operant chamber, limited access; and (d) DID-multiple scheduled access conditions; such that these protocols result in BACs that exceed 80 mg% and rats often displaying overt intoxication.

Moreover, binge-like alcohol drinking is displayed by both peri-adolescent and adult as well as male and female rats from these selectively bred lines. Genomic [messenger-ribonucleic acid (mRNA) levels detected by microarray and reverse transcription-polymerase chain reaction (RT-PCR)] and proteomic (protein levels detected by 2-dimensional gel electrophoresis and Western blots) studies using these binge-drinking protocols have provided evidence that the GABAergic (including neurosteroid), glutamatergic, DAergic, serotonergic, and cholinergic neurotransmitter systems within multiple brain regions of the mesocorticolimbic system mediate this type of drinking behavior. In vivo microdialysis studies targeting subregions of the mesocorticolimbic system of P rats that have experienced these binge-drinking protocols has confirmed a role for the glutamatergic, DAergic and serotonergic systems in this behavior. Pharmacological studies using ligands targeting the above neurotransmitter systems as well as neuropeptide systems discussed in this chapter have provided even further evidence that these neurotransmitter and neuropeptide systems mediate, at least in part, binge alcohol-drinking and its effects. In conclusion, these findings support current theories on the role of neurotransmission in the mesocorticolimbic system and the associated extended amygdala as it pertains to binge drinking, alcohol abuse and dependence. While this research has provided possible pharmacological targets for the treatment of alcohol abuse and dependence, further research is needed to develop greater resolution in determining small-molecule/drugable targets. Towards this end, these selectively bred rat lines and associated alcohol drinking protocols will continue to play a crucial role in this research.

ACKNOWLEDGMENTS

This work was supported in part by National Institute on Alcohol Abuse and Alcoholism grants AA13522 (RLB) and AA20396 (EAE).

REFERENCES

Abizaid A, Liu ZW, Andrews ZB, Shanabrough M, Borok E, Elsworth JD, Roth RH, Sleeman MW, Picciotto MR, Tschop MH, Gao XB, Horvath TL. (2006). Ghrelin modulates the activity and synaptic input organization of midbrain dopamine neurons while promoting appetite. *J. Clin. Invest.* 116:3229-3239.

Addolorato G, Capristo E, Leggio L, Ferrulli A, Abenavoli L, Malandrino N, Farnetti S, Domenicali M, D'Angelo C, Vonghia L, Mirijello A, Cardone S, Gasbarrini G. (2006). Relationship between ghrelin levels, alcohol craving, and nutritional status in current alcoholic patients. *Alcohol Clin. Exp. Res.* 30:1933-1937.

Adriani W, Laviola G. (2004). Windows of vulnerability to psychopathology and therapeutic strategy in the adolescent rodent model. *Behav. Pharmacol.* 15:341-352.

Agabio R, Maccioni P, Carai MA, Gessa GL, Froestl W, Colombo G. (2012). The development of medications for alcohol-use disorders targeting the GABAB receptor system. *Rec. Patents CNS Drug Disc.* 7:113-128.

Ahmed SH. (2011). Escalation of drug use. In MC Olmstead (ed.), *Animal Models of Drug Addiction.* New York: Humana Press/Springer Science; pp. 267-292.

Albuquerque EX, Pereira EFR, Alkondon M, Rogers SW. (2009). Mammalian nicotinic acetylcholine receptors: from structure to function. *Physiol. Rev.* 89:73-120.

Allen YS, Roberts GW, Bloom SR, Crow TJ, Polak JM. (1994). Neuropeptide Y in the stria terminalis: evidence for an amygdalofugal projection. *Brain Res.* 321:357-362.

American Psychiatric Association. (2000). *Diagnostic and Statistical Manual of Mental Disorders* (4th ed.). Washington, DC: American Psychiatric Association.

Andersen SL. (2003). Trajectories of brain development: points of vulnerability or windows of opportunity. *Neurosci. Biobehav. Rev.* 27:3-18.

Andrews MM, Meda SA, Thomas AD, Potenza MN, Krystal JH, Worhunsky P, Stevens MC, O'Malley S, Book GA, Reynolds B, Pearlson GD. (2011). Individuals family history positive for alcoholism show functional magnetic resonance imaging differences in reward sensitivity that are related to impulsivity factors. *Biol. Psychiatry* 69:675-683.

Anthony JC, Petronis KR. (1995). Early-onset drug use and risk of later drug problems. *Drug Alcohol Depend.* 40:9-15.

Azmitia EC, Segal M. (1978). An autoradiographic analysis of the differential ascending projections of the dorsal and median raphe nuclei in the rat. *J. Comp. Neurol.* 179: 641-67.

Babor TF, Hofmann M, DelBoca FK, Hesselbrock V, Meyer RE, Dolinsky ZS, Rounsaville B. (1992). Types of alcoholics, I. Evidence for an empirically derived typology based on indicators of vulnerability and severity. *Arch. Gen. Psychiatry* 49:599-608.

Backstrom P, Bachteler D, Koch S, Hyytia P, Spanagel R. (2004). mGluR5 antagonist MPEP reduces ethanol-seeking and relapse behavior. *Neuropsychopharmacology* 29:921-928.

Badanich KA, Maldonado AM, Kirstein CL. (2007). Chronic ethanol exposure during adolescence increases basal dopamine in the nucleus accumbens septi during adulthood. *Alcohol Clin. Exp. Res.* 31:895-900.

Badaoui A, De Saeger C, Duchemin J, Gihousse D, de Timary P, Stärkel P. (2008). Alcohol dependence is associated with reduced plasma and fundic ghrelin levels. *Eur. J. Clin. Invest.* 38: 397-403.

Badia-Elder NE, Gilpin NW, Stewart RB. (2007). Neuropeptide Y modulation of ethanol intake: Effects of ethanol drinking history and genetic background. *Peptides* 28:339-344.

Barnes NM, Sharp T. (1999). A review of central 5-HT receptors and their function. *Neuropharmacology* 38:1083-1152.

Barron S, Lewis B, Wellmann K, Carter M, Farook J, Ring J, Rogers DT, Holley R, Crooks P, Littleton J. (2012). Polyamine modulation of NMDARs as a mechanism to reduce effects of alcohol dependence. *Rec. Patents CNS Drug Disc.* 7:129-144.

Barson JR, Carr AJ, Soun JE, Sobhani NC, Rada P, Leibowitz SF, Hoebel BG. (2010). Opioids in the hypothalamic paraventricular nucleus stimulate ethanol intake. *Alcohol Clin. Exp. Res.* 34:214-222.

Bartlett S, Heilig M. (2013). Translational approaches to medications development. *Curr. Topics Behav. Neurosci.* 13:543-582.

Bava S, Tapert SF. (2010). Adolescent brain development and the risk for alcohol and other drug problems. *Neuropsychol. Rev.* 20:398-413.

Beart PM, McDonald D. (1982). 5-Hydroxytryptamine and 5-hydroxytryptaminergic dopaminergic interactions in the ventral tegmental area of rat brain. *J. Pharm. Pharmacol.* 34:591-593.

Bell RL, Franklin KM, Hauser SR, Zhou FC. (2012a). Introduction to the special issue "Pharmacotherapies for the treatment of alcohol abuse and dependence" and a summary of patents targeting other neurotransmitter systems. *Rec. Patents CNS Drug Disc.* 7:93-112.

Bell RL, Kimpel MW, McClintick JN, Strother WN, Carr LG, Liang T, Rodd ZA, Mayfield RD, Edenberg HJ, McBride WJ. (2009). Gene expression changes in the nucleus accumbens of alcohol-preferring rats following chronic ethanol consumption. *Pharmacol. Biochem. Behav.* 94:131-147.

Bell RL, Kimpel MW, Rodd ZA, Strother WN, Bai F, Peper CL, Mayfield RD, Lumeng L, Crabb DW, McBride WJ, Witzmann FA. (2006a). Protein expression changes in the nucleus accumbens and amygdala of inbred alcohol-preferring rats given either continuous or scheduled access to ethanol. *Alcohol* 40:3-17.

Bell RL, McKinzie DL, Murphy JM, McBride WJ. (2000). Sensitivity and tolerance to the motor impairing effects of moderate doses of ethanol. *Pharmacol. Biochem. Behav.* 67:583-586.

Bell RL, Rodd ZA, Boutwell CL, Hsu CC, Lumeng L, Murphy JM, Li TK, McBride WJ. (2004). Effects of long-term episodic access to ethanol on the expression of an alcohol deprivation effect in low alcohol-consuming rats. *Alcohol Clin. Exp. Res.* 28:1867-1874.

Bell RL, Rodd ZA, Lumeng L, Murphy JM, McBride WJ. (2006b). The alcohol-preferring P rat and animal models of excessive alcohol drinking. *Addict. Biol.* 11:270-288.

Bell RL, Rodd ZA, Murphy JM, McBride WJ. (2005). Use of selectively bred alcohol-preferring rats to study alcohol abuse, relapse and craving. In VR Preedy, RR Watson (eds.), *Comprehensive handbook of alcohol related pathology* (Vol. 3). New York: Academic Press; pp. 1515-1533.

Bell RL, Rodd ZA, Sable HJK, Schultz JA, Hsu CC, Lumeng L, Murphy JM, McBride WJ. (2006c). Daily patterns of ethanol drinking in periadolescent and adult alcohol-preferring (P) rats. *Pharmacol. Biochem. Behav.* 83:35-46.

Bell RL, Rodd ZA, Schultz JA, Peper CL, Lumeng L, Murphy JM, McBride WJ. (2008). Effects of short deprivation and re-exposure intervals on the ethanol drinking behavior of selectively bred high alcohol-consuming rats. *Alcohol* 42:407-416.

Bell RL, Rodd ZA, Smith RJ, Toalston JE, Franklin KM, McBride WJ. (2011). Modeling binge-like ethanol drinking by peri-adolescent and adult P rats. *Pharmacol. Biochem. Behav.* 100:90-97.

Bell RL, Sable HJK, Colombo G, Hyytia P, Rodd ZA, Lumeng L. (2012b). Animal models for medications development targeting alcohol abuse using selectively bred rat lines: neurobiological and pharmacological validity. *Pharmacol. Biochem. Behav.* 103:119-55.

Bell RL, Stewart RB, Woods JE, 2nd, Lumeng L, Li TK, Murphy JM, McBride WJ. (2001). Responsivity and development of tolerance to the motor impairing effects of moderate doses of ethanol in alcohol-preferring (P) and -nonpreferring (NP) rat lines. *Alcohol Clin. Exp. Res.* 25:644-650.

Benes FM, Taylor JB, Cunningham MC. (2000). Convergence and plasticity of monoaminergic systems in the medial prefrontal cortex during the postnatal period: implications for the development of psychopathology. *Cereb. Cortex* 10:1014-1027.

Benjamin D, Grant ER, Pohorecky LA. (1993). Naltrexone reverses ethanol-induced dopamine release in the nucleus accumbens in awake, freely moving rats. *Brain Res.* 621:137-140.

Bennett B, Downing C, Parker C, Johnson TE. (2006). Mouse genetic models in alcohol research. *Trends Genet.* 22:367-374.

Berglind WJ, Whitfield TW Jr., LaLumiere RT, Kalivas PW, McGinty JF. (2009). A single intra-PFC infusion of BDNF prevents cocaine-induced alterations in extracellular glutamate within the nucleus accumbens. *J. Neurosci.* 29:3715-3719.

Bertholomey ML, Henderson AN, Badia-Elder NE, Stewart RB. (2011). Neuropeptide Y (NPY)-induced reductions in alcohol intake during continuous access and following alcohol deprivation are not altered by restraint stress in alcohol-preferring (P) rats. *Pharmacol. Biochem. Behav.* 97:453-461.

Besheer J, Grondin JJ, Cannady R, Sharko AC, Faccidomo S, Hodge CW. (2010). Metabotropic glutamate receptor 5 activity in the nucleus accumbens is required for the maintenance of ethanol self-administration in a rat genetic model of high alcohol intake. *Biol. Psychiatry* 67:812-822.

Blednov YA, Walker D, Martinez M, Harris RA. (2006). Reduced alcohol consumption in mice lacking preprodynorphin. *Alcohol* 40:73-86.

Blomqvist O, Ericson M, Engel JA, Soderpalm B. (1997). Accumbal dopamine overflow after ethanol: localization of the antagonizing effect of mecamylamine. *Eur. J. Pharmacol.* 334:149-156.

Blomqvist O, Ericson M, Johnson DH, Engel JA, Soderpalm B. (1996). Voluntary ethanol intake in the rat: Effects of nicotinic acetylcholine receptor blockade or subchronic nicotine treatment. *Eur. J. Pharmacol.* 314:257-267.

Blumenthal SJ. (1997). Women and substance abuse: a new national focus. *National Institute on Drug Abuse Conference on Substance Abuse in Women.* Available at: http://www.nida.nih.gov (See NIDA Notes on Women and Gender)

Boehm SL, 2nd, Moore EM, Walsh CD, Gross CD, Cavelli AM, Gigante E, Linsenbardt DN. (2008). Using drinking in the dark to model prenatal binge-like exposure to ethanol in C57BL/6J mice. *Dev. Psychobiol.* 50:566-578.

Boyce-Rustay JM, Cunningham CL. (2004). The role of NMDA receptor binding sites in ethanol place conditioning. *Behav. Neurosci.* 118:822-834.

Brienza RS, Stein MD. (2002). Alcohol use disorders in primary care: do gender-specific differences exist? *J. Gen. Intern. Med.* 17:387-397.

Brodie MS, Shefner SA, Dunwiddie TV. (1990). Ethanol increases the firing rate of dopamine neurons of the rat ventral tegmental area in vitro. *Brain Res.* 508:65-69.

Brodie MS, Trifunović RD, Shefner SA. (1995). Serotonin potentiates ethanol-induced excitation of ventral tegmental area neurons in brain slices from three different rat strains. *J. Pharmacol. Exp. Ther.* 273:1139-1146.

Brunelle C, Assad J-M, Barrett SP, Avila C, Conrod PJ, Tremblay RE, Pihl RO. (2004). Heightened heart rate response to alcohol intoxication is associated with a reward-seeking personality profile. *Alcohol Clin. Exp. Res.* 28:394-401.

Brunelle C, Barrett SP, Pihl RO. (2007). Relationship between the cardiac response to acute intoxication and alcohol-induced subjective effects throughout the blood alcohol concentration curve. *Human Psychopharmacology* 22:437-43.

Capaldi DM, Feingold A, Kim HK, Yoerger K, Washburn IJ. (2013). Heterogeneity in growth and desistance of alcohol use for men in their 20s: prediction from early risk factors and association with treatment. *Alcohol Clin. Exp. Res.* 37:E347-355.

Carlezon WA, Jr, Wise RA. (1996). Rewarding actions of phencyclidine and related drugs in nucleus accumbens shell and frontal cortex. *J. Neurosci.* 16:3112-3122.

Carroll MR, Rodd ZA, Murphy JM, Simon JR. (2006). Chronic ethanol consumption increases dopamine uptake in the nucleus accumbens of high alcohol drinking rats. *Alcohol* 40:103-109.

Casey BJ, Giedd JN, Thomas KM. (2000). Structural and functional brain development and its relation to cognitive development. *Biol. Psychiatry* 54:241-247.

Chambers RA, Taylor JR, Potenza MN. (2003). Developmental neurocircuitry of motivation in adolescence: a critical period of addiction vulnerability. *Am. J. Psychiatry* 160:1041-1052.

Chandler LJ, Newsom H, Sumners C, Crews F. (1993). Chronic ethanol exposure potentiates NMDA excitotoxicity in cerebral cortical neurons. *J. Neurochem.* 60:1578-1581.

Charlet K, Beck A, Heinz A. (2013). The dopamine system in mediating alcohol effects in humans. *Curr. Topics Behav. Neurosci.* 13:461-488.

Cherpitel CJ, Moskalewicz J, Swiatkiewicz G. (2004). Drinking patterns and problems in emergency services in Poland. *Alcohol Alcohol.* 39:256-261.

Chin VS, Van Skike CE, Matthews DB. (2010). Effects of ethanol on hippocampal function during adolescence: a look at the past and thoughts on the future. *Alcohol* 44:3-14.

Chou SP, Pickering RP. (1992). Early onset of drinking as a risk factor for lifetime alcohol-related problems. *Br. J. Addict.* 87:1199-1204.

Chugani HT, Phelps ME, Mazziotta JC. (1987). Positron emission tomography study of human brain functional development. *Ann. Neurol.* 22:487-497.

Ciccocioppo R, Angeletti S, Colombo G, Gessa G, Massi M. (1999). Autoradiographic analysis of 5-HT2A binding sites in the brain of Sardinian alcohol-preferring and nonpreferring rats. *Eur. J. Pharmacol.* 373:3-9.

Ciccocioppo R, Martin-Fardon R, Weiss F. (2002). Effect of selective blockade of mu (1) or delta opioid receptors on reinstatement of alcohol-seeking behavior by drug-associated stimuli in rats. *Neuropsychopharmacology* 27:391-399.

Cicero TJ. (1979). A critique of animal analogues of alcoholism. In E Majchrowicz, EP Noble (eds.), *Biochemistry and Pharmacology of Ethanol* (Vol. 2). New York: Plenum Press; pp. 533-60.

Clapp JD, Lange J, Min JW, Shillington A, Johnson M, Voas R. (2003). Two studies examining environmental predictors of heavy drinking by college students. *Prev. Sci.* 4:99-108.

Clark DB, Kirisci L, Tarter RE. (1998). Adolescent versus adult onset and the development of substance use disorders in males. *Drug Alcohol Depend.* 49:115-21.

Clark DB, Thatcher DL, Tapert SF. (2008). Alcohol, psychological dysregulation, and adolescent brain development. *Alcohol Clin. Exp. Res.* 32:375-385.

Clark JT, Kalra PS, Crowley WR, Kalra SP. (1984). Neuropeptide Y and human pancreatic polypeptide stimulate feeding behavior in rats. *Endocrin.* 115:427-429.

Clermont Y, Perry B. (1957). Quantitative study of the cell population of the seminiferous tubules in immature rats. *Amer. J. Anat.* 100:241-260.

Cloninger CR. (1987). Neurogenetic adaptive mechanisms in alcoholism. *Science* 236:410-416.

Coleman J, Williams A, Phan TH, Mummalaneni S, Melone P, Ren Z, Zhou H, Mahavadi S, Murthy KS, Katsumata T, DeSimone JA, Lyall V. (2011). Strain differences in the neural, behavioral, and molecular correlates of sweet and salty taste in naive, ethanol- and sucrose-exposed P and NP rats. *J. Neurophysiol.* 106:2606-2621.

Conrod PJ, Pihl RO, Stewart SH, Dongier M. (2000). Validation of a system of classifying female substance abusers on the basis of personality and motivational risk factors for substance abuse. *Psychol. Addict. Behav.* 14:243-256.

Corominas M, Roncero C, Casas M. (2010). Corticotropin releasing factor and neuroplasticity in cocaine addiction. *Life Sci.* 86:1-9.

Corrigall WA, Coen KM, Adamson KL. (1994). Self-administered nicotine activates the mesolimbic dopamine system through the ventral tegmental area. *Brain Res.* 653:278-284.

Courtney KE, Polich J. (2009). Binge drinking in young adults: data, definitions, and determinants. *Psychol. Bull.* 135:142-156.

Covington HE, III, Miczek KA. (2011). Binge drug taking. In MC Olmstead (ed.), *Animal Models of Drug Addiction*. New York: Humana Press/Springer Science; pp. 403-430.

Cozzoli DK, Goulding SP, Zhang PW, Xiao B, Hu JH, Ary AW, Obara I, Rahn A, Abou-Ziab H, Tyrrel B, Marini C, Yoneyama N, Metten P, Snelling C, Dehoff MH, Crabbe JC, Finn DA, Klugmann M, Worley PF, Szumlinski KK. (2009). Binge drinking upregulates accumbens mGluR5-Homer2-PI3K signaling: functional implications for alcoholism. *J. Neurosci.* 29:8655-8668.

Crabbe JC. (2008). Review. Neurogenetic studies of alcohol addiction. *Philos. Trans. R Soc. Lond. B Biol. Sci.* 363:3201-3211.

Crabbe JC. (2012). Translational behavior-genetic studies of alcohol: are we there yet? *Genes Brain Behav.* 11:375-386.

Crabbe JC, Bell RL, Ehlers CL. (2010a). Human and laboratory rodent low response to alcohol: is better consilience possible? *Addict. Biol.* 15:125-144.

Crabbe JC, Harris RA, Koob GF. (2011). Preclinical studies of alcohol binge drinking. *Ann. New York Acad. Sci.* 1216:24-40.

Crabbe JC, Kendler KS, Hitzemann RJ. (2013). Modeling the diagnostic criteria for alcohol dependence with genetic animal models. *Curr. Topics Behav. Neurosci.* 13:187-221.

Crabbe JC, Metten P, Rhodes JS, Yu C-H, Brown LL, Phillips TJ, Finn DA. (2009). A line of mice selected for high blood ethanol concentrations shows drinking in the dark to intoxication. *Biol. Psychiatry* 65:662-670.

Crabbe JC, Phillips TJ, Belknap JK. (2010b). The complexity of alcohol drinking: studies in rodent genetic models. *Behav. Genet.* 40:737-750.

Crabbe JC, Phillips TJ, Harris RA, Arends MA, Koob GF. (2006). Alcohol-related genes: contributions from studies with genetically engineered mice. *Addict. Biol.* 11:195-269.

Crabbe JC, Phillips TJ, Kosobud A, Belknap JK. (1990). Estimation of genetic correlation: interpretation of experiments using selectively bred and inbred animals. *Alcohol Clin. Exp. Res.* 14:141-151.

Cranford JA, McCabe SE, Boyd CJ. (2006). A new measure of binge drinking: prevalence and correlates in a probability sample of undergraduates. *Alcohol Clin. Exp. Res.* 30:1896-1905.

Cudd TA. (2005). Animal models systems for the study of alcohol teratology. *Exp. Biol. Med.* 230:389-393.

Dani JA, Harris RA. (2005). Nicotine addiction and comorbidity with alcohol abuse and mental illness. *Nat. Neurosci.* 8:1465-1470.

Dawson DA, Grant BF, Stinson FS, Chou PS. (2004). Another look at heavy episodic drinking and alcohol use disorders among college and noncollege youth. *J. Stud. Alcohol* 65:477-488.

Dayas CV, Liu X, Simms JA, Weiss F. (2007). Distinct patterns of neural activation associated with ethanol seeking: effects of naltrexone. *Biol. Psychiatry* 61:979-989.

Deehan GA, Jr, Bordie MS, Rodd ZA. (2013). What is in that drink: the biological actions of ethanol, acetaldehyde, and salsolinol. *Curr. Topics Behav. Neurosci.* 13:163-184.

de Oliveira RW, Nakamura-Palacios EM. (2003). Haloperidol increases the disruptive effect of alcohol on spatial working memory in rats: a dopaminergic modulation in the medial prefrontal cortex. *Psychopharmacology* (Berl) 170:51-61.

De Witte P. (2004). Imbalance between neuroexcitatory and neuroinhibitory amino acids causes craving for ethanol. *Addict. Behav.* 29:1325-1339.

Dhaher R, Hauser SR, Getachew B, Bell RL, McBride WJ, McKinzie DL, Rodd ZA. (2010). The orexin-1 receptor antagonist SB-334867 reduces alcohol relapse drinking, but not alcohol-seeking, in alcohol-preferring (P) rats. *J. Addict. Med.* 4:153-159.

Dhaher R, McConnell KK, Rodd ZA, McBride WJ, Bell RL. (2012a). Daily patterns of ethanol drinking in adolescent and adult, male and female, high alcohol drinking (HAD) replicate lines of rats. *Pharmacol. Biochem. Behav.* 102:540-548.

Dhaher R, Toalston JE, Hauser SR, Bell RL, McKinzie DL, McBride WJ, Rodd ZA. (2012b). Effects of naltrexone and LY255582 on ethanol maintenance, seeking and relapse responding by alcohol-preferring (P) rats. *Alcohol* 46:17-27.

Di Chiara G, Imperato A. (1988). Drugs abused by humans preferentially increase synaptic dopamine concentrations in the mesolimbic system of freely moving rats. *Proc. Natl. Acad. Sci. USA* 85:5274-5278.

Dick DM, Bierut LJ. (2006). The genetics of alcohol dependence. *Curr. Psychiatry Rep.* 8:151-157.

Ding ZM, Katner SN, Rodd ZA, Truitt W, Hauser SR, Deehan GA, Jr, Engleman EA, McBride WJ. (2012a). Repeated exposure of the posterior ventral tegmental area to nicotine increases the sensitivity of local dopamine neurons to the stimulating effects of ethanol. *Alcohol* 46:217-223.

Ding ZM, Oster SM, Hall SR, Engleman EA, Hauser SR, McBride WJ, Rodd ZA. (2011). The stimulating effects of ethanol on ventral tegmental area dopamine neurons projecting to the ventral pallidum and medial prefrontal cortex in female Wistar rats: regional difference and involvement of serotonin-3 receptors. *Psychopharmacology* (Berl) 216:245-255.

Ding ZM, Rodd ZA, Engleman EA, Bailey JA, Lahiri DK, McBride WJ. (2012b). Alcohol drinking and deprivation alter basal extracellular glutamate concentrations and clearance in the mesolimbic system of alcohol-preferring (P) rats. *Addict. Biol.* : In Press.

Ding ZM, Toalston JE, Oster SM, McBride WJ, Rodd ZA. (2009). Involvement of local serotonin-2A but not serotonin-1B receptors in the reinforcing effects of ethanol within the posterior ventral tegmental area of female Wistar rats. *Psychopharmacology* 204:381-390.

Döhler KD, Wuttke W. (1975). Changes with age in levels of serum gonadotropins, prolactin and gonadal steroids in prepubertal male and female rats. *Endocrin.* 97:898-907.

Donovan JE. (2009). Estimated blood alcohol concentrations for child and adolescent drinking and their implications for screening instruments. *Pediat.* 123:e975-e981.

Duka T, Tasker R, Stephens DN. (1998). Alcohol choice and outcome expectancies in social drinkers. *Behav. Pharmacol.* 9:643-653.

Duka T, Gentry J, Malcolm R, Ripley TL, Borlikova G, Stephens DN, Veatch LM, Becker HC, Crews FT. (2004). Consequences of multiple withdrawals from alcohol. *Alcohol Clin. Exp. Res.* 28:233-246.

Duka T, Townshend JM, Collier K, Stephens DN. (2002). Kindling of withdrawal: a study of craving and anxiety after multiple detoxifications in alcoholic inpatients. *Alcohol Clin. Exp. Res.* 26:785-795.

Duka T, Townshend JM, Collier K, Stephens DN. (2003). Impairment in cognitive functions after multiple detoxifications in alcoholic inpatients. *Alcohol Clin. Exp. Res.* 27:1563-1572.

Dumas TC. (2004). Early eyelid opening enhances spontaneous alternation and accelerates the development of perforant path synaptic strength in the hippocampus of juvenile rats. *Develop. Psychobiol.* 45:1-9.

Dundon W, Lynch KG, Pettinati HM, Lipkin C. (2004). Treatment outcomes in type A and B alcohol dependence 6 months after serotonergic pharmacotherapy. *Alcohol Clin. Exp. Res.* 28:1065-1073.

Ehlers CL, Criado JR. (2010). Adolescent ethanol exposure: does it produce long-lasting electrophysiological effects? *Alcohol* 44:27-38.

Ehlers CL, Li TK, Lumeng L, Hwang BH, Somes C, Jimenez P, Mathé AA. (1998). Neuropeptide Y levels in ethanol-naive alcohol-preferring and nonpreferring rats and in Wistar rats after ethanol exposure. *Alcohol Clin. Exp. Res.* 22:1778-1782.

Ehlers CL, Walter NAR, Dick DM, Buck KJ, Crabbe JC. (2010). A comparison of selected quantitative trait loci associated with alcohol use phenotypes in humans and animal models. *Addict. Biol.* 15:185-199.

Eiler WA, II, June HL. (2007). Blockade of GABAA receptors within the extended amygdala attenuates D2 regulation of alcohol-motivated behaviors in the ventral tegmental area of alcohol-preferring (P) rats. *Neuropharmacol.* 52:1570-1579.

Engleman EA, Ding ZM, Oster SM, Toalston JE, Bell RL, Murphy JM, McBride WJ, Rodd ZA. (2009). Ethanol is self-administered into the nucleus accumbens shell, but not the core: evidence of genetic sensitivity. *Alcohol Clin. Exp. Res.* 33:2162-2171.

Engleman EA, Ingraham CM, McBride WJ, Lumeng L, Murphy JM. (2006). Extracellular dopamine levels are lower in the medial prefrontal cortex of alcohol-preferring rats compared to Wistar rats. *Alcohol* 38:5-12.

Engleman EA, Keen EJ, Tilford SS, Thielen RJ, Morzorati SL. (2011). Ethanol drinking reduces extracellular dopamine levels in the posterior ventral tegmental area of nondependent alcohol-preferring rats. *Alcohol* 45:549-557.

Engleman EA, McBride WJ, Li T-K, Lumeng L, Murphy JM. (2003). Ethanol drinking experience attenuates (-)sulpiride-induced increase in extracellular dopamine levels in the nucleus accumbens of alcohol-preferring (P) rats. *Alcohol Clin. Exp. Res.* 27:424-431.

Engleman EA, McBride WJ, Wilber AA, Shaikh SR, Eha RD, Lumeng L, Li TK, Murphy JM. (2000). Reverse microdialysis of a dopamine uptake inhibitor in the nucleus accumbens of alcohol-preferring rats: effects on dialysate dopamine levels and ethanol intake. *Alcohol Clin. Exp. Res.* 24:795-801.

Engleman EA, Rodd ZA, Bell RL, Murphy JM. (2008). The role of 5-HT3 receptors in drug abuse and as a target for pharmacotherapy. *CNS Neurol. Disord. Drug Targets* 7:454-467.

Engleman EA, Thielen RJ, O'Brien CE, Hill TE, Lumeng L, Li T-K, McBride WJ, Murphy JM. (2002). Chronic Ethanol drinking and prolonged or repeated deprivations reduce dopamine (DA) transmission in the nucleus accumbens (ACB). *Soc. Neurosci. Abstracts*, vol 28, #309.1.

Enna SJ. (1997). GABAB receptor agonists and antagonists: pharmacological properties and therapeutic possibilities. *Expert. Opin. Invest. Drugs* 6:1319-25.

Enoch MA, Zhou Z, Kimura M, Mash DC, Yuan Q, Goldman D. (2012). GABAergic gene expression in postmortem hippocampus from alcoholics and cocaine addicts; corresponding findings in alcohol-naive P and NP rats. *PLoS One* 7(1):e29369.

Ericson M, Molander A, Lof E, Engel JA, Soderpalm B. (2003). Ethanol elevates accumbal dopamine levels via indirect activation of ventral tegmental nicotinic acetylcholine receptors. *Eur. J. Pharmacol.* 467:85-93.

Epstein EE, Kahler CW, McCrady BS, Lewis KD, Lewis S. (1995). An empirical classification of drinking patterns among alcoholics: binge, episodic, sporadic, and steady. *Addict. Behav.* 20:23-41.

Everitt BJ, Belin D, Economidou D, Pelloux Y, Dalley JW, Robbins TW. (2008). Neural mechanisms underlying the vulnerability to develop compulsive drug-seeking habits and addiction. *Phil. Trans R Soc. B* 363:3125-35.

Fadda F, Mosca E, Colombo G, Gessa GL. (1990). Alcohol-preferring rats: genetic sensitivity to alcohol-induced stimulation of dopamine metabolism. *Physiol. Behav.* 47:727-729.

Fadda F, Rossetti ZL. (1998). Chronic ethanol consumption: from neuroadaptation to neurodegeneration. *Prog. Neurobiol.* 56:385-431.

Farren CK, O'Malley S. (1997). Sequential use of naltrexone in the treatment of relapsing alcoholism. *Am. J. Psychiatry* 154:714.

Fleming RL, Acheson SK, Moore SD, Wilson WA, Swartzwelder HS. (2012). In the rat, chronic intermittent ethanol exposure during adolescence alters the ethanol sensitivity of tonic inhibition in adulthood. *Alcohol. Clin. Exp. Res.* 36:279-285.

Flory K, Lynam D, Milich R, Leukefeld C, Clayton R. (2004). Early adolescent through young adult alcohol and marijuana use trajectories: Early predictors, young adult outcomes, and predictive utility. *Dev. Psychopath.* 16:193-213.

Floyd DW, Jung KY, McCool BA. (2003). Chronic ethanol ingestion facilitates N-methyl-D-aspartate receptor function and expression in rat lateral/basolateral amygdala neurons. *J. Pharmacol. Exp. Ther.* 307:1020-1029.

Foster KL, McKay PF, Seyoum R, Milbourne D, Yin W, Sarma PV, Cook JM, June HL. (2004). GABA(A) and opioid receptors of the central nucleus of the amygdala selectively regulate ethanol-maintained behaviors. *Neuropsychopharmacology* 29:269-284.

Franklin KM, Engleman EA, Ingraham CM, McClaren JA, Keith CM, McBride WJ, Murphy JM. (2009). A single, moderate ethanol exposure alters extracellular dopamine levels and dopamine receptor function in the nucleus accumbens of Wistar rats. *Alcohol Clin. Exp. Res.* 33:1721-1730.

Galea LAM. (2008). Gonadal hormone modulation of neurogenesis in the dentate gyrus of adult male and female rodents. *Brain Res. Rev.* 57:332-341.

Galef BG, Jr. (1981). The ecology of weaning: parasitism and the achievement of independence by altricial mammals. In DJ Gubernick, PH Klopfer (eds.), *Parental Care in Mammals*. New York: Plenum Press; pp. 211-241.

Gass JT, Olive MF. (2008). Glutamatergic substrates of drug addiction and alcoholism. *Biochem. Pharmacol.* 75:218-65.

George O, Sanders C, Freiling J, Grigoryan E, Vu S, Allen CD, Crawford E, Mandyam CD, Koob GF. (2012). Recruitment of medial prefrontal cortex neurons during alcohol withdrawal predicts cognitive impairment and excessive alcohol drinking. *Proc. Natl. Acad. Sci. USA* 109:18156-18161.

Gessa GL, Muntoni F, Collu M, Vargiu L, Mereu G. (1985). Low doses of ethanol activate dopaminergic neurons in the ventral tegmental area. *Brain Res.* 348:201-203.

Giacchino JL, Henriksen SJ. (1998). Opioid effects on activation of neurons in the medial prefrontal cortex. *Prog. Neuro-Psychopharmacol. Biol. Psychiatry* 22:1157-1178.

Gierski F, Hubsch B, Stefaniak N, Benzerouk F, Cuervo-Lombard C, Bera-Potelle C, Cohen R, Kahn J-P, Limosin F. (2013). Executive functions in adult offspring of alcohol-dependent probands: toward a cognitive phenotype? *Alcohol Clin. Exp. Res.* 37:E356-E363.

Gilman JM, Ramchandani VA, Crouss T, Hommer DW. (2012). Subjective and neural responses to intravenous alcohol in young adults with light and heavy drinking patterns. *Neuropsychopharmacology* 37:467-477.

Gilpin NW, Roberto M. (2012). Neuropeptide modulation of central amygdala neuroplasticity is a key mediator of alcohol dependence. *Neurosci. Biobehav. Rev.* 36:873-888.

Gilpin NW, Stewart RB, Badia-Elder NE. (2008). Neuropeptide Y administration into the amygdala suppresses ethanol drinking in alcohol-preferring (P) rats following multiple deprivations. *Pharmacol. Biochem. Behav.* 90:470-474.

Gonzales RA, Weiss F. (1998). Suppression of ethanol-reinforced behavior by naltrexone is associated with attenuation of the ethanol-induced increase in dialysate dopamine levels in the nucleus accumbens. *J. Neurosci.* 18:10663-10671.

Goodman A. (2008). Neurobiology of addiction. An integrative review. *Biochem. Pharmacol.* 75:266-322.

Gore FM, Bloem PJN, Patton GC, Ferguson J, Joseph V, Coffey C, Sawyer SM, Mathers CD. (2011). Global burden of disease in young people aged 10-24 years: a systematic analysis. *Lancet* 377:2093-3102.

Gotti C, Clementi F. (2004). Neuronal nicotinic receptors: From structure to pathology. *Prog. Neurobiol.* 74:363-396.

Grace AA, Floresco SB, Goto Y, Lodge DJ. (2007). Regulation of firing of dopaminergic neurons and control of goal-directed behaviors. *Trends Neurosci.* 30:220-227.

Grant BF, Dawson DA. (1997). Age at onset of alcohol use and its association with DSM-IV alcohol abuse and dependence: results from the National Longitudinal Alcohol Epidemiologic Survey. *J. Subst. Abuse* 9:103-110.

Gray TS, Morley JE. (1986). Neuropeptide Y: anatomical distribution and possible function in mammalian nervous system. *Life Sci.* 38:389-401.

Griffin JF. (2002). A strategic approach to vaccine development: Animal models, monitoring vaccine efficacy, formulation and delivery. *Adv. Drug Del. Rev.* 54:851-861.

Guan XM, McBride WJ. (1989). Serotonin microinfusion into the ventral tegmental area increases accumbens dopamine release. *Brain Res. Bull.* 23:541-547.

Guan XM, Yu H, Palyha OC, McKee KK, Feighner SD, Sirinathsinghji DJ, Smith RG, Van der Ploeg LH, Howard AD. (1997). Distribution of mRNA encoding the growth hormone secretagogue receptor in brain and peripheral tissues. *Brain Res. Mol. Brain Res.* 48:23-29.

Guccione L, Paolini AG, Penman J, Djouma E. (2012). The effects of calorie restriction on operant-responding for alcohol in the alcohol-preferring (iP) rat. *Behav. Brain Res.* 230:281-287.

Guerri C, Pascual M. (2010). Mechanisms involved in the neurotoxic, cognitive, and neurobehavioral effects of alcohol consumption during adolescence. *Alcohol* 44:15-26.

Gupta T, Syed YM, Revis AA, Miller SA, Martinez M, Cohn KA, Demeyer MR, Patel KY, Brzezinska WJ, Rhodes JS. (2008). Acute effects of acamprosate and MPEP on ethanol drinking-in-the-dark in male C57BL/6J mice. *Alcohol Clin. Exp. Res.* 32:1992-1998.

Hall FS, Sora I, Uhl GR. (2001). Ethanol consumption and reward are decreased in mu-opiate receptor knockout mice. *Psychopharmacology* (Berl) 154:43-49.

Halliday GM, Törk I. (1989). Serotonin-like immunoreactive cells and fibres in the rat ventromedial mesencephalic tegmentum. *Brain Res. Bull.* 22:725-735.

Hansson AC, Bermúdez-Silva FJ, Malinen H, Hyytiä P, Sanchez-Vera I, Rimondini R, Rodriguez de Fonseca F, Kunos G, Sommer WH, Heilig M. (2007). Genetic impairment of frontocortical endocannabinoid degradation and high alcohol preference. *Neuropsychopharmacology* 32:117-126.

Hargreaves GA, Wang EYJ, Lawrence AJ, McGregor IS. (2011). Beer promotes high levels of alcohol intake in adolescent and adult alcohol-preferring rats. *Alcohol* 45:485-498.

Harwood H, Fountain D, Livermore G. (2000). The economic costs of alcohol and drug abuse in the United States 1992 (updated for 1998). *Report prepared for the National Institute on Drug Abuse and the National Institute on Alcohol Abuse and Alcoholism.* NIH Publication No. 98-4327.

Hauser SR, Bracken AL, Deehan Jr. GA, Toalston JE, Ding Z-M, Truitt WA, Bell RL, McBride WJ, Rodd ZA. (2013). Selective breeding for high alcohol preference increases the sensitivity of the posterior VTA to the reinforcing effects of nicotine. *Addict. Biol. In Press.*

Hauser SR, Ding ZM, Getachew B, Toalston JE, Oster SM, McBride WJ, Rodd ZA. (2011). The posterior ventral tegmental area mediates alcohol-seeking behavior in alcohol-preferring rats. *J. Pharmacol. Exp. Ther.* 336:857-865.

Hauser SR, Getachew B, Oster SM, Dhaher R, Ding ZM, Bell RL, McBride WJ, Rodd ZA. (2012a). Nicotine modulates alcohol-seeking and relapse by alcohol-preferring (P) rats in a time-dependent manner. *Alcohol Clin. Exp. Res.* 36:43-54.

Hauser SR, Katner SN, Deehan GA Jr, Ding ZM, Toalston JE, Scott BJ, Bell RL, McBride WJ, Rodd ZA. (2012b). Development of an oral operant nicotine/ethanol co-use model in alcohol-preferring (P) rats. *Alcohol Clin. Exp. Res.* 36:1963-1972.

Hawkins JD, Graham JW, Maguin E, Abbott R, Hill KG, Catalano RF. (1997). Exploring the effects of age of alcohol use initiation and psychosocial risk factors on subsequent alcohol misuse. *J. Stud. Alcohol* 58:280-290.

He J, Crews FT. (2007). Neurogenesis decreases during brain maturation from adolescence to adulthood. *Pharmaol. Biochem. Behav.* 86:327-333.

Heather N, Tebbutt JS, Mattick RP, Zamir R. (1993). Development of a scale for measuring impaired control over alcoholism: a preliminary report. *J. Stud. Alcohol* 54:700-709.

Hedner T, Iversen K, Lundborg P. (1984). Central GABA mechanisms during postnatal development in the rat: Neurochemical characteristics. *J. Neural. Trans.* 59:105-118.

Hegarty AA, Vogel WH. (1993). Modulation of the stress response by ethanol in the rat frontal cortex. *Pharmacol. Biochem. Behav.* 45:327-334.

Heilig M, Egli M. (2006). Pharmacological treatment of alcohol dependence: Target symptoms and target mechanisms. *Pharmacol. Ther.* 111:855-876.

Heilig M, McLeod S, Brot M, Heinrichs SC, Menzaghi F, Koob GF, Britton KT. (1993). Anxiolytic-like action of neuropeptide Y: mediation by Y1 receptors in amygdala, and dissociation from food intake effects. *Neuropsychopharmacology* 8:357-363.

Heilig M, Widerlöv E. (1990). Neuropeptide Y: an overview of central distribution, functional aspects, and possible involvement in neuropsychiatric illnesses. *Acta. Psychiatr. Scand.* 82:95-114.

Heilig M, Widerlöv E. (1995). Neurobiology and clinical aspects of neuropeptide Y. *Crit. Rev. Neurobiol.* 9:115-136.

Hendrickson LM, Zhao-Shea R, Tapper AR. (2009). Modulation of ethanol drinking-in-the-dark by mecamylamine and nicotinic acetylcholine receptor agonists in C57BL/6J mice. *Psychopharmacology* (Berl) 204:563-572.

Herman MA, Kallupi M, Luu G, Oleata CS, Heilig M, Koob GF, Ciccocioppo R, Roberto M. (2012). Enhanced GABAergic transmission in the central nucleus of the amygdala of genetically selected Marchigian Sardinian rats: Alcohol and CRF effects. *Neuropharmacology* 67C:337-348.

Hernandez L, Paredes D, Rada P. (2011). Feeding behavior as seen through the prism of brain microdialysis. *Physiol. Behav.* 104:47-56.

Herve D, Pickel VM, Joh TH, Beaudet A. (1987). Serotonin axon terminals in the ventral tegmental area of the rat: fine structure and synaptic input to dopaminergic neurons. *Brain Res.* 435:71-83.

Hingson RW, Heeren T, Winter MR. (2006). Age at drinking onset and alcohol dependence: Age at onset, duration, and severity. *Arch. Ped. Adol. Med.* 160:739-746.

Hodge CW, Chappelle AM, Samson HH. (1996). Dopamine receptors in the medial prefrontal cortex influence ethanol and sucrose-reinforced responding. *Alcohol Clin. Exp. Res.* 20:1631-1638.

Hodge CW, Cox AA. (1998). The discriminative stimulus effects of ethanol are mediated by NMDA and GABA(A) receptors in specific limbic brain regions. *Psychopharmacology* (Berl) 139:95-107.

Holdstock L, King AC, De Wit H. (2000). Subjective and objective responses to ethanol in moderate/heavy and light social drinkers. *Alcohol Clin. Exp. Res.* 24:789-794.

Hunt WA. (1993). Neuroscience research: how has it contributed to our understanding of alcohol abuse and alcoholism? A review. *Alcohol Clin. Exp. Res.* 17:1055-1065.

Hwang BH, Zhang JK, Ehlers CL, Lumeng L, Li TK. (1999). Innate differences of neuropeptide Y (NPY) in hypothalamic nuclei and central nucleus of the amygdala between selectively bred rats with high and low alcohol preference. *Alcohol Clin. Exp. Res.* 23:1023-1030.

Hwang BH, Suzuki R, Lumeng L, Li TK, McBride WJ. (2004). Innate differences in neuropeptide Y (NPY) mRNA expression in discrete brain regions between alcohol-preferring (P) and -nonpreferring (NP) rats: a significantly low level of NPY mRNA in dentate gyrus of the hippocampus and absence of NPY mRNA in the medial habenular nucleus of P rats. *Neuropeptides* 38:359-368.

Ikemoto S. (2007). Dopamine reward circuitry: two projection systems from the ventral midbrain to the nucleus accumbens-olfactory tubercle complex. *Brain Res. Rev.* 56:27-78.

Imperato A, Di Chiara G. (1986). Preferential stimulation of dopamine release in the nucleus accumbens of freely moving rats by ethanol. *J. Pharmacol. Exp. Ther.* 239:219-228.

Insel TR, Miller LP, Gelhard RE. (1990). The ontogeny of excitatory amino acid receptors in rat forebrain. I. N-methyl-D-aspartate and quisqualate receptors. *Neurosci.* 35:31-43.

Iyer RN, Bradberry CW. (1996). Serotonin-mediated increase in prefrontal cortex dopamine release: pharmacological characterization. *J. Pharmacol. Exp. Ther.* 277:40-47.

Jerlhag E, Egecioglu E, Dickson SL, Andersson M, Svensson L, Engel JA. (2006). Ghrelin stimulates locomotor activity and accumbal dopamine-overflow via central cholinergic systems in mice: implications for its involvement in brain reward. *Addict. Biol.* 11:45-54.

Jerlhag E, Egecioglu E, Dickson SL, Douhan A, Svensson L, Engel JA. (2007). Ghrelin administration into tegmental areas stimulates locomotor activity and increases extracellular concentration of dopamine in the nucleus accumbens. *Addict. Biol.* 12:6-16.

Jerlhag E, Egecioglu E, Dickson SL, Engel JA. (2010). Ghrelin receptor antagonism attenuates cocaine- and amphetamine-induced locomotor stimulation, accumbal dopamine release, and conditioned place preference. *Psychopharmacology* 211:415-422.

Jerlhag E, Egecioglu E, Dickson SL, Engel JA. (2011). Glutamatergic regulation of ghrelin induced activation of the mesolimbic dopamine system. *Addict. Biol.* 16:82-91.

Jerlhag E, Egecioglu E, Dickson SL, Svensson L, Engel JA. (2008). Alpha-conotoxin MII-sensitive nicotinic acetylcholine receptors are involved in mediating the ghrelin-induced locomotor stimulation and dopamine overflow in nucleus accumbens. *Eur. Neuropsychopharmacology* 18:508-518.

Jerlhag E, Engel JA. (2011). Ghrelin receptor antagonism attenuates nicotine-induced locomotor stimulation, accumbal dopamine release and conditioned place preference in mice. *Drug Alcohol Depend.* 117:126-131.

Ji D, Gilpin NW, Richardson HN, Rivier CL, Koob GF. (2008). Effects of naltrexone, duloxetine, and a corticotropin-releasing factor type 1 receptor antagonist on binge-like alcohol drinking in rats. *Behav. Pharmacol.* 19:1-12.

Johnson BA. (2004). Role of the serotonergic system in the neurobiology of alcoholism: implications for treatment. *CNS Drugs* 18:1105-1118.

Johnson BA. (2010). Medication treatment of different types of alcoholism. *Am. J. Psychiatry* 167:630-639.

Johnson BA, Ait-Daoud N, Ma JZ, Wang Y. (2003). Ondansetron reduces mood disturbance among biologically predisposed, alcohol-dependent individuals. *Alcohol Clin. Exp. Res.* 27:1773-1779.

Johnston LD, O'Malley PM, Bachman JG. (1991). *Drug use among American high school seniors, college students and young adults*, 1975-1990. Volume I. High school seniors (DHHS Publication No. ADM 91-1813). Washington, DC: Superintendent of Documents, U.S. Government Printing Office.

Johnston LD, O'Malley, PM, Bachman JG. (1993). *National Survey Results on Drug Use from the Monitoring the Future Study*, 1975–1992. Volume I: Secondary school students (NIH Publication No. 93-3597). Rockville, MD: National Institute on Drug Abuse.

Johnston LD, O'Malley PM, Bachman JG. (1999). *National Survey Results on Drug Use from the Monitoring the Future Study*, 1975–1997. Rockville, MD: National Institute on Drug Abuse.

Johnston, LD, O'Malley PM, Bachman JG, Schulenberg JE. (2008). *National Survey Results on Drug Use from the Monitoring the Future Study*, 1975-2007. Volume I: Secondary school students (NIH Publication No. 08-6418A). Bethesda, MD: National Institute on Drug Abuse.

Jones AW. (2010). Evidence-based survey of the elimination rates of ethanol from blood with applications in forensic casework. *Forensic. Sci. Int.* 200:1-20.

June HL, Cummings R, Eiler, WJA, II, Foster KL, McKay PF, Seyoum R, Garcia M, McCane S, Grey C, Hawkins SE, Mason D. (2004). Central opioid receptors differentially regulate the nalmefene-induced suppression of ethanol- and saccharin-reinforced behaviors in alcohol-preferring (P) rats. *Neuropsychopharmacology* 29:285-299.

June HL, Devaraju SL, Eggers MW, Williams JA, Cason CR, Greene TL, Leveige T, Braun MR, Torres L, Murphy JM. (1998). Benzodiazepine receptor antagonists modulate the actions of ethanol in alcohol-preferring and -nonpreferring rats. *Eur. J. Pharmacol.* 342:139-151.

June HL, McCane SR, Zink RW, Portoghese PS, Li TK, Froehlich JC. (1999). The delta 2-opioid receptor antagonist naltriben reduces motivated responding for ethanol. *Psychopharmacology* (Berl) 147:81-89.

Jupp B, Lawrence AJ. (2010). New horizons for therapeutics in drug and alcohol abuse. *Pharmacol. Ther.* 125:138-168.

Kageyama H, Kitamura Y, Hosono T, Kintaka Y, Seki M, Takenoya F, Hori Y, Nonaka N, Arata S, Shioda S. (2008). Visualization of ghrelin-producing neurons in the hypothalamic arcuate nucleus using ghrelin-EGFP transgenic mice. *Regul. Pept.* 145:116-121.

Kahkonen S, Wilenius J, Nikulin VV, Ollikainen M, Ilmoniemi RJ. (2003). Alcohol reduces prefrontal cortical excitability in humans: a combined TMS and EEG study. *Neuropsychopharmacology* 28:747-754.

Kalivas PW. (2009). The glutamate homeostasis hypothesis of addiction. *Nat. Rev. Neurosci.* 10:561-572.

Kalivas PW, Volkow N, Seamans J. (2005). Unmanageable motivation in addiction: a pathology in prefrontal-accumbens glutamate transmission. *Neuron* 45:647-650.

Kamdar NK, Miller SA, Syed YM, Bhayana R, Gupta T, Rhodes JS. (2007). Acute effects of naltrexone and GBR 12909 on ethanol drinking-in-the-dark in C57BL/6J mice. *Psychopharmacology* (Berl) 192:207-217.

Kampov-Polevoy AB, Matthews DB, Gause L, Morrow AL, Overstreet DH. (2000). P rats develop physical dependence on alcohol via voluntary drinking: Changes in seizure thresholds, anxiety, and patterns of alcohol drinking. *Alcohol Clin. Exp. Res.* 24:278-284.

Kandel D, Chen K, Warner LA, Kessler RC, Grant B. (1997). Prevalence and demographic correlates of symptoms of last year dependence on alcohol, nicotine, marijuana and cocaine in the U.S. population. *Drug Alcohol Depend.* 44:11-29.

Kapasova Z, Szumlinski KK. (2008). Strain differences in alcohol-induced neurochemical plasticity: a role for accumbens glutamate in alcohol intake. *Alcohol Clin. Exp. Res.* 32:617-631.

Kasanetz F, Manzoni OJ. (2009). Maturation of excitatory synaptic transmission of the rat nucleus accumbens from juvenile to adult. *J. Neurophysiol.* 101:2516-2527.

Katner SN, McBride WJ, Lumeng L, Li TK, Murphy JM. (1997). Alcohol intake of P rats is regulated by muscarinic receptors in the pedunculopontine nucleus and VTA. *Pharmacol. Biochem. Behav.* 58:497-504.

Katner SN, Oster SM, Ding Z-M, Deehan GA, Toalston JE, Hauser SR, McBride WJ, Rodd ZA. (2011). Alcohol-preferring (P) rats are more sensitive than Wistar rats to the reinforcing effects of cocaine self-administered directly into the nucleus accumbens shell. *Pharmacol. Biochem. Behav.* 99:688-695.

Kemppainen H, Raivio N, Suo-Yrjo V, Kiianmaa K. (2012). Opioidergic modulation of ethanol self-administration in the ventral pallidum. *Alcohol Clin. Exp. Res.* 36:286-293.

Kenna GA, Swift RM, Hillemacher T, Leggio L. (2012). The relationship of appetitive, reproductive and posterior pituitary hormones to alcoholism and craving in humans. *Neuropsychology Rev.* 22:211-228.

Kennedy GC. (1967). Ontogeny of mechanisms controlling food and water intake. In CF Code (ed.), *Handbook of Physiology: Alimentary Canal. Food and Water Intake* (Vol. 1). Washington, DC: American Physiological Society; pp. 337-352.

King AC, De Wit H, McNamara PJ, Cao D. (2011). Rewarding, stimulant, and sedative alcohol responses and relationship to future binge drinking. *Arch. Gen. Psychiatry* 68:389-399.

King AC, Houle T, De Wit H, Holdstock L, Schuster A. (2002). Biphasic alcohol response differs in heavy versus light drinkers. *Alcohol Clin. Exp. Res.* 26:827-835.

Knight JR, Wechsler H, Kuo M, Seibring M, Weitzman ER, Schuckit MA. (2002). Alcohol abuse and dependence among U.S. college students. *J. Stud. Alcohol.* 63:263-270.

Knoll J, Miklya I, Knoll B, Dallo J. (2000). Sexual hormones terminate in the rat: The significantly enhanced catecholaminergic/serotoninergic tone in the brain characteristic to the post-weaning period. *Life Sci.* 67:765-773.

Kojima M, Kangawa K. (2005). Ghrelin: structure and function. *Physiol. Rev.* 85:495-522.

Kokavec A, Crowe SF. (1999). A comparison of cognitive performance in binge versus regular chronic alcohol misusers. *Alcohol Alcohol.* 34:601-608.

Koob GF. (2004). A role for GABA mechanisms in the motivational effects of alcohol. *Biochem. Pharmacol.* 68:1515-1525.

Koob GF. (2009). Dynamics of neuronal circuits in addiction: Reward, antireward, and emotional memory. *Pharmacopsychiatry* 42(Suppl 1):S32-S41.

Koob GF. (2013). Theoretical frameworks and mechanistic aspects of alcohol addiction: alcohol addiction as a reward deficit disorder. *Curr. Topics Behav. Neurosci.* 13:3-30.

Koob GF, Le Moal M. (2006). *Neurobiology of addiction*. New York: Elsevier Academic Press.

Koob GF, Le Moal M. (2008). Neurobiological mechanisms for opponent motivational processes in addiction. *Phil. Trans. R Soc. B* 363:3113-3123.

Koob GF, Roberts AJ, Schulteis G, Parsons LH, Heyser CJ, Hyytiä P, Merlo-Pich E, Weiss F. (1998). Neurocircuitry targets in ethanol reward and dependence. *Alcohol Clin. Exp. Res.* 22:3-9.

Koob GF, Volkow ND. (2010). Neurocircuitry of addiction. *Neuropsychopharmacology* 35:217-238.

Korpi ER, Sinkkonen ST. (2006). GABA(A) receptor subtypes as targets for neuropsychiatric drug development. *Pharmacol. Ther.* 109:12-32.

Kryger R, Wilce PA. (2010). The effects of alcoholism on the human basolateral amygdala. *Neurosci.* 167:361-371.

Kuntsche E, Rehm J, Gmel G. (2004). Characteristics of binge drinkers in Europe. *Soc. Sci. Med.* 59:113-127.

Kupila J, Karkkainen O, Laukkanen V, Tupala E, Tiihonen J, Storvik M. (2013). mGluR1/5 receptor densities in the brains of alcoholic subjects: A whole-hemisphere autoradiography study. *Psychiatry Res.* : In Press.

Lallemand F, Eard RJ, De Witte P, Verbanck P. (2011). Binge drinking +/- chronic nicotine administration alters extracellular glutamate and arginine levels in the nucleus accumbens of adult male and female Wistar rats. *Alcohol Alcohol.* 46:373-382.

Lancaster FE. (1994). Gender differences in the brain: implications for the study of human alcoholism. *Alcohol Clin. Exp. Res.* 18:740-746.

Landgren S, Engel JA, Hyytiä P, Zetterberg H, Blennow K, Jerlhag E. (2011). Expression of the gene encoding the ghrelin receptor in rats selected for differential alcohol preference. *Behav. Brain Res.* 221:182-188.

Lange JE, Voas RB. (2000). Defining binge drinking quantities through resulting BACs. *Ann. Proc. Assoc. Adv. Auto Med.* 44:389-404.

Le AD, Poulos CX, Harding S, Watchus J, Juzytsch W, Shaham Y. (1999). Effects of naltrexone and fluoxetine on alcohol self-administration and reinstatement of alcohol seeking induced by priming injections of alcohol and exposure to stress. *Neuropsychopharmacology* 21:435-444.

Leggio L, Ferrulli A, Cardone S, Nesci A, Miceli A, Malandrino N, Capristo E, Canestrelli B, Monteleone P, Kenna GA, Swift RM, Addolorato G. (2011). Ghrelin system in alcohol-dependent subjects: role of plasma ghrelin levels in alcohol drinking and craving. *Addict. Biol.* 17:452-464.

Lesch OM, Walter H. (1996). Subtypes of alcoholism and their role in therapy. *Alcohol Alcohol.* Suppl 1:63-67.

Lester D, Freed EX. (1973). Criteria for an animal model of alcoholism. *Pharmacol. Biochem. Behav.* 1:103-107.

Li Z, Zharikova A, Vaughan CH, Bastian J, Zandy S, Esperon L, Axman E, Rowland NE, Peris J. (2010). Intermittent high-dose ethanol exposures increase motivation for operant ethanol self-administration: Possible neurochemical mechanism. *Brain Res.* 1310:142-153.

Liu J, Yang AR, Kelly T, Puche A, Esoga C, June HL Jr, Elnabawi A, Merchenthaler I, Sieghart W, June HL Sr, Aurelian L. (2011). Binge alcohol drinking is associated with GABAA alpha2-regulated Toll-like receptor 4 (TLR4) expression in the central amygdala. *Proc. Natl. Acad. Sci. USA* 108:4465-4470.

Lyness WH, Smith F. (1992). Influence of dopaminergic and serotonergic neurons on intravenous ethanol self-administration in the rat. *Pharmacol. Biochem. Behav.* 42: 187-192.

Lyons AM, Lowery EG, Sparta DR, Thiele TE. (2008). Effects of food availability and administration of orexigenic and anorectic agents on elevated ethanol drinking associated with drinking in the dark procedures. *Alcohol Clin. Exp. Res.* 32:1962-1968.

Maldonado-Devincci AM, Badanich KA, Kirstein CL. (2010). Alcohol during adolescence selectively alters immediate and long-term behavior and neurochemistry. *Alcohol* 44: 57-66.

Malinen H, Hyytia P. (2008). Ethanol self-administration is regulated by CB1 receptors in the nucleus accumbens and ventral tegmental area in alcohol-preferring AA rats. *Alcohol Clin. Exp. Res.* 32:1976-1983.

Marczinski CA, Grant EC, Grant VJ. (2009). *Binge drinking in adolescents and college students*. New York: Nova Science Publishers.

Margolis EB, Fields HL, Hjelmstad GO, Mitchell JM. (2008). Delta-opioid receptor expression in the ventral tegmental area protects against elevated alcohol consumption. *J. Neurosci.* 28:12672-12681.

Marini V, Fucile C, Zuccoli ML, Testino G, Sumberaz A, Robbiano L, Martelli A, Mattioli F. (2013). Involvement of the mu-opioid receptor gene polymorphism A118G in the efficacy of detoxification of alcohol dependent patients. *Addict. Behav.* 38:1669-1671.

Marszalec W, Aistrup GL, Narahashi T. (1999). Ethanol-nicotine interactions at alpha bungarotoxin insensitive nicotinic acetylcholine receptors in rat cortical neurons. *Alcohol Clin. Exp. Res.* 23:439-445.

Martin-Fardon R, Weiss F. (2013). Modeling relapse in animals. *Curr. Topics Behav. Neurosci.* 13:403-432.

Martinic M, Measham F. (2008). *Swimming with crocodiles: The culture of extreme drinking*. New York: Routledge/Taylor and Francis Group.

Mason BJ, Higley AE. (2013). A translational approach to novel medications development for protracted abstinence. *Curr. Topics Behav. Neurosci.* 13:647-670.

McBride WJ. (2002). Central nucleus of the amygdala and the effects of alcohol and alcohol-drinking behavior in rodents. *Pharmacol. Biochem. Behav.* 71:509-515.

McBride WJ, Chernet E, Dyr W, Lumeng L, Li TK. (1993a). Densities of dopamine D2 receptors are reduced in CNS regions of alcohol-preferring P rats. *Alcohol* 10:387-390.

McBride WJ, Chernet E, Rabold JA, Lumeng L, Li TK. (1993b). Serotonin-2 receptors in the CNS of alcohol-preferring and -nonpreferring rats. *Pharmacol. Biochem. Behav.* 46:631-636.

McBride WJ, Kimpel MW, Schultz JA, McClintick JN, Edenberg HJ, Bell RL. (2010). Changes in gene expression in regions of the extended amygdala of alcohol-preferring rats following binge-like alcohol drinking. *Alcohol* 44:171-183.

McBride WJ, Li T-K. (1998). Animal models of alcoholism: Neurobiology of high alcohol-drinking behavior in rodents. *Crit. Rev. Neurobiol.* 12:339-369.

McBride WJ, Lovinger DM, Machu T, Thielen RJ, Rodd ZA, Murphy JM, Roache JD, Johnson BA. (2004). Serotonin-3 receptors in the actions of alcohol, alcohol reinforcement, and alcoholism. *Alcohol Clin. Exp. Res.* 28:257-267.

McBride WJ, Murphy JM, Ikemoto S. (1999). Localization of brain reinforcement mechanisms: intracranial self-administration and intracranial place-conditioning studies. *Behav. Brain. Res.* 101:129-152.

McCool BA, Christian DT, Diaz MR, Läck AK. (2010). Glutamate plasticity in the drunken amygdala: the making of an anxious synapse. *Int. Rev. Neurobiol.* 91:205-233.

McKinney WT. (2001). Overview of the past contributions of animal models and their changing place in psychiatry. *Sem. Clin. Psychiatry* 6:68-78.

McKinzie DL, Nowak KL, Yorger L, McBride WJ, Murphy JM, Lumeng L, Li T-K. (1998). The alcohol deprivation effect in the alcohol-preferring P rat under free-drinking and operant access conditions. *Alcohol Clin. Exp. Res.* 22:1170-1176.

Melendez RI, Hicks MP, Cagle SC, Kalivas PW. (2005). Ethanol exposure decreases glutamate uptake in the nucleus accumbens. *Alcohol Clin. Exp. Res.* 29:326-333.

Melendez RI, Rodd-Henricks ZA, Engleman EA, Li T-K, McBride WJ, Murphy JM. (2002). Microdialysis of dopamine in the nucleus accumbens of alcohol-preferring (P) rats during anticipation and operant self-administration of ethanol. *Alcohol Clin. Exp. Res.* 26:318-325.

Melis M, Camarini R, Ungless MA, Bonci A. (2002). Long-lasting potentiation of GABAergic synapses in dopamine neurons after a single in vivo ethanol exposure. *J. Neurosci.* 22:2074-2082.

Melon LC, Boehm SL, II. (2011). GABAA receptors in the posterior, but not anterior, ventral tegmental area mediate Ro15-4513-induced attenuation of binge-like ethanol consumption in C57BL/6J female mice. *Behav. Brain Res.* 220:230-237.

Miller ET, Turner AP, Marlatt GA. (2001). The harm reduction approach to the secondary prevention of alcohol problems in adolescents and young adults: considerations across a developmental spectrum. In PM Monti, SM Colby, TA O'Leary, (eds.), *Adolescents, Alcohol, and Substance Abuse: Reaching Teens through Brief Interventions*. New York: Guilford Press; pp. 58-79.

Miller JW, Naimi TS, Brewer RD, Jones SE. (2007). Binge drinking and associated health risk behaviors among high school students. *Pediatr.* 119:76-85.

Milner LC, Buck KJ. (2010). Identifying quantitative trait loci (QTLs) and genes (QTGs) for alcohol-related phenotypes. *Intl. Rev. Neurobiol.* 91:173-204.

Mokdad A, Marks J, Stroup D, Gerberding J. (2004). Actual causes of death in the United States, 2000. *J. Am. Med. Assoc.* 291:1238-1245.

Moll GH, Mehnert C, Wicker M, Bock N, Rothenberger A, Ruther E, Huether G. (2000). Age-associated changes in the densities of presynaptic monoamine transporters in different regions of the rat brain from early juvenile life to late adulthood. *Brain Res. Dev. Brain Res.* 119:251-257.

Moore EM, Boehm SL, II. (2009). Site-specific microinjection of baclofen into the anterior ventral tegmental area reduces binge-like ethanol intake in male C57BL/6J mice. *Behav. Neurosci.* 123:555-563.

Morganstern I, Liang S, Ye Z, Karatayev O, Leibowitz SF. (2012). Disturbances in behavior and cortical enkephalin gene expression during the anticipation of ethanol in rats characterized as high drinkers. *Alcohol* 46:559-568.

Moss HB, Chen CM, Yi HY. (2007). Subtypes of alcohol dependence in a nationally representative sample. *Drug Alcohol Depend.* 91:149-158.

Murphy JM, McBride WJ, Lumeng L, Li TK. (1982). Regional brain levels of monoamines in alcohol-preferring and -nonpreferring lines of rats. *Pharmacol. Biochem. Behav.* 16:145-149.

Murphy JM, McBride WJ, Lumeng L, Li TK. (1987). Contents of monoamines in forebrain regions of alcohol-preferring (P) and -nonpreferring (NP) lines of rats. *Pharmacol. Biochem. Behav.* 26:389-392.

Murphy JM, Stewart RB, Bell RL, Badia-Elder NE, Carr LG, McBride WJ, Lumeng L, Li TK. (2002). Phenotypic and genotypic characterization of the Indiana University rat lines selectively bred for high and low alcohol preference. *Behav. Genet.* 32:363-388.

Myrick H, Anton RF, Li X, Henderson S, Randall PK, Voronin K. (2008). Effect of naltrexone and ondansetron on alcohol cue-induced activation of the ventral striatum in alcohol-dependent people. *Arch. Gen. Psychiatry* 65:466-475.

Navarro M, Cubero I, Ko L, Thiele TE. (2009). Deletion of agouti-related protein blunts ethanol self-administration and binge-like drinking in mice. *Genes Brain Behav.* 8:450-458.

Nayak SV, Ronde P, Spier AD, Lummis SCR, Nichols RA. (2000). Nicotinic receptors co-localize with 5-HT3 serotonin receptors on striatal nerve terminals. *Neuropharmacol* 39:2681-2690.

Neighbors C, Oster-Aaland L, Bergstrom RL, Lewis MA. (2006). Event- and context-specific normative misperceptions and high-risk drinking: 21st birthday celebrations and football tailgating. *J. Stud. Alcohol* 67:282-289.

Nelson CB, Heath AC, Kessler RC. (1998). Temporal progression of alcohol dependence symptoms in the U.S. household population: results from the National Comorbidity Survey. *J. Consult. Clin. Psychol.* 66:474-483.

Nestler EJ, Hyman SE. (2010). Animal models of neuropsychiatric disorders. *Nat. Neurosci.* 13:1161-1169.

Nevo I, Hamon M. (1995). Neurotransmitter and neuromodulatory mechanisms involved in alcohol abuse and alcoholism. *Neurochem. Intl.* 26:305-336; discussion 337-342.

Newburn T, Shiner M. (2001). Teenage kicks? *Young people and alcohol*: A review of the literature. York, UK: Joseph Rowntree Foundation.

Newlin DB, Thomson JB. (1990). Alcohol challenge with sons of alcoholics: a critical review and analysis. *Psychol. Bull.* 108:383-402.

Newlin DB, Thomson JB. (1999). Chronic tolerance and sensitization to alcohol in sons of alcoholics: II. Replication and reanalysis. *Exp. Clin. Psychopharmacol.* 7:234-243.

NIAAA. (2012). Underage drinking. NIAAA Fact Sheet. Available at http://pubs.niaaa.nih.gov/publications/UnderageDrinking/Underage_Fact.pdf. Published March 2012.

NIAAA National Advisory Council. (2004). *NIAAA Council approves definition of binge drinking*. NIAAA Newsletter3:5.

Nie Z, Madamba SG, Siggins GR. (1994). Ethanol inhibits glutamatergic neurotransmission in nucleus accumbens neurons by multiple mechanisms. *J. Pharmacol. Exp. Ther.* 271:1566-1573.

Nie Z, Yuan X, Madamba SG, Siggins GR. (1993). Ethanol decreases glutamatergic synaptic transmission in rat nucleus accumbens in vitro: naloxone reversal. *J. Pharmacol. Exp. Ther.* 266:1705-1712.

Nielsen CK, Simms JA, Li R, Mill D, Yi H, Feduccia AA, Santos N, Bartlett SE. (2012). Delta-opioid receptor function in the dorsal striatum plays a role in high levels of ethanol consumption in rats. *J. Neurosci.* 32:4540-4552.

Nisell M, Nomikos GG, Svensson TH. (1994). Systemic nicotine-induced dopamine release in the rat nucleus accumbens is regulated by nicotinic receptors in the ventral tegmental area. *Synapse* 16:36-44.

Nixon K, Morris SA, Liput DJ, Kelso ML. (2010). Roles of neural stem cells and adult neurogenesis in adolescent alcohol use disorders. *Alcohol* 44:39-56.

Noori HR, Spanagel R, Hansson AC. (2012). Neurocircuitry for modeling drug effects. *Addict. Biol.* 17:827-864.

Nowak KL, McBride WJ, Lumeng L, Li TK, Murphy JM. (1998). Blocking GABA(A) receptors in the anterior ventral tegmental area attenuates ethanol intake of the alcohol-preferring P rat. *Psychopharmacology* 139:108-116.

Nowak KL, McBride WJ, Lumeng L, Li TK, Murphy JM. (2000). Involvement of dopamine D2 autoreceptors in the ventral tegmental area on alcohol and saccharin intake of the alcohol-preferring P rat. *Alcohol Clin. Exp. Res.* 24:476-483.

Obara I, Bell RL, Goulding SP, Reyes CM, Larson LA, Ary AW, Truitt WA, Szumlinski KK. (2009). Differential effects of chronic ethanol consumption and withdrawal on homer/glutamate receptor expression in subregions of the accumbens and amygdala of P rats. *Alcohol Clin. Exp. Res.* 33:1924-1934.

Okoro CA, Brewer RD, Naimi TS, Moriarty DG, Giles WH, Mokdad AH. (2004). Binge drinking and health-related quality of life: do popular perceptions match reality. *Am. J. Prev. Med.* 26:230-233.

Oster SM, Toalston JE, Kuc KA, Pommer TJ, Murphy JM, Lumeng L, Bell RL, McBride WJ, Rodd ZA. (2006). Effects of multiple alcohol deprivations on operant ethanol self-administration by high-alcohol-drinking replicate rat lines. *Alcohol* 38:155-164.

Oswald LM, Wand GS. (2004). Opioids and alcoholism. *Physiol. Behav.* 81:339-358.

Palmer AA, Low MJ, Grandy DK, Phillips TJ. (2003). Effects of a Drd2 deletion mutation on ethanol-induced locomotor stimulation and sensitization suggest a role for epistasis. *Behav. Genet.* 33:311-324.

Palmiter RD, Erickson JC, Hollopeter G, Baraban SC, Schwartz MW. (1998). Life without neuropeptide Y. *Recent Prog. Horm. Res.* 53:163-199.

Pandey SC. (2003). Anxiety and alcohol abuse disorders: a common role for CREB and its target, the neuropeptide Y gene. *Trends Pharmacol. Sci.* 24:456-460.

Pandey SC, Carr LG, Heilig M, Ilveskoski E, Thiele TE. (2003). Neuropeptide Y and alcoholism: genetic, molecular, and pharmacological evidence. *Alcohol Clin. Exp. Res.* 27:149-154.

Pandey SC, Zhang H, Roy A, Xu T. (2005). Deficits in amygdaloid cAMP-responsive element binding protein signaling play a role in genetic predisposition to anxiety and alcoholism. *J. Clin. Invest.* 115:2762-2773.

Parent A, Descarries L, Beaudet A. (1981). Organization of ascending serotonin systems in the adult rat brain. A radioautographic study after intraventricular administration of [3H] 5 hydroxytryptamine. *Neurosci.* 6:115-138.

Parks MH, Dawant BM, Riddle WR, Hartmann SL, Dietrich MS, Nickel MK, Price RR, Martin PR. (2002). Longitudinal brain metabolic characterization of chronic alcoholics with proton magnetic resonance spectroscopy. *Alcohol Clin. Exp. Res.* 26:1368-1380.

Pascual M, Boix J, Felipo V, Guerri C. (2009). Repeated alcohol administration during adolescence causes changes in the mesolimbic dopaminergic and glutamatergic systems and promotes alcohol intake in the adult rat. *J. Neurochem.* 108: 920-931.

Perello M, Zigman JM. (2012). The role of ghrelin in reward-based eating. *Biol. Psychiatry* 73:347-353.

Perry DC, Xiao Y, Nguyen HN, Musachio JL, Dávila-García MI, Kellar KJ. (2002). Measuring nicotinic receptors with characteristics of alpha4beta2, alpha3beta2 and alpha3beta4 subtypes in rat tissues by autoradiography. *J. Neurochem.* 82:468-481.

Pessia M, Jiang ZG, North RA, Johnson SW. (1994). Actions of 5-hydroxytryptamine on ventral tegmental area neurons of the rat in vitro. *Brain Res.* 654:324-330.

Peters J, LaLumiere RT, Kalivas PW. (2008). Infralimbic prefrontal cortex is responsible for inhibiting cocaine seeking in extinguished rats. *J. Neurosci.* 28:6046-6053.

Phillips AG, Vacca G, Ahn S. (2008). A top-down perspective on dopamine, motivation and memory. *Pharmacol. Biochem. Behav.* 90:236-249.

Philpot R, Kirstein C. (2004). Developmental differences in the accumbal dopaminergic response to repeated ethanol exposure. *Ann. N. Y. Acad. Sci.* 1021:422-426.

Pidoplichko VI, Noguchi J, Areola OO, Liang Y, Peterson J, Zhang T, Dani JA. (2004). Nicotinic cholinergic synaptic mechanisms in the ventral tegmental area contribute to nicotine addiction. *Learn. Mem.* 11:60-69.

Pitkanen T, Lyyra AL, Pulkkinen L. (2005). Age of onset of drinking and the use of alcohol in adulthood: a follow-up study from age 8—42 for females and males. *Addict.* 100:652-661.

Pivac N, Mück-Seler D, Mustapić M, Nenadić-Sviglin K, Kozarić-Kovacić D. (2004). Platelet serotonin concentration in alcoholic subjects. *Life Sci.* 76:521-531.

Plant M, Plant M. (2006). *Binge Britain: Alcohol and the National Response.* New York: Oxford University Press.

Prelipceanu D, Mihailescu R. (2005). Non A non B variants in the binary typology of alcoholics. *Addict. Dis. Treat.* 4:149-156.

Presley CA, Meilman PW, Lyerla R. (1994). Development of the Core Alcohol and Drug Survey: Initial findings and future directions. *J. Amer. Coll. Health* 42:248-255.

Prime Minister's Strategy Unit. (2004). *Alcohol Harm Reduction Strategy for England.* Department of Health, London, UK.

Quine S, Stephenson JA. (1990). Predicting smoking and drinking intentions and behavior of pre-adolescents: The influence of parents, siblings, and peers. *Family Sys. Med.* 8: 191-200.

Quintanilla ME, Bustamante D, Tampier L, Israel Y, Herrera-Marschitz M. (2007). Dopamine release in the nucleus accumbens (shell) of two lines of rats selectively bred to prefer or avoid ethanol. *Eur. J. Pharmacol.* 573:84-92.

Rahman S, McBride WJ. (2002). Involvement of GABA and cholinergic receptors in the nucleus accumbens on feedback control of somatodendritic dopamine release in the ventral tegmental area. *J. Neurochem.* 80:646-654.

Rahman S, Prendergast MA. (2012). Cholinergic receptor system as a target for treating alcohol abuse and dependence. *Rec. Patents CNS Drug Disc.* 7:145-150.

Ray LA, Bujarski S, MacKillop J, Courtney KE, Monti PM, Miotto K. (2013). Subjective response to alcohol among alcohol-dependent individuals: effects of the mu-opioid receptor (OPRM1) gene and alcoholism severity. *Alcohol Clin. Exp. Res.* 37:E116-E124.

Reed T, Page WF, Viken RJ, Christian JC. (1996). Genetic predisposition to organ-specific endpoints of alcoholism. *Alcohol Clin. Exp. Res.* 20:1528-1533.

Rehm J, Room R, Graham K, Monteiro M, Gmel G, Sempos CT. (2003). The relationship of average volume of alcohol consumption and patterns of drinking to burden of disease: an overview. *Addict.* 98:1209-1228.

Research Society on Alcoholism. (2009). *Impact of Alcoholism and Alcohol Induced Disease on America.* Austin, TX: Research Society on Alcoholism.

Rezvani AH, Lawrence AJ, Arolfo MP, Levin ED, Overstreet DH. (2012). Novel medication targets for the treatment of alcoholism: preclinical studies. *Rec. Patents CNS Drug Disc.* 7:151-162.

Rhodes JS, Best K, Belknap JK, Finn DA, Crabbe JC. (2005). Evaluation of a simple model of ethanol drinking to intoxication in C57BL/6J mice. *Physiol. Behav.* 84:53-63.

Rice OV, Patrick J, Schonhar CD, Ning H, Ashby CR, Jr. (2012). The effects of the preferential dopamine D(3) receptor antagonist S33138 on ethanol binge drinking in C57BL/6J mice. *Synapse* 66:975-978.

Roberts AJ, McDonald JS, Heyser CJ, Kieffer BL, Matthes HW, Koob GF, Gold LH. (2000). mu-Opioid receptor knockout mice do not self-administer alcohol. *J. Pharmacol. Exp. Ther.* 293:1002-1008.

Robison AJ, Nestler EJ. (2011). Transcriptional and epigenetic mechanisms of addiction. *Nat. Rev. Neurosci.* 12:623-637.

Rodd ZA, Bell RL, Kuc KA, Murphy JM, Lumeng L, Li TK, McBride WJ. (2003). Effects of repeated alcohol deprivations on operant ethanol self-administration by alcohol-preferring (P) rats. *Neuropsychopharmacology* 28:1614-1621.

Rodd ZA, Bell RL, Kuc KA, Murphy JM, Lumeng L, McBride WJ. (2008). Effects of concurrent access to multiple ethanol concentrations and repeated deprivations on alcohol intake of high-alcohol-drinking (HAD) rats. *Addict. Biol.* 14:152-164.

Rodd ZA, Bell RL, Kuc KA, Zhang Y, Murphy JM, McBride WJ. (2005a). Intracranial self-administration of cocaine within the posterior ventral tegmental area of Wistar rats: evidence for involvement of serotonin-3 receptors and dopamine neurons. *J. Pharmacol. Exp. Ther.* 313:134-145.

Rodd ZA, Bell RL, McQueen VK, Davids MR, Hsu CC, Murphy JM, Li TK, Lumeng L, McBride WJ. (2005b). Chronic ethanol drinking by alcohol-preferring rats increases the sensitivity of the posterior ventral tegmental area to the reinforcing effects of ethanol. *Alcohol Clin. Exp. Res.* 29:358-366.

Rodd ZA, Bell RL, McQueen VK, Davids MR, Hsu CC, Murphy JM, Li TK, Lumeng L, McBride WJ. (2005c). Prolonged increase in the sensitivity of the posterior ventral tegmental area to the reinforcing effects of ethanol following repeated exposure to cycles of ethanol access and deprivation. *J. Pharmacol. Exp. Ther.* 315:648-657.

Rodd ZA, Bell RL, Melendez RI, Kuc KA, Lumeng L, Li T-K, Murphy JM, McBride WJ. (2004a). Comparison of intracranial self-administration of ethanol within the posterior ventral tegmental area between alcohol-preferring and Wistar rats. *Alcohol Clin. Exp. Res.* 28: 1212-1219.

Rodd ZA, Bell RL, Oster SM, Toalston JE, Pommer TJ, McBride WJ, Murphy JM. (2010). Serotonin-3 receptors in the posterior ventral tegmental area regulate ethanol self-administration of alcohol-preferring (P) rats. *Alcohol* 44:245-255.

Rodd ZA, Bell RL, Sable HJ, Murphy JM, McBride WJ. (2004b). Recent advances in animal models of alcohol craving and relapse. *Pharmacol. Biochem. Behav.* 79:439-450.

Rodd ZA, McKinzie DL, Bell RL, McQueen VK, Murphy JM, Schoepp DD, McBride WJ. (2006). The metabotropic glutamate 2/3 receptor agonist LY404039 reduces alcohol-seeking but not alcohol self-administration in alcohol-preferring (P) rats. *Behav. Brain Res.* 171:207-215.

Rodd ZA, Melendez RI, Bell RL, Kuc KA, Zhang Y, Murphy JM, McBride WJ. (2004c). Intracranial self-administration of ethanol within the ventral tegmental area of male Wistar rats: evidence for involvement of dopamine neurons. *J. Neurosci.* 24:1050-1057.

Rodd-Henricks ZA, Bell RL, Kuc KA, Murphy JM, McBride WJ, Lumeng L, Li TK. (2001). Effects of concurrent access to multiple ethanol concentrations and repeated deprivations on alcohol intake of alcohol-preferring rats. *Alcohol Clin. Exp. Res.* 25:1140-1150.

Rodd-Henricks ZA, McKinzie DL, Crile RS, Murphy JM, McBride WJ. (2000a). Regional heterogeneity for the intracranial self-administration of ethanol within the ventral tegmental area of female Wistar rats. *Psychopharmacology* (Berl) 149:217-224.

Rodd-Henricks ZA, McKinzie DL, Edmundson VE, Dagon CL, Murphy JM, McBride WJ, Lumeng L, Li TK. (2000b). Effects of 5-HT(3) receptor antagonists on daily alcohol intake under acquisition, maintenance, and relapse conditions in alcohol-preferring (P) rats. *Alcohol* 21:73-85.

Rodd-Henricks ZA, McKinzie DL, Murphy JM, McBride WJ, Lumeng L, Li TK. (2000c). The expression of an alcohol deprivation effect in the high-alcohol-drinking replicate rat lines is dependent on repeated deprivations. *Alcohol Clin. Exp. Res.* 24:747-753.

Rodd-Henricks ZA, McKinzie DL, Shaikh SR, Murphy JM, McBride WJ, Lumeng L, Li TK. (2000d). Alcohol deprivation effect is prolonged in the alcohol preferring (P) rat after repeated deprivations. *Alcohol Clin. Exp. Res.* 24:8-16.

Rohsenow DJ, Howland J, Winter M, Bliss CA, Littlefield CA, Heeren TC, Calise TV. (2012). Hangover sensitivity after controlled alcohol administration as predictor of post-college drinking. *J. Abnorm. Psychol.* 121:270-275.

Rominger A, Cumming P, Xiong G, Koller G, Boning G, Wulff M, Zwergal A, Forster S, Reilhac A, Munk O, Soyka M, Wangler B, Bartenstein P, la Fougere C, Pogarell O.

(2012). [18F]Fallypride PET measurement of striatal and extrastriatal dopamine D 2/3 receptor availability in recently abstinent alcoholics. *Addict. Biol.* 17:490-503.

Rossow I, Kuntsche E. (2013). Early onset of drinking and risk for heavy drinking in young adulthood—a 13-year prospective study. *Alcohol Clin. Exp. Res.* 37:E297-E304.

Rutledge PC, Park A, Sher KJ. (2008). 21st birthday drinking: extremely extreme. *J. Consult. Clin. Psychol.* 76:511-516.

Sabino V, Kwak J, Rice KC, Cottone P. (2013). Pharmacological Characterization of the 20% Alcohol Intermittent Access Model in Alcohol-Preferring Rats: A Model of Binge-Like Drinking. *Alcohol Clin. Exp. Res. In Press.*

Sahr AE, Thielen RJ, Lumeng L, Li TK, McBride WJ. (2004). Long-lasting alterations of the mesolimbic dopamine system after periadolescent ethanol drinking by alcohol-preferring rats. *Alcohol Clin. Exp. Res.* 28:702-711.

Sajja RK, Rahman S. (2011). Lobeline and cytisine reduce voluntary ethanol drinking behavior in male C57BL/6J mice. *Prog. Neuropsychopharmacol. Biol. Psychiatry* 35:257-264.

SAMHSA. (2012). *Report to Congress on the Prevention and Reduction of Underage Drinking.* Available at: http://store.samhsa.gov/product/Report-to-Congress-on-the-Prevention-and-Reduction-of-Underage-Drinking-2012/PEP12-RTCUAD Published November 2012.

Samson HH, Chappell A. (2003). Dopaminergic involvement in medial prefrontal cortex and core of the nucleus accumbens in the regulation of ethanol self-administration: a dual-site microinjection study in the rat. *Physiol. Behav.* 79:581-590.

Sari Y, Bell RL, Zhou FC. (2006). Effects of chronic alcohol and repeated deprivations on dopamine D1 and D2 receptor levels in the extended amygdala of inbred alcohol-preferring rats. *Alcohol Clin. Exp. Res.* 30:46-56.

Sari Y, Sakai M, Weedman JM, Rebec GV, Bell RL. (2011). Ceftriaxone, a beta-lactam antibiotic, reduces ethanol consumption in alcohol-preferring rats. *Alcohol Alcohol.* 46:239-246.

Schellekens H, Finger BC, Dinan TG, Cryan JF. (2012). Ghrelin signaling and obesity: at the interface of stress, mood and food reward. *Pharmacol. Ther.* 135:316-326.

Schlaepfer IR, Hoft NR, Ehringer MA. (2008). The genetic components of alcohol and nicotine co-addiction: from genes to behavior. *Curr. Drug Abuse Rev.* 1:124-134.

Schmidt LG, Dufeu P, Heinz A, Kuhn S, Rommelspacher H. (1997). Serotonergic dysfunction in addiction: effects of alcohol, cigarette smoking and heroin on platelet 5-HT content. *Psychiatry Res.* 72:177-185.

Schochet TL, Bremer QZ, Brownfield MS, Kelley AE, Landry CF. (2008). The dendritically targeted protein Dendrin is induced by acute nicotine in cortical regions of adolescent rat brain. *Eur. J. Neurosci.* 28:1967-1979.

Schroeder JP, Overstreet DH, Hodge CW. (2005). The mGluR5 antagonist MPEP decreases operant ethanol self-administration during maintenance and after repeated alcohol deprivations in alcohol-preferring (P) rats. *Psychopharmacology* (Berl) 179:262-270.

Schucki MA. (1998). Binge drinking: The five/four measure. *J. Stud. Alcohol* 59:123-124.

Schultz W. (2011). Potential vulnerabilities of neuronal reward, risk, and decision mechanisms to addictive drugs. *Neuron* 69:603-617.

Schwandt ML, Lindell SG, Chen S, Higley JD, Suomi SJ, Heilig M, Barr CS. (2010). Alcohol response and consumption in adolescent rhesus macaques: life history and genetic influences. *Alcohol* 44:67-80.

Sinclair JD, Senter RJ. (1967). Increased preference for ethanol in rats following alcohol deprivation. *Psychonom. Sci.* 8:11–12.

Sinha R, Fox HC, Hong K-IA, Hansen J, Tuit K, Kreek MJ. (2011). Effects of adrenal sensitivity, stress- and cue-induced craving, and anxiety on subsequent alcohol relapse and treatment outcomes. *Arch. Gen. Psychiatry* 68:942-952.

Smith AD, Weiss F. (1999). Ethanol exposure differentially alters central monoamine neurotransmission in alcohol-preferring versus -nonpreferring rats. *J. Pharmacol. Exp. Ther.* 288:1223-1228.

Smith RF. (2003). Animal models of periadolescent substance abuse. *Neurotoxicol. Teratol.* 25:291-301.

Smith TL. (1997). Regulation of glutamate uptake in astrocytes continuously exposed to ethanol. *Life Sci.* 61:2499-2505.

Smith TL, Zsigo A. (1996). Increased Na(+)-dependent high affinity uptake of glutamate in astrocytes chronically exposed to ethanol. *Neurosci. Lett.* 218:142-144.

Soderpalm B, Ericson M. (2013). Neurocircuitry involved in the development of alcohol addiction: the dopamine system and its access points. *Curr. Topics Behav. Neurosci.* 13:127-161.

Soderpalm B, Ericson M, Olausson P, Blomqvist O, Engel JA. (2000). Nicotinic mechanisms involved in the dopamine activating and reinforcing properties of ethanol. *Behav. Brain Res.* 113:85-96.

Spanagel R. (2009). Alcoholism: a systems approach from molecular physiology to addictive behavior. *Physiol. Rev.* 89:649-705.

Spanagel R, Holter SM. (1999). Long-term alcohol self-administration with repeated alcohol deprivation phases: an animal model of alcoholism? *Alcohol Alcohol.* 34:231-243.

Spanagel R, Vengeliene V. (2013). New pharamcological strategies for relapse prevention. *Curr. Topics Behav. Neurosci.* 13:583-609.

Sparrow AM, Lowery-Gionta EG, Pleil KE, Li C, Sprow GM, Cox BR, Rinker JA, Jijon AM, Peňa J, Navarro M, Kash TL, Thiele TE. (2012). Central neuropeptide Y modulates binge-like ethanol drinking in C57BL/6J mice via Y1 and Y2 receptors. *Neuropsychopharmacology* 37:1409-1421.

Spear LP. (2000). The adolescent brain and age-related behavioral manifestations. *Neurosci. Biobehav. Rev.* 24:417-463.

Spear LP. (2004a). Adolescent brain development and animal models. *Ann. N. Y. Acad. Sci.* 1021:23-26.

Spear LP. (2004b). Adolescence and the trajectory of alcohol use: Introduction to part IV. *Ann. N. Y. Acad. Sci.* 1021:202-205.

Spear LP. (2007). The developing brain and adolescent-typical behavior patterns: An evolutionary approach. In D Romer, EF Walker (eds.), *Adolescent Psychopathology and the Developing Brain*. New York: Oxford University Press; pp. 9-30.

Spear LP. (2010). *The Behavioral Neuroscience of Adolescence*. New York: W.W. Norton.

Spear LP, Brake SC. (1983). Periadolescence: age-dependent behavior and psychopharmacological responsivity in rats. *Dev. Psychobiol.* 16: 83-109.

Spear LP, Varlinskaya EI. (2006). Adolescence: Alcohol sensitivity, tolerance, and intake. In M Galanter (ed.) *Alcohol Problems in Adolescents and Young Adults*. New York: Springer; pp. 143-159.

Spence JP, Lai D, Shekhar A, Carr LG, Foroud T, Liang T. (2013). Quantitative trait locus for body weight identified on rat chromosome 4 in inbred alcohol-preferring and -nonpreferring rats: Potential implications for neuropeptide Y and corticotrophin releasing hormone 2 receptor. *Alcohol* 47:63-67.

Spence JP, Liang T, Habegger K, Carr LG. (2005). Effect of polymorphism on expression of the neuropeptide Y gene in inbred alcohol-preferring and -nonpreferring rats. *Neurosci.* 131:871-876.

Spence JP, Liang T, Liu L, Johnson PL, Foroud T, Carr LG, Shekhar A. (2009). From QTL to candidate gene: a genetic approach to alcoholism research. *Curr. Drug Abuse Rev.* 2: 127-134.

Sprow GM, Thiele TE. (2012). The neurobiology of binge-like ethanol drinking: evidence from rodent models. *Physiol. Behav.* 106:325-331.

Stephens DN, Duka T. (2008). Cognitive and emotional consequences of binge drinking: role of amygdala and prefrontal cortex. *Phil. Trans. R Soc. B* 363:3169-3179.

Stewart RB, Gatto GJ, Lumeng L, Li T-K, Murphy JM. (1993). Comparison of alcohol-preferring P and –nonpreferring NP rats on tests relating to anxiety and on the anxiolytic effects of ethanol. *Alcohol* 10:1-10.

Strother WN, Lumeng L, Li TK, McBride WJ. (2005). Dopamine and serotonin content in select brain regions of weanling and adult alcohol drinking rat lines. *Pharmacol. Biochem. Behav.* 80:229-237.

Sun X, Milovanovic M, Zhao Y, Wolf ME. (2008). Acute and chronic dopamine receptor stimulation modulates AMPA receptor trafficking in nucleus accumbens neurons cocultured with prefrontal cortex neurons. *J. Neurosci.* 28:4216-4230.

Suzuki R, Lumeng L, McBride WJ, Li TK, Hwang BH. (2004). Reduced neuropeptide Y mRNA expression in the central nucleus of amygdala of alcohol preferring (P) rats: its potential involvement in alcohol preference and anxiety. *Brain Res.* 1014:251-254.

Szumlinski KK, Diab ME, Friedman R, Henze LM, Lominac KD, Bowers MS. (2007). Accumbens neurochemical adaptations produced by binge-like alcohol consumption. *Psychopharmacology* 190:415-431.

Tabakoff B, Saba L, Printz M, Flodman P, Hodgkinson C, Goldman D, Koob G, Richardson HN, Kechris K, Bell RL, Hubner N, Heinig M, Pravenec M, Mangion J, Legault L, Dongier M, Conigrave KM, Whitfield JB, Saunders J, Grant B, Hoffman PL. (2009). Genetical genomic determinants of alcohol consumption in rats and humans. *BMC Biol.* 7:70.

Tanchuck MA, Yoneyama N, Ford MM, Fretwell AM, Finn DA. (2011). Assessment of GABA-B, metabotropic glutamate, and opioid receptor involvement in an animal model of binge drinking. *Alcohol* 45:33-44.

Thielen RJ, Engleman EA, Rodd ZA, Murphy JM, Lumeng L, Li T-K, McBride WJ. (2004). Ethanol drinking and deprivation alter dopaminergic and serotonergic function in the nucleus accumbens of alcohol-preferring rats. *J. Pharmacol. Exp. Ther.* 309:216-225.

Thoma R, Mullins P, Ruhl D, Monnig M, Yeo RA, Caprihan A, Bogenschutz M, Lysne P, Tonigan S, Kalyanam R, Gasparovic C. (2011). Perturbation of the glutamate-glutamine system in alcohol dependence and remission. *Neuropsychopharmacology* 36:1359-1365.

Toalston JE, Oster SM, Kuc KA, Pommer TJ, Murphy JM, Lumeng L, Bell RL, McBride WJ, Rodd ZA. (2008). Effects of alcohol and saccharin deprivations on concurrent ethanol and saccharin operant self-administration by alcohol-preferring (P) rats. *Alcohol* 42:277-284.

Townshend JM, Duka T. (2002). Patterns of alcohol drinking in a population of young social drinkers: a comparison of questionnaire and diary measures. *Alcohol Alcohol.* 37:187-192.

Townshend JM, Duka T. (2003). Mixed emotions: alcoholics' impairments in the recognition of specific emotional facial expressions. *Neuropsychologia* 41:773-782.

Townshend JM, Duka T. (2005). Binge drinking, cognitive performance and mood in a population of young social drinkers. *Alcohol Clin. Exp. Res.* 29:317-325.

Trommer BL, Liu YB, Pasternak JF. (1996). Long-term depression at the medial perforant path-granule cell synapse in developing rat dentate gyrus. *Brain Res. Dev. Brain Res.* 96:97-108.

Tu Y, Kroener S, Abernathy K, Lapish C, Seamans J, Chandler LJ, Woodward JJ. (2007). Ethanol inhibits persistent activity in prefrontal cortical neurons. *J. Neurosci.* 27:4765-4775.

Tyler DB, van Harreveld A. (1942). The respiration of the developing brain. *Amer. J. Physiol.* 136:600-603.

Van den Oever MC, Lubbers BR, Goriounova NA, Li KW, Van der Schors RC, Loos M, Riga D, Wiskerke J, Binnekade R, Stegeman M, Schoffelmeer AN, Mansvelder HD, Smit AB, De Vries TJ, Spijker S. (2010a). Extracellular matrix plasticity and GABAergic inhibition of prefrontal cortex pyramidal cells facilitates relapse to heroin seeking. *Neuropsychopharmacology* 35:2120-2133.

Van den Oever MC, Spijker S, Smit AB, De Vries TJ. (2010b). Prefrontal cortex plasticity mechanisms in drug seeking and relapse. *Neurosci. Biobehav. Rev.* 35:276-284.

Vengeliene V, Bachteler D, Danysz W, Spanagel R. (2005). The role of the NMDA receptor in alcohol relapse: a pharmacological mapping study using the alcohol deprivation effect. *Neuropharmacology* 48:822-829.

Vengeliene V, Bilbao A, Molander A, Spanagel R. (2008). Neuropharmacology of alcohol addiction. *Br. J. Pharmacol.* 154:299-315.

Vengeliene V, Siegmund S, Singer MV, Sinclair JD, Li TK, Spanagel R. (2003). A comparative study on alcohol-preferring rat lines: effects of deprivation and stress phases on voluntary alcohol intake. *Alcohol Clin. Exp. Res.* 27:1048-1054.

Vik PW, Tate SR, Carrelo P. (2000). Detecting college binge drinkers using an extended time frame. *Addict. Behav.* 25:607-612.

Volkow ND, Li TK. (2005). Drugs and alcohol: treating and preventing abuse, addiction and their medical consequences. *Pharmacol. Ther.* 108:3-17.

Volpicelli JR, Alterman AI, Hayashida M, O'Brien CP. (1992). Naltrexone in the treatment of alcohol dependence. *Arch. Gen. Psychiatry* 49:876-880.

Waller MB, McBride WJ, Lumeng L, Li TK. (1982). Induction of dependence on ethanol by free-choice drinking in alcohol-preferring rats. *Pharmacol. Biochem. Behav.* 16:501-507.

Ward RJ, Lallemand F, de Witte P. (2009). Biochemical and neurotransmitter changes implicated in alcohol-induced brain damage in chronic or 'binge drinking' alcohol abuse. *Alcohol Alcohol.* 44:128-135.

Wechsler H, Austin SB. (1998). Binge drinking: the five/four measure. *J. Stud. Alcohol.* 59:122-124.

Wechsler H, Davenport A, Dowdall G, Moeykens B, Castillo S. (1994). Health and behavioral consequences of binge drinking in college: a national survey of students at 140 campuses. *JAMA* 272:1672-1677.

Wechsler H, Dowdall GW, Davenport A, Castillo S. (1995). Correlates of college student binge drinking. *Am. J. Pub. Health* 85:921-926.

Wechsler H, Lee JE, Kuo M, Lee H. (2000). College binge drinking in the 1990s: a continuing problem. Results of the Harvard School of Public Health 1999 College Alcohol Study. *J. Am. Coll. Health* 48:199-210.

Wechlser H, Nelson TF. (2006). Relationship between level of consumption and harms in assessing drink cut-points for alcohol research: commentary on "Many college freshmen drink at levels far beyond binge threshold" by White et al. *Alcohol Clin. Exp. Res.* 30:922-927.

Weerts EM, Wand GS, Kuwabara H, Munro CA, Dannals RF, Hilton J, Frost JJ, McCaul ME. (2011). Positron emission tomography imaging of mu- and delta-opioid receptor binding in alcohol-dependent and healthy control subjects. *Alcohol Clin. Exp. Res.* 35(12):2162-2173.

Weiss F, Parsons LH, Schulteis G, Hyytia P, Lorang MT, Bloom FE, Koob GF. (1996). Ethanol self-administration restores withdrawal-associated deficiencies in accumbal dopamine and 5-hydroxytryptamine release in dependent rats. *J. Neurosci.* 16:3474-3485.

Weissenborn R, Duka T. (2003). Acute alcohol effects on cognitive function in social drinkers: their relationship to drinking habits. *Psychopharmacology* 165:306-312.

Weitlauf C, Woodward JJ. (2008). Ethanol selectively attenuates NMDAR-mediated synaptic transmission in the prefrontal cortex. *Alcohol Clin. Exp. Res.* 32:690-698.

Wettstein JG, Earley B, Junien JL. (1995). Central nervous system pharmacology of neuropeptide Y. *Pharmacol. Ther.* 65:397-414.

White AM, Kraus CL, Swartzwelder H. (2006). Many college freshmen drink at levels far beyond the binge threshold. *Alcohol Clin. Exp. Res.* 30:1006-1010.

Wilsnack SC, Klassen AD, Schur BE, Wilsnack RW. (1991). Predicting onset and chronicity of women's problem drinking: a five-year longitudinal analysis. *Am. J. Public Health* 81:305-318.

Windle M, Scheidt DM. (2004). Alcoholic subtypes: are two sufficient? *Addict.* 99:1508-1519.

Winters KC. (2001). Assessing adolescent substance use problems and other areas of functioning: state of the art. In PM Monti, SM Colby, TA O'Leary (eds.), *Adolescents, Alcohol, and Substance Abuse: Reaching Teens through Brief Interventions*. New York: Guilford Press; pp. 80-108.

Witt ED. (1994). Mechanisms of alcohol abuse and alcoholism in adolescents: a case for developing animal models. *Behav. Neural. Biol.* 62:168-177.

Witt ED. (2006). Neurobiology. In M Galanter (ed.), *Alcohol Problems in Adolescents and Young Adults*. New York: Springer; pp. 119-122.

Witt ED. (2010). Research on alcohol and adolescent brain development: opportunities and future directions. *Alcohol* 44:119-124.

Won YK, Liu J, Olivier K, Jr., Zheng Q, Pope CN. (2001). Age-related effects of chlorpyrifos on acetylcholine release in rat brain. *Neurotoxicology* 22:39-48.

Wonnacott S. (1997). Presynaptic nicotinic ACh receptors. *Trends Neurosci.* 20:92-98.

Wrase J, Reimold M, Puls I, Kienast T, Heinz A. (2006). Serotonergic dysfunction: brain imaging and behavioral correlates. *Cogn. Affect. Behav. Neurosci.* 6:53-61.

Yang ARST, Yi HS, Mamczarz J, June HL, Jr, Hwang BH, June HL, Sr. (2009). Deficits in substance P mRNA levels in the CeA are inversely associated with alcohol-motivated responding. *Synapse* 63:972-981.

Yau WY, Zubieta JK, Weiland BJ, Samudra PG, Zucker RA, Heitzeg MM. (2012). Nucleus accumbens response to incentive stimuli anticipation in children of alcoholics: relationships with precursive behavioral risk and lifetime alcohol use. *J. Neurosci.* 32:2544-2551.

Yoshimoto K, McBride WJ. (1992). Regulation of nucleus accumbens dopamine release by the dorsal raphe nucleus in the rat. *Neurochem. Res.* 17:401-407.

Yoshimoto K, McBride WJ, Lumeng L, Li TK. (1992). Ethanol enhances the release of dopamine and serotonin in the nucleus accumbens of HAD and LAD lines of rats. *Alcohol Clin. Exp. Res.* 16:781-785.

Yu Z-Y, Wang W, Fritschy J-M, Witte OW, Redecker C. (2006). Changes in neocortical and hippocampal GABA-A receptor subunit distribution during brain maturation and aging. *Brain Res.* 1099:73-81.

Zhang H, Sakharkar AJ, Shi G, Ugale R, Prakash A, Pandey SC. (2010). Neuropeptide Y signaling in the central nucleus of amygdala regulates alcohol-drinking and anxiety-like behaviors of alcohol-preferring rats. *Alcohol Clin. Exp. Res.* 34:451-461.

Zhou FC, Bledsoe S, Lumeng L, Li TK. (1991). Immunostained serotonergic fibers are decreased in select brain regions of alcohol-preferring rats. *Alcohol* 8: 425-431.

Zigman JM, Jones JE, Lee CE, Saper CB, Elmquist JK. (2006). Expression of ghrelin receptor mRNA in the rat and the mouse brain. *J. Comp. Neurol.* 494:528-548.

Zorrilla EP, Valdez GR, Weiss F. (2001). Changes in levels of regional CRF-like-immunoreactivity and plasma corticosterone during protracted drug withdrawal in dependent rats. *Psychopharmacology* 158:374-381.

Zucker RA. (1987). Alcohol and addictive behaviors. In PC Rivers (ed.), *Nebraska Symposium on Motivation* (Vol. 34). Lincoln, NE: University of Nebraska Press; pp. 27-84.

Zucker RA. (1995). Pathways to alcohol problems and alcoholism: A developmental account of the evidence for multiple alcoholisms and for contextual contributions to risk. In RA Zucker, GM Boyd, J Howard (eds.) *The Development of Alcohol Problems: Exploring the Biopsychosocial Matrix of Risk*. NIAAA Research Monograph 26. Rockville, MD: U.S. Dept. of Health and Human Services, National Institute on Alcohol Abuse and Alcoholism; pp. 255-289.

In: Binge Eating and Binge Drinking
Editor: Simon B. Harris

ISBN: 978-1-62618-580-7
© 2013 Nova Science Publishers, Inc.

Chapter 2

BINGE EATING DISORDER: CAUSES, COFACTORS AND COMPLICATIONS

Summar Reslan[1,*], *Karen K. Saules*[1]
and Valentina Ivezaj[2]

[1]Department of Psychology, Eastern Michigan University,
Ypsilanti, MI, US
[2]Department of Psychiatry, Yale School of Medicine,
New Haven, CT, US

ABSTRACT

Rates of obesity and overweight have been rising steadily for nearly three decades, and the associated psychosocial and medical complications are creating a public health crisis. Although obesity rates have no doubt been impacted by a host of environmental, behavioral, and genetic variables, a very important contributor has been Binge Eating Disorder (BED). BED is associated with myriad mental and physical health problems, many of which can be both causes and consequences of disordered eating behavior, resulting in a complex interplay of etiologic and associated features. In particular, a lifetime history of BED is associated with obesity in its most severe form, and BED is also highly comorbid with other documented mortality risk factors (e.g., tobacco use and alcohol abuse).

This chapter provides an overview of BED, with an emphasis on our current understanding of the disorder. First, historical changes in the conceptualization of BED are covered, including the changes to the BED diagnosis in the Diagnostic and Statistical Manual of Mental Disorders (DSM-5). Next, we review BED's psychosocial cofactors (e.g., sex, ethnicity, body image) and comorbid conditions. Finally, we conclude by drawing parallels between BED, binge eating (BE), and addictive behavior, suggesting related directions for future research.

---

[*] Phone: (734) 487-4987; Fax: (734) 487-4989; E-mail: shabhab1@emich.edu.

INTRODUCTION

Binge eating disorder (BED), both in its subthreshold and full forms, has become a major focus of the eating disorder (ED) field over the last two decades. Interest in BED has grown in light of increasing awareness of its maladaptive psychological (e.g., depression) and weight-related comorbidities (e.g., obesity, diabetes, hypertension, and dyslipidemia; Striegel, Bedrosian, Wang and Schwartz, 2012). In particular, interest in BED over time has paralleled concerns about the dramatically increasing prevalence of overweight and obesity in recent decades (Flegal, Carroll, Ogden, and Curtin, 2010; Hedley, Ogden, and Johnson, 2004; Ogden et al., 2006). However, the negative psychological cofactors associated with BED may affect both obese (Specker, de Zwaan, Raymond, and Mitchell, 1994; Yanovski, Nelson, Dubbert, and Spitzer, 1993) and normal weight individuals (Telch and Agras, 1994; Yanovski et al., 1993). Nonetheless, the majority of BED research to date has focused on obese populations (Barry, Grilo, and Masheb, 2003; Devlin, 2007).

In the early 1990's, Robert Spitzer invited researchers to test the validity of BED as a potential disorder for inclusion in the fourth edition of the Diagnostic and Statistical Manual of Mental Disorders (DSM-IV; Spitzer et al., 1991). This call for BED research resulted in an exponential increase in research focusing on BED over the past two decades (Dingemans, van Hanswijck de Jonge, and van Furth, 2005). To encourage this additional research, BED was listed as a provisional disorder within the DSM-IV-Text Revision (DSM-IV-TR) Appendix B under the heading "Criteria Sets and Axes Provided for Further Study" (American Psychiatric Association [APA], 2000).

Definitions

Binge eating (BE) is defined as the consumption of an objectively large amount of food and experiencing lack of control over eating during the eating episode. The DSM-IV-TR defined BED as involving recurrent BE episodes combined with other associated features. The full DSM-IV-TR BED criteria are delineated in Table 1. For the remainder of this chapter, because the literature to date has used the DSM-IV-TR criteria to diagnose BED, our references to BED refer to those criteria, except when making specific reference to the recently released DSM-5. The definition of subthreshold BED varies throughout the literature (e.g., Clyne, Latner, Gleaves, and Blampied, 2010; Hudson, Hiripi, Pope Jr., and Kessler, 2007; Stice, Marti, and Rohde, 2012; Stice, Marti, Shaw, and Jaconis, 2009). Some define subthreshold BED as BE less than twice per week but no less than once in the last 28 days, plus subjective binge episodes (i.e., eating a *subjectively* large amount of food and lack of control over eating; Clyne et al., 2010). Others define subthreshold BED based on the frequency of objective BE (Stice et al., 2012; Stice et al., 2009); others exclude three of five associated features and distress over eating when defining subthreshold BED (Hudson et al., 2007). Although a consensus has not been reached on the definition of subthreshold BED, this term is always applicable to those who endorse most but not all diagnostic criteria for BED. For the remainder of this chapter, the definition of subthreshold BED will be contingent on that used in the study referenced. An attempt will be made to highlight the meaning of subthreshold BED when it is used, but for greater clarification, please refer to the original article in which it was cited.

Table 1. DSM-IV-TR BED Criteria

A. Recurrent episodes of binge eating. An episode of binge eating is characterized by both of the following:
(1) eating, in a discrete period of time (e.g., within any 2-hour period), an amount of food that is definitely larger than most people would eat in a similar period of time and under similar circumstances
(2) a sense of lack of control over eating during the episode (e.g., a feeling that one cannot stop eating or control what or how much ones is eating)

B. The binge-eating episodes are associated with three (or more) of the following:
(1) eating much more rapidly than normal
(2) eating until feeling uncomfortably full
(3) eating large amounts of food when not feeling physically hungry
(4) eating alone because of being embarrassed by how much one is eating
(5) feeling disgusted with oneself, depressed, or very guilty after overeating

C. Marked distress regarding binge eating is present.

D. The binge eating occurs, on average, at least 2 days a week for 6 months.
Note: The method of determining frequency differs from that used for Bulimia Nervosa; future research should address whether the preferred method of setting a frequency threshold is counting the number of days on which binges occur or counting the number of episodes of binge eating.

E. The binge eating is not associated with the regular use of inappropriate compensatory behaviors (e.g., purging, fasting, excessive exercise) and does not occur exclusively during the course of Anorexia Nervosa or Bulimia Nervosa.

Note. From the American Psychiatric Association, 2000, p. 787.

There were three ED classifications in the DSM-IV-TR, Anorexia Nervosa (AN), Bulimia Nervosa (BN), and Eating Disorder Not Otherwise Specified (EDNOS; APA, 2000). Thus, until very recently, individuals meeting criteria for BED were diagnosed with EDNOS, given that the BED criteria themselves were only offered as "provisional" and intended to promote "further study."

The majority of individuals seeking treatment for an ED have thus fallen into the EDNOS category rather than meeting criteria for the more long-standing disorders of BN or AN (e.g., Ricca et al., 2001; Striegel-Moore and Bulik, 2007; Turner and Bryant-Waugh, 2004; Zimmerman et al., 2008).

Individuals with BED have composed the majority of cases seen in treatment from the EDNOS category (Crow, Agras, Halmi, Mitchell, and Kraemer, 2002). Thus, with the advent of BED as a recognized disorder in the DSM-5 (APA, 2013), BED is likely to become the most prevalent ED seen in clinical practice.

Historical Background on the Evolution of the BED Criteria

Although overeating accompanied by a sense of loss of control and distress among the obese was first described in 1959 by Albert Stunkard, the study of BE, subthreshold BED, and BED was neglected for approximately three decades. It was not until the late 1980s and early 1990s that the controversy began over whether BED should be regarded as a distinct diagnosis, as opposed to a substhreshold variant of BN or simply an unhealthy eating pattern, not a psychiatric condition (Devlin, Walsh, Sptizer, and Hasin, 1992; Spitzer et al., 1991). Evidence from the first multisite field trial of BED prompted the ED Task Force to recommend the inclusion of BED in DSM-IV either as a new disorder or as a disorder requiring further study (Spitzer et al., 1991). In the first multisite study, Spitzer et al. (1991) found varying prevalence of BED depending on the sample. Specifically, 71.2% of an Overeaters Anonymous sample, 30% of a weight control sample, and 2% of a community sample met BED criteria. These rates were replicated, and results were expanded in a second multisite study (Spitzer et al., 1993). Early research also found that BED was associated with functional impairment in work and social settings, body image concerns, and a history of psychopathology (e.g., depression, alcohol abuse), even after accounting for obesity and BN (Spitzer et al., 1993). The validity of BED seemed promising, but some argued that classifying BED as a new ED was premature (Fairburn, Welch, and Hay, 1993). In consideration of this controversy, BED was included as a provisional disorder requiring further study in the DSM-IV-TR.

Many researchers have successfully argued in favor of an official BED diagnosis in DSM-5 (Castonguay, Eldredge, and Agras, 1995; Hudson et al., 2007; Reichborn-Kjennerud, Bulik, Tambs, and Harris, 2004; Striegel-Moore and Franko, 2008; Striegel-Moore and Wonderlich, 2007). Evidence has converged to substantiate the validity of BED primarily on the basis that BED and BN differ in important ways (e.g., Barry et al., 2003; Fairburn and Cooper, 2011; Wonderlich, Gordon, Mitchell, Crosby, and Engel, 2009). That literature will be reviewed next.

Difference between BED and BN

Similarities and differences exist between BN and BED (Grilo, 2002). See Table 2 for the full list of DSM-IV-TR BN criteria. The similarities between BN and BED include the presence of BE and comparable problematic eating attitudes and shape concerns, both of which are important as they support that BED is indeed an ED.

After controlling for age and depression, treatment-seeking women with BN are similar to treatment-seeking women with BED on general personality measures that assess ineffectiveness, perfectionism, interpersonal distrust, and interoceptive awareness (Barry et al., 2003).

In a community-based sample, those with BED, purging BN, and nonpurging BN did not differ on rates of current or lifetime history of Axis I disorders (Striegel-Moore et al., 2001). Despite these similarities, important differences between BED and BN have also been highlighted. The most salient difference between BN and BED is that, by definition, individuals meeting criteria for BED do not regularly engage in compensatory behaviors such as laxative use, purging, or excessive exercise following a binge episode. Age, sex, ethnicity, and levels of dietary restraint also differ between those with BN and BED (Devlin, Goldfein, and Dobrow, 2003; Pike, Dohm, Striegel-Moore, Wilfley, and Fairburn, 2001). BN commonly occurs among adolescent females, whereas the age of onset for BED tends to be older (Fairburn and Cooper, 2011; Smink, Hoeken, and Hoek, 2012). Both BN and BED are far more prevalent among females (Hudson et al., 2007; Franko et al., 2012; Striegel, Bedrosian, Wang, and Schwartz, 2012), but 7.5% of men have been found to binge eat (Striegel et al.., 2012).

Table 2. Diagnostic Criteria for BN

A. Recurrent episodes of binge eating. An episode of binge eating is characterized by both of the following:
(1) eating, in a discrete period of time, an amount of food that is definitely larger than most people would eat during a similar period of time and under similar circumstances
(2) a sense of lack of control over eating during the episode

B. Recurrent inappropriate compensatory behavior in order to prevent weight gain, such as self-induced vomiting; misuse of laxatives, diuretics, enemas, or other medications; fasting; or excessive exercise.

C. The binge eating and inappropriate compensatory behaviors both occur, on average, at least twice a week for 3 months.

D. Self-evaluation is unduly influenced by body shape and weight.

E. The disturbance does not occur exclusively during episodes of Anorexia Nervosa.

Note. From the American Psychiatric Association, 2000, p. 594. The changes to the BN diagnosis in the DSM-5 (APA, 2013) are twofold: 1. The frequency of BE and purging is decreased from two times per week for three months to once a week for three months, and 2. The "non-purging" BN subtype is eliminated and merged with BED (Wolfe, Hannon-Engel, and Mitchell, 2012). However, we present the DSM-IV-TR criteria here because the literature to date has primarily relied on the earlier definition.

Although dieting tends to precede BE among those meeting criteria for BN, many individuals with BED engage in BE before dieting, and they endorse lower levels of dietary restraint (Barry et al., 2003; Wilfley, Schwartz, Spurrell, and Fairburn, 2000), defined as the extent to which one attempts to exert control over food intake with the goal of influencing body weight. A history of purging among those with BED is not associated with the severity of this condition or later comorbidity (Peterson et al., 1998). In a community-based sample, very few BED cases had a history of BN, and AN was associated with BN but not BED (Striegel-Moore et al., 2001). Together, this evidence supports the lack of cross-over between BED and other EDs.

Other notable differences include that those with BED report that they enjoy the senses associated with eating (e.g., taste and smell) more so than do those with BN (Mitchell et al., 1999). Individuals with BED also consume less food during binge episodes (Brody, Walsh, and Devlin, 1994; Goldfein, Walsh, LaChaussee, Kissileff, and Devlin, 1993), but they consume more food during non-binge times than those with BN (Mitchell, Crow, Peterson, Wonderlich, and Crosby, 1998). Those with BED more frequently engage in grazing (i.e., continuous snacking throughout the entire day) rather than the "feast or famine" behavior that is characteristic of those with BN (Marcus et al., 1992).

Recently, differences in the activation of specific neural regions have been purported to differentiate between BN and BED (e.g., Celone, Thompson-Brenner, Ross, Pratt, and Stern, 2011; Dodds et al., 2012; Karhunen et al., 2000; Lock, Garrett, Beenhakker, and Reiss, 2011; Schienle, Schäfer, Hermann, and Vaitl, 2009; Weygandt, Schaefer, Schienle, and Haynes, 2012). Neuroimaging studies have revealed differences in brain activation in response to visual food cues among patients with BN and BED (Karhunen et al., 2000; Schienle et al., 2009), and visual food cues have been found to be encoded in distinct reward-related brain areas for those with BN and BED (Weygandt et al., 2012). Increased activation in response to food cues in frontal regions involved in selective attention (i.e., the anterior cingulated cortex) and subcortical areas such as the insula were characteristic of those with BN, while patients with BED exhibited increased activation in the prefrontal regions, especially the orbitofrontal cortex, which are involved in the processing of the hedonic value of primary reinforcers such as food (Karhunen et al., 2000; Schienle et al., 2009). Grey matter volume in the ventral striatum has also been implicated as a structural brain difference that can help distinguish between those with BN and BED (Schäfer, Vaitl, and Schienle, 2010), and the volume of the ventral striatum, which includes the nucleus accumbens, was found to be larger for those with BN relative to those with BED and normal-weight controls. It is suggested that greater striatal grey matter volume is the result of recurrent purging among those with BN, a behavior that is typically absent among those with BED and normal-weight controls (Schäfer et al., 2010). Further exploration of these differences in neural activity and brain structure may be a viable direction for future research to advance our understanding of etiologic mechanisms and further assist in distinguishing between BN and BED. The differences will also likely become more pronounced in future work because non-purging BN has been eliminated from the DSM-5 (APA, 2013; Wolfe et al., 2012), and these individuals now fall into the BED diagnostic category. In previous work, the BN group included non-purging BN, a group that we now classify as having BED, which would likely have attenuated the findings described above.

Critical Examination of BED Criteria

Critical examination of BED criteria is also essential to advance the ED field and to further validate the legitimacy of the BED diagnosis. The definition of BE has been a matter of considerable debate (Wolfe, Wood Baker, Smith, and Kelly-Weeder, 2009). Criterion A specifies that a binge episode should consist of an unusually large amount of food in a discrete period of time (often considered to be less than two hours) with the associated sense of loss of control. This combination is typically referred to as an objective binge episode or OBE. Inherent problems are associated with this definition, especially the criterion of the consumption of an unusually large amount of food in a discrete period of time. Approximately one quarter of obese individuals who binge eat engage in binges that span the entire day (Marcus et al., 1992), which is inconsistent with the two-hour specification included in the definition of an objective binge episode. There has also been debate about what constitutes an objectively large amount of food. This criterion is vague (Devlin et al.,

2003) and subjective (Mathes, Brownley, Mo, and Bulik, 2009), and may lead to inconsistencies in the definition of a binge.

In contrast to the OBE definition of consuming an *objectively* large amount of food while also experiencing a loss of control over eating, *subjective* binge eating refers to eating a *subjectively* large amount of food and feeling a loss of control over eating. Individuals who engage in objective binge eating do not necessarily differ on measures of depression and psychological distress relative to individuals who engage in subjective binge eating (Brownstone et al., 2013; Niego et al., 1997; Watson, Fursland, Bulik, and Nathan, 2012). Therefore, the size of a binge may not be as crucial as the associated feeling of loss of control over eating (i.e., Criterion A2).

According to Devlin et al. (2003), the initial reasons for the inclusion of "loss of control" in the criteria for BED were twofold. First, this descriptor was included to discriminate those who engage in disordered eating behavior from those who occasionally overeat. Second, this criterion was included to match the BN definition of a binge. Devlin et al. (2003) raised concerns that these reasons were arbitrary. Despite these concerns, however, research has substantiated the importance of including "loss of control" as a criterion for BED (Grilo and White, 2011). Specifically, loss of control has been found to be crucial to predicting the negative psychological outcomes associated with BE among adults (e.g., Colles, Dixon, O'Brien, 2008; Johnson, Boutelle, Torgrud, Davig, and Turner, 2000; Johnson, Carr-Nangle, Nangle, Antony, and Zayfert, 1997) and adolescents (e.g., Sonneville et al., 2012). Evidence has thus emerged to validate that a sense of loss of control over eating is a crucial component of BED. Support has also emerged to validate other criteria of BED, namely Criterion B (i.e., associated symptoms of BED) and C (i.e., marked distress regarding BE).

Criterion B outlines five associated symptoms (see Table 1); three or more of these five associated symptoms must be endorsed in order to meet the BED diagnostic criteria. Although additional empirical support for the requirement of three out of five associated symptoms is needed (Ackard, Fulkerson, and Neumark-Sztainer, 2007; Striegel-Moore and Franko, 2008; Striegel-Moore and Marcus, 1995), all of the associated symptoms have been found to have predictive value and the number of symptoms present is associated with the severity of BED (White and Grilo, 2011).

Criterion C, endorsing marked levels of distress regarding the binge episode, was also initially thought to be arbitrary (Devlin et al., 2003). It is unclear whether distress before, during, after a binge episode, or in some combination is important to the diagnosis of BED. There is some evidence to suggest that sex differences may moderate the importance of the level of distress associated with BE. Men are less likely to endorse distress associated with BE, and subsequently, fail to meet diagnostic criteria for BED at rates as high as women (Hudson et al., 2007).

Recently, Grilo and White (2011) found that endorsing marked levels of distress in response to BE is essential to the diagnosis of BED, even after controlling for demographic differences (i.e., age, sex, and ethnicity). They concluded that if marked distress about BE were not required for a BED diagnosis, a substantial increase in the number of persons with BED would occur, but this group would be similar in ED psychopathology and associated depression to obese persons who do not binge eat (Grilo and White, 2011). Thus, marked distress following BE may be a crucial component of the diagnostic criteria for BED.

With respect to Criterion D, the frequency criterion, a note included in the provisional criteria for BED reads, "The method of determining frequency differs from that used for BN;

future research should address whether the preferred method of setting a frequency threshold is counting the number of days on which binges occur or counting the number of episodes of binge eating" (APA, 2000, p. 787). Thus, the frequency criterion has been subject to a variety of critiques. It has been argued that this frequency criterion does not fully capture those at risk for psychological distress associated with BE (Colles et al., 2008), and individuals experience psychological distress when the frequency of binge episodes ranges from at least *once a week* for six months (Striegel-Moore, Wilson, Wilfley, Elder, and Brownell, 1998) to at least *once a month* for six months (Striegel-Moore, Wilfley, Pike, Dohm, and Fairburn, 2000). Many researchers feel that this frequency criterion is problematic (e.g., Bruce and Agras, 1992; Hay and Fairburn, 1998; Grissett and Fitzgibbon, 1996; Striegel-Moore et al., 1998; Wilson and Sysko, 2009), and this critique has been addressed by those who formulated the DSM-5 criteria for BED (discussed below).

In addition to the critiques of the DSM-IV-TR BED criteria noted above, the exclusion of the overvaluation of weight and shape to the diagnosis of BED is a matter of debate. Given that body image concerns represent a major cofactor with EDs and that the overvaluation of weight and shape has been shown to be comparable between BED and BN participants, Masheb and Grilo (2000) suggest that the exclusion of this criterion is a significant oversight. Multiple recommendations have been made to remedy this situation. It has been suggested that heightened concern with body shape and weight be added to the criteria for BED (Goldschmidt et al., 2010; Masheb and Grilo, 2000).

It has also been suggested that the overvaluation of weight and shape should be included as a specifier of BED and not part of the diagnostic criteria because about half of individuals with BED do not endorse these weight concerns (e.g., Grilo et al., 2009; Grilo, White, Gueorguieva, Wilson, and Masheb, 2012; Hrabosky, Masheb, White, and Grilo, 2007). Recent research suggests that body mass index (BMI) is not related to heightened concern with body shape and weight among those with BED and supports that a high degree of weight concern is associated with BED itself, not with simply being overweight (Grilo, Masheb, and White, 2010). There has also been discussion about a dimensional classification of BED for future editions of the DSM (Brown and Barlow, 2005; Thomas, Vartanian, and Brownell, 2009; Widiger and Samuel, 2005).

A dimensional classification system would involve organizing psychopathology along a continuum as opposed to classifying individuals into formal diagnostic categories. Regarding the debate over the inclusion of the overvaluation of shape and weight, a dimensional classification for this construct may be have merit, as grading the severity of this symptom among those with BED may be informative (Ahrberg, Trojca, Nasrawi, and Vocks, 2011). In sum, a subgroup of individuals with BED endorse overvaluation of shape and weight concern, and greater consideration of the clinical implications of this symptom of BED is warranted. Converging lines of research created a strong argument that an official BED diagnosis was warranted for the DSM-5 (Wilfley, Wilson, and Agras, 2003; Wonderlich et al., 2009). Endorsing a lack of control over eating and marked levels of distress in response to overeating are essential to the diagnosis of BED (Colles et al., 2008; Grilo and White, 2011; Johnson et al., 2000), but the utility of other BED criteria (i.e., consuming an objectively large amount of food, frequency and duration criteria, and endorsing three of five associated symptoms) requires additional validation.

The Future of BED

With the publication of the DSM-5, BED has become an official diagnosis (APA, 2013; Hudson, Coit, Lalonde, and Pope Jr., 2012; Sysko et al., 2012; Trace et al., 2012). Despite debate about the criteria that compose BED, all DSM-IV-TR BED criteria remain in DSM-5 (Table 1) with the exception of the frequency and duration requirements. Specifically, BED criteria are now met by having had symptoms only once per week for three months (Table 3). Although the lifetime prevalence of symptoms of BE is relatively common (Reba-Harrelson et al., 2009), the diagnosis of BED is less common due in part to the imposed frequency and duration stipulations (Striegel-Moore and Franko, 2003). However, the empirical evidence to support the validity of the DSM-IV-TR "two days per week for six months" criteria of BED is lacking (Crow et al., 2002; Striegel-Moore et al., 2000). For example, individuals who binge eat twice per week are similar to individuals who binge eat less frequently on demographic characteristics, body mass index, ED symptomatology, and psychiatric distress (Striegel-Moore et al., 2000). Changing the DSM-5 frequency threshold to engaging in BE one day per week thus has empirical support (Trace et al., 2012; Wilfley, Bishop, Wilson, Agras, 2007), although some suggest that changes to the frequency and duration criterion will have only a minimal effect on the prevalence of BED (Fairburn and Cooper, 2011; Hudson et al., 2012). Nonetheless, trained interviewers can reliably diagnose BED using the proposed DSM-5 criteria, and the classification of BED as a standalone diagnosis reduces the proportion of individuals with an EDNOS diagnosis (Birgegard, Norring, and Clinton, 2012; Sysko et al., 2012).

Table 3. DSM-5 BED Criteria

A. Recurrent episodes of binge eating. An episode of binge eating is characterized by both of the following:
(1) eating, in a discrete period of time (e.g., within any 2-hour period), an amount of food that is definitely larger than most people would eat in a similar period of time and under similar circumstances
(2) a sense of lack of control over eating during the episode (e.g., a feeling that one cannot stop eating or control what or how much ones is eating)

B. The binge-eating episodes are associated with three (or more) of the following:
(1) eating much more rapidly than normal
(2) eating until feeling uncomfortably full
(3) eating large amounts of food when not feeling physically hungry
(4) eating alone because of being embarrassed by how much one is eating
(5) feeling disgusted with oneself, depressed, or very guilty after overeating

C. Marked distress regarding binge eating is present.

D. The binge eating occurs, on average, at least 1 day a week for 3 months.

E. The binge eating is not associated with the regular use of inappropriate compensatory behaviors (e.g., purging, asting, excessive exercise) and does not occur exclusively during the course of Anorexia Nervosa or Bulimia Nervosa.

Note. From the American Psychiatric Association, 2013, www.dsm5.org.

PREVALENCE OF BED

In non-weight loss treatment seeking samples, the diagnosis of BED ranges from 3% to 6% (e.g., Grucza, Przybeck, Cloninger, 2007).

Of those seeking mental health treatment, 1% meet criteria for BED (Hoek and van Hoeken, 2003). Thus, because the prevalence of BED among those seeking treatment (1%) is less than the prevalence of BED in the general population (3% to 6%), it is reasonable to hypothesize that those with BED may be under-utilizing mental health services. Few studies have focused on the specific impact that BED may have on health-care service utilization (e.g., Becker, Franko, Speck, and Herzog, 2003; Hepworth and Paxton, 2007; Hoffman et al., 2006; Reslan, 2010). The majority of individuals who binge eat and subsequently develop BED or BN experience severe role impairment but rarely seek treatment (Hudson et al., 2007; Reslan, 2010). That is, less than one half of those with BN or BED have ever sought treatment for their ED; however, the majority of people with AN, BN, or BED have sought treatment at some point for an emotional problem (Hudson et al., 2007). Additional study of BED is warranted because current research has found that BED is a pervasive, stable, and chronic condition (Hudson et al., 2007).

PSYCHOSOCIAL COFACTORS WITH BED

Diversity

Sex and BED. BED prevalence differs by sex. Lifetime prevalence for subthreshold BED (defined here as BE at least twice a week for at least three months and not occurring solely during the course of AN or BN) and BED are reportedly 0.6% and 3.5%, respectively, for women and 1.9% and 2% for men (Hudson et al., 2007). Males report BE about as often as females when subthreshold and clinical levels of BED are combined. Many similarities are observed between men and women with BED. Specifically, treatment seeking men and women with BED generally do not differ in terms of age at first overweight (Barry, Grilo, and Masheb, 2002; Guerdjikova, McElroy, Kotwal, and Keck, 2007), age at onset of BE or dieting, weight cycling (Barry et al., 2002), measures of current ED symptoms (Barry et al., 2002; Guerdjikova et al., 2007), depression (Barry et al., 2002; Guerdjikova et al., 2007; Tanofsky, Wilfley, Spurrell, Welch, and Brownell, 1997), or anxiety (Guerdjikova et al., 2007; Tanofsky et al., 1997). Males, however, are not as likely to meet BED criteria as females. Diagnostic emphasis of BED as involving three of five associated symptoms and distress over eating may result in heightened diagnosis of BED among females, even if they manifest the same rate of BE as males. Notably, however, in terms of public health consequences, it is BE, not necessarily BED, that leads to adverse consequences such as obesity (Riener, Schindler, and Ludvik, 2006) and related health problems. Medical concerns such as neck pain, shoulder pain, and chronic pain were higher among individuals engaging in BE than those who did not, and these concerns were more frequent from men than women with BE (Reichborn-Kjennerud et al., 2004), highlighting the significance of identifying BED criteria that are also applicable to men. In fact, a recent report indicates that men and women who binge eat have comparable levels of physical and emotional impairment across multiple domains; based on these results, Striegel et al. (2012) have called for greater inclusion of men in BE research.

Sex differences in the experience of a "binge" may also contribute to the disproportionate likelihood of females meeting the diagnostic criteria for BED, rather than actual differences in rates of BE. Men and women have different definitions for what constitutes an eating binge (Reslan and Saules, 2011). Research consistently shows that, relative to males, females are more inclined to label their own eating as a binge. Females with BED identified lack of control over eating and the quantity of food consumed as fundamental when defining an eating binge (LaPorte, 1997; Lewinsohn, Seeley, Moerk, and Striegel-Moore, 2002; Reslan and Saules, 2011; Telch and Stice, 1998). Conversely, males require a larger quantity of food, increased speed of consumption, and feeling gastrointestinal consequences before labeling their behavior as a binge episode (LaPorte, 1997).

The events that precipitate an eating binge for males and females have been observed to differ (Barry et al., 2002; Reagan and Hersch, 2005; Womble et al., 2007). BE is associated with negative emotions (e.g., anger) in men, while BE has been linked to diet failures in women (Barry et al., 2002). Additionally, men often have a history of substance abuse preceding their binge patterns, whereas women report using BE as a coping mechanism (Barry et al., 2002; Grilo, White, and Masheb, 2009; Tanofsky et al., 1997). The social environment plays a large role in determining patterns of overeating among women (Reagan and Hersch, 2005). In addition to sex, other demographic factors are associated with differential prevalence of BED, namely ethnicity and sexual orientation.

Ethnicity and BED. There is a cultural misperception that pathological eating behaviors rarely occur among ethnic minorities. This expectation may be based on the abundance of research on EDs that has been conducted among Caucasian samples (Pike and Walsh, 1996; Striegel-Moore, and Smolak, 2000). More recent research investigating ethnic differences in eating pathology, however, indicates that there is a higher prevalence of BED among ethnic minorities than among Caucasians (e.g., Franko et al., 2012; Hudson et al., 2007; Reslan and Saules, in press; Striegel-Moore and Franko, 2008). BED is the most prevalent ED among African Americans, although sex differences in the prevalence of BED among African Americans have been observed, with African American men meeting BED criteria less often than do African American women (Taylor, Caldwell, Baser, Faison, and Jackson, 2007). Among clinical samples of women, African American women report more binge episodes per week ($M = 4.4$, $SD = 2.4$) than do Caucasian women ($M = 4.2$, $SD = 3.9$; Grilo, Lozano, and Masheb, 2005). In addition, amongst women in the San Francisco area, approximately 2% of Caucasian women but 5% of both African American and Hispanic women met criteria for BED (Bruce and Agras, 1992). Among Latinos, lifetime rates of BE and BED, as well as its clinical features and psychiatric comorbidity, are similar to those observed among Caucasian samples (Palavras, Kaio, Mari, and Claudino, 2011). In a BED treatment-seeking sample, Hispanic adults were found to have significantly greater body shape and eating concerns than did their Caucasian and African American counterparts (Franko et al., 2012).

The cultural misperception that pathological eating behavior, namely BED, is more common among Caucasians may have emerged because ethnic minorities are less likely to seek treatment for these disordered eating patterns than are Caucasians (e.g., Reslan, 2010; Striegel-Moore et al., 2003). Research suggests that when ethnic minorities do seek mental health treatment, they are less likely to receive treatment for an ED. This finding holds even among those who self-report an eating problem (Becker et al., 2003). Specifically, African

Americans, Latinos, and Native Americans are significantly less likely to receive a recommendation or referral for further evaluation of their eating pathology than are Caucasians (Becker et al., 2003; Striegel-Moore et al., 2003). The majority of research has found differential patterns of psychological treatment seeking and referral for members of different ethnicities; however, minimal research has investigated differences within members of the same ethnic group with regard to treatment seeking. Few studies suggest that there are differential treatment-seeking patterns among members of the same ethnicity that are a function of both age and weight. For example, African American women with BED do not typically seek treatment until they are older and heavier (Grilo et al., 2005), a similar pattern observable among Caucasian treatment seekers (Eisenberg, Golberstien, and Gollust, 2007).

Sexual orientation. Some studies suggest an association between sexual orientation and EDs, particularly BE (Feldman and Meyer, 2007). Specifically, gay men are more likely to engage in BE than heterosexual men (French, Story, Remafedi, Resnick, and Blum, 1996; Yager, Kurtzman, Landsverk, and Wiesmeier, 1988). Gay and bisexual men are more likely to be diagnosed with EDs than heterosexual men (Feldman and Meyer, 2007), and although lesbians and heterosexual women have comparable rates of BN, lesbians endorse higher rates of BED.

This elevated rate of BED among the lesbian community has been attributed to negative affect and discrimination (Heffernan, 1996). Specifically, BED among lesbians was strongly related to the use of food for negative affect regulation, and it has been proposed that discrimination contributes to negative self-awareness, stress, and lack of social support among lesbians (Heffernan, 1996). Additional research in this domain is requisite, given that sexual orientation is not commonly discussed in the BED literature.

Body Image and BED

Three of the most common types of body image disturbance include body image distortion, or the difference between perceived and actual body size, body image discrepancy, or the difference between current and ideal body size, and body image dissatisfaction, or the level of dissatisfaction with one's current body size (Sorbara and Geliebter, 2002). Body image disturbance, most notably body image dissatisfaction, is strongly associated with the onset of BE and BED (Johnson and Wardle, 2005).

Those who binge eat exhibit more body image discrepancy and report more body image dissatisfaction than those who do not engage in BE (Sorbara and Geliebter, 2002). Females with BED report lower self-esteem, which may be attributable in part to body image dissatisfaction (Pesa, Syre, and Jones, 2000).

Unlike the criteria for BN, "self-evaluation influenced by body shape and weight" is not a requirement for the diagnosis of BED. However, research suggests that at least among the obese, body image dissatisfaction is greater among individuals who meet criteria for BED versus those who do not meet the diagnostic criteria for this disorder (Masheb and Grilo, 2003).

In related work, Saules et al. (2009) found that believing oneself to be overweight predicted BE in a sample of college students even after controlling for BMI, depression, and sex. Ethnicity also influences the association between heightened concern with body shape and weight and BED (Reslan and Saules, in press). Specifically, heightened concern with body shape and weight is related to increased odds for BED among Caucasians, Hispanics, and Arab-Americans, but it is unrelated to risk for BED among African Americans, Native Americans, Asian-Americans, and Pacific Islanders.

Impulsivity and BED

In general, those with EDs, particularly those with BN (Claes et al., 2005; Killen et al., 1996; Steiger, Lehoux, and Gauvin, 1999), manifest poorer impulse control than those without EDs (Killen et al., 1996). Some research indicates that the urge to binge eat is different among those with BN who are high in impulsivity in comparison to those with BN who are low in impulsivity (Steiger et al., 1999). Among those with BN and high impulsivity, BE is more often associated with diminished inhibitory control, whereas among those with BN but low impulsivity, the urge to binge is more often associated with poor dietary restraint (Steiger et al., 1999).

As impulsivity is a multifaceted construct, one study sought to investigate which dimensions of impulsivity are prominent amongst those with BN (Fischer, Smith, and Anderson, 2003). For that investigation, impulsivity was defined in two ways. First, impulsivity was defined as a lack of premeditation: that is, having the inability to delay action before thinking about consequences, or in other words, the inability to plan. Second, impulsivity was defined as a sense of urgency: that is, having a predisposition to act in the face of negative emotion.

Results indicated that when one is referring to heightened levels of impulsivity among individuals with BN, impulsivity should be conceptualized as a sense of urgency, or the predisposition to act rashly in the face of negative emotions, not as a lack of planning (Fischer et al., 2003).

No specific research studies have investigated the direct relationship between BED and impulsivity; however, some research indicates that BE is strongly associated with heightened levels of impulsivity (Claes et al., 2005; de Zwaan et al., 1994). A review article by Dawe and Loxton (2004) concludes that BE is typically accompanied by a feeling a loss of control, which is influenced by impulsivity.

A behavioral manifestation of impulsivity is heightened reward sensitivity, which Dawe and Loxton (2004) suggest increases vulnerability to BE. Heightened reward sensitivity to food cues has also been observed among individuals with BED using functional magnetic resonance imaging (fMRI; Schienle et al., 2009).

According to reinforcement sensitivity theory (Gray, 1991), differences in reward sensitivity are mediated by the behavioral approach system (BAS), or the motivational system that responds to signals of reward. Activity in the BAS or greater BAS sensitivity motivates or increases movement toward a desired goal. For example, individuals with BED have an elevated sensitivity for primary rewards such as food relative to those who are overweight without BED, those who are normal weight without BED, and those who are normal weight with BN (Schienle et al., 2009).

CONDITION COMMONLY COMORBID WITH BED

Psychiatric Comorbidity

Psychiatric comorbidity is elevated among those who meet criteria for BED. Among treatment-seeking individuals with BED, 67% report having at least one additional lifetime psychiatric disorder, and 37% report having at least one current psychiatric disorder (Grilo, White, Barnes, and Masheb, 2012). Specifically, BED is highly comorbid with substance use disorders (specifically, alcoholism and tobacco use; Grilo et al., 2012), bipolar disorder (Krüger, Shugar, and Cooke, 1996; McElroy, Kotwal, and Keck, 2006), major depressive disorder, panic disorder, and phobias (Anthony, Johnson, Carr-Nagle, and Abel, 1994; Bijl and Ravelli, 2000; Bulik, Sullivan, Kendler, 2003; Mussell et al., 1996). The most well established link between BED and psychiatric comorbidity is that with anxiety and depressive disorders. Specifically, compared to the general population, symptoms of depression and anxiety are elevated among both men and women with BED (Reichborn-Kjennerud et al., 2004).

Depression. Those with BED have high rates of depressive disorders. In one study of those who engage in binge eating, 36% of males and 47% of women met screening criteria for depressive disorders (Reichborn-Kjennerug et al., 2004). Furthermore, depression is associated with poorer weight-loss treatment outcomes (Linde et al., 2004). Some research suggests that obesity treatment can lessen depression (Stunkard, Faith, and Allison, 2003); however, this relationship appears to be moderated by a variety of factors, including BE. In a systematic literature review examining the relationship between depression and BED, approximately 71% of the studies reviewed supported the association between depression and BED (Araujo, Santos, and Nardi, 2010). Notably, these studies were not longitudinal or prospective, leaving the directionality of the relationship between depression and BED unknown. In a laboratory study of the association between internalizing behaviors (i.e., depression and anxiety), BED, and caloric intake, the association between internalizing behaviors and caloric intake was fully mediated by BED (Peterson, Latendresse, Bartholome, Warren, and Raymond, 2012). Unfortunately, the question of whether BED precedes or follows depression and/or anxiety remains unanswered.

Anxiety. BE is also associated with anxiety (e.g., Marcus et al., 1990; Reichborn-Kjennerud et al., 2004). Individuals with BED report more anxiety than those with subthreshold BED and non-BED controls (Antony et al., 1994). Moreover, anxiety and mood disorders are the most common comorbid disorders among individuals seeking treatment for BED (Grilo et al., 2009). Anxiety is suggested to be the most common precursor to binge episodes among overweight individuals with BED (Masheb and Grilo, 2006). Community samples of those with BED have higher rates of anxiety disorders than those observed among BED treatment-seeking samples, suggesting that anxiety may serve as a barrier to BED treatment (Wilfley, Pike, Dohm, Striegel-Moore, and Fairburn, 2001).

Attention Deficit Hyperactivity Disorder (ADHD). In a study of 86 adults who met DSM-IV criteria for ADHD, 8.3% also met criteria for BED (Mattos et al., 2004). This prevalence was higher than expected, relative to the general population BED prevalence of 3% to 6% (Grucza et al., 2007). Because only a couple DSM-IV criteria for BED involve impulsivity (Table 1), the association between ADHD and BED is not thought to be an artifact of similar symptomatology; rather, this relationship is thought to represent true comorbidity between these disorders (Cortese, Bernardina, and Mouren, 2007). In the first nationally representative sample examining the relationship between ADHD and obesity, BED was found to mediate the relationship between adult ADHD and obesity (Pagato et al., 2009). The authors attributed this finding to difficulty following through with planned meals secondary to disinhibition.

There are two prominent hypotheses that attempt to explain the co-occurrence of ADHD and BED. The first suggests that both the impulsive and inattentive components of ADHD may foster disordered eating patterns because deficient inhibitory control, which manifests as poor planning and difficulty managing behavior effectively, can lead to the overconsumption of food for hedonic not homeostatic motivations. Stated differently, those with ADHD may more commonly eat for pleasure and not solely eat to replenish their bodies' depleted resources. The second hypothesis suggests that ADHD and BE share common neurobiological mechanisms (Cortese et al., 2007). Those with ADHD may present with behaviors consistent with the reward deficiency syndrome (Blum et al., 2000), or insufficient dopamine activation that leads to the use of "unnatural" immediate rewards such as substance use (which is also highly comorbid with ADHD) and compulsive overeating to compensate for this deficiency (Comings and Blum, 2000; Davis et al., 2009). Future research is needed to fully test these hypotheses and advance our understanding of the association between ADHD and BED.

Personality disorders. Certain personality disorders are common among those with BED. Among those seeking treatment for BED, as many as 30-50% meet criteria for at least one personality disorder (Grilo and Masheb, 2002). The most common personality disorders among individuals with BED are avoidant, obsessive compulsive, and borderline personality disorders (Mitchell et al., 2008). About 15% of individuals with BED meet obsessive compulsive personality disorder (Grilo, 2004; Wilfley et al., 2000). Those with BN are also generally thought of as having general personality impairments (Schmidt and Telch, 1990), but the possible difference in rates of personality disorders between BED and BN individuals awaits further study.

Obesity

Numerous studies have referred to the problem of obesity as an "epidemic" (Mokdad, Marks, Stroup, and Gerberding, 2000; Mokdad et al., 1999; Popkin and Doak, 1998). Reports from the American Medical Association indicate that in 2009-2010, 69% of adults were overweight or obese and 36% of adults were obese (Flegal, Carroll, Kit, and Ogden, 2012). While escalating rates of overweight and obesity may be leveling off, obesity rates at the higher end of the BMI spectrum are increasing much faster than rates of moderate obesity. Specifically, from 2000-2005, prevalence of BMI greater than 30 increased by 24%; BMI greater than 40 increased by 50%, and BMI greater than 50 increased by 75% (Sturm, 2007). A large body of research links obesity to a number of negative health consequences, behavioral changes (i.e., BE), and severe psychopathology (Dansky et al., 1998; Kruger et al., 1994; McElroy et al., 2001). A number of long-term health consequences are associated with obesity. The estimated number of deaths attributed to obesity alone is approximately 111,909 annually (Flegal, Graubard, Williamson, and Gail, 2005). Obesity is strongly associated with the development of type 2 diabetes, coronary heart disease, certain forms of cancer, sleep and breathing disorders, and decreased life expectancy (Kopelman, 2000). Research suggests that being overweight or obese typically takes a lifelong course. That is, elevated body weight continues to increase until approximately age 50 to 60 (Kopelman, 2000). Thus, early interventions to combat this problem are clearly necessary.

A research emphasis has been placed on examining modifiable behavioral risk factors related to obesity such as physical inactivity, poor diet (Mokdad et al., 2004), and notably, BE (Tanofsky-Kraff and Yanovski, 2004). Due to the rapid increase in obesity rates that are not solely due to genetics, Striegel-Moore and Bulik (2007) argue that research focusing on eating disturbances and obesity is necessary. Comparing obese individuals with and without BED became a crucial step in validating BED as its own disorder. Initially, it was unclear if BE itself was problematic or simply a characteristic of obesity (Mitchell, Devlin, de Zwaan, Crow, and Peterson, 2008).

Comorbidity of BED and obesity. There is a robust association between BED and obesity (Grilo, Masheb, Brody, Burke-Martindale, and Rothschild; 2005; Reas, White, and Grilo, 2006; Striegel-Moore et al., 1998; Womble et al., 2001). A lifetime history of BED is associated with obesity in its most severe form (BMI greater than or equal to 40 kg/m^2; Hudson et al., 2007). Individuals with BED have a greater vulnerability to obesity than healthy controls (Fairburn et al., 1998), and a moderate overlap between the genetic liability for obesity and BED has been noted (Bulik et al., 2003). Although obesity is not a requirement for BED, approximately 70% of those with BED are obese (Grucza et al., 2007). Additionally, 15% to 30% of obese treatment-seekers report some form of BE behavior (Womble et al., 2001). There is a striking difference between the prevalence of BED in the general population versus that among obese individuals seeking weight loss treatment, i.e., 2% to 6% (de Zwaan, 2001; Grucza et al., 2007) versus 20-30% (Spitzer et al., 1991; Spitzer et al., 1993), respectively. Many obese individuals meet BED criteria, but BED and obesity do not always co-occur. As BMI increases, however, the relationship between BED and obesity strengthens (Hudson et al., 2006; Telch, Agras, and Rossiter, 1988). When examining the prevalence of BED in the general population, one study found that a little over half of individuals meeting BED criteria were overweight/obese, leaving a substantial number of individuals with BED who were of normal weight (Didie and Fitzgibbon, 2005). Based on this finding, Mitchell et al. (2008) concluded that normal-weight individuals may not be as distressed (yet) to seek treatment.

Co-occurring conditions among obese individuals with BED. Relative to obese individuals without BED, obese individuals with BED report a higher lifetime prevalence of psychiatric disorders such as depression and anxiety (Clark, Forsyth, Lloyd-Richardson, and King, 2000; Kolotkin et al., 2004; Marcus et al., 1990; Mussell et al., 1996; Specker et al., 1994; Yanovski et al., 1993), poorer eating self-efficacy (Clark et al., 2000), lower body satisfaction (Mussell et al., 1996), poorer subjective sleep quality and physical functioning (Rieger, Wilfley, Stein, Marino, and Crow, 2005; Vardar, Caliyurt, Arikan, and Tuglu, 2004), greater work and sexual impairment, and poorer quality of life (Rieger et al., 2005). Histrionic personality disorder, borderline personality disorder, and avoidant personality disorder were also more common among obese individuals with BED than among obese individuals without BED (Specker et al., 1994; Yanovski et al., 2003). When examining patterns of eating among obese individuals with and without BED, those with BED ate significantly more food than those without BED. These findings are consistent across laboratory studies (Cooke et al., 1997; Goldfein et al., 1993; Guss, Kissileff, Walsh, and Devlin, 1994; Sysko, Devlin, Walsh,

Zimmerli, and Kissileff, 2007; Walsh and Boudreau, 2003) and those that analyzed self-report data (Yanovski and Sebring, 1994). These findings lend support to the severity of BED and suggest that this disorder is associated with myriad negative sequelae that while not simply a function of obese status, are certainly compounded by obesity.

BED among those who are normal weight. There is a robust relationship between obesity and BED, but it is important to note that BED is a psychiatric disorder independent of weight status (Didie and Fitzgibbon, 2005; Telch and Agras, 1994; Yanovski et al., 1993). Epidemiological studies indicate that many individuals meeting BED criteria are normal-weight. BED among normal weight individuals may eventually lead to obesity; evidence from longitudinal studies (Fairburn, Cooper, Doll, Normal, and O'Connor, 2000; Hasler et al., 2004) and treatment studies (Raymond, de Zwaan, Mitchell, Ackard, and Thuras, 2002; Wilfley et al., 2002) support this hypothesis. One study noted that individuals who met BED criteria became obese many years following the onset of this disorder (Mussell et al., 1995). Prospective longitudinal studies are needed to further test this hypothesis as there is a dearth of research on normal-weight individuals with BED.

Medical Conditions Associated with BED

The research on psychological problems associated with BED is vast; however, there is a major gap in the literature regarding the association between medical complications and BED irrespective of weight. Obesity-related medical problems are well documented, but research on BED and medical complications is scant (Mitchell et al., 2008). A review of all existing studies of the effects of BED on physical health revealed only two investigations reporting the association between BED and medical complaints independent of obesity status (Bulik and Reichborn-Kjennerud, 2003; Reichborn-Kjennerud et al., 2004). Earlier menarche and sleep problems were significantly associated with BED among women after controlling for BMI (Bulik and Reichborn-Kjennerud, 2003). Among males with BED, most observed health concerns were not solely a function of obesity, and BED status was significantly associated with alcohol concerns, use of pain medication, daily smoking and decreased exercise after controlling for BMI (Reichborn-Kjennerud et al., 2004). Future research should further investigate the extent to which BED is associated with medical conditions, after controlling for BMI.

Substance Use Disorders

The co-occurrence of disordered eating and substance use disorders is high (Polivy and Herman, 2002). Notably, unlike illicit drugs and nicotine, alcohol contains calories, which may contribute to higher body weight and influence eating behavior. The estimated comorbidity of alcohol abuse and disordered eating in a community sample falls between 30% to 50% (Dansky, Brewerton, and Kilpatrick, 2000), while 71% of women seeking treatment for problematic alcohol use report compulsive overeating (Stewart et al., 2006). Fifty-eight to sixty-eight percent of individuals who use tobacco endorse disordered eating (Anzengruber et al., 2006).

There is an association between BED and substance use disorders, but the relationship is much stronger among those with BN, especially for alcohol use disorders (Fitzgibbon, Sanchez-Johnsen, and Martinovich, 2003). Those with purging BN are much more likely to report drug and alcohol abuse history than are those with BED (Spitzer et al., 1993). According to Mitchell et al. (2008), dieting first (before BE onset) is a pattern more strongly associated with substance use disorders, whereas bingeing first is more related to depression. Those with BED are more likely to binge first, whereas many individuals with BN are more likely to diet first, which may help account for some of the differences in substance use disorders between BED and BN samples.

Cigarette smoking is also related to BE (Crisp et al., 1999; Saules et al., 2009). It has been postulated that smoking and BE may be used to alleviate negative affect (White and Grilo, 2007), especially among treatment seeking obese women (White and Grilo, 2006). Nicotine suppresses appetite and body weight. As such, weight concerns are commonly associated with the onset of smoking (Tomeo, Field, Berkey, Colditz, and Frazier, 1999) and often pose a barrier to smoking cessation, particularly among women (Saules, Pomerleau and Tate, 2008). This subset of smokers has been referred to as "weight control smokers" (Pomerleau and Kurth, 1996). Unfortunately, weight gain is a very reliable consequence of smoking cessation (Perkins, 1993; Saules et al., 2008). Given the strong association between BED and obesity referenced earlier, and the fact that weight gain following smoking cessation is typically due to increased caloric intake (e.g., Hatsukami, LaBounty, Hughes, and Laine, 1993; Kos et al., 1997) and shifts in food preferences, it is not surprising that following smoking cessation, individuals with BED regain more weight than individuals who are overweight but do not have BED (White et al., 2010). The strength of the relationship between cigarette smoking and BED status is influenced by ethnicity (Reslan and Saules, in press). Specifically, cigarette smoking increases risk for BED among only Arab-Americans and Pacific Islanders, but not among any other ethnic group.

BE, BED AND ADDICTION

Despite emphasis on the study and treatment of substance and non-substance related addictions by the Society of Addiction Psychology (APA Division 50) and the American Society for Addiction Medicine (ASAM), no gold standard definition for an "addiction" currently exists (Walters and Gilbert, 2000). The ASAM proposes that addiction is a chronic disease of brain reward, motivation, memory and related circuitry (ASAM, 2012). However, this definition lacks an appreciation of the associated social and psychological components of addiction, and it is not included in any formal diagnostic manual. Diagnostic criteria for substance dependence is sometimes used as the operational definition of an addiction (e.g., Ifland et al., 2009).

Given the lack of consensus on what is meant by "addiction," for the remainder of this chapter, *addiction* will be defined as the compulsive pursuit of a desired substance (e.g., food or drugs) with associated biological, social, and psychological components (APA, 2013). The most widely cited clinical features of addiction include impaired control over substance intake despite detrimental consequences, tolerance and withdrawal, as well as relapse and craving, broadly defined as a strong desire to use or consume a particular substance (World Health

Organization, 1992). Exposure to a stimulus, as well as persistently engaging in behaviors seeking to repeat this experience, are essential to the development of addiction (West, 2001), as continued exposure to a substance with addictive potential can cause neurobiological changes (e.g., activation and adaptation of reward circuitry; Shafer et al., 2004). Drugs have notoriously been thought to possess these addictive properties, but only recently have variants of disordered eating been identified as possessing similar addictive features.

In recent years, parallels between BED and drug-addictive behavior have been drawn, with emphasis on shared clinical features and neurobiological mechanisms (Davis and Carter, 2009; Volkow, Wang, Fowler, and Teland, 2008). Both BE and initial drug use involve activation of endogenous opioids and mesolimbic dopamine (DA; Mathes et al., 2009; Pecina and Smith, 2010; Pelchat, 2002; Volkow et al., 2008; Volkow and Wise, 2005). Activation of the mesolimbic DA system mediates the primary reinforcing characteristics of addictive substances (e.g., Dayas, Liu, Simms, and Weiss 2007; Di Chiara, 2002; Heinz et al., 2004; Volkow, Fowler, Wang, and Goldstein, 2002) and food (e.g., Avena, Hoebel, and Rada 2008; Calantuoni et al., 2001; Liang et al., 2006; Small, Jones-Gotman, and Dagher, 2003; Spangler et al., 2004).

Chronic use of addictive substances (Brown et al., 2012; Dettling et al., 1995; Martinez et al., 2007; Stice, Yokum, and Burger, in press; Volkow et al., 1996; Wang, Volkow, Fowler, and Logan, 1997) and chronic overeating (Alsio et al., 2010; Burger and Stice, 2012; Stice, Spoor, Bohon, and Small, 2008; Stice Spoor, Bohon, Veldhuizen, and Small, 2008; Stice, Yokum, Blum, and Bohon, 2010; Volkow et al., 2008; Wang et al., 2001) lead to the downregulation, or reduction, of mesolimbic DA. Thus, neurobiological support exists for consideration of BED as possibly sharing features with other addictive disorders.

Food Addiction

Although the concept of "food addiction," emerged in the diet industry, it is now popular among the general public. The empirical support for this construct is limited, but it is an increasingly popular topic for debate in the scientific community (Avena, Gearhardt, Gold, Wang, and Potenza, 2012; Benton, 2010; Davis et al., 2011; Ziauddeen, Farooqi, and Fletcher, 2012). To clarify, "food addiction" has been conceptualized in accordance with the seven DSM-IV-TR (APA, 2000) symptoms of psychoactive substance dependence (Gearhardt, Corbin, and Brownell, 2009).

Recently, meeting "diagnostic" criteria for "food addiction" has been linked to BED (Davis et al., 2011), but it is argued that BED and food addiction represent related yet independent conditions (Gearhardt, White, and Potenza, 2011).

The majority of the empirical support for the notion of "food addiction" has come from animal literature (Avena, 2010). After a month of unrestricted sugar access, rats show a series of behaviors similar to the behaviors of rats addicted to drugs (e.g., Avena, Bocarsly, Rada, Kim, and Hoebel, 2008).

Specifically, sugar addicted rats exhibit increased daily sugar consumption and increased speed of consumption, and physiological signs of withdrawal (e.g., teeth chattering, forepaw tremors, and headshakes) are observed when the rats access to food is restricted for 24 hours (Avena, Long, and Hoebel, 2005; Avena et al., 2008). Thus, unrestricted sugar access can result in sugar binges when it becomes freely available. Both food and drugs of abuse, however, share common reward substrates (Avena et al., 2008; Davis et al., 2012; Pelchat, 2009), and drugs of abuse may compete with food for brain reward sites, and at times, alcohol and other drug use may function as a substitute for excessive eating. For example, rats maintained on intermittent sugar access show an increase in alcohol (Avena, Carrillo, Needham, Leibowitz, and Hoebel, 2004) and cocaine (Carroll, Anderson, and Morgan, 2007) consumption when deprived of sugar.

The extent to which these parallels between eating and addictive behaviors support the case for "food addiction" remains an empirical question, and one that no doubt will spur lively debate and scientific inquiry in the coming years.

CONCLUSION

Our current understanding of BED has evolved over the last two decades, and it will likely continue to evolve with the addition of BED as a formal diagnosis in the DSM-5 (APA, 2013). Better understanding of issues related to diversity, body image, and impulsivity, as well as comorbid conditions including obesity, mood disorders, anxiety, medical consequences, and substance use disorders will be critical to enhance our ability to prevent and treat BED. Taken together, the information reviewed supports that BED warrants its own diagnostic category, given the important differences between BED and the related yet distinct conditions of BN and obesity. Although now considered a formal diagnostic condition in the DSM-5, validation of the modified criteria warrant additional research. More diverse samples including normal weight individuals and older adults should also be studied to fully understand BED. The concept of a food addiction has popular appeal and some scientific support, but the association between addiction, BE, and BED warrants further study. Empirical findings support the parallels in the clinical features of BED and addiction, and given recent advancements in the study of food addiction, it is anticipated that this topic will continue to gain attention.

REFERENCES

Ackard, D. M., Fulkerson, J. A., and Neumark-Sztainer, D. (2007). Prevalence and utility of DSM-IV eating disorder diagnostic criteria among youth. *International Journal of Eating Disorders, 40*, 409-417.

Ahrberg, M., Trojca, D., Nasrawi, N., and Vocks, S. (2011). Body image disturbance in binge eating disorder: A review. *European Eating Disorders Review*, Advanced online publication, doi:10.1002/erv.1100

Alsio, J., Olszweski, P. K., Norback, A. H., Gunnarsson, Z. E. A., Levine, A. S., Pickering, C., and Schioth, H. B. (2010). Dopamine D1 receptor gene expression decreases in the nucleus accumbens upon long-term exposure to palatable food and differ depending on diet-induced obesity phenotype in rats. *Neuroscience, 171*, 779-787.

American Psychiatric Association [APA]. (2000). Diagnostic and statistical manual of mental disorders (Revised 4th ed.). Washington, DC: Author.

American Psychiatric Association [APA]. (2013). Diagnostic and statistical manual of mental disorders (5th ed.). Washington, DC: Author.
American Psychiatric Association [APA]. (2012). *DSM-5 development.* Retrieved November 20, 2012, from http://www.dsm5.org/ Pages/Default.aspx
American Society of Addiction Medicine [ASAM]. (2011). Definition of addiction (short version), Retrieved December 25, 2012, from http://www.asam.org/
Antony, M. M., Johnson, W. G., Carr-Nangle, R. E., and Abel, J. L. (1994). Psychopathology correlates of binge eating and binge eating disorder. *Comprehensive Psychiatry, 35*, 386-392.
Anzengruber, D., Klump, K. L., Thornton, L., Brandt, H., Crawford, S., Fichter, M. M., ... Bulik, C. M. (2006). Smoking in eating disorders. *Eating Behaviors, 7*, 291-299.
Araujo, D. M. R., Santos, G. F. D. S., and Nardi, A. E. (2010). Binge eating disorder and depression: A systematic review. *The World Journal of Biological Psychiatry, 10*, 1-9.
Avena, N. M. (2010). The study of food addiction using animal models of binge eating. *Appetite, 55*, 734-737.
Avena, N. M., Bocarsly, M. E., Rada, P., Kim, A., and Hoebel, B. G. (2008). After daily bingeing on sucrose solution, food deprivation induces anxiety and accumbens dopamine/acetylcholine imbalance. *Physiology and Behavior, 94*, 309-315.
Avena, N. M., Carrillo, C. A., Needham, L., Leibowitz, S. f., and Hoebel, B. G. (2004). Sugar-dependent rats show enhanced intake of unsweetened ethanol. *Alcohol, 34*, 203-209.
Avena, N. M., Gearhardt, A. N., Gold, M. S., Wang, G. J., and Potenza, M. N. (2012). Tossing the baby out with the bathwater after a brief rinse? The potential downside of dismissing food addiction based on limited data. *Nature Reviews Neuroscience, 13*, 514.
Avena, N. M., Long, K. A., and Hoebel, B. G. (2005). Sugar-dependent rats show enhanced responding for sugar after abstinence: Evidence of a sugar deprivation effect. *Physiology and Behavior, 84*, 359-362.
Avena, N. M., Rada, P., and Hoebel, B. G. (2008). Evidence for sugar addiction: Behavioral and neurochemical effects of intermittent, excessive sugar intake. *Neuroscience and Biobehavioral Review, 32*, 20-39.
Barry, D. T., Grilo, C. M., and Masheb, R. M. (2003). Comparison of patients with bulimia nervosa, obese patients with binge eating disorder, and nonobese patients with binge eating disorder. *The Journal of Nervous and Mental Disease, 191*, 589-594.
Barry, D. T., Grilo, C. M., and Masheb, R. M. (2002). Gender differences in patients with binge eating disorder. *International Journal of Eating Disorders, 31*, 63-70.
Becker, A. E., Franko, D. L., Speck, A., and Herzog, D. B. (2003). Ethnicity and differential access to care for eating disorder symptoms. *International Journal of Eating Disorders, 33*, 205-212.
Benton, D. (2010). The plausibility of sugar addiction and its role in obesity and eating disorders. *Clinical Nutrition, 29*, 288-303.
Bijl, R. V., and Ravelli, A. (2000). Psychiatric morbidity, service use, and need for care in the general population: Results of The Netherlands mental Health Survey and Incidence Study. *American Journal of Public Health, 90*, 602-607.
Birgegard, A., Norring, C., and Clinton, D. (2012). DSM-IV versus DSM-5: Implementation of proposed DSM-5 criteria in a large naturalistic database. *International Journal of Eating Disorders, 45*, 353-361.

Blum, K., Braverman, E. R., Holder, J. M., Lubar, J. F., Monastra, V. J., Miller, D., ... Comings, D. E. (2000). Reward deficiency syndrome: A biogenic model for the diagnosis and treatment of impulsive, addictive, and compulsive behaviors. *Journal of Psychoactive Drugs, 32*, 1-112.

Brody, M. L., Walsh, B. T., and Devlin, M. J. (1994). Binge eating disorder: Reliability and validity of a new diagnostic category. *Journal of Consulting and Clinical Psychology, 62*, 381-386.

Brown, T. A., and Barlow, D. H. (2005). Categorical vs dimensional classification of mental disorders in DSM-V and beyond. *Journal of Abnormal Psychology, 114*, 551-556. Brown, A. K., Mandelkern, M. A., Farahi, J., Robertson, C., Ghahremani, D. G., Sumerel, B., London E. D. (2012). Sex differences in striatal dopamine D2/D3 receptor availability in smokers and non-smokers. *International Journal of Neuropsychopharmacology, 15*, 989-994.

Brownstone, L. M., Bardone-Cone, A. M., Fitzsimmons-Craft, E. E., Printz, K. S., Le Grange, D., Mitchell, J. E., Joiner, T. E. (2013). *International Journal of Eating Disorders, 46*, 66-76.

Bruce, B., and Agras, W. S. (1992). Binge eating in females: A population-based investigation. *International Journal of Eating Disorders, 12*, 365-373.

Bulik, C. M., and Reichborn-Kjennerud, T. (2003). Medical morbidity in binge eating disorder. *International Journal of Eating Disorders, 34*, S39-S46.

Bulik, C. M., Sullivan, P. F., and Kendler, K. S. (2003). Genetic and environmental contributions to obesity and binge eating. *International Journal of Eating Disorders, 33*, 293-298.

Burger, K. S., and Stice, E. (2012). Frequent ice cream consumption is associated with reduced striatal response to receipt of an ice cream-based milkshake. *The American Journal of Clinical Nutrition*, Advanced online publication, doi:10.3945ajcn.111.027003

Carroll, M. E., Anderson, M. M., and Morgan, A. D. (2007). Regulation of intravenous cocaine self-administration in rats selectively bred for high (HiS) and low (LoS) saccharin intake. *Psychopharmacology (Berl), 190*, 331-341.

Castonguay, L. G., Eldredge, K. L., and Agras, W. S. (1995). Binge eating disorder: Current state and future directions. *Clinical Psychology Review, 15*, 865-890.

Celone, K. A., Thompson-Brenner, H., Ross, R. S., Pratt, E. M., and Stern, C. E. (2011). An fMRI investigation of the fronto-striatal learning system in women who exhibit eating disorder behaviors. *Neuroimage, 56*, 1749-1757.

Claes, L., Vandereycken, W., and Vertommen, H. (2005). Impulsivity-related traits in eating disorder patients. *Personality and Individual Differences, 39*, 739-749.

Clark, M. M., Forsyth, L. H., Lloyd-Richardson, E. E., and King, T. K. (2000). Eating self-efficacy and binge eating disorder in obese women. *Journal of Applied Biobehavioral Research, 5*, 154-161.

Clyne, C., Latner, J. D., Gleaves, D. H., and Blampied, N. M. (2010). Treatment of emotional dysregulation in full syndrome and subthreshold binge eating disorder. *Eating Disorders: The Journal of Treatment and Prevention, 18*, 408-424.

Colantuoni, C., Rada, P., McCarthy, J., Patten, C., Avena, N. M., Chadeayne, A., and Hoebel, B. G. (2002). Evidence that intermittent, excessive sugar intake causes endogenous opioid dependence. *Obesity Research, 10*, 478-488.

Colantuoni, C., Schwenker, J., McCarthy, J., Rada, P., Ladenheim, B., Cadet, J. L., Hoebel, B. G. (2001). Excessive sugar intake alters binding to dopamine and mu-opioid receptors in the brain. *Neuroreport, 12*, 3549-3552.

Colles, S. L., Dixon, J. B., and O'Brien, P. E. (2008). Grazing and loss of control related to eating: Two high-risk factors following bariatric surgery. *Obesity, 16*, 615-622. Comings, D. E., and Blum, K. (2000). Reward deficiency syndrome: Genetic aspects of behavioral disorders. *Progress in Brain Research, 126*, 325-341.

Cooke, E. A., Guss, J. L., Kissileff, H. R., Devlin, M. J., and Walsh, T. (1997). Patterns of food selection during binges in women with binge eating disorder. *International Journal of Eating Disorders, 22*, 187-193.

Cortese, S., Bernardina, B. D., and Mouren, M. C. (2007). *Nutrition Reviews, 65*, 404-411.

Crisp, A., Sedgwick, P., Halek, C., Joughin, N., and Humphrey, H. (1999). Why may teenage girls persist in smoking? *Journal of Adolescence, 22*, 657-672.

Crow, S. J., Agras, W. S., Halmi, K., Mitchell, J. E., and Kraemer, H. C. (2002). Full syndromal versus subthreshold anorexia nervosa, bulimia nervosa, and binge eating disorder. A multicenter study. *International Journal of Eating Disorders, 32*, 309-318.

Dansky, B. S., Brewerton, T. D., and Kilpatrick, D. G. (2000). Comorbidity of bulimia nervosa and alcohol use disorders: Results from the National Women's Study. *International Journal of Eating Disorders, 27*, 180-190.

Davis, C., and Carter, J. C. (2009). Compulsive overeating as an addiction disorder. A review of theory and evidence. *Appetite, 53*, 1-8.

Davis, C., Curtis, C., Levitan, R. D., Carter, J. C., Kaplan, A. S., and Kennedy, J. L. (2011). Evidence that 'food addiction' is a valid phenotype of obesity. *Appetite, 57*, 711-717.

Davis, C., Levitan, R. D., Yilmaz, Z., Kaplan, A. S., Carter, J. C., and Kennedy, J. L. (2012).Binge eating disorder and the dopamine D2 receptor: Genotypes and sub-phenotypes. *Progress in Neuro-Psychopharmacology and Biological Psychiatry, 38*, 328-335.

Davis, C., Patte, K., Levitan, R. D., Carter, J., Kaplan, A. S., Zai, C., Reid, C., Kennedy, J. L. (2009). A psycho-genetic study of associations between the symptoms of binge eating disorder and those of attention deficit (hyperactivity) disorder. *Journal of Psychiatric Research, 43*, 687-696.

Dawe, S., and Loxton, N. J. (2004). The role of impulsivity in the development of substance use and eating disorders. *Neuroscience and Biobehavioral Reviews. Special Issue: Festschrift in Honour of Jeffrey Gray- Issue 1: Anxiety and Neuroticism, 28*, 343-351.

Dayas, C. V., Liu, X., Simms, J. A., and Weiss, F. (2007). Distinct patterns of neural activation associated with ethanol seeking: Effects of naltrexone. *Biological Psychiatry, 61*, 979-989.

Dettling, M., Heinz, A., Dufeu, P., Rommelspacher, H., Gräf, K. J., and Schmidt, L. G. (1995).

Dopamingergic responsivity in alcoholism: Trait, state, or residual marker? *American Journal of Psychiatry, 152*, 1317-1321.

Devlin, M. J. (2007). Is there a place for obesity in DSM-V? *International Journal of Eating Disorders, 40*, S83-S88.

Devlin, M. J., Goldfein, J. A., and Dobrow, I. (2003). What is this thing called BED? Current status of binge eating disorder nosology. *International Journal of Eating Disorders, 34* S2-S18.

Devlin, M. J., Walsh, B. T., Spitzer, R. L., and Hasin, D. (1992). Is there another binge eating disorder? A review of the literature on overeating in the absence of bulimia nervosa. *International Journal of Eating Disorders, 11*, 333-340.

Di Chiara, G. (2002). Nucleus accumbens shell and core dopamine: Differential role in behavior and addiction. *Behavior and Brain Research, 137*, 75-114.

de Zwaan, M. (2001). Binge eating disorder and obesity. *International Journal of Obesity and Related Metabolic Disorders, 25*, S51-S55.

de Zwaan, M., Mitchell, J. E., Seim, H. C., Specker, S. M., Pyle, R. L., Raymound, N. C., and Crosby, R. B. (1994). Eating related and general psychopathology in obese females with binge eating disorder. *International Journal of Eating Disorders, 15,* 43-52.

Didie, E. R., and Fitzgibbon, M. (2005). Binge eating and psychological distress: Is the degree of obesity a factor? *Eating Behaviors, 6*, 35-41.

Dingemans, A. E., van Hanswijck, P., and van Furth, E. F. (2005). The empirical status of binge eating disorder. In Norring and Palmer. *EDNOS Eating Disorders Not Otherwise Specified: Scientific and clinical perspectives on the other eating disorders* (63-82). New York: Routledge Taylor and Francis Group.

Dodds, C. M., O'Neill, B., Beaver, J., Makwana, A., Bani, M., Merlo-Pich, E., ... Nathan, P. J. (2012). Effect of the dopamine D_3 receptor antagonist GSK598809 on brain responses to rewarding food images in overweight and obese binge eaters. *Appetite, 59*, 27-33.

Eisenberg, D., Golberstein, E., and Gollust, S. E. (2007). Help-seeking and access to mental health care in a university student population. *Medical Care, 45*, 584-601.

Fairburn, C. G., and Cooper, Z. (2011). Eating disorders, DSM-5, and clinical reality. *The British Journal of Psychiatry, 198*, 8-10.

Fairburn, C. G., Cooper, Z., Doll, H. A., Normal, P., O'Connor, M. E. (2000). The natural course of bulimia nervosa and binge eating disorder in young women. *Archives of General Psychiatry, 57*, 659-665.

Fairburn, C. G., Doll, H. A., Welch, S. L., Hay, P. J., Davies, B. A., and O'Connor, M. E. (1998). Risk factors for binge eating disorder: A community-based, case-control study. *Archives of General Psychiatry, 55*, 425-432.

Fairburn, C. G., Welch, S. L., and Hay, P. J. (1993). The classification of recurrent overeating: The "Binge Eating Disorder" proposal. *International Journal of Eating Disorders, 13*, 155-159.

Feldman, M. B., and Meyer, I. H. (2007). Eating disorders in diverse lesbian, gay, and bisexual populations. *International Journal of Eating Disorders, 40*, 218-226.

Fischer, S., Smith, G. T., and Anderson, K. G. (2003). Clarifying the role of impulsivity in bulimia nervosa. *International Journal of Eating Disorders, 33*, 406-411.

Fitzgibbon, M. L., Sanchez-Johnsen, L. A. P., and Martinovich, Z. (2003). A test of the continuity perspective across bulimic and binge eating pathology. *International Journal of Eating Disorders, 34*, 83-97.

Flegal, K. M., Carroll, M D., Kit, B. K., and Odgen, C. L. (2012). Prevalence and trends in the distribution of body mass index among US adults, 1999-2010. *JAMA, 307*, 491-497.

Flegal, K. M., Carroll, M. D., Ogden, C. L., and Curtin, L. R. (2010). Prevalence and trends in obesity among US adults, 1999-2008. *JAMA, 303*, 235-241.

Flegal, K. M., Graubard, B. I., Williamson, D. F., and Gail, M. H. (2005). Excess deaths associated with underweight, overweight, and obesity. *JAMA, 293*, 1861-1867.

Franko, D. L., Thompson-Brenner, H., Thompson, D. R., Boisseau, C. L., Davis, A., Forbush, K. T., Wilson, G. T. (2012). Racial/ethnic differences in adults in randomized clinical trials of binge eating disorder. *Journal of Consulting and Clinical Psychology, 80*, 186-195.

French, S. A., Story, M., Remafedi, G., Resnick, M. D., and Blum, R. W. (1996). Sexual orientation and prevalence of body dissatisfaction and eating disordered behaviors: A population-based study of adolescents. *International Journal of Eating Disorders, 19*, 119-126.

Gearhardt, A. N., Corbin, W. R., and Brownell, K. D. (2009). Preliminary validation of the Yale Food Addiction Scale. *Appetite, 52*, 430-439.

Gearhardt, A.N., White, M.A., and Potenza, M.N. (2011). Binge eating disorder and food addiction. *Current Drug Abuse Reviews*, 4, 201-207.

Goldfein, J. A., Walsh, B. T., LaChaussee, J. L., Kissileff, H. R., and Devlin, M. J. (1993). Eating behavior in binge eating disorder. *International Journal of Eating Disorders, 14*, 427-431.

Goldschmidt, A. B., Hildert, A., Manwaring, J. L., Wilfley, D. E., Pike, K. M., Fairburn, C. G., and Striegel-Moore, R. H. (2010). The significance of overevaluation of shape and weight in binge eating disorder. *Behavior Research and Therapy, 48*, 187-193.

Gray, J. A. (1991). Neural systems of motivation, emotion and affect. In J. Madden (Ed.), *Neurobiology of Learning, Emotion and Affect* (pgs. 273-306). New York: Raven Press.

Grilo, C. M. (2002). Binge eating disorder. In CG Fairburn, KD Brownell (Eds), Eating disorder and obesity (2nd ed. pgs. 178-182). New York: Guilford Press.

Grilo, C. M. (2004). Diagnostic efficiency of DSM-IV criteria for obsessive compulsive personality disorder in patients with binge eating disorder. *Behaviour Research and Therapy, 42*, 57-65.

Grilo, C. M., Crosby, R. D., Masheb, R. M., White, M. A., Peterson, C. B., Wonderlich, S. A., ... Mitchell, J. E. (2009). Overvaluation of shape and weight in binge eating disorder, bulimia nervosa, and sub-threshold bulimia nervosa. *Behavior and Research Therapy, 47*, 692-696.

Grilo, C. M., Lozano, C., and Masheb, R. M. (2005). Ethnicity and sampling bias in binge eating disorder: Black women who seek treatment have different characteristics than those who do not. *International Journal of Eating Disorders, 38*, 257-262.

Grilo, C. M. and Masheb, R. M. (2002). Childhood maltreatment and personality disorders in adult patients with binge eating disorder. *Pscyhiatric Scandinavia, 106*, 183-188.

Grilo, C. M., Masheb, R. M., Brody, M., Burke-Martindale, C. H., and Rothschild, B. S. (2005). Binge eating and self-esteem predict body image dissatisfaction among obese men and women seeking bariatric surgery. *International Journal of Eating Disorders, 37*, 347-351.

Grilo, C.M., Masheb, R.M., and White, M.A (2010). Significance of overevaluation of shape/weight in binge eating disorder: comparative study with overweight and bulimia nervosa. *Obesity, 18*, 499-504.

Grilo, C. M., and White, M. A. (2011). A controlled evaluation of the distress criterion for binge eating disorder. *Journal of Consulting and Clinical Psychology, 79*, 509-514.

Grilo, C. M., White, M. A., Barnes, R. D., and Masheb, R. M. (2012). Psychiatric disorder co-morbidity and correlates in an ethnically diverse sample of obese patients with binge eating disorder in primary care settings. *Comprehensive Psychiatry*, Advanced online publication, PMID: 22943959.

Grilo, C. M., White, M. A., Gueroguieva, R., Wilson, G. T., and Masheb, R. M. (2012). Predictive significance of the overvaluation of shape/weight in obese patients with binge eating disorder: Findings from a randomized controlled trial with 12-month follow-up. *Psychological Medicine*, Advanced online publication, doi:10.1017/S0033291712002097

Grilo, C. M., White, M. A., and Masheb, R. M. (2009). DSM-IV psychiatric disorder comorbidity and its correlates in binge eating disorder. *International Journal of Eating Disorders, 42*, 228-234.

Grissett, N. L., and Fitzgibbon, M. L. (1996). The clinical significance of binge eating in an obese population: Support for BED and questions regarding its critical. *Addictive Behaviors, 21*, 57-66.

Grucza, R. A., Przybeck, T. R., Cloninger, C. R. (2007). Prevalence and correlates of binge eating disorder in a community sample. *Comprehensive Psychiatry, 48*, 124-131.

Guerdjikova, A. I., McElroy, S. L., Kotwal, R., and Keck, P. E. (2007). Comparison of obese men and women with binge eating disorder seeking weight management. *Eating and Weight Disorders, 12*, e19-e23.

Guss, J. L., Kissileff, H. R., Walsh, B. T., and Devlin, M. J. (1994). Binge eating behavior in patients with eating disorders. *Obesity Research, 2*, 355-363.

Hatsukami, D., LaBounty, L., Hughes, J., and Laine, D. (1993). Effects of tobacco abstinence on food intake among cigarette smokers. *Health Psychology, 12*, 499-502.

Hasler, G., Pine, D. S., Gamma, A., Milos, G., Adjacic, V., Eich, D., ... Angst, J. (2004). The association between psychopathology and being overweight: A 20-year prospective study. *Psychological Medicine, 34*, 1047-1057.

Hay, P., and Fairburn, C. (1998). The validity of the DSM-IV scheme for classifying bulimic eating disorders. *International Journal of Eating Disorders, 23*, 7-15.

Hedley, A. A., Ogden, C. L., and Johnson, C. L. (2004). Prevalence of overweight and obesity among US children, adolescents, and adults, 1999-2002. *JAMA, 291*, 2847-2850.

Heffernan, K. (1996). Eating disorders and weight concerns among lesbians. *International Journal of Eating Disorders, 19*, 127-138.

Heinz, A., Siessmeiser, T., Wrase, J., Hermann, D., Klein, S., Grusser, S. M., ...Bartenstein, P. (2004). Correlation between dopamine D92) receptors in the ventral striatum and central processing of alcohol cues and craving. *The American Journal of Psychiatry, 161*, 1783-1789.

Hepworth, N., and Paxton, S. J. (2007). Pathways to help-seeking in bulimia nervosa and binge eating problems: A concept mapping approach. *International Journal of Eating Disorders, 40*, 493-504.

Hoek, H. W., and van Hoeken, D. (2003). Review of the prevalence and incidence of eating disorders. *International Journal of Eating Disorders, 34*, 383-396.

Hoffman, D. J., Policastro, P., Quick, V., and Lee, S. (2006). Changes in body weight and fat mass of men and women in the first year of college: A study of the "freshman 15". *Journal of American College Health, 55*, 41-45.

Hrabosky, J. I., and Grilo, C. M. (2007). Body image and eating disordered behavior in a community sample of Black and Hispanic women. *Eating Behaviors, 8*, 106-114.

Hudson, J. I., Coit, C. E., Lalonde, J. K., and Pope H. G. Jr. (2012). By how much will the proposed new DSm-5 criteria increase the prevalence of binge eating disorder? *International Journal of Eating Disorders, 45*, 139-141.

Hudson, J. I., Hiripi, E., Pope, H. G. Jr., and Kessler, R. C. (2007). The prevalence and correlates of eating disorders in the National Comorbidity Survey Replication. *Biological Psychiatry, 61*, 348-358.

Hudson, J. I., Lalonde, J. K., Berry, J. M., Pindyck, L. J., Bulik, C. M., Crow, S. J., … Pope, H. G. Jr. (2006). Binge-eating disorder as a distinct familial phenotype in obese individuals. *Archives of General Psychiatry, 6*, 313-319.

Ifland, J. R., Preuss, H. G., Marcus, M. T., Rourke, K. M., Taylor, W. C., Burau, K., Manso, (2009). Refined food addiction: A classic substance use disorder. *Medical hypotheses, 72*, 518-526.

Johnson, W. G., Boutelle, K. N., Torgrud, L., Daviq, J. P., and Turner, S. (2000). What is a binge? The influence of amount, duration, and loss of control criteria on judgments of binge eating. *International Journal of Eating Disorders, 27*, 471-479.

Johnson, W. G., Carr-Nangle, R. E., Nangle, D. W., Antony, M. M., and Zayfert, C. (1997). What is binge eating? A comparison of binge eating, peer, and professional judgments of eating episodes. *Addictive Behaviors, 22*, 631-635.

Johnson, F., and Wardle, J. (2005). Dietary restraint, body dissatisfaction, and psychological distress: A prospective analysis. *Journal of Abnormal Psychology, 114*, 119-125.

Karhunen, L. J., Vanninen, E. J., Kuikka, J. T., Lappalainen, R. I., Tiihonen, J., and Uusitupa, M. I. J. (2000). Regional cerebral blood flow during exposure to food in obese binge eating women. *Psychiatry Research: Neuroimaging Section, 99*, 29-42.

Killen, J. D., Taylor, B., Hayward, C., Hydel, F. K., Wilson, D. M., Hammer, L., Strachowski, D. (1996). Weight concerns influence the development of eating disorders: A 4-year prospective study. *Journal of Consulting and Clinical Psychology, 64*, 936-940.

Kolotkin, R. L., Westman, E. C., Ostbye, T., Crosby, R. D., Eisenson, H. J., and Binks, M. (2004). Does binge eating disorder impact weight-related quality of life? *Obesity Research, 12*, 999-1005.

Kopelman, P. G. (2000). The nature of obesity as a medical problem. *Nature, 404*, 635-643.

Kos, J., Hasenfratz, M., and Bättig, K. (1997). Effects of a two day abstinence from smoking on dietary, cognitive, subjective, and physiologic parameters among younger and older female smokers. *Physiology and Behaviour, 61*, 671-678.

Krüger, S., Shugar, G., and Cooke, R. G. (1996). Comorbidity of binge eating disorder and the partial binge eating syndrome with bipolar disorder. *International Journal of Eating Disorders, 19*, 45-52.

LaPorte, D. J. (1997). Gender differences in perceptions and consequences of an eating binge. *Gender Roles, 36*, 479-489.

Lewinsohn, P. M., Seeley, J. R., Moerk, K. C., and Striegel-Moore, R. H. (2002). Gender differences in eating disorders symptoms in young adults. *International Journal of Eating Disorders, 32*, 426-440.

Liang, N. C., Hajnal, A., and Norgren, R. (2006). Sham feeding corn oil increases accumbens dopamine in the rat. *American Journal of Physiology – Regulatory, Integrative, and Comparative Physiology, 291*, R1236-1239.

Linde, J. A., Jeffery, R. W., Levy, R. L., Sherwood, N. E., Utter, J., Pronk, N. P., and Boyle, R. G. (2004). Binge eating disorder, weight control self-efficacy, and depression in overweight men and women. *International Journal of Obesity, 28*, 418-425.

Lock, J., Garrett, A., Beenhakker, J., Reiss, A. (2011). Aberrant brain activation during a response inhibition task in adolescent eating disorder subtypes. *The American Jouranl of Psychiatry, 168*, 55-64.

Marcus, M. D., Smith, D., Santelli, R., and Kaye, W. (1992). Characterization of eating disordered behavior in obese binge eaters. *International Journal of Eating Disorders, 12*, 249-255.

Marcus, M. D., Wing, R. R., Ewing, L., Kern, E., Gooding, W., and McDermott, M. (1990). Psychiatric disorders among obese binge eaters. *International Journal of Eating Disorders, 9*, 69-77.

Martinez, D., Narendran, R., Foltin, R., Slifstein, M., Hwang, D., Broft, A., ... Laruelle, M. (2007). Amphetamine-induced dopamine release: Markedly blunted in cocaine dependence and predictive of the choice to self-administer cocaine. *The American Journal of Psychiatry, 164*, 622-629.

Masheb, R. M., and Grilo, C. M. (2000). Binge eating disorder: A need for additional diagnostic criteria. *Comprehensive Psychiatry, 41*, 159-162.

Masheb, R. M. and Grilo, C. M. (2006). Emotional overeating and its associations with eating disorder psychopathology among overweight patients with binge eating disorder. *International Journal of Eating Disorders, 39*, 141-146.

Masheb, R. M., and Grilo, C. M. (2003). The nature of body image disturbance in patients with binge eating disorder. *International Journal of Eating Disorders, 33*, 333-341.

Mathes, W. F., Brownley, K. A., Mo, X., and Bulik, C. M. (2009). The biology of binge eating. *Appetite, 52*, 545-553.

Mattos, P., Saboya, E., Ayrao, V., Segenreich, D., Duchesne, M., and Coutinho, G. (2004). Comorbid eating disorders in a Brazalian attention-deficit/hyperactivity disorder adult clinical sample. *Revista brasileira de psiquiatria, 26*, 248-250.

McElroy, S. L., Kotwal, R., and Keck, P. E., Jr. (2006). Comorbidity of eating disorders with bipolar disorder and treatment implications. *Bipolar Disorders, 8*, 686-695.

Mitchell, J. E., Crow, S., Peterson, C. B., Wonderlich, S., and Crosby, R. D. (1998). Feeding laboratory studies in patients with eating disorders: A review. *International Journal of Eating Disorders*, 24, 115-124.

Mitchell, J. E., Devlin, M. J., de Zwaan, M., Crow, S. J., and Peterson, C. B. (2008). Binge-eating disorder: Clinical foundations and treatment. New York: Guildford Press.

Mitchell, J. E., Mussell, M. P., Peterson, C. B., Crow, S., Wonderlich, S. A., Crosby, R. D., ... Weller, C. (1999). Hedonics of binge eating in women with bulimia nervosa and binge eating disorder. *International Journal of Eating Disorders, 26*, 165-170.

Mokdad, A. H., Marks, J. S., Stroup, D. F., Gerberding, J. L. (2000). Actual causes of death in the United States, 2000. *Journal of the American Medical Association, 291*, 1238-1245.

Mokdad, A. H., Serdula, M. K., Dietz, W. H., Bowman, B. A., Marks, J. S., and Koplan, J. P.(1999). The spread of the obesity epidemic in the United States, 1991-1998. *Journal of the American Medical Association, 282*, 1519-1522.

Mussell, M. P., Mitchell, J. E., Weller, C. L., Raymond, N. C., Crow, S. J., and Crosby, R. D. (1995). Onset of binge eating, dieting, obesity, and mood disorders among subjects seeking treatment for binge eating disorder. *International Journal of Eating Disorders, 17*, 395-401.

Mussell, M. P., Peterson, C. B., Weller, C. L., Crosby, R. D., de Zwaan, M., and Mitchell, J. E. (1996). Differences in body image and depression among obese women with and without binge eating disorder. *Obesity Research, 4*, 431-439.

Niego, S. H., Pratt, E. M., and Agras, W. S. (1997). Subjective or objective binge: Is the distinction valid? *International Journal of Eating Disorders, 22*, 291-298.

Ogden, C. L., Carroll, M. D., Curtin, L. R., McDowell, M. A., Tabak, C. J., and Flegal, K. M. (2006). Prevalence of overweight and obesity in the United States, 1999-2004. *Journal of the American Medical Association, 295*, 1549-1555.

Pagoto, S. L., Curtin, C., Lemon, S. C., Bandini, L. G., Schneider, K. L., Bodenlos, J. S., and Ma, Y. (2009). Association between adult attention deficit/hyperactivity disorder and obesity in the US population. *Obesity, 17*, 539-544.

Palavras, M. A., Kaio, G. H., Mari, Jde J., and Claudino, A. M. (2011). A review of Latin American studies on binge eating disorder. *Revista brasileira de psiquiatria, 33*, S81-S108.

Pecina, S., and Smith, K. S. (2010). Hedonic and motivational roles of opioids in food reward: Implications for overeating disorders. *Pharmacology Biochemistry and Behavior, 97*, 34-46.

Pelchat, M. L. (2009). Food addiction in humans. *The Journal of Nutrition, 139*, 620-622.

Pelchat, M. L. (2002). Of human bondage: Food craving, obsession, compulsion, and addiction. *Physiology and Behavior, 76*, 347-352.

Perkins, K. A. (1993). Weight gain following smoking cessation. *Journal of Consulting and Clinical Psychology, 61*, 768-777.

Pesa, J. A., Syre, T. R., and Jones, E. (2000). Psychosocial differences associated with body weight among female adolescents: The importance of body image. *Journal of Adolescent Health, 26*, 330-337.

Peterson, R. E., Latendresse, S. J., Bartholome, L. T., Warren, C. S., and Raymond, N. C. (2012). Binge eating disorder mediates links between symptoms of depression, anxiety, and caloric intake in overweight and obese women. *Journal of Obesity*, Advanced online publication, doi:10.1155/2012/407103

Peterson, C. B., Mitchell, J. E., Engbloom, S., Nugent, S., Mussell, M. P., Crow, S. J., and Miller, J. P. (1998). Binge eating disorder with and without a history of purging symptoms. *International Journal of Eating Disorders, 24*, 251-257.

Pike, K. M., Dohm, F. A., Striegel-Moore, R. H., Wilfley, D. E., and Fairburn, C. G. (2001). A comparison of black and white women with binge eating disorder. *American Journal of Psychiatry, 158*, 1455-1460.

Pike, K. M., and Walsh, B. T. (1996). Ethnicity and eating disorders: implications for incidence and treatment. *Psychopharmacological Bulletin, 32*, 265–273.

Polivy, J., and Herman, C. P. (2002). Causes of eating disorders. *Annual Review of Psychology, 53*, 187-213.

Pomerleau, C. S., and Kurth, C. L. (1996). Willingness of female smokers to tolerate postcessation weight gain. *Journal of Substance Abuse, 8*, 371-378.

Popkin, B. M., and Doak, C. M. (1998). The obesity epidemic is a worldwide phenomenon. *Nutrition Reviews, 56*, 106-114.

Raymond, N. C., de Zwaan, M., Mitchell, J. E., Ackard, D. and Thuras, P. (2002). Effect of a very low calorie diet on the diagnostic category of individuals with binge eating disorder. *International Journal of Eating Disorders, 31*, 49-56.

Reagan, P. and Hersch, J. (2005). Influence of race, gender, and socioeconomic status on binge eating frequency in a population-based sample. *International Journal of Eating Disorders, 38*, 252-256.

Reas, D. L., White, M. A., and Grilo, C. M. (2006). Body checking questionnaire: Psychometric properties and clinical correlates in obese men and women with binge eating disorder. *International Journal of Eating Disorders, 39*, 326-331.

Reba-Harrelson, L., Von Holle, A., Hamer, R. M., Swann, R., Reyes, M. L., and Bulik, C. M. (2009). Patterns and prevalence of disordered eating and weight control behaviors in women ages 25-45. *Eating and Weight Disorders, 14*, e190-198.

Reichborn-Kjennerud, T., Bulik, C. M., Tambs, K., and Harris, J. R. (2004). Psychiatric and medical symptoms in binge eating in the absence of compensatory behaviors. *Obesity Research, 12*, 1445–1454.

Rieger, E., Wilfley, D. E., Stein, R. I., Marino, V., and Crow, S. J. (2005). A comparison of quality of life in obese individuals with and without binge eating disorder. *International Journal of Eating Disorders, 37*, 234-240.

Reslan, S. (2010). Relationships between binge eating, psychological and behavioral covariates, and health care utilization on college campuses: Results from a national sample of college students. (Master's Thesis). Retrieved from Eastern Michigan University Digital Commons database. Paper 282. http:// commons.emich.edu/theses/282.

Reslan, S., and Saules, K. K. (in press). Assessing the prevalence and predictors of overweight, obesity, and Binge Eating Disorder as a function of ethnicity. *Eating and Weight Disorders*.

Reslan, S., and Saules, K. K. (2011). College students' definitions of an eating "binge" differ as a function of gender and binge eating disorder status. *Eating Behaviors, 12*, 225-227.

Ricca, V., Mannucci, E., Mezzani, B., Di Bernardo, M., Zucchi, T., Paionni, A. … Faravelli, C. (2001). Psychopathological and clinical features of outpatients with an eating disorder not otherwise specified. *Eating and Weight Disorders, 6*, 157-165.

Riener, R., Schindler, K., and Ludvik, B. (2006). Psychosocial variables, eating behavior, depression, and binge eating in morbidly obese subjects. *Eating Behaviors, 7*, 309-314.

Saules, K. K., Collings, A. S., Hoodin, F., Angelella, N. E., Alschuler, K., Ivezaj, V., … Wiedemann, A. A. (2009). The contributions of weight problem perception, BMI, gender, mood, and smoking status to binge eating among college students. *Eating Behaviors, 10*, 1-9.

Saules, K. K., Tate, J. C., and Pomerleau, C. S. (2008). Weight control smoking in women. In K. P. Tolson and E. B. Veksler (Eds.), Research Focus on Smoking and Women's Health. New York: Nova Science Publishers, Inc.

Schafer, J. L., and Graham, J. W. (2002). Missing data: Our view of the state of the art. *Psychological Methods, 7*, 147-177.

Schäfer, A., Vaitl, D., and Schienle, A. (2010). Regional grey matter volume abnormalities in bulimia nervosa and binge-eating disorder. *Neuroimage, 50*, 639-643.

Schienle, Schäfer, A., Hermann, A., and Vaitl, D. (2009). Binge-eating disorder: Reward sensitivity and activation to images of food. *Biological Psychiatry, 65*, 654-661.

Schmidt, N. B., and Telch, M. J. (1990) Prevalence of personality disorders among bulimics, non-bulimic binge eaters, and normal controls. *Journal of Psychopathology and Behavioral Assessment, 12*, 169-185.

Small, D. M., Jones-Gotman, M., and Dagher, A. (2003. Feeding induced dopamine release in dorsal striatum correlates with meal pleasantness ratings in healthy human volunteers. *NeuroImage, 19*, 1709-1715.

Smink, F. R. E., van Hoeken, D., and Heok, H. W. (2012). Epidemiology of eating disorders: Incidence, prevalence, and mortality rates. *Current Psychiatry Reports, 14*, 406-414.

Sonnevile, K. R., Horton, N. J., Micali, B., Crosby, R. D., Swanson, S. A., Solmi, F., and Field, A. (2012). Longitudinal associations between binge eating and overeating and adverse outcomes among adolescents and young adults. *Archives of Pediatrics and Adolescent Medicine, 10*, 1-7.

Sobara, M., and Geliebter, A. (2002). Body image disturbance in obese outpatients before and after weight loss in relation to race, gender, binge eating, and age of onset of obesity. *International Journal of Eating Disorders, 31*, 416-423.

Spandler, R., Wittkowski, K. M., Goddard, N. L., Avena, N. M., Hoebel, B. G., and Leibowitz, S. F. (2004). Opiate-like effects of sugar on gene expression in reward areas of the rat brain. *Molecular Brain Research, 124*, 134-142.

Specker. S., de Zwaan, M., Raymond, N., and Mitchell, J. (1994). Psychopathology in subgroups of obese women with and without binge eating disorder. *Comprehensive Psychiatry, 35*, 185-190.

Spitzer, R. L., Devlin, M. J., Walsh, B. T., Hasin, D., Wing, R., Marcus, M. D., ... Nonas, C. (1991). Binge eating disorder: To be or not to be in DSM-IV. *International Journal of Eating Disorders, 10*, 627-629.

Spitzer, R. L., Yanovski, S. Z., Wadden T., Wing, R., Marcus M., Stunkard, A., ... Horne, R. L. (1993). Binge eating disorder: Its further validation in a multisite study. *International Journal of Eating Disorders, 13*, 137-153.

Stewart, S. H., Brown, C. G., Devoulyte, K., Theakston, J., and Larsen, S. E. (2006). Why do women with alcohol problems binge eat? Exploring connections between binge eating and heavy drinking in women receiving treatment for alcohol problems. *Journal of Health Psychology, 11*, 409-425.

Stice, E., Marti, C. N., and Rohde, P. (2012). Prevalence, incidence, impairment, and course of the proposed DSM-5 eating disorder diagnosis in an 8-year prospective community study of young women. *Journal of Abnormal Psychology*. Advanced online publication. doi: 10.1037/a0030679.

Stice, E., Marti, C. N., Shaw, H., and Jaconis, M. (2009). An 8-year longitudinal study of the natural history of threshold, subthreshold, and partial eating disorders from a community sample of adolescents. *Journal of Abnormal Psychology, 138*, 587-597.

Stice, E., Spoor, S., Bohon, C., and Small, D. M. (2008). Relation between obesity and blunted striatal response to food is moderated by TaqIA A1 allele. *Science, 322*, 449-452.

Stice, E., Spoor, S., Bohon, C., Veldhuizen, M. G., and Small, D. M. (2008). Relation of reward from food intake and anticipated food intake to obesity: A functional magnetic resonance imaging study. *Journal of Abnormal Psychology, 117*, 924-935.

Stice, E., Yokum, S., Blum, K., and Bohon, C. (2010). Weight gain is associated with reduced striatal response to palatable food. *The Journal of Neuroscience, 30*, 105-109.

Stice, E., Yokum, S., and Burger, K. S. (in press). Elevated reward region responsivity predicts future substance use onset but not overweight/obesity onset. *Biological Psychiatry*.

Steiger, H., Lehoux, P. M., and Gauvin, L. (1999). Impulsivity, dietary control and the urge to binge in bulimic syndromes. *International Journal of Eating Disorders, 26*, 261-274.

Striegel, R. H., Bedrosian, R., Wang, C., and Schwartz, S. (2012). Why men should be included in research on binge eating: Results from a comparison of psychosocial impairment in men and women. *International Journal of Eating Disorder, 45*, 233-240.

Striegel-Moore, R. H., and Bulik, C. M. (2007). Risk factors for eating disorders. *The American Psychologist, 62*, 181-198.

Striegel-Moore, R. H., Cachelin, F. M., Dohm, F. A., Pike, K. M., Wilfley, D. E., and Fairburn, C. G. (2001). Comparison of binge eating disorder and bulimia nervosa in a community sample. *International Journal of Eating Disorders, 29*, 157-165.

Striegel-Moore, R. H., Dohm, F. A., Kraemer, H. C., Taylor, C. B., Daniels, S., Crawford, P. B., and Schreiber, G. B. (2003). Eating disorders in white and black women. *American Journal of Psychiatry, 160*, 1326-1331.

Striegel-Moore, R. H., and Franko, D. L. (2003). Epidemiology of binge eating disorder, *International Journal of Eating Disorders, 34*, S19-S29.

Striegel-Moore, R. H., and Franko, D. L. (2008). Should binge eating disorder be included in the DSM-V? A critical review of the state of the evidence. *Annual Review of Clinical Psychology, 4*, 305-324.

Striegel-Moore, RH, and Marcus, M (1995). Eating disorders in women: Current issues and debates. In A. L. Stanton and S. J. Gallant (Eds.), The psychology of women's health: Progress and challenges in research and application (pgs. 445-487). Washington, DC: American Psychological Association.

Striegel-Moore, R. H., Smolak, L. (2000). The influence of ethnicity on eating disorders in women. In R. M. Eisler and M. Hersen. (Eds.), Handbook of Gender, Culture, and Health (pp. 227-254). Mahwah, NJ: Lawrence Erlbaum Associates.

Striegel-Moore, R. H., Wilfley, D. E., Pike, K. M., Dohm, F. A., and Fairburn, C. G. (2000). Recurrent binge eating in black American women. *Archives of Family Medicine, 9*, 83-87.

Striegel-Moore, R. H., Wilson, G. T., Wilfley, D. E., Elder, K. A., and Brownell, K. D. (1998). Binge eating in the obese community sample. *International Journal of Eating Disorders, 23*, 27-37.

Striegel-Moore, R. H., and Wonderlich, S. (2007). Diagnosis and classification of eating disorders: Finding a way forward. *International Journal of Eating Disorders, 40*, S1.

Stunkard, A. J. (1959). Eating patterns and obesity. *Psychiatric Quarterly, 33*, 284-295.

Stunkard, A. J., Faith, M. S., and Allison, K. C. (2003). Depression and obesity. *Biological Psychiatry, 54*, 330-337.

Sturm, R. (2007). Increases in morbid obesity in the USA: 2000-2005. *Public Health, 121*, 492-496.

Sysko, R., Devlin, M. J., Walsh, B. T., Zimmerli, E., and Kissileff, H. R. (2007). Satiety and test meal intake among women with binge eating disorder. *International Journal of Eating Disorders, 40*, 554-561.

Sysko, R., Roberto, C. A., Barnes, R. D., Grilo, C. M., Attia, E., and Walsh, T. (2012). Test-retest reliability of the proposed DSM-5 eating disorder diagnostic criteria. *Psychiatry Research, 196*, 302-308.

Tanofsky, M. B., Wilfley, D. E., Spurrell, E. B., Welch, R., and Brownell, K. D. (1997). Comparison of men and women with binge eating disorder. *International Journal of Eating Disorders, 21*, 49-54.

Tanofsky-Kraff, M., and Yanovski, S. Z. (2004). Eating disorder or disordered eating? Non-normative eating patterns in obese individuals. *Obesity Research, 12*, 1361-1366.

Taylor, J. Y., Caldwell, C. H., Baser, R. E., Jackson, J. S., Faison, N. (2007). Prevalence of eating disorders among Blacks in a national survey of American life. *International Journal of Eating Disorders. Special Issue on Diagnosis and Classification, 40*, S10-S14.

Telch, C. F., and Agras, W. S. (1994). Obesity, binge eating and psychopathology: Are they related? *International Journal of Eating Disorders, 15*, 53-61.

Telch, C. F., Agras, W. S., and Rossiter, E. M. (1988). Binge eating increases with increasing adiposity. *International Journal of Eating Disorders, 7*, 115-119.

Telch, C. F., and Stice, E. (1998). Psychiatric comorbidity in women with binge eating disorder: Prevalence rates from a non-treatment seeking sample. *Journal of Consulting and Clinical Psychology, 66*, 768-776.

Thomas, J. J., Vartanian, L. R., and Brownell, K. D. (2009). The relationship between eating disorder not otherwise specified (EDNOS) and officially recognized eating disorders: Meta-analysis and implications for DSM. *Psychological Bulletin, 135*, 407-423.

Tomeo, C. A., Field, A. E., Berkey, C. S., Colditz, G. A., and Frazier, A. L. (1999). Weight concerns, weight control behaviors, and smoking initiation. *Pediatrics, 104*, 918-924.

Trace, S. E., Thornton, L. M., Root, T. L., Mazzeo, S. E., Lichtenstein, P., Pedersen, N. L., and Bulik, C. M. (2012). Effects of reducing the frequency and duration criteria for binge eating and binge eating disorder: Implications for DSM-5. *International Journal of Eating Disorders, 45*, 531-536.

Turner, H., and Bryant-Waugh, R. (2004). Eating disorder not otherwise specified (EDNOS): Profiles of clients presenting at a community eating disorder service. *European Eating Disorders Review, 12*, 18-26.

Vardar, E., Caliyurt, O., Arikan, E., and Tuglu, C. (2004). Sleep quality and psychopathological features in obese binge eaters. *Stress and Health, 20*, 35-41.

Volkow, N. D., Fowler, J. S., Wang, G. J., and Goldstein, R. Z. (2002). Role of dopamine, the frontal cortex and memory circuits in drug addiction: Insight from imaging studies. *Neurobiology of Learning and Memory, 78*, 610-624.

Volkow, N. D., Wang, G. J., Fowler, J. S., Logan, J., Hitzmann, R., Ding, Y. S., ... Piscani, K. (1996). Decreases in dopamine receptors but not in dopamine transporters in alcoholics. *Alcoholism: Clinical and Experimental Research, 20*, 1594-1598.

Volkow, N. D., Wang, G. J., Fowler, J. S., and Telang, F. (2008). Overlapping neuronal circuits in addiction and obesity: Evidence of systems pathology. *Philosophical Transactions of the Royal Society B: Biological, 363*, 3191-3200.

Volkow, N. D., and Wise, R. A. (2005). How can drug addiction help us understand obesity? *Nature Neuroscience, 8*, 555-560.

Walsh, B. T., and Boudreau, G. (2003). Laboratory studies of binge eating disorder. *International Journal of Eating Disorders, 34*, S30-S38.

Walters, G. D., and Gilbert, A. A. (2000). Defining addiction: Contrasting views of clients and experts. *Addiction Research and Theory, 8*, 211-220.

Wang, G., Volkow, N. D., Fowler, J. S., and Logan, J. (1997). Dopamine D2 receptor availability in opiate dependent subjects before and after naloxone-precipitated withdrawal. *Neuropsychopharmacology, 16*, 174-182.

Wang, G. J., Volkow, N. D., Logan, J., Pappas, N. R., Wong, C. T., Zhu, W., ... Fowler, J. S. (2001). Brain dopamine and obesity. *Lancet, 357*, 354-357.

Watson, H. J., Fursland, A., Bulik, C. M., and Nathan, P. (2012). Subjective binge eating with compensatory behaviors: A variant presentation of bulimia nervosa. *International Journal of Eating Disorders*, Advanced online publication. doi: 10.1002/eat.22052

West, R. (2001). Theories of addiction. *Addiction, 96*, 3-13.

Weygandt, M., Schaefer, A., Schienle, A., and Haynes, J. D. (2012). Diagnosing different binge-eating disorders based on reward-related brain activation patterns. *Human Brain Mapping, 33*, 2135-2146.

White, M. A., and Grilo, C. M. (2011). Diagnostic efficiency of DSM-IV indicators for binge eating episodes. *Journal of Consulting and Clinical Psychology, 79*, 75-83.

White, M. A., and Grilo, C. M. (2006). Psychiatric comorbidity in binge-eating disorder as a function of smoking history. *Journal of Clinical Psychiatry, 67*, 594-599.

White, M. A., and Grilo, C. M. (2007). Symptom severity in obese women with binge eating disorder as a function of smoking history. *International Journal of Eating Disorders, 40*, 77-81.

White, M. A., Masheb, R. M., and Grilo, C. M. (2010). Self-reported weight gain following smoking cessation: A function of binge eating behavior. *International Journal of Eating Disorders, 43*, 572-575.

Widiger, T.A., and Samuel, D.B. (2005). Diagnostic categories or dimensions: A question for. DSM-V. *Journal of Abnormal Psychology*, 114, 494-504.

Wilfley, D. E., Bishop, M. E., Wilson, G. T., and Agras, W. S. (2007). Classification of eating disorders: Toward DSM-V. *International Journal of Eating Disorders, 40*, S123-129.

Wilfley, D. E., Pike, K. M., Dohm, F. A., Striegel-Moore, R. H., and Fairburn, C. G. (2001). Bias in binge eating: How representative are recruited samples? *Journal of Consulting and Clinical Psychology, 69*, 383-388.

Wilfley, D. E., Schwartz, M. B., Spurrell, E. B., and Fairburn, C. G. (2000). Using the eating disorder examination to identify the specific psychopathology of binge eating disorder. *International Journal of Eating Disorders, 27*, 259-269.

Wilfley, D. E., Welch, R. R., Stein, R. I., Spurrell, E. B., Cohen, L. R., Saelens, B. E., ... Matt, G. E., (2002). A randomized comparison of group cognitive-behavioral therapy and group interpersonal therapy for the treatment of overweight individuals with binge eating disorder. *Archives of General Psychiatry, 59*, 713-721.

Wilfley, D. E., Wilson, G. T., and Agras, W. S. (2003). The clinical significance of binge eating disorder. *International Journal of Eating Disorders, 34*, S96-S106.

Wilson, G. T., and Sysko, R. (2009). Frequency of binge eating episodes in bulimia nervosa and binge eating disorder: Diagnostic considerations. *International Journal of Eating Disorders, 42*, 603-610.

Wolfe, B. E., Baker, C. W., Smith, A. T., and Kelly-Weeder, S. (2009). Validity and utility of the current definition of binge eating. *International Journal of Eating Disorders, 42*, 674-686.

Wolfe, B. E., Hannon-Engel, S. L., and Mitchell, J. E. (2012). Bulimia nervosa in DSM-5. *Psychiatric Annals, 42*, 406-409.

Womble L. G., Williamson, D. A., Martin, C. K., Zucker, N. L., Thaw, J. M., Netermeyer, R., ... Greenway, F. L. (2001). Psychosocial variables associated with binge eating in obese males and females. *International Journal of Eating Disorders, 30*, 252-256.

Wonderlich, S. A., Gordon, K. H., Mitchell, J. E., Crosby, R. D., and Engel, S. G. (2009). The validity and clinical utility of binge eating disorder. *International Journal of Eating Disorders, 42*, 687-705.

World Health Organization. (1992). International statistical classification of diseases and related health problems (10 ed. Vol. II, Instructional Manual). Geneva: World Health Organization.

Yager, J., Kurtzman, F., Landsverk, J., and Wiesmeier, E. (1988). Behaviors and attitudes related to eating disorders in homosexual male college students. *The American Journal of Psychiatry, 145*, 495-497.

Yanovski, S. Z., Nelson, J. E., Dubbert, B. K., Billinda, K., and Spitzer, R. L. (1993). Association of binge eating disorder and psychiatric comorbidity in obese subjects. *The American Journal of Psychiatry, 150*, 1472-1479.

Yanovski, S. Z., Nelson, J. E., Dubbert, B. K., and Spitzer, R. L. (1993). Association of binge eating disorder and psychiatric comorbidity in obese subjects. *American Journal of Psychiatry, 150*, 1472-1479.

Yanovski, S. Z., and Sebring, N. G. (1994). Recorded food intake of obese women with binge eating disorder before and after weight loss. *International Journal of Eating Disorders, 15*, 135-150.

Ziauddeen, H., Farooqi, I. S., and Fletcher, P. C. (2012). Obesity and the brain: How convincing is the addiction model? *Nature Reviews Neuroscience, 13*, 279-286.

Zimmerman, M., Francione-Witt, C., Chelminski, I., Young, D., and Tortolani, C. (2008). Problems applying the DSM-IV eating disorders diagnostic criteria in a general psychiatric outpatient practice. *Journal of Clinical Psychiatry, 69*, 381-384.

In: Binge Eating and Binge Drinking
Editor: Simon B. Harris

ISBN: 978-1-62618-580-7
© 2013 Nova Science Publishers, Inc.

Chapter 3

UNDERSTANDING THE HIGH CO-PREVALENCE OF PROBLEMATIC EATING AND DRINKING

Kenny A. Karyadi[*]*, Ayca Coskunpinar, Andree Entezari, Conner Long, and Melissa A. Cyders*
Department of Psychology,
Indiana University-Purdue University at Indianapolis,
Indianapolis, IN, US

ABSTRACT

Prior studies have indicated a high prevalence of comorbidity between problematic levels of eating and drinking. This high co-prevalence has been partly attributed to the disinhibiting effects of alcohol on eating behaviors. Specifically, alcohol consumption has been shown to increase food intake by disinhibiting eating behaviors. Alternately, it is also possible that food and alcohol consumption might become associated through repeated pairings. Through these repeated pairings, food cues and food consumption might elicit alcohol cravings and subsequent alcohol use. Similarly, alcohol cues and alcohol consumption might elicit food cravings and subsequent food intake. Finally, other common factors might explain both eating and drinking behaviors. In particular, the tendency to cope with distress through food and alcohol consumption has been shown to increase the risk for problematic levels of eating and drinking. The current chapter will review evidence supporting and theories underlying these pathways in order to better understand the high co-prevalence of problematic eating and drinking.

INTRODUCTION

In the United States, there is a high prevalence of both eating disorders and alcohol use disorders. For eating disorders, prevalence rates range from .3% to .9% for anorexia nervosa, .5% to 1.5% for bulimia nervosa, and 1.5% to 2.0% for binge eating disorder (Hudson, Hiripi,

---
[*] Corresponding Author's Email: kkaryadi@iupui.edu.

Pope, & Kessler, 2007). For alcohol use disorders, the prevalence of lifetime alcohol abuse and alcohol dependence is 17.8% and 12.5%, respectively (Hasin, Stinson, Ogburn, & Grant, 2007). Furthermore, individuals with alcohol use disorders are more likely to experience increased negative alcohol consequences—including physical and sexual assaults, driving under the influence, and alcohol-related deaths (Hingson, Heeren, Winter, & Wechsler, 2005; Hingson, Zha, & Weitzman, 2009; Knight et al., 2002). Similarly, individuals with eating disorders might also experience problems from their eating behaviors—including physical problems, psychological problems, and higher mortality risk (Hudson et al., 2007; Steinhausen, 2009). Finally, only a minority of people with eating disorders (Hoek & van Hoeken, 2003) and with alcohol use disorders (Hasin et al., 2007) seek treatment. The high prevalence of these disorders, the problems associated with these disorders, and low treatment rates are indicative of a need to better understand the mechanisms underlying these disorders.

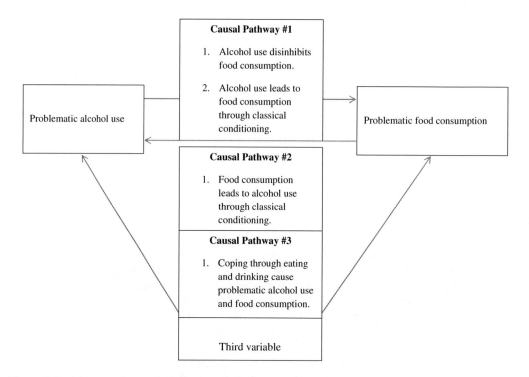

Figure 1. Pathways to Comorbid Problematic Eating and Drinking.

Research suggests that the high prevalence of problematic eating and alcohol use might be partly due to an elevated comorbidity between the two problematic behaviors (Sinha & O'Malley, 2000). For instance, prior studies have indicated that problematic alcohol users are more likely to engage in problematic eating behaviors compared to non-problematic alcohol users (Stewart, Brown, Devoulyte, Theakston, & Larsen, 2006; Taylor, Peveler, Hibbert, & Fairburn, 1993). Similarly, prior studies have also indicated that problematic eaters are more likely to engage in problematic alcohol use behaviors compared to non-problematic eaters (Braun, Sunday, & Halmi, 1994; Dansky et al., 1998; Jones, Cheshire, & Moorhouse, 1985; Lundholm, 1989). Taken together, these findings indicate that there might be underlying mechanisms connecting these two problematic behaviors. Indeed, prior studies have suggested multiple possible mechanisms for the co-occurrence between problematic eating and drinking.

In particular, there are three possible pathways that we will discuss here that might explain how problematic eating and drinking can co-occur (see Figure 1).

First, problematic alcohol use behaviors might lead to problematic eating behaviors (causal pathway #1). For instance, prior studies have indicated that alcohol use increases food intake by disinhibiting eating behaviors (Caton, Ball, Ahern, & Hetherington, 2004; Hetherington, Cameron, Wallis, & Pirie, 2001; Hoffman & Friese, 2008; Stewart et al., 2006; Yeomans, Caton, & Hetherington, 2003). Furthermore, through repeated pairings between alcohol use and eating, alcohol cues and alcohol consumption consumption can elicit food cravings and food consumption (Hetherington et al., 2001). Second, problematic eating behaviors might cause and maintain problematic alcohol use behaviors (causal pathway #2). In particular, through repeated pairings between alcohol use and eating, food cues and food consumption can come to elicit alcohol cravings and alcohol consumption (Hetherington et al., 2001). Third, problematic eating and alcohol use behaviors might be predicted by a third factor (causal pathway #3). For instance, the tendency to cope with distress through the consumption of food or alcohol might precede the development of both problematic eating and alcohol use behaviors (Stewart et al., 2006).

The present chapter will attempt to elucidate these pathways in order to better understand the co-occurrence between problematic eating and alcohol use. At the same time, these pathways are not mutually exclusive, meaning that the viability of one pathway does not necessarily influence the viability of another pathway. Specifically, the relationship between problematic eating and drinking can be explained through multiple pathways. However, although we discuss how some pathways might interact to influence comorbid eating and drinking problems, there are likely other pathways that we did not review or propose here. In general, the present chapter will review human studies that examine (1) eating and alcohol use disorders, and (2) subclinical levels of problematic eating and drinking behaviors. By reviewing these studies, the chapter will attempt to elucidate three pathways that might underlie the co-occurrence between problematic eating and alcohol use behaviors.

CAUSAL PATHWAY #1: DISINHIBITING EFFECTS OF ALCOHOL ON EATING BEHAVIORS

Introduction

One way in which problematic alcohol use can lead to problematic eating behaviors is through the disinhibiting effects of alcohol. As is well documented, alcohol has an impact on decision-making and behaviors, and can lead to a disinhibition of certain habits and behaviors. In particular, consumption of alcohol can disinhibit eating behaviors, thus leading to increased food intake. Such disinhibition can manifest as increased caloric consumption while drinking and/or intoxicated. In this section, we will discuss four separate mechanisms that might explain alcohol's disinhibition of eating behaviors. In order to better understand the co-occurrence between problematic eating and drinking behaviors, we will also discuss findings and theories underlying each of these mechanisms.

Disinhibition of Eating Behaviors

Several previous studies have shown an increase in eating behaviors following low to moderate alcohol consumption. For instance, in a sample of male subjects, lunch intake was greatest following the consumption of alcohol compared to no alcohol consumption (Caton et al., 2004; Hetherington et al., 2001). Furthermore, among overweight female college students, participants who consumed alcohol ate significantly more than participants who did not consume alcohol (Hoffmann & Friese, 2008). Finally, among participants with bulimia nervosa, acute alcohol intoxication has been documented to reduce restrictions in food intake (Bruce et al., 2011). In sum, various eating behaviors (e.g. dieting, bulimia and food preoccupation) have been associated with alcohol consumption and intoxication (Lavik, Clausen, & Pedersen, 1991). Although the relationship between food and alcohol consumption has been well documented, the mechanisms through which alcohol can disinhibit eating behaviors have not been well-understood. Here, we will discuss four possible mechanisms that might explain the disinhibition of eating behaviors following alcohol consumption. First, alcohol use might directly facilitate impulsive behaviors, including impulsive eating behaviors. Second, alcohol users might have fewer cognitive resources for behavioral control. Third, alcohol might make strongly represented dieting rules temporarily inaccessible. Fourth, alcohol use might impair an individual's ability to monitor their eating behaviors.

Mechanism #1: Increase in Impulsiveness

Impulsivity, which can be broadly conceptualized as the tendency to engage in risky behaviors without forethought (Cyders & Coskunpinar, 2011), might be influenced by alcohol consumption. Indeed, research has shown that alcohol use directly increases the participation in multiple impulsive behaviors (Reed, Levin, & Evans, 2012; Reynolds, Richards, & deWit, 2006). Although trait level impulsivity has been shown to be associated with both alcohol consumption and eating behaviors (Acton, 2003; Dick et al., 2010; Fischer, Settles, Collins, Gunn, & Smith, 2012; Mulder, 2002), we focus on state-level impulsivity in this chapter. This is because research has shown that consumption of alcohol increases state level impulsivity (Reed et al., 2012). In turn, state-level impulsivity has been shown to predict food intake (Guerrieri, Nederkoorn, & Jansen, 2007) and has been associated with several facets of unhealthy eating, such as over-eating (Jasinska et al., 2012).

In sum, these findings suggest that the relationship between alcohol use and increased food intake can be partly explained through alcohol induced impulsivity. While consuming alcohol, individuals appear to become more impulsive.

Due to this alcohol-induced increase in state-level impulsivity, individuals might be less likely to see potential negative consequences from their behaviors and might consequently engage in increased food intake. Based on previous research (Guerrieri et al., 2007; Reed et al., 2012), it is plausible that alcohol consumption increases eating behavior indirectly through increasing impulsiveness. In order to better establish this mechanism, future studies should examine whether alcohol-induced state-level impulsivity directly leads to increased food intake in an experimental paradigm. Research to date suggests viability of this mechanism.

Mechanism #2: Reduction in Behavioral Control

Alcohol might also increase food consumption by reducing behavioral control. Indeed, previous research suggests that alcohol might temporarily weaken the behavioral inhibition system (Quay, 1997), which can be defined as a neuropsychological system that determines sensitivity to punishment. Furthermore, empirical studies have demonstrated reduced inhibitory control following alcohol consumption (Fillmore & Vogel-Sprott, 1990; Mulvihill, Skilling, & Vogal-Sprott, 1997; Weafer & Fillmore, 2012). Similarly, imaging studies have also demonstrated reduced inhibition on task performance following alcohol consumption (Easdon & Vogel-Sprott, 2000). Finally, consumption of alcohol increases activation in certain parts of the middle temporal gyrus, middle frontal gyrus, and the striatum—which demonstrates the effect of alcohol on behavioral inhibition on a neurophysiological level (Easdon & Vogel-Sprott, 2000).

Taken together, these findings indicate that alcohol can impair one's behavioral control. In turn, impairments in behavioral control can increase food intake (Svaldi, Brand, & Tuschen-Caffier, 2010). High levels of behavioral control or behavioral inhibition might drive individuals to naturally avoid situations that would cause negative experiences, such as fear and anxiety (Quay, 1997). However, a decrease in behavioral control due to alcohol consumption might impair their ability to judge and avoid these situations. These individuals might then engage in increased food intake because they are less likely to consider increased food intake as a possible cause of negative experiences. However, no studies have examined whether alcohol-induced impairments in behavioral control might lead to increased food intake. Future studies should examine, experimentally, the role of behavioral control as a mediator in the relationship between alcohol use and food consumption. This role appears viable based on the existing limited research, but future research needs to be conducted to better elucidate this role.

Mechanism #3: Suppression of Dieting Standards

One's awareness of their current behavior and how their current behavior compares to relevant behavioral standards is known as monitoring (Carver & Scheier, 1981). Accordingly, a lapse in monitoring leads to a failure to adhere to certain behavioral standards. In particular, a decrease in one's ability to monitor their eating behaviors tends to lead to a failure to adhere to dieting standards (Ward & Mann, 2000). These dieting standards might entail remembering how much food one has consumed, how much more food one can consume, food that one cannot or should not consume, and the pre-set food portion that one is allowed to eat. Individuals need to remember these standards during food intake in order to continue to utilize them properly. In remembering these standards, individuals must rely on their memory systems. However, the consumption of alcohol can impair these memory systems. Indeed, alcohol intoxication has been shown to significantly hinder recall from long-term memory (Nelson, McSpadden, Fromme, & Marlatt, 1986; Saults, Cowan, Sher, & Moreno, 2007) and to impair working memory (Nelson et al., 1986). Alcohol-induced impairments in these memory systems might lead to a failure to adhere to dieting related standards and to a consequent increase in food intake.

Long-term memory is crucial for remembering any stored information, whereas working memory stores information for 20-30 seconds for fast recall. The functional roles of these systems suggest that long term memory is crucial in remembering dieting standards, and that working memory is crucial in the successful maintenance and application of dieting standards to eating behaviors (Hoffmann & Friese, 2008; Saults et al., 2007). However, under the influence of alcohol, individuals might have a more difficult time retrieving dieting standards from long-term memory, and maintaining and applying dieting standards using their working memory (Baumeister, Heatherton, & Tice, 1994; Nelson et al., 1986). As a result, their ability to access and adhere to their usual dieting standards becomes impaired (Ward & Mann, 2000). Impairments in their ability to access and adhere to dieting standards might consequently facilitate increased food intake. In this way, alcohol disinhibits eating behaviors by impairing memory systems, which are responsible for regulating dieting standards. However, no studies have examined whether alcohol-induced impairments in memory systems might lead directly to increased food intake. Future studies should examine this experimentally in order to determine whether memory system impairments might mediate the relationship between alcohol and food consumption. Research to date suggests that this hypothesis is viable, but not well-tested.

Mechanism #4: Impaired Monitoring of Eating Behaviors

Alcohol consumption has been associated with decreased levels of self-awareness (Wolfe & Maisto, 2000). In particular, alcohol might increase food intake by reducing self-awareness of a wide range of behaviors (Hull & Bond, 1986). Indeed, previous research has shown that alcohol induced impairments in self-awareness can increase food consumption (Heatherton, Polivy, Herman, & Baumeister, 1991; Polivy & Herman, 1976a; Polivy & Herman, 1976b; Ward & Mann, 2000). Furthermore, individuals who had to watch a video of their failing on a problem-solving task (low self-awareness condition) showed disinhibited eating (Heatherton et al., 1991). Similarly, low levels of self-awareness have also been associated with problematic eating behaviors (Ruderman & Grace, 1987; Ruderman & Grace, 1988). These findings suggest that alcohol induced impairments in self-awareness might lead to problematic eating behaviors. Past research has validated the role of alcohol in reducing self-awareness and subsequently increasing food intake. Of all the mechanisms reviewed, this mechanism appears to have the most consistent approach. However, future work to examine how this might or might not lead to more problematic levels of food consumption would be warranted.

Conclusion

In sum, prior findings suggest the viability of the model, wherein alcohol use disinhibits eating behaviors (Sinha & O'Malley, 2000; Stewart et al., 2006). This causal relationship between alcohol and food consumption can potentially be explained through various mechanisms. In particular, alcohol might have disinhibiting effects on eating behavior by (1) impairing long-term and working memory, (2) impairing self-awareness, (3) reducing behavioral inhibition, and (4) increasing impulsivity. Although there is some support for the proposed mechanisms above, future studies need to provide more direct tests of these hypotheses, including experimental manipulations of alcohol consumption and its effects on both food consumption and the above-proposed mediators. Additionally, research should examine the relationship between alcohol and food consumption in more realistic settings. Even though self-report measures have various benefits (e.g. cost efficient and easy to administer, easy interpretation), social desirability and accuracy of recalling past information can compromise the accuracy of the relationship between these two constructs. Furthermore, in order to better explain and generalize the mechanisms proposed above, future research should examine this relationship in different populations (e.g. bulimia nervosa, dieters) and under different conditions (e.g., social drinking vs. intoxication). Finally, there should be more research comparing eating behaviors of control participants to participants who have eating disorders under different levels of alcohol consumption. Future studies will provide a better understanding of how these mechanisms might explain increased food consumption under the influence of alcohol.

CAUSAL PATHWAYS #1 AND #2: RECIPROCAL INFLUENCES BETWEEN DRINKING AND EATING

Introduction

Alcohol use and eating behaviors might causally influence and maintain each other through classical conditioning processes. In order to discuss how classical conditioning processes might influence the co-occurrence between problematic eating and drinking, we will first explain classical conditioning. After, we will discuss how alcohol use and eating can be considered classically conditioned behaviors. Furthermore, we will discuss the viability of pathways that suggest that alcohol and eating behaviors can become paired through classical conditioning processes. In particular, we will examine whether alcohol cues and consumption can elicit food cravings and food consumption, and whether food cues and consumption can elicit alcohol cravings and alcohol consumption. Finally, we will discuss whether classical conditioning can explain the high co-prevalence between problematic eating and alcohol use behaviors.

Classical Conditioning

Classical conditioning is a form of learning that involves the process of association. A meaningful stimulus (unconditioned stimulus) that is able to naturally elicit a response (unconditioned response) becomes associated with a neutral stimulus. By repeatedly pairing the neutral stimulus and the unconditioned stimulus, this neutral stimulus eventually becomes a powerful enough stimulus (conditioned stimulus) that is able to elicit a response by itself (conditioned response). This process of association is most famously demonstrated in Ivan Pavlov's classic experiments. Pavlov noticed that dogs naturally produce the salivation reflex (unconditioned response) when presented with food (unconditioned stimulus), but not when presented with the noise of a buzzer (neutral stimulus). After the buzzer is repeatedly paired with the food, the buzzer becomes powerful enough (conditioned stimulus) to elicit the salivation reflex by itself (conditioned response). Since Pavlov's experiments, it has been discovered that this classical conditioning process can influence a variety of stimuli and behaviors.

Alcohol Use and Classical Conditioning

Alcohol use behaviors can be driven by this classical conditioning process (Childress, Ehrman, Rohsenow, Robbins, & O'Brien, 1992; Drummond, Tiffany, Glautier, & Remington, 1995). Alcohol can be considered an unconditioned stimulus that can elicit unconditioned responses, such as relaxation and motor impairment, through its consumption (Glautier, Drummond & Remington, 1994). There are also neutral stimuli (e.g. smell, taste, sight of alcohol) that can become paired with alcohol, alcohol use, and alcohol effects (Childress et al., 1992; Drobes & Tiffany, 1997). These alcohol-related stimuli have the potential of becoming conditioned stimuli that can come to elicit conditioned responses. In turn, these conditioned responses can take on multiple forms, all of which have the potential of influencing alcohol intake (Field, Moggs, & Bradley, 2005; Tiffany, 1990). See Figure 2 for an example of how alcohol and alcohol-related stimuli can become classically conditioned.

First, for problematic alcohol users, abstinence from alcohol can elicit an unconditioned withdrawal state. Alcohol-related stimuli, such as environments that individuals typically drink in, might become repeatedly paired with alcohol abstinence. Consequently, when not followed by alcohol consumption, exposure to these conditioned stimuli may come to induce a conditioned withdrawal response and subsequent cravings for alcohol (Cooney, Litt, Morse, Bauer, & Gaupp, 1997; Siegel, 1983; McCusker & Brown, 1990). In turn, alcohol consumption might become re-instated in order to reduce alcohol cravings and withdrawal stress (Edwards, 1990; Tiffany, 1990).

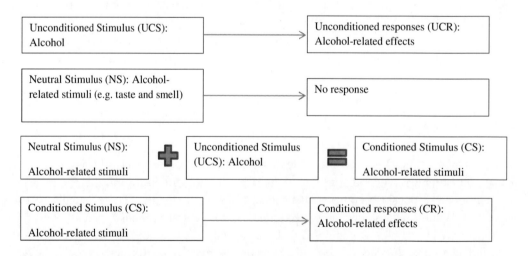

Figure 2. Alcohol and Classical Conditioning.

Second, alcohol use can have a variety of effects, such as increased heart and pulse rate. Stimuli that have been reliably paired with alcohol use can become conditioned stimuli that prepare the body for these effects by producing opposite effects, called conditioned compensatory responses (Siegel, 1983; Tiffany, 1990). These conditioned stimuli have been shown to produce skin temperature, pulse rate response, and heart rate response that were opposite in direction to the effects of alcohol (Newlin, 1985; Newlin, 1986; Staiger & White, 1988). These compensatory responses prepare the body for the effects of alcohol but, when alcohol is not consumed, these responses can be experienced as withdrawal and cravings (Siegel, 1983). Withdrawal and cravings, in turn, can facilitate alcohol consumption.

Third, stimuli that have been reliably paired with alcohol use can also elicit effects similar to alcohol (Stewart, de Wit, & Eikelboom, 1984). For instance, stimuli that have been paired with alcohol use have been shown to elicit a conditioned heart rate response in the same direction as the heart rate response produced by alcohol consumption (Staiger & White, 1988). Moreover, individuals who were given placebo drinks that resemble alcohol (e.g. in sight, taste, and smell) reported intoxication levels and alcohol content ratings similar to individuals who were given actual alcoholic drinks (Lapp, Collins, Zywiak, & Izzo, 1994; Ross & Pihl, 1989). Conditioned alcohol-related stimuli might produce effects similar to alcohol's direct effects and might consequently influence consumption rates (Asp, 1977; Marlatt, Demming, & Reid, 1973).

Finally, alcohol use has been known to produce a variety of desirable effects, such as relaxation and euphoria. Stimuli, such as the sight and smell of alcohol, can become paired with these pleasant effects. They can become conditioned incentives that are often highly salient and attention grabbing, and that can consequently incentivize further alcohol use (Field et al., 2005). For instance, alcoholic individuals responded more slowly to alcohol-related words than to neutral words, indicative of an attentional bias toward alcohol-related stimuli (Johnsen, Laberg, Cox, Vaksdal, & Hugdahl, 1994). Furthermore, higher attentional bias for alcohol pictures among heavy drinkers might contribute to higher levels of cravings (Field, Mogg, Zetteler, & Bradley, 2004). Finally, attentional biases to alcohol-related stimuli might increase the risk of relapse among alcohol abusers (Cox, Hogan, Kristian, & Race, 2002).

Eating and Classical Conditioning

Similar to alcohol use behaviors, food intake can also be influenced by classical conditioning process (Kennedy, Katz, Ralevsky, & Mendlowitz, 1995; Schmidt & Marks, 1988).

Food can be considered an unconditioned stimulus that can elicit unconditioned responses, such as insulin release and salivation (Jansen, 1998), through its consumption. These same responses can be brought under the control of cues typically associated with food consumption—such as the smell, sight, taste, and thought of food (Wardle, 1990; Woods, 1991).

In other words, through repeated pairings between these cues and food intake, the cues may start to act as conditioned stimuli that can trigger conditioned responses. Similar to alcohol-related conditioned responses, these learned conditioned responses can take on multiple forms and can increase the likelihood of excessive food intake (Jansen, 1990; Wardle, 1990). See Figure 3 for an example of how food and food-related stimuli can become classically conditioned.

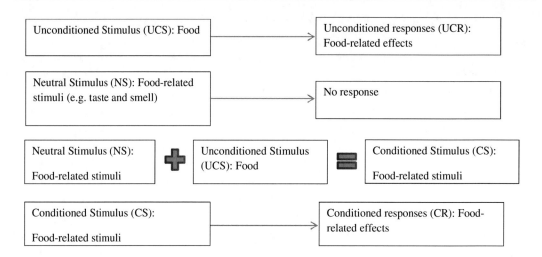

Figure 3. Food and Classical Conditioning.

First, food consumption can have a variety of effects, such as increased salivation and insulin release. Cues that have been reliably paired with food intake can become conditioned stimuli that prepare the body for these effects by producing opposite effects or compensatory physiological responses (Powley, 1977).

These compensatory physiological responses prepare individuals to eat and can consequently facilitate increased food intake. For instance, food related stimuli (e.g. thought, smell, taste, and sight) have been shown to increase acid secretion and serum gastrin concentrations, both of which might prepare individuals for food consumption (Feldman & Richardson, 1986). Furthermore, among women, food cues produced changes in heart rate, salivation, blood pressure, skin conductance, and gastric activity—all of which might influence food craving and food intake (Nederkoorn, Smulders, & Jansen, 2000). Finally, taste exposure to high fat food produced greater pancreatic polypeptide level and facilitated greater food intake compared to taste exposure to low fat food (Crystal & Teff, 2006).

Second, like alcohol use, food consumption can also produce a variety of desirable effects, such as satiety and euphoria. Cues, such as the sight and smell of food, can become paired with these effects and can consequently become conditioned incentives. These conditioned incentives are often highly salient and attention grabbing, and can consequently incentivize food consumption. For instance, despite feeding and decreased self-report of hunger, obese individuals had higher attentional biases toward food related images (Castellanos et al., 2009).

Similarly, among women with eating disorders, attentional biases were found for food-related pictures (Shafran, Lee, Cooper, Palmer, & Fairburn, 2007). In addition, among young females, attentional biases for food cues were associated with increased subjective appetite (Hepworth, Mogg, Brignell, & Bradley, 2010).

Finally, satiated rats were found to eat a large meal when exposed to a tune previously paired with food consumption (Weingarten, 1983). These findings indicate that conditioned incentives can increase subjective appetite and consequent food intake.

Reciprocal Effects between Alcohol and Eating Behaviors

Pairing Between Alcohol and Eating Behaviors

Taken together, prior findings suggest that classical conditioning process can exert an influence on both eating and alcohol use behaviors. Furthermore, multiple studies have indicated an association between alcohol use and eating (Yeomans et al., 2003). For instance, among males, lunch intake was greatest following the consumption of alcohol compared to no alcohol consumption (Caton et al., 2004; Hetherington et al., 2001). Furthermore, among overweight females, participants who consumed alcohol ate significantly more (Hoffman & Friese, 2008). However, although these findings indicate that alcohol use and eating behaviors can co-occur, it is not clear whether this co-occurrence is due to classical conditioning processes (Hetherington et al., 2011). Unfortunately, no studies have ever examined the role of classical conditioning in the co-occurrence between eating and drinking behaviors. Based on prior research, we can infer possible classical conditioning mechanisms that might underlie this co-occurrence. In these mechanisms, both food and alcohol consumption and stimuli have the potential of increasing food and alcohol intake.

Mechanism #1: Food As a Conditioned Stimulus

First, for problematic drinkers, abstinence from alcohol can elicit an unconditioned withdrawal state (Wikler, 1973). Food consumption and food related stimuli might become repeatedly paired with this state of abstinence and might subsequently elicit a conditioned withdrawal response. When not immediately followed by alcohol consumption, food consumption or exposure to food stimuli may come to induce conditioned alcohol withdrawal and subsequent alcohol craving. In turn, individuals might use alcohol in order to reduce alcohol cravings and withdrawal. Using animals, future studies should examine whether food consumption and food stimuli that are paired with alcohol abstinence and subsequent withdrawal would later elicit conditioned withdrawal and a subsequent increase in alcohol consumption.

Second, stimuli that have been reliably paired with alcohol use can start to prepare the body for alcohol's effects by producing conditioned compensatory responses (Siegler, 1983). After repeated pairings, food consumption and food related stimuli might produce changes in bodily tension, skin temperature, pulse rate response, and heart rate response opposite in direction to the effects of alcohol. These compensatory changes prepare the body for the effects of alcohol. When not followed by alcohol consumption, these compensatory changes can be experienced as withdrawal and cravings, which can in turn facilitate alcohol consumption. Using individuals with comorbid eating and drinking problems, future studies should examine whether food consumption and food related stimuli can produce these compensatory responses, and whether such responses might be associated with increased alcohol use.

Third, after being repeatedly paired with alcohol use, food consumption and food related stimuli might elicit an intoxication level in the same direction as the effect of alcohol (Stewart et al., 1984). The intoxication level produced by food consumption and food stimuli will presumably be lower than the intoxication level produced by alcohol. Since low level of intoxication has been shown to prime further alcohol use (Le et al., 1998), food elicited intoxication might prime further alcohol use for the purpose of increasing intoxication level. Using human subjects, future studies should examine whether food consumption and food related stimuli that have been paired with alcohol use would produce changes in intoxication level, and whether changes in intoxication level might facilitate further alcohol consumption.

Fourth, food consumption and food related stimuli might become reliably paired with the pleasant effects of alcohol and can consequently become conditioned incentives for alcohol use behaviors (Field et al., 2005). Specifically, these food related conditioned incentives might be highly salient and attention grabbing. Moreover, through their association with the positive effects of alcohol, these conditioned incentives have the potential of facilitating alcohol cravings and incentivizing alcohol use. Using individuals with comorbid eating and drinking problems, future studies should examine whether food consumption and food stimuli that have been paired with positive alcohol effects can influence subsequent alcohol craving and alcohol consumption.

Overall, these possible mechanisms suggest that food consumption and food related stimuli can elicit increased alcohol cravings and alcohol consumption. However, no studies have examined the viability of these mechanisms in explaining the high co-prevalence of eating and drinking problems in the population. For instance, among newly abstinent drinkers, comorbid eating disorders characterized by increased food consumption and increased exposure to food related stimuli might be risk factors that trigger increased alcohol cravings and that might consequently re-instate alcohol consumption. Among individuals with comorbid eating and drinking problems, food consumption and food related stimuli might produce alcohol-related compensatory responses, alcohol intoxication level, and incentivization of alcohol use—all of which might maintain problematic drinking behaviors. Future studies should examine these mechanisms, particularly their contribution to comorbid eating and drinking problems.

Mechanism #2: Alcohol As a Conditioned Stimulus

First, stimuli that have been associated with food intake can induce compensatory physiological responses (Powley, 1977). In this way, alcohol consumption and alcohol-related stimuli that have been paired with food intake might produce compensatory changes that prepare for the effects of eating and that can consequently facilitate increased food intake. For instance, alcohol consumption and alcohol-related stimuli might produce changes in acid secretion, serum gastrin concentrations, heart rate, salivation, blood pressure, and skin conductance—all of which might influence food craving and food intake. Using individuals with comorbid eating and drinking problems, future studies should examine whether alcohol consumption and alcohol stimuli that have been paired with food intake would produce these compensatory changes, and whether these compensatory changes would elicit increased food cravings and intake.

Second, alcohol consumption and alcohol-related stimuli might become paired with the pleasant effects of eating and might consequently become conditioned incentives for food intake. These conditioned incentives might be attractive and attention grabbing. Moreover, through their association with the positive effects of eating, they also have the potential of increasing food cravings and food intake. Although no studies have ever examined this, similar mechanisms have been suggested for the pairing between alcohol use and smoking (Burton & Tiffany, 1997; Stewart et al., 1984). Using individuals with comorbid eating and drinking problems, future studies should examine whether alcohol consumption and alcohol-related stimuli could elicit attentional biases for food, and whether such biases would facilitate increased food cravings and food intake.

Third, abstinence from food could elicit an unconditioned withdrawal state, particularly hunger. Alcohol use and alcohol-related stimuli might become repeatedly paired with food abstinence and might subsequently elicit a conditioned withdrawal state. Over time, alcohol use and alcohol-related stimuli could directly elicit this withdrawal state, which can in turn trigger eating behaviors. Although no studies have ever examined this, there is indirect evidence from the smoking literature. Alcohol use and alcohol stimuli have been shown to evoke conditioned withdrawal from cigarettes, which can consequently trigger smoking cravings and smoking (Ludwig & Wikler, 1974; Poulos, Hinson, & Siegel, 1981). Based on those studies, future studies should examine whether alcohol use and alcohol stimuli could also elicit conditioned withdrawal for food, and whether such withdrawal might influence food cravings and food intake.

In sum, these possible mechanisms suggest that alcohol use and alcohol-related stimuli can elicit increased food cravings and food consumption. However, no studies have examined whether these are viable mechanisms that might explain the high co-occurrence between eating and drinking problems in the population. Among individuals recovering from eating disorders, comorbid alcohol use disorders characterized by excessive consumption and increased exposure to alcohol-related stimuli might trigger food cravings and might re-instate unhealthy food consumption. Among individuals with comorbid eating and drinking problems, alcohol consumption and alcohol-related stimuli might produce food related compensatory responses and incentivization of food consumption, both of which might maintain unhealthy eating behaviors. Future studies should examine whether these mechanisms might be more salient among individuals with comorbid eating and drinking disorders.

Conclusion

In summary, multiple studies have indicated that classical conditioning can influence both eating and drinking behaviors. Alcohol-related conditioned stimuli have been shown to elicit conditioned withdrawal (Wikler, 1973), conditioned compensatory responses (Siegel, 1983), conditioned alcohol responses (Stewart et al., 1984), and increased alcohol-related salience (Field et al., 2004)—all of which have the potential of facilitating alcohol consumption. Food related conditioned stimuli have been shown to elicit compensatory physiological responses (Powley, 1977) and increased food-related salience (Castellanos et al., 2009), both of which might facilitate food consumption.

Similarly, the co-occurrence between eating and alcohol use behaviors might also be influenced by classical conditioning process. For instance, food consumption and food related stimuli might elicit alcohol withdrawal state, conditioned compensatory alcohol responses, unconditioned alcohol responses—all of which might influence alcohol consumption. Similarly, alcohol consumption and alcohol-related stimuli might elicit conditioned compensatory food responses and food withdrawal state, both of which might influence food consumption. Finally, food and alcohol consumption and stimuli might become conditioned incentives that directly elicit increased food and alcohol consumption. Unfortunately, no studies have examined these classical conditioning mechanisms. Elucidating these mechanisms, and examining how these mechanisms might contribute to the high co-prevalence of eating and drinking problems, should be the goals of future studies.

CAUSAL PATHWAY #3: A THIRD FACTOR PREDICTOR

Introduction

The tendency to cope through eating and drinking might explain the comorbidity between problematic eating and alcohol use behaviors. In order to discuss this risk factor, we will first review separate eating and alcohol use literatures. We will then discuss possible mechanisms that might explain why eating to cope might lead to problematic eating behaviors and why drinking to cope might lead to problematic drinking behaviors. Furthermore, we will review literatures indicating that drinking and eating to cope lead to comorbid problematic eating and drinking behaviors. Finally, we will discuss possible mechanisms that might explain why drinking and eating to cope might lead to comorbid eating and drinking problems.

One Potential Third Factor: Drinking and Eating to Cope

The high comorbidity between problematic eating and alcohol use might be attributed to common risk factors. One possible common risk factor is the tendency to cope with distressing emotions through eating and drinking (Stewart et al., 2006; Lesieur & Blume, 1993). Indeed, both eating and drinking have been linked in their separate literatures as ways of coping with distressing feelings (Ferriter & Ray, 2011; Stewart et al., 2006). However, due to the diversity in these literatures, this tendency to cope through eating and drinking has taken on several different labels. For instance, this tendency might be labeled as a way of regulating emotions (Agras & Telch, 1998; Mizes, 1985; Sherwood, Crowther, Wills, & Ben-Porath, 2000), a way to self-medicate (Suh, Ruffins, Robins, Albanese, & Khantzian, 2008; Peveler & Fairburn, 1990), and a maladaptive coping method (Cooper, 1994; Cooper, Russell, & George, 1988). Despite the label differences, this tendency to cope with distress through alcohol and food consumption has been consistently linked to higher problematic eating and drinking (Birch, Stewart, & Brown, 2007; Ferriter & Ray, 2011; Stewart et al., 2006).

Problematic Drinking

Some distressed individuals tend to drink reactively as a way of coping with distress. However, the use of alcohol to cope with distress might be problematic (Cooper et al., 1988; Kassel, Bornovalova, & Mehta, 2006). For instance, among alcoholic inpatients, negative mood induced alcohol cravings predicted relapse after inpatient discharge (Cooney et al.,

1997). In addition, stressors were more highly predictive of drinking problems among African American and Caucasian drinkers who relied on avoidant forms of coping (Cooper, Russell, Skinner, Frone, & Mudar, 1992). Similarly, among African American adolescents, drinking for the purpose of coping was associated with alcohol misuse (Bradizza, Reifman, & Barnes, 1999). Furthermore, among undergraduate students, problematic drinking was shown to be a way of coping with negative mood (Kassel, Jackson, & Unrod, 2000). Finally, among college students, the tendency to behave rashly in face of strong negative emotions or negative urgency has been associated with increased problematic drinking, possibly for the purpose of coping with negative emotions (Coskunpinar, Dir, & Cyders, in press). In sum, these findings indicate that distress coping through alcohol use might drive problematic levels of drinking.

There are multiple mechanisms that might underlie the association between distress coping through alcohol use. For instance, individuals might find that alcohol is effective in alleviating distress and might develop problematic drinking through a negative reinforcement pathway. The relief of distress associated with alcohol use might encourage increased alcohol use, which might consequently lead to an increase in problematic levels of drinking over time (Grant, Stewart, O'Connor, Blackwell, & Conrod, 2007; Kushner, Abrams, & Borchardt, 2000; Schuckit, Smith, & Chacko, 2006; Stewart, Peterson, & Pihl, 1995; Weiner, Pentz, Turner, & Dwyer, 2001). Similarly, some individuals might have high expectations about the effectiveness of alcohol for reducing distress (Cooper et al., 1992; Kassel et al., 2000). Due to these high expectations, these individuals might be more likely to consistently use alcohol for the purpose of coping and to consequently develop problematic levels of drinking over time. Finally, distressing emotions might impair decision making processes by making some individuals more likely to focus on their immediate emotional needs without regards for long-term consequences (Cyders & Smith, 2008; Cyders et al., 2007; Cyders & Coskunpinar, 2010). The increased focus on emotional needs might drive risky alcohol use behaviors for the purpose of coping and might lead to alcohol-related problems (Cooper, Frone, Russell, & Mudar, 1995; Cyders, Flory, Rainer, & Smith, 2009; Fischer, Anderson, & Smith, 2004; Smith et al., 2007).

Problematic Eating

Some individuals might consume more food when they are distressed (Mayer, Waller, & Walters, 1998; Polivy & Herman 1993) as a way of coping (Mayhew & Edelman, 1989; Troop, Holbrey, Trowler, & Treasure, 1994). However, eating to cope can be considered maladaptive when it leads to problematic eating behaviors. For instance, individuals who engage in problematic eating behaviors often report doing so in response to psychological stress (Crowther, Snaftner, Bonifazi, & Shepherd, 2001; Freeman & Gil, 2004) and for the purpose of alleviating negative affect (Deaver, Miltenberger, Smyth, & Crosby, 2003; Heatherton & Baumeister 1991). Moreover, negative mood induced problematic eating behaviors have been suggested to decrease anxiety among individuals with binge eating disorders (Agras & Telch, 1998). In addition, among undergraduate students, urgency was associated with increased problematic eating behaviors, possibly for the purpose of coping with strong negative emotions (Fischer & Smith, 2008). Similarly, difficulties coping with or regulating negative emotions were associated with problematic eating among undergraduate college students (Whiteside et al., 2007). Finally, among individuals with eating and anxiety disorders, negative emotion driven eating tendencies were associated with problematic eating (Arnow, Kenardy, & Agras, 1994). These findings indicate that distress coping through food consumption might drive problematic levels of eating.

There are also multiple mechanisms that might explain the relationship between eating to cope and problematic eating behaviors. For instance, eating to cope might lead to the development and maintenance of problematic eating behaviors through a negative reinforcement pathway. In particular, some individuals might continue to eat to cope because they have found eating to be an effective way of reducing emotional distress (Agras & Telch, 1998). Due to this increased reliance on eating to cope, these individuals might develop problematic patterns of eating (Hohlstein, Smith, & Atlas, 1998). Similarly, some individuals might have positive expectations about the effectiveness of food consumption for reducing emotional distress (Hohlstein et al., 1998). Indeed, high expectations that eating helps manage negative affect have been shown to characterize individuals with disordered eating behaviors (Hayaki, 2009). These high expectations might reinforce increased eating and might lead to the development of problematic patterns of eating. Finally, the experience of negative emotions might impair decision making processes by making some individuals more likely to focus on their immediate emotional needs without considering long-term consequences (Fischer et al., 2012). Consequently, increased focus on emotional needs might lead to problematic patterns of eating for the purpose of coping (Fischer & Smith, 2008; Fischer et al., 2004).

Drinking and Eating to Cope As a Common Risk Factor

Comorbidity

In sum, prior studies indicated that this tendency to cope through food or alcohol consumption has been linked with problematic drinking and eating in separate literatures, suggesting that this tendency can be an important common risk factor (Cyders & Smith, 2008). Indeed, recent investigations supported that distress coping through food or alcohol consumption might contribute to the comorbidity of alcohol problems and eating disorders (Benjamin & Wulfert, 2005; Fischer et al., 2012). For instance, negative emotions and negative urgency have been found to be highly elevated among girls who engage in binge eating and drinking (Fischer et al., 2012). Furthermore, individuals who experience both higher levels of negative affect and negative urgency are at risk for comorbid eating and alcohol use problems (Fischer, Smith, Annus, & Hendricks, 2007; Rush, Becker, & Curry, 2009). Finally, negative affect and negative urgency might be common dispositional features among individuals who engage in binge eating and drinking (Dir, Karyadi, & Cyders, *under review;* Ferriter & Ray, 2011).

Other conceptualizations of the tendency to cope through food or alcohol consumption have also been linked with comorbid problematic eating and drinking (Lesieur & Blume, 1993). For instance, in a large sample of men and women, both binge eating and drinking were driven by stressful experiences and might reflect a way of coping with stressful experiences (Laitinen, Ek, & Sovio, 2002). Furthermore, heavy drinking and binge eating might be equally likely to occur during relief situations involving unpleasant emotions and emotional discomfort (Birch et al., 2007). In addition, emotional instability was shown to be strongest simultaneous predictor of both binge eating and heavy drinking behaviors

(Benjamin & Wulfert, 2005). Finally, avoidance coping was more highly endorsed among individuals who engage in problematic eating or drinking as compared to individuals who do not (Ferriter & Ray 2011). Taken together, various conceptualizations of this tendency to cope through food or alcohol consumption have been simultaneously associated with both problematic drinking and eating behaviors.

Mechanisms

Multiple mechanisms might explain the relationship between distress coping through ingestion behaviors and comorbid eating and drinking problems. For instance, distress coping might contribute to the development of comorbid eating and drinking problems through negative reinforcement pathways. In particular, the effectiveness of food in providing emotional relief (Agras & Telch, 1998) might result in increased reliance on consuming food to cope and might consequently result in problematic patterns of food consumption (Hohlstein et al., 1998). Similarly, the effectiveness of alcohol in reducing emotional distress might also encourage increased reliance on alcohol to cope, which might consequently lead to the development of problematic levels of drinking (Grant et al., 2007). Considering that some individuals are equally likely to use both alcohol and food for coping purposes (Birch et al., 2007), these individuals might be more likely to develop an increased reliance on both food and alcohol for coping purposes. This increased reliance might consequently lead to comorbid eating and drinking problems over time. However, the roles of these negative reinforcement pathways are unclear. Using a sample of high-risk individuals, future studies should further examine whether distress coping through ingestion behaviors might predict comorbid eating and drinking problems.

Furthermore, distress coping might contribute to comorbid eating and drinking problems through positive expectancies about the effects of food and alcohol on distress. Specifically, some individuals might have high expectations about the effectiveness of alcohol for reducing distress, and might be more likely to use alcohol whenever they are distressed and to consequently develop problematic levels of drinking (Cooper et al., 1995; Kassel et al., 2000). Similarly, some individuals might also have positive expectations about the effectiveness of food for reducing distress (Hohlstein et al., 1998), and might become more likely to consume food whenever distressed and to consequently develop problematic patterns of eating (Hayaki, 2009). It is possible that some individuals might utilize both alcohol and food for the purpose of coping (Birch et al., 2007), suggesting that they might have high expectations about the effectiveness of both food and alcohol for reducing emotional distress. Due to these expectations, these individuals might be more likely to consume both alcohol and food whenever they are distressed, and to consequently develop comorbid eating and drinking problems. Future studies should examine whether high expectations about the effects of food and alcohol consumption on distress might lead to a simultaneous increase in problematic eating and drinking.

Finally, distress coping might contribute to the development of comorbid eating and drinking problems through increased dysregulation in face of distress. Specifically, the experience of strong emotions might make some individuals more likely to focus on their immediate emotional need, particularly their need to alleviate negative emotions, without consideration of long-term consequences (Fischer et al., 2004; Smith et al., 2007). In turn, this need to alleviate distressing emotions might drive individuals to consume alcohol (Cyders et al., 2007; Smith et al., 2007) or to consume food (Fischer & Smith, 2008; Fischer et al., 2004). If food or alcohol is successful in reducing distress, these individuals might quickly associate distress reduction with these ingestion behaviors. Because these individuals tend to disregard long-term consequences of their behaviors in favor of immediate emotional relief, they might be more likely to develop problematic patterns of eating or drinking over time (Fischer et al., 2004; Fischer et al., 2012). Considering that some individuals are equally likely to use both food and alcohol to cope (Birch et al., 2007; Fischer et al., 2012), it is possible that the experience of distress and the consequent need to immediately alleviate distress might lead to comorbid eating and drinking problems. Future studies should examine whether such distress reactivity is a common factor among individuals with comorbid eating and drinking problems.

Conclusions

Both eating and drinking have been identified as ways of coping with distressing feelings (Ferriter & Ray, 2011; Stewart et al., 2006). However, this tendency to cope through eating or drinking might be problematic. In particular, the tendency to cope with distress through eating has been linked with higher problematic eating (Birch et al., 2007; Whiteside et al., 2007). Furthermore, the tendency to cope with distress through drinking has been linked to higher problematic drinking (Bradizza et al., 1999; Kassel et al., 2000). Finally, distress coping through food or alcohol consumption might also contribute to the comorbidity between problematic eating and drinking (Benjamin & Wulfert, 2005; Fischer et al., 2012). This relationship between distress coping and the problematic levels of consumption might be explained through (1) negative reinforcement pathways, (2) positive expectations about the effectiveness of food or alcohol in reducing distress, and (3) increased dysregulation in face of distressing emotions. Future studies should examine these mechanisms in order to elucidate effective treatment and prevention approaches for individuals with problematic eating and drinking behaviors. However, although eating and drinking to cope might explain the comorbidity between problematic eating and drinking, it should be noted that it is only one possible third factor. In order to further elucidate the mechanisms that might underlie comorbid problematic eating and drinking, future studies should examine other possible third factors, such as impulse control problems and dependence to non-alcoholic substances (Hudson et al., 2007).

A FINAL POTENTIAL PATHWAY:
A MODEL OF INTEGRATED MECHANISMS

Introduction

In sum, there are multiple mechanisms that might explain the comorbidity between problematic eating and drinking behaviors. First, alcohol use has been shown to increase food intake by disinhibiting eating behaviors. Alcohol might disinhibit eating behaviors by (1) suppressing dieting standards, (2) impairing one's ability to monitor eating behaviors, (3) reducing cognitive resources for controlling eating behaviors, and (4) directly fostering impulsive eating behaviors (Hoffman & Friese, 2008). Second, alcohol and eating behaviors might become paired through classical conditioning processes. Through these processes, food consumption and food related stimuli might elicit (1) an alcohol withdrawal state (see Wikler, 1973), (2) conditioned compensatory alcohol responses (see Siegler, 1983), and (3) increased alcohol incentivization (see Field et al., 2005)—all of which might increase alcohol cravings and consumption. Similarly, alcohol consumption and alcohol-related stimuli might elicit (1) conditioned compensatory food responses (see Powley, 1977), (2) a food withdrawal state (see Poulos et al., 1981), and (3) food incentivization (see Stewart et al., 1984)—all of which might increase food cravings and consumption. Finally, the tendency to cope with distress through food and alcohol consumption might be a common risk factor that connects both problematic eating and drinking (Benjamin & Wulfert, 2003; Fischer et al., 2012). Although these mechanisms suggest multiple differing pathways, there might also be interactions among these mechanisms that can influence comorbid eating and drinking problems.

Disinhibition and Coping

Individuals who drink to cope have been shown to have higher rates of drinking (Smith et al., 2007). Such high rates of drinking can strengthen the disinhibiting effects of alcohol on eating behaviors. For instance, higher rates of alcohol consumption among these individuals can increase the likelihood that strongly represented dieting standards become obscured (Baumeister et al., 1994).

As a result, these individuals might become more likely to engage in increased food consumption due to the lack dieting standards. Furthermore, higher rates of consumption among these individuals can also increase the likelihood that they become impaired in the ability to monitor eating behaviors (Heatherton et al., 1991).

In turn, decreased monitoring of eating behaviors might increase unhealthy patterns of food consumption. In addition, higher alcohol consumption might increase the likelihood that these individuals have fewer cognitive resources for behavioral control (Quay, 1997). Consequently, due to the lack of behavioral control, these individuals might become less likely to control their eating behaviors and more likely to engage in excess eating behaviors. Finally, higher rates of alcohol consumption can directly facilitate increased impulsive eating behaviors by emphasizing immediate pleasures that can be gained from eating and by obscuring negative consequences associated with overeating (Fischer et al., 2012). No studies have examined whether individuals who drink to cope might be at increased risk for disinhibited eating due to their higher rates of drinking.

Future studies should examine these disinhibition processes among individuals who drink to cope. By doing so, future studies can further elucidate whether the prevention of these disinhibition processes can lead to a reduction in disinhibited eating among individuals who drink to cope. In turn, future studies can further clarify whether preventing disinhibition processes among these individuals might also reduce their risk for comorbid eating and drinking problems.

Disinhibition and Classical Conditioning

Alcohol's disinhibition of eating behaviors might foster classical conditioning processes, which might further maintain the eating-drinking association. Since alcohol consumption has been shown to disinhibit eating behaviors (Hoffman & Friese, 2008), alcohol consumption and alcohol-related stimuli might trigger food cravings and food consumption more easily. For instance, alcohol use and alcohol-related stimuli might come to (1) prepare the body for the effects of eating (see Powley, 1977), (2) elicit food-related withdrawal (see Poulos et al., 1981), and (3) increase the incentivization of food (see Stewart et al., 1984)—all of which might increase food cravings and food consumption. However, after food and alcohol consumption have been repeatedly paired, food consumption and food-related stimuli might also exert similar effects on alcohol cravings and alcohol consumption. Food consumption and food-related stimuli might come to (1) prepare the body for the effects of alcohol use (see Siegler, 1983), (2) elicit alcohol withdrawal symptoms (see Wikler, 1973), and (3) increase the incentivization of alcohol (see Field et al., 2005)—all of which might increase alcohol cravings and consumption. Future studies should examine whether alcohol's disinhibition of eating behaviors might lead to the development of classically conditioned learning, which can maintain comorbid problematic eating and drinking behaviors. In particular, future studies can elucidate whether reducing or preventing alcohol's disinhibition of eating behaviors might prevent classically conditioned learning. In turn, future studies can clarify whether such prevention of classically conditioned learning can reduce the risk for comorbid eating and drinking problems.

Coping and Classical Conditioning

Individuals who drink or eat to cope with distress have been shown to have higher rates of both problematic drinking and eating (Cyders et al., 2007; Fischer et al., 2009; Smith et al., 2007). In turn, higher rates of consumption among these individuals can facilitate learning processes (Settles et al., 2010), which might lead to the development of comorbid eating and drinking problems. For instance, because of higher rates of consumption, these individuals might be more likely to develop alcohol and food withdrawal following abstinence. In turn, food consumption might become more easily paired with alcohol withdrawal (see Wikler, 1973) and alcohol consumption might become more easily paired with food withdrawal (see Poulos et al., 1981). Furthermore, the high rates of consumption among these individuals indicate that they are more likely to experience pleasant effects from eating and drinking. In this way, food might become more easily paired with the pleasant effects of alcohol use (see Field et al., 2005) and alcohol might become more easily paired with the pleasant effects of eating (see Stewart et al., 1984). Finally, higher rates of food and alcohol consumption can foster the development of compensatory responses. As a result, food might come to trigger compensatory responses that prepare the body for alcohol (see Siegler, 1983) and alcohol might come to trigger compensatory responses that prepare the body for food (see Powley, 1977). All these processes can trigger increased food and alcohol cravings and consumption, but no studies have examined them. Future studies should examine these processes among individuals who drink or eat to cope.

In particular, future studies can elucidate whether teaching these individuals more adaptive coping methods can reduce their levels of problematic eating or drinking. Future studies can clarify whether such reduction in problematic consumption following the acquisition of more adaptive coping methods might prevent classically conditioned learning processes, and the consequent risk for developing comorbid eating and drinking problems.

CONCLUSION

Research to date has been limited, but does suggest certain mechanisms that could be explaining how eating and drinking are related, both at subclinical and clinical levels. However, this chapter suggests that the relationship between problematic eating and alcohol use is one that deserves more empirical attention. As such, future research should address these relationships more fully, testing not only each of the pathways we have proposed here, but other pathways or mechanisms that we have yet to identify. It is our hope that this chapter will increase the interest in the important relationship between problematic eating and alcohol use, and will stimulate future programs of research to better understand how these two behaviors are related. As we have mentioned throughout the chapter, the pathways and mechanisms that we have proposed and reviewed here are not mutually exclusive or exhaustive. It is our hope that research will spring from the ideas presented in this chapter to develop and empirically test an integrated model of the relationship between eating and drinking behaviors.

To date, certain areas in this field are more developed than others. For instance, research to support how distress coping similarly predicts eating and drinking behaviors is well developed. Comorbidity between eating disorders and alcohol use disorders is similarly well documented. However, although partial pathways are well studied (such as the effect of alcohol use on increased state-level impulsivity), most of the full mediational pathways (e.g. alcohol's disinhibition of food consumption through increases on state-level impulsivity) have yet to be empirically examined. It is our view that well-designed, controlled experimental paradigms to examine these in vivo (in the moment) relationship mechanisms between eating and drinking are necessary. Furthermore, it is our view that new and innovative technologies (e.g. eye-tracking technology to measure alcohol or food cue reactivity) play important roles in the advancement of this literature.

There is a high co-occurrence between not only eating disorders and alcohol use disorders, but also between eating and drinking behaviors in our everyday lives. As such, understanding how these behaviors operate might help individuals and researchers better understand how to intervene upon eating and drinking problems. For instance, obesity is a growing epidemic, especially in the United States. If increased food consumption is related to or caused in part by alcohol consumption, interventions for problematic eating that do not account for alcohol use are likely to be ineffective. On the other hand, if food consumption in part causes increased alcohol consumption due to classical conditioning mechanisms, understanding how eating cues can trigger alcohol consumption should be incorporated into alcohol use relapse prevention programs. The first step is better understanding these causal pathways and mechanisms. Only then can we design and implement treatments that will address an adequate number of mechanisms in order to prevent future problematic behavior.

Until we understand these relationships, our treatments are likely to not be fully sufficient. Given the high public impact of obesity and alcohol use problems, this is an area that deserves much more empirical attention than it is currently receiving.

The current review chapter does have some limitations that will be discussed here. First, the current review is not meant to be an exhaustive review of all potential pathways and mechanisms linking problematic eating and drinking behaviors. There are likely many more factors that we have not discussed, including genetic proclivity factors and other personality-based risk factors as third factor predictors. However, as we mentioned above, this is the first attempt to review the existing literature on the relationship between problematic eating and drinking, and to move the field forward to a cumulative science on this relationship. We urge researchers to find factors, mechanisms, and pathways that we have failed to develop. We also urge researchers to propose, study, and report these findings in order to add to the forward momentum of scientific theory and data in this area. Second, the current chapter did not distinguish between clinical and subclinical level of eating and drinking problems, although it is likely that such distinctions could be differentiated through different causal mechanisms. Third, the current chapter did not present new empirical research findings to test any of the above-proposed pathways and roles. As such, the chapter is thought to be a review aimed at speaking on the current state of the literature and not as a final assessment of the viability of these pathways. Bootstrapping these theories and findings in future work is necessary. Fourth, only human studies were reviewed here; thus, a review of animal studies that could inform the relationship between problematic eating and drinking is warranted in the future.

REFERENCES

Acton, G. S. (2003). Measurement of impulsivity in a hierarchical model of personality traits: Implications for substance use. *Substance Use and Misuse 38*, 67-83.

Agras, W. S., & Telch, C. F. (1998). The effects of caloric deprivation and negative affect on binge eating in obese binge-eating disordered women. *Behavior Therapy, 29*, 491-503.

Arnow, B., Kenardy, J., Agras. W. S. (1994). The emotional eating scale: The development of a measure to assess coping with negative affect by eating. *International Journal of Eating Disorders, 18*, 79-90.

Asp, D. R., (1977). Effects of alcoholics' expectation of a drink. *Journal of Studies on Alcohol and Drugs, 38*, 1790.

Baumeister, R. F., Heatherton, T. F., & Tice, D. M. (1994). *Losing control: How and why people fail at self-regulation.* San Diego, CA: Academic Press.

Benjamin, L., & Wulfert, E. (2005). Dispositional correlates of addictive behaviours in college women: Binge eating and heavy drinking. *Eating Behaviors, 6*, 197-209.

Birch, C. D., Stewart, S. H., & Brown, C. G. (2007). Exploring differential patterns of situational risk for binge eating and heavy drinking. *Addictive Behaviors, 32*, 433-448.

Bradizza, C. M., Reifman, A., Barnes, G. M. (1999). Social and coping reasons for drinking: Predicting alcohol misuse in adolescents. *Journal of Studies on Alcohol and Drugs, 60*, 491-499.

Braun, D. L., Sunday, S. R., & Halmi, K. A. (1994). Psychiatric comorbidity in patients with eating disorders. *Psychological Medicine, 24,* 859-867.

Bruce, K. R., Steiger, H., Israel, M., Kin, N. M. K. N. Y., Hakin, J., Schwartz, D., Richardson, J., & Mansour, S. A. (2011). Effects of acute alcohol intoxication on eating-related urges among women with bulimia nervosa. *International Journal of Eating Disorders, 44,* 333-339.

Burton, S. M., & Tiffany, S. T. (1997). The effect of alcohol consumption on craving to smoke. *Addiction, 92,* 15-26.

Carver, C. S. & Scheier, M. F. (1981). *Attention and self-regulation: A control theory approach to human behavior.* New York: Springer-Verlag.

Castellanos, E. H., Charboneau, E., Dietrich, M. S., Park, S., Bradley, B. P., Mogg, K., & Cowan, R. L. (2009). Obese adults have visual attentional bias for food images: Evidence for altered reward system function. *International Journal of Obesity, 33,* 1063-1073.

Caton, S. J., Ball, M., Ahern, A., & Hetherington, M. M. (2004). Dose-dependent effects of alcohol on appetite and food intake. *Physiology and Behavior, 81,* 51-58.

Childress, A. R., Ehrman, R., Rohsenow, D. J., Robbins, S. J., & O'Brien, C. (1992). Classically conditioned factors in drug dependence. In J. Lowinson, P. Ruiz, R. Millman, & J. Langrod (Eds.), *Substance abuse: A comprehensive textbook* (56-69). Baltimore: Williams and Wilkins.

Cooney, N. L., Litt, M. D., Morse, P. A., Bauer, L. O., & Gaupp, L. (1997). Alcohol cue reactivity, negative-mood reactivity, and relapse in treated alcoholic men. *Journal of Abnormal Psychology, 106,* 243-250.

Cooper, M. L. (1994). Motivations for alcohol use among adolescents: Development and validation of a four-factor model. *Psychological Assessment, 62,* 117-128.

Cooper, M. L., Frone, M. R., Russell, M., & Mudar, P. (1995). Drinking to regulate positive and negative emotions: A motivational model of alcohol use. *Journal of Personality and Social Psychology, 69,* 990-1005.

Cooper, M. L., Russell, M., & George, W. H. (1988). Coping, expectancies, and alcohol abuse: A test of social learning formulations. *Journal of Abnormal Psychology, 97,* 218-230.

Cooper, M. L., Russell, M., Skinner, J. B., Frone, M. R., & Mudar, P. (1992). Stress and alcohol use: Moderating effects of gender, coping, and alcohol expectancies. *Journal of Abnormal Psychology, 10,* 139-152.

Coskunpinar, A., Dir, A., & Cyders, M. A. (in press). Multidimensionality in impulsivity and alcohol use: From small to robust effect sizes. *Addiction.*

Cox, W. M., Hogan, L. M., Kristian, M. R., & Race, J. H. (2002). Alcohol attentional bias as a predictor of alcohol abusers' treatment outcome. *Drug and Alcohol Dependence, 68,* 237-243.

Crowther, J. H., Shaftner, J., Bonifazi, D. Z., & Shepherd, K. L. (2001). The role of daily hassles in binge eating. *International Journal of Eating Disorders, 29,* 449-454.

Crystal, S. R., & Teff, K. L. (2006). Tasting fat: Cephalic phase hormonal responses and food intake in restrained and unrestrained eaters. *Physiology and Behavior, 89,* 213-220.

Cyders, M. A., & Coskunpinar, A. (2010). Is urgency emotionality? Separating urgent behaviors from effects of emotional experiences. *Personality and Individual Differences, 48,* 839-844.

Cyders, M. A., & Coskunpinar, A. (2011). Measurement of constructs using self-report and behavioral lab tasks: Is there overlap in nomothetic span and construct representation for impulsivity? *Clinical Psychology Review, 31*, 965-982.

Cyders, M. A., & Smith, G. T. (2008). Emotion-based dispositions to rash action: Positive and negative urgency. *Psychological Bulletin, 134*, 807-828.

Cyders, M. A., Flory, K., Rainer, S., & Smith, G. T. (2009). The role of personality dispositions to risky behavior in predicting first-year college drinking. *Addiction, 104*, 193-202.

Cyders, M. A., Smith, G. T., Spillane, N. S., Fischer, S., Annus, A. M., & Peterson, C. (2007). Integration of impulsivity and positive mood to predict risky behavior: Development and validation of a measure of positive urgency. *Psychological Assessment, 19*, 107-118.

Dansky, B. S., Brewerton, T. D., Kilpatrick, D. G., O'Neil, P. M., Resnick, H. S., Best, C. L., & Saunders, B. E. (1998). The nature and prevalence of binge eating disorder in a national sample of women. In T. A. Widiger, A. J. Frances, H. A. Pincus, R. Ross, M. B. First, W. F. Davis, & M. Kline (Eds.), DSM-IV sourcebook (pp. 515–531). Washington: APA Press.

Deaver, C. M., Miltenberger, R. G., Smyth, J., Meidinger, A., & Crosby, R. (2003). An evaluation of affect and binge eating. *Behavior Modification, 27*, 578-599.

Dick, D.M., Smith, G.T., Olausson, P., Mitchell, S.H., Leeman, R.F., O'Malley, S.S., & Sher, K. (2010). Understanding the construct of impulsivity and its relationship to alcohol use disorders. *Addictive Biology, 15*, 217-226.

Dir, A. L., Karyadi, K. A., & Cyders, M. A. (under review). The uniqueness of negative urgency as a common risk factor for self-harm behaviors, alcohol consumption, and eating problems.

Drobes, D. J., & Tiffany, S. T. (1997). Induction of smoking urge through imaginal and in vivo procedures: physiological and self-report manifestations. *Journal of Abnormal Psychology, 106*, 15–25.

Drummond, D.C., Tiffany, S.T., Glautier, S. & Remington, B. (1995). *Addictive behaviour. Cue exposure theory and practice.* West Sussex: Wiley Series in Clinical Psychology.

Easdon, C. M., & Vogal-Sprott, M. (2000). Alcohol and behavior control: Impaired response inhibition and flexibility in social drinkers. *Experimental and Clinical Psychopharmacology, 8*, 387-394.

Edwards, G. (1990). Withdrawal symptoms and alcohol dependence: Fruitful mysteries. *British Journal of Addictions, 85*, 447-461.

Feldman, M., & Richardson, C. T. (1986). Role of thought, sight, smell, and taste of food in the cephalic phase of gastric acid secretion in humans. *Gastroenterology, 90*, 428-433.

Ferriter, C., & Ray, L. A. (2011). Binge eating and binge drinking: An integrative review. *Eating Behaviors, 12*, 99-107.

Field, M., Mogg, K., & Bradley, B. P. (2005). Craving and cognitive biases for alcohol cues in social drinkers. *Alcohol and Alcoholism, 6*, 504-510.

Field, M., Mogg, K., Zetteler, J., & Bradley, B. P. (2004). Attentional biases for alcohol cues in heavy and light social drinkers: The roles of initial orienting and maintained attention. *Psychopharmacology, 176*, 88-93.

Fillmore, M. T., & Vogel-Sprott, M. (1990). An alcohol model of impaired inhibitory control and its treatment in humans. *Experimental and Clinical Psychopharmacology, 7*, 49-55.

Fischer, S. F., Anderson, K. G., & Smith, G. T. (2004). Coping with distress by eating or drinking: Role of trait urgency and expectancies. *Psychology of Addictive Behaviors, 18,* 269-274.

Fischer, S., & Smith, G. T. (2008). Binge eating, problem drinking, and pathological gambling: Linking behavior to shared traits and social learning. *Personality and Individual Differences, 44,* 789-800.

Fischer, S., Settles, R., Collins, B., Gunn, R., & Smith, G. T. (2012). The role of negative urgency and expectancies in problem drinking and disordered eating: Testing a model of comorbidity in pathological and at-risk samples. *Psychology of Addictive Behaviors, 26,* 112-123.

Fischer, S., Smith, G. T., Annus, A., & Hendricks, M. (2007). The relationship of neuroticism and urgency to negative consequences of alcohol use in women with bulimic symptoms. *Personality and Individual Differences, 43,* 1199-1209.

Freeman, L. M., Y., & Gil, K M. (2004). Daily stress, coping, and dietary restraint in binge eating. *International Journal of Eating Disorders, 36,* 204-212.

Glautier, S.C., Drummond, C., & Remington, B. (1994). Alcohol as an unconditioned stimulus in human classical conditioning. *Psychopharmacology, 116,* 360-368.

Grant, V. V., Stewart, S. H., O'Connor, R. M., Blackwell, E., & Conrod, P. J. (2007). Psychometric evaluation of the five-factor Modified Drinking Motives Questionnaire—revised in undergraduates. *Addictive Behaviors, 32,* 2611-2632.

Guerrieri, R., Nederkoorn, C., & Jansen, A. (2007). The interaction between impulsivity and varied food environment: Its influence on food intake and overweight. *International Journal of Obesity, 32,* 708-714.

Hasin, D. S., Stinson, F. S., Ogburn, E., & Grant, B. F. (2007). Prevalence, correlates, disability, and comorbidity of the DSM-IV alcohol abuse and dependence in the United States. *Archives in General Psychiatry, 64,* 830-842.

Hayaki, J. (2009). Negative reinforcement eating expectancies, emotion dysregulation, and symptoms of bulimia nervosa. *International Journal of Eating Disorders, 42,* 552-556.

Heatherton, T. F., & Baumeister, R. F. (1991). Binge eating as escape from self-awareness. *Psychological Bulletin, 110,* 86-108.

Heatherton, T. F., Polivy, J., Herman, P., & Baumeister, R. F. (1991). Self-awareness, task failure, and disinhibition: How attentional focus affects eating. *Journal of Personality, 61,* 49-61.

Hepworth, R., Mogg, K., Brignell, C., & Bradley, B. P. (2010). Negative mood increases selective attention to food cues and subjective appetite. *Appetite, 54,* 134-142.

Hetherington, M. M., Cameron, F., Wallis, D. J., & Pirie, L. M. (2001). Stimulation of appetite by alcohol. *Physiology and Behavior, 74,* 283-289.

Hingson, R. W., Heeren, T., Winter, M., & Wechsler, H. (2005). Magnitude of alcohol-related mortality and morbidity among US college students ages 18-24: Changes from 1998 to 2001. *Annual Review of Public Health, 26,* 259-279.

Hingson, R. W., Zha, W., & Weitzman, E. R. (2009). Magnitude and trends in alcohol-related mortality and morbidity among U.S. college students ages 18-24, 1998-2005. *Journal of Studies on Alcohol and Drugs, 16,* 12-20.

Hoek, H. W., & van Hoeken, D. (2003). Review of the prevalence and incidence of eating disorders. *International Journal of Eating Disorders, 34,* 383-396.

Hoffmann, W., & Friese, M. (2008). Impulses got the better of me: Alcohol moderates the influence of implicit attitudes toward food cues on eating behavior. *Journal of Abnormal Psychology, 117*, 420-427.

Hohlstein, L. A., Smith, G. T., & Atlas, J. G. (1998). An application of the expectancy theory to eating disorders: Development and validation of measures of eating and dieting expectancies. *Psychological Assessment, 10*, 49-58.

Hudson, J. I., Hiripi, E., Pope, H. G., & Kessler, R. C. (2007). The prevalence and correlates of eating disorders in the National Comorbidity Survey replication. *Biological Psychiatry, 61*, 348-358.

Hull, J. G., & Bond, C. J. (1986). Social behavioral consequences of alcohol consumption and expectancy: A meta-analysis. *Psychological Bulletin, 99*, 374-360.

Jansen, A. (1990). *Binge eating. Notes and data.* (Dissertation). Retrieved from Datawyse(ISBN 90-5291-027-8).

Jansen, A. (1998). A learning model of binge eating: Cue reactivity and cue exposure. *BehaviorTherapy and Research, 36*, 257-272.

Jasinska, A. J., Yasuda, M., Burant, C. F., Gregor, N., Khatri, S., Sweet, M., & Falk, E. B. (2012). Impulsivity and inhibitory control deficits are associated with unhealthy eating in young adults. *Appetite, 59*, 738-747.

Johnsen, B. H., Laberg, J. C., Cox, W. M., Vaksdal, A., & Hugdahl, K. (1994). Alcoholic subjects' attentional bias in the processing of alcohol-related words. *Psychology of Addictive Behaviors, 8*, 111-115.

Jones, D. A., Cheshire, N., & Moorhouse, H. (1985). Anorexia nervosa, bulimia and alcoholism—association of eating disorder and alcohol. *Journal of Psychiatric Research, 19*, 377-380.

Kassel, J. D., Bornovalova, M., & Mehta, N. (2007). Generalized expectancies for negative mood regulation predict change in anxiety and depression among college students. *Behaviour Research and Therapy, 45*, 939-950.

Kassel, J. D., Jackson, S. I., & Unrod, M. (2000). Generalized expectancies for negative mood regulation and problem drinking among college students. *Journal of Studies on Alcohol and Drugs, 61*, 332-340.

Kennedy, S. H., Katz, R., Neitzert, C. S., Ralevsky, E., & Mendlowitz, S. (1995). Exposure with response prevention treatment of anorexia nervosa–bulimic subtype and bulimia nervosa. *Behaviour Research and Therapy, 33*, 685–689.

Knight, J. R., Wechsler, H., Kuo, M., Seibring, M., Weitzman, E. R., & Schuckit, M. A. (2002). Alcohol abuse and dependence among US college students. *Journal of Studies on Alcohol, 63*, 263-270.

Kushner, M. G., Abrams, K., & Borchardt, C. (2000). The relationship between anxiety disorders and alcohol use disorders: A review of major perspectives and findings. *Clinical Psychology Review, 20*, 149-171.

Laitinen, J., Ek, E., & Sovio, U. (2002). Stress-related eating and drinking behavior and body mass index and predictors of this behavior. *Preventive Medicine, 34*, 29-39.

Lapp, W. M., Collins, L., Zywiak, W. H., & Izzo, C. V. (1994). Psychopharmacological effects of alcohol on time perception: The extended balanced placebo design. *Journal of Studies on Alcohol, 55*, 96-112.

Lavik, N. J., Calusen, S. E., & Pedersen, W. (1991). Eating behavior, drug use, psychopathology and parental bonding in adolescents in Norway. *Acta Psychiatrica Scandinavica, 84*, 387-390.

Le, A. D., Quan, B., Juzytch, W., Fletcher, P. J., Joharchi, N., & Shaham, Y. (1998). Reinstatement of alcohol seeking by priming injections of alcohol and exposure to stress in rats. *Psychopharmacology, 135*, 169-174.

Lesieur, H. R., & Blume, S. B. (1993). Pathological gambling, eating disorders, and the psychoactive substance use disorders. *Journal of Addictive Diseases, 12*, 89-102.

Ludwig, A. M., Wikler, A. (1974). Craving and relapse to drink. *Quarterly Journal of Studies on Alcohol, 35*, 108-130.

Lundholm, J. K. (1989). Alcohol use among university females: Relationship to eating disordered behavior. *Addictive Behaviors, 14*, 181-185.

Marlatt, G. A., Demming, B., & Reid, J. B. (1973). Loss of control drinking in alcoholics: An experimental analogue. *Journal of Abnormal Psychology, 81*, 233-241.

Mayer, C., Waller, G., & Walters, A. (1998). Emotional states and bulimic psychopathology. In H. W. Hoek, J. L. Treasure, & M. A. Katzman (Eds.), *Neurobiological in the treatment of eating disorders* (pp. 271-289). Chichester: Wiley.

Mayhew, R., & Edelman, R. (1989). Self-esteem, irrational beliefs, and coping strategies in relation to eating problems in a nonclinical population. *Personality and Individual Differences, 10*, 581-584.

McCusker, C. G., & Brown, K. (1990). Alcohol-predictive cues enhance tolerance and precipitate "craving" for alcohol in social drinkers. *Journal of Studies on Alcoholism, 51*, 494-499.

Mizes, J. S. (1985). Bulimia: A review of its symptomatology and treatment. *Advances in Behaviour Research and Therapy, 7*, 91-142.

Mulder, R. T. (2002). Alcoholism and personality. *Australian and New Zealand Journal of Psychiatry, 36*, 44-52.

Mulvihill, L. E., Skilling, T. A., & Vogal-Sprott, M. (1997). Alcohol and the ability to inhibit behavior in men and women. *Journal of Studies on Alcohol and Drugs, 58*, 600-605.

Nederkoorn, C., Smulders, F. T. Y., & Jansen, A. (2000). Cephalic phase responses, craving and food intake in normal subjects. *Appetite, 35*, 45-55.

Nelson, T. O., McSpadden, M., Fromme, K., & Marlatt, G. A. (1986). Effects of alcohol intoxication on metamemory and on retrieval from long-term memory. *Journal of Experimental Psychology: General, 115*, 247-254.

Newlin, D. B. (1985). Human conditioned compensatory response to alcohol cues: Initial evidence. *Alcohol, 2*, 507-509.

Newlin, D. B. (1986). Conditioned compensatory response to alcohol placebo in humans. *Psychopharmacology, 88*, 247-251.

Peveler, R. C., & Fairburn, C. G. (1990). Measurement of neurotic symptoms by self-report questionnaire: SCL-90R. *Psychological Medicine, 20*, 873-879.

Polivy, J., & Herman, C. P. (1976a). The effects of alcohol on eating behavior: Disinhibition or Sedation? *Addictive Behaviors, 1*, 121-125.

Polivy, J., & Herman, C. P. (1976b). Effects of alcohol on eating behavior: Influence of mood and perceived intoxication. *Journal of Abnormal Psychology, 85*, 601-606.

Polivy, J., & Herman, C. P. (1993). Etiology of binge eating: Psychological mechanisms. In C. G. Fairburn & G. T. Wilson (Eds.), *Binge eating: Nature, assessment, and treatment* (pp. 173-205). New York: Guilford Press.

Poulos, C. W., Hinson, R., & Siegel, S. (1981). The role of Pavlovian processes in drug tolerance and dependence: Implications for treatment. *Addictive Behaviors, 6,* 205-211.

Powley, T. L. (1977). The ventromedial hypothalamic syndrome, satiety and cephalic phase hypothesis. *Psychological Review, 84,* 89-126.

Quay, H. C. (1997). Inhibition and attention deficit hyperactivity disorder. *Journal of Abnormal Child Psychology, 25,* 7-13.

Reed, S. C., Levin, F. R., & Evans, S. M. (2012). Alcohol increases impulsivity and abuse liability in heavy drinking women. *Experimental and Clinical Psychopharmacology, 20,* 454-465.

Reynolds, B., Richards, J. B., & de Wit, H. (2006). Acute-alcohol effects on the Experiential Discounting Task (EDT) and a question-based measure of delay discounting. *Pharmacology Biochemistry and Behavior, 83,* 194-202.

Ross, D. F., & Pihl, R. O. (1989). Modification of the balanced-placebo design for use at high blood alcohol levels. *Addictive Behaviors, 14,* 91-97.

Ruderman, A. J., & Grace, P. S. (1987). Restraint, bulimia, and psychopathology. *Addictive Behaviors, 12,* 249-255.

Ruderman, A. J., & Grace, P. S. (1988). Bulimics and restrained eaters: a personality comparison. *Addictive Behaviors, 13,* 359-368.

Rush, C. C., Becker, S. J., & Curry, J. F. (2009). Personality factors and styles among college students who binge eat and drink. *Psychology of Addictive Behaviors, 23,* 140-145.

Saults, J. S., Cowan, N., Sher, K. J., & Moreno, M. V. (2007). Differential effects of alcohol on working memory: Distinguishing multiple processes. *Experimental and Clinical Psychopharmacology, 15,* 576-587.

Schmidt, U., & Marks, I. (1989). Exposure plus prevention of bingeing vs. exposure plus prevention of vomiting in bulimia nervosa. *The Journal of Nervous and Mental Disease, 177,* 259–266.

Schuckit, M. A., Smith, T. L., & Chacko, Y. (2006). Evaluation of depression-related model of alcohol problems in 430 probands from the San Diego prospective study. *Drug and Alcohol Dependence, 82,* 194-203.

Settles, R. F., Cyders, M. A., & Smith, G. T. (2010). Longitudinal validation of the acquired preparedness model of drinking risk. *Psychology of Addictive Behaviors, 24,* 198-208.

Shafran, R., Lee, M., Cooper, Z., Palmer, R. L., & Fairburn, C. G. (2007). Attentional bias in eating disorders. *International Journal of Eating disorders, 40,* 369-380.

Sherwood, N. E., Crowther, J. H., Wills, L., & Ben-Porath, Y. S. (2000). The perceived function of eating for bulimic, subclinical bulimic, and non-eating disordered women. *Behavior Therapy, 31,* 777-793.

Siegel, S. (1983). Classical conditioning, drug tolerance and drug dependence. *Research Advances in Alcohol and Drug Problems, 7,* 207–246.

Sinha, R., & O'Malley, S. S. (2000). Alcohol and eating disorders: Implications for alcohol treatment and health services research. *Alcoholism: Clinical and Experimental Research, 24,* 1312-1319.

Smith, G. T., Fischer S., Cyders, M. A., Annus, A. M., Spillane, N. S., & McCarthy, D. M. (2007). On the validity and utility of discriminating among impulsivity-like traits. *Assessment, 14,* 155-170.

Staiger, P. K., & White, J. M. (1988). Conditioned alcohol-like and alcohol-opposite responses in humans. *Psychopharmacology, 95,* 87-91.

Steinhausen, H. C. (2009). Outcomes of eating disorders. *Child and Adolescent Psychiatric Clinics of North America, 18,* 225-242.

Stewart, J., de Wit, H., & Eikelboom, R. (1984). The role of unconditioned and conditioned drug effects in the self-administration of opiates and stimulants. *Psychological Review, 91,* 251–268.

Stewart, S. B., Brown, C. G., Devoulyte, K., Theakston, J., Larsen, S. E. (2006). Why do women with alcohol problems binge eat? Exploring connections between binge eating and heavy drinking in women receiving treatment for alcohol problems. *Journal of Health Psychology, 31,* 409-425.

Stewart, S. H., Peterson, J. B., & Pihl, R. O. (1995). Anxiety sensitivity and self-reported alcohol consumption rates in university women. *Journal of Anxiety Disorders, 9,* 283-292.

Suh, J. J., Ruffins, S., Robins, C. E., Albanese, M. J., & Khantzian, E. J. (2008). Self-medication hypothesis: Connecting affective experience and drug choice. *Psychoanalytic Psychology, 25,* 518-532.

Svaldi, J., Brand, M., & Tuschen-Caffier, B. (2010). Decision-making impairments in women with binge eating disorder. *Appetite, 54,* 84-92.

Taylor, A. V., Peveler, R. C., Hibbert, G. A., & Fairburn, C. G. (1993). Eating disorders among women receiving treatment for an alcohol problem. *International Journal of Eating Disorders, 14,* 147-151.

Tiffany, S. T. (1990). A cognitive model of drug urges and drug-use behavior: Role of automatic and non-automatic processes. *Psychological Review, 97,* 147-168.

Troop, N. A., Holbrey, A., Trowler, R., & Treasure, J. L. (1994). Ways of coping in women with eating disorders. *Journal of Nervous and Mental Disease, 182,* 535-540.

Ward, A. & Mann, T. (2000). Don't mind if I do: Disinhibited eating under cognitive load. *Journal of Personality and Social Psychology, 78,* 753-763.

Wardle, J. (1990). Conditioning processes and cue exposure in the modification of excessive eating. *Addictive Behaviors, 15,* 387–393

Weafer, J. & Fillmore, M. T. (2012). Comparison of alcohol impairment of behavioral and attentional inhibition. *Drug and Alcohol Dependence, 126,* 176-182.

Weiner, M. D. W., Pentz, M. A., Turner, G. E., & Dwyer, J. H. (2001). From early to late adolescence: Alcohol use and anger relationships. *Journal of Adolescent Health, 28,* 450-457.

Weingarten, H. (1983). Conditioned cues elicit feeding in sated rats: A role for learning in meal initiation. *Science, 220,* 431–432.

Whiteside, U., Chen, E., Neighbors, C., Hunter, D., Lo, T., & Larimer, M. (2007). Difficulties regulating emotions: Do binge eaters have fewer strategies to modulate and tolerate negative affect? *Eating Behaviors, 8,* 162-169.

Wikler, A. (1973). Conditioning of successive adaptive responses to the initial effects of drugs. *Conditioned Reflex, 8,* 193–210.

Wolfe, W. L., & Maisto, S. A. (2000). The relationship between eating disorders and substance use: Moving beyond co-prevalence research. *Clinical Psychology Review, 20,* 617-631.

Woods, S. C. (1991). The eating paradox: How we tolerate food. *Psychological Review, 4,* 488–505.

Yeomans, M. R., Caton, S., & Hetherington, M. M. (2003). Alcohol and food intake. *Current Opinion in Clinical Nutrition & Metabolic Care,* 6, 63.

In: Binge Eating and Binge Drinking
Editor: Simon B. Harris

ISBN: 978-1-62618-580-7
© 2013 Nova Science Publishers, Inc.

Chapter 4

BINGE DRINKING: A NEUROCOGNITIVE PROFILE

Eduardo López-Caneda[1], Nayara Mota[2], Teresa Velasquez[3] and Alberto Crego[3]

[1] Department of Clinical Psychology and Psychobiology,
University of Santiago de Compostela, Galicia, Spain
[2] Department of Fundamentals of Psychology,
Rio de Janeiro State University, Brazil
[3] Neuropsychophysiology Lab, Center for Research in Psychology,
School of Psychology, University of Minho, Braga, Portugal

ABSTRACT

Binge Drinking (BD) is a highlighted topic on current research, possibly due to its intrinsic integration of biological and social health concerning vulnerabilities. Especially prevalent during adolescence, a neurodevelopmental period marked by accentuated social relevance on decisions, BD has an underestimated financial, social and health cost. Described as the consumption of high quantity of alcohol in a short period of time, BD has shown to be related to differential brain activity and neuropsychological performance.

Thus, there is growing scientific evidence reporting a wide range of neurocognitive impairments in adolescents and young people with a BD pattern, involving especially cognitive processes such as attention, executive functions, and learning and memory. However, the potential mid and long-term effects of BD remain unclear, so further studies should be conducted to elucidate the evolution of this neurocognitive profile, as well as to provide a more precise estimation of its reflection on the social functionality of binge drinkers. Therefore, the aim of the proposed chapter is to provide an updated scientific comprehension of BD neurocognitive profile, complemented by a discussion of some aspects related to it. Firstly, a definition and description of the binge drinking phenomena will be conducted. Secondly, it will be presented a review about neurodevelopment on adolescence and youth, period in which BD episodes are more common, followed by the principal outcomes about BD observed in animal studies.

Then, a comprehension of neurostructural impact of BD, as well as a description of neurocognitive profile associated to BD will be offered, mentioning neurofunctional and neuropsychological consequences of this alcohol consumption pattern. Finally, future perspectives will be proposed, considering the evolution of BD neurocognitive profile and its related aspects.

1. THE BINGE DRINKING PATTERN

Through the last decades, a specific pattern of intensive alcohol consumption became increasingly popular in the majority of western countries, with a high prevalence especially among young people and adolescents [1-3]. This pattern has been defined as "Binge Drinking" (BD) and it is characterized by the intake of large amounts of alcohol in a short period of time, which tends to lead to alcoholic intoxication, with periods of abstinence between these intensive alcohol consumption episodes [for a review, see 4, 5].

This pattern has been associated with alcohol consumption at weekends, preference for alcoholic drinks with a higher amount of alcohol, peaks of prevalence among adolescents and college students, equalization of consumption between gender and also with low risk perception concerning alcohol use.

The establishment of a precise definition of binge drinking (frequency and amount, regularity, etc.) and its prevalence in population is important since this type of consumption has social and sanitary consequences that can be as serious (if not worse) as the costs resultant from regular alcohol consumption [6-9], including the possible development of alcohol abuse/dependence'[10-12].

1.1. Conceptual Definition

Generally, the term Binge Drinking has two distinct meanings. One refers to a pattern of intensive consumption of alcohol in a large period of time (at least two days in a row) that interferes significantly with the person's life, and is associated with clinical definitions of alcohol abuse or dependence [13, 14]. The other one, which is also called *heavy drinking* [15-17] or *heavy episodic drinking* [18, 19], refers to the intake of large amounts of alcohol in a single occasion, in a short period of time, which leads to intoxication or drunkenness. In this chapter we will refer to this second definition.

Ham and Hope [20] have noted that an adequate definition of BD pattern should integrate distinct variables, such as quantity, speed and frequency of consumption. They have also pointed out negative outcomes associated with alcohol consumption (such as academic failure, sexual assault, fights, problems with authority and reckless driving). However, although the numerous definitions proposed until now have included these variables, it has not been always done in an integrated way.

In the seventies, the epidemiologic study of 'Monitoring the Future Study' [21] introduced the term Binge Drinking to describe a prevalent pattern of alcohol consumption in the population between 18 and 24 years old (especially under 21). This pattern was characterized by the intake of large quantities of alcohol in a short period of time, which frequently leads to intoxication.

In the nineties, based on an investigation of *Harvard School of Public Health College Alcohol Study* [22] which arose the importance of gender differences in alcohol consumption among college students, the concept of BD was operationalized as the intake of 5 or more alcoholic drinks in men and 4 or more alcoholic drinks in women (5+/4+) in a single occasion, at least once in the last two weeks. Wechsler's group established these criteria based on data collected in a survey about alcohol consumption habits, which indicated that men show significant problems related to alcohol consumption with 5 drinks per occasion, and women with 4 drinks [23].

Despite the extent of Wechsler's proposal, a great controversy concerning some of its aspects still remains. Some critics have been pointed out to some elements, such as a) the establishment of a quantity of alcoholic drinks that are too small to be classified as disruptive alcohol consumption, b) the absence of specification regarding the period of time that constitutes "a single occasion", and c) the lack of a universal operational definition of an alcoholic drink (in grams of alcohol).

Regarding the quantity, or the cut-off of alcoholic beverages consumed in a single occasion in order to define the BD pattern, some authors have proposed hat if what is intended is to relate BD pattern with activities that undertake more risk, or which have grimmer consequences – traffic incidents, aggression or sexual assault –, it would be advisable to increase the number of alcoholics drinks consumed in a single occasion of reference [24, 25]. However, although the rise in this number in the BD definition would certainly be useful to identify in a more accurate way the young who could fulfill the criteria for alcohol abuse and/or dependence according to Diagnostic and Statistical Manual of Mental Disorders – DSM-IV [26], it would not be accurate at all to the establishment of a breaking point of risk in general population [27]. For this, the criterion most employed and the one that gathers the most consent in the study of neurocognitive impairment of BD pattern in non-clinical population is still the one proposed by Wechsler and colleagues (5+/4+) [22, 28].

Respect to the speed of consumption and the controversy of the meaning of "a single occasion", several studies have highlighted the need to register blood alcohol concentration (BAC) levels, in order to determine with more accuracy the limit starting from which a BD pattern is established [14, 29, 30]. For this, the National Institute on Alcohol Abuse and Alcoholism (NIAAA) has redefined the term BD, taking in consideration the BAC: "Binge drinking means drinking so much within about 2 hours that blood alcohol concentration (BAC) levels reach 0.08g/dl. For women, this usually occurs after about 4 drinks, and for men, after about 5" [31].

With regard to the lack of a universal operational definition of alcoholic beverage, it is important to note that the quantity of alcohol grams in a regular alcoholic drink varies considerably between countries [32]. Considering these differences, the adaptation of the 5+/4+ criteria is required for the country in which the study takes place. For instance, even though in Portugal it could be employed the same cuttoff as in the USA (since a drink contains the same quantity of grams of alcohol in both countries), in the UK the pattern of BD is usually defined by the consumption of 8 or more drinks for men and 6 or more for women in a single occasion [33, 34].

Another relevant variable for a complete and precise definition of the BD pattern is the frequency with which the BD episodes take place [35]. As in the case of the quantity, also there is not a clear criteria concerning frequency and there is great variability between studies in the adoption of this criteria.

Even though the time frame mostly used to establish the presence of BD is two weeks, some studies have employed periods of 1 month, 3 months or 1 year. Results collected in these studies have demonstrated that, on the one hand, a too short timeframe (2 weeks) could underestimate the prevalence of BD pattern due to the variability that college students show in their frequency of consumption; on the other hand a too vast timeframe (3 months) could overestimate this prevalence. In this sense, a study with college students has demonstrated that, with a timeframe of two weeks, about 50% presented a BD pattern in alcohol consumption; however, if the timeframe was extended to 3 months, this percentage would raise up to 80% [36]. In line with these findings, a study conducted by Labrie et al. in 2007 [37] found that a third of the participants (college students) who had been classified as non-BD in the last 2 weeks of the month, were classified as BD in the first 2 weeks. Also, this group – named the 'inconsistent' group – presented a higher rank of negative consequences associated to alcohol consumption, similar to those classified as BD.

In the initial epidemiologic study conducted by Wechsler et al. [22], two distinct groups of BD were established according to the frequency of consumption: occasional BD (the subjects who consumed alcohol in an intensive way (5+/4+) 1 or 2 times in the last two weeks) and frequent BD (the ones who consumed the same quantities considered before, but 3 or more times in the last two weeks). However, this classification has been questioned, since the description of frequent BD could cover who fulfill the criteria for alcohol abuse and/or dependence according to DSM-IV [38].

Therefore, despite the inexistence of an universal criteria to characterize the BD pattern, the most extended and accepted approach is to consider the presence of at least one episode of intensive consumption in 2 weeks or 1 month.

Ultimately, when we intend to study the binge drinking pattern, it turns out to be necessary the inclusion of several aspects such as quantity, speed of consumption and frequency. The combination of these variables, as well as the adaptation of them to the country where the study takes place, is what makes to the establishment of an operative and equanimous definition of the term BD more difficult.

1.2. Epidemiology

According to epidemiological reports of national and international institutions, higher prevalence of BD is observed in adolescents and youths aged until 25 years, especially between college students, among which binge drinking prevalence rate reaches 40-50% [1-3, 13, 28, 39, 40]. From this age, it is observed a gradual reduction, what some authors have associated with increased responsibilities that come with this age [20].

In United States, although among young adults aged 18 to 22 the rate of binge drinking appears to be declining somewhat, it remains very high. In 2002, the binge drinking rate within this age group was 41% compared to 36.9% in 2011. Among full-time college students, the rate decreased from 44.4% to 39.1%. Among part-time college students and others not in college, the rate decreased from 38.9% to 35.4% percent during the same time period [3].

Results from the 2011 National Survey on Drug Use and Health have shown that 22.6% of people over age 12 have a BD pattern, defined as consumption of five or more alcoholic drinks on the same occasion (in two hours) at least once in the past month. These results vary significantly depending on age. Thus, rates of binge alcohol use in 2011 were 1.1% among 12 or 13 year olds, 5.7% among 14 or 15 year olds, 15% among 16 or 17 year olds, 31.2%

among persons aged 18 to 20, and peaked among those aged 21 to 25 at 45.4%. In older ages the percentage drops both progressively and significantly. Regarding gender, although recent reports have shown a trend to similar rates between genders, BD pattern still remains higher in men than in women. Thus, 17.5% of men between 12 and 20 years have this pattern, while only 14% of women in this age exhibit this habit of consumption [3].

Accordingly, the high prevalence of BD among adolescents and young people urges a thorough analysis of the consequences that may arise from this drinking pattern. In the following pages, we will address the neurocognitive implications that BD can have on a still-developing brain, as is the case of the adolescent brain.

2. ADOLESCENCE, BRAIN DEVELOPMENT AND VULNERABILITY TO ALCOHOL EFFECTS

Human adolescence is a period full of changes, characterized by a wide variety of behavioral, emotional, cognitive and psychosocial transitions from childhood to adulthood [41]. These transitions are subject to multiple maturational processes that can influence positively or negatively the life courses trajectories. Although the biggest proportion of brain development occurs before the age of five years [42, 43], human neuromaturation is far from finishing in childhood. On the contrary, neurodevelopment is an intricate process that extends throughout adolescence and into young adulthood [44, 45]. Thus, significant exposure to alcohol or other drugs during this period may adversely affect a wide range of neuromaturational process and, consequently, determine the subsequent behavioral, cognitive and/or affective development of individuals.

2.1. Main Maturational Events during Adolescence

Firstly through post-mortem studies [46-48] and later by means of magnetic resonance imaging (MRI) technique [49-51], it has been demonstrated that brain structure – specially the prefrontal cortex (PFC) – undergo considerable changes during adolescence. Among these changes, there are two major developmental processes that characterize the adolescent period. The first of these events is known as *myelination*. Myelin is an insulating layer that forms around axons.

The formation of this layer entails an increase in the action potentials conduction speed and, consequently, in the neural information transmission speed. Myelinated axons are commonly known as white matter. While myelination in sensory and motor brain regions occurs relatively early during development, the prefrontal cortex (PFC), as well as other high-order association cortices, continue to be myelinated during adolescence and young adulthood [52, 53]. Studies using MRI as well as diffusion tensor imaging (DTI), another non-invasive imaging technique more sensitive than conventional imaging to tissue microstructure measures [54], have showed that this myelination process follows a linear course, increasing throughout individual development, and that certain white matter connections, as the association fibers of the prefrontal cortex, show volume increased even after 30 years old [45, 50].

In addition to the changes that take place in the white matter, grey matter experience, in turn, profound modifications during the adolescent period and, as in the myelination process, these variations take place essentially in high-order association cortices, such as the PFC, the inferior temporal cortex and the posterior parietal cortex [51]. Nevertheless, while the increase in white matter seems to be linear, changes in grey matter volume show an inverted U-shape. Thus, a grey matter increment arises at the onset of puberty, which has been related with a wave of synaptic proliferation. Later, during adolescence, a gradual decrease in synaptic density and, therefore, in grey matter volume, takes place as result of *synaptic pruning*, i.e., the elimination of infrequently used connections. This synaptic reorganization has been linked to an improvement in neural networks functioning as well as to increased neuronal efficiency [55-57].

Given the relationship between cognitive development and brain maturation, synaptic pruning and myelination may directly influence developmental advances in maturation of cognitive processes such as attention, working memory or inhibitory control, which are partially supported by PFC and other high-order association cortices.

In this context of development of brain structure and functioning, alcohol consumption may have a severe negative impact on neuromaturation and, consequently, impair the normal functioning of cognitive processes that are essential for a correct adjustment to adult life.

2.2. Alcohol Effects in the Adolescent Brain: Evidence from Animal Studies

Given that alcohol use during adolescence may alter developmental processes ongoing in certain brain regions, it is not surprising that similar amounts of alcohol may entail different consequences in adolescents compared to adults. In the last decade, several animal studies have showed that, effectively, adolescence is a particularly sensitive period to the harmful effects of alcohol. Thus, it has been shown that adolescent rats exhibit substantially more alcohol-induced damage than similarly treated adults, especially in developmental regions such as the PFC [58]. Also parts of the limbic system, such as the hippocampus, an essential structure for memory, are markedly impaired in adolescent rats exposed to alcohol [59]. Accordingly, it has been observed that young rats are more likely to exhibit cognitive impairments in learning and memory tasks as a result of excessive alcohol consumption [60, 61], and that it may persist in the long-term [62-64]. Likewise, binge alcohol exposure markedly disrupted neurogenesis in hippocampus [65], to a greater extent in adolescents than in adult rats [66]. Finally, it has been demonstrated that BD episodes may be more harmful for the brain than an equivalent amount of alcohol without withdrawal episodes [67, 68].

Ultimately, taking into account that 1) adolescence is a period marked by profound changes in the brain necessary for the proper functioning of cognitive abilities such as working memory or inhibitory control [55, 69, 70]; 2) alcohol is the most widely used drug among adolescents and young people [71, 72]; 3) BD is the most common form of problematic drug consumption among these subjects [1-3]; 4) this intensive pattern of consumption turns out to be more harmful than the regular consumption of alcohol [73-75]; and 5) the adolescent brain appears to be more vulnerable to the effects of alcohol compared with the adult brain [58, 59]; considering, therefore, all these factors, persistence of a BD pattern during these years of transition to adulthood is of particular concern. Human studies that we will see in the next chapters have confirmed and justified these concerns.

3. Neuropsichological Profile of Binge Drinking

As a highly accepted and widespread social practice, binge drinking´s intellectual consequences among youth are commonly underestimated. Last decade literature has uncovered differences on neurocognitive functioning among healthy binge drinkers, not expected before. Next, it is presented a description of neuropsychological profile characteristic of binge drinking on youth.

3.1. Attention

Attention is a multifaceted process that represents the capacity to highlight relevant information from stimulus or situations [76]. It activates frontoparietal regions, as well as anterior cingulate cortex [77, 78]. In a neuropsychological approach, it can be expressed as focalized, selective, divided or sustained attention. Focalized attention is the ability to guide someone´s own activation to a pre-defined aspect or stimulus. Binge drinkers show less focalized attention, both to orally and to visually presented information (Digit and Corsi forward tasks), compared to abstainers [79]. Another type of attention studied among binge drinkers is sustained attention, that is, the capacity to maintain response to attributes or stimuli for a prolonged period. It is inferior among this young subpopulation, as assessed by Paced Auditory Serial Addition Test (PASAT) [80].

3.2. Processing Speed

Another neuropsychological index is processing speed, facilitated by a high integration (complexity and connection) of white matter [81]. Subjacent to many functions, it is characterized by the time duration of different neuropsychological processes, like attention, perception and visuoconstructive praxis.

Binge drinkers perform slower than abstainers or light drinkers on different tasks, such as planning, reading, and visual (color and abstract forms) discrimination and recognition [79, 80, 82-84].

3.3. Visuo-Spatial Perception

Perception is a wide and non-automatic process of identifying different elements, accessed by visual, auditory, tactile or interoceptive sense. It orchestrates the activation of different and specialized brain regions in occipital, parietal and temporal areas [85,86]. As our quotidian activities are highly dependent on visual information, the most studied dimension is visual perception.

This function seems to be preserved from the impact of binge drinking pattern. There are no differences on visual pattern or spatial localization recognition in function of binge drinking pattern [79, 80, 84].

3.4. Memory

Memory is a crucial neuropsychological function, which expresses the capacity to retain information and use it for adaptive purposes [87]. It comprises encoding, consolidation and evocation of information. According to Ryle´s (1949) model, it can be declarative, when information can be stated, or non-declarative (procedural), when information refers to skills, habits and dispositions [88]. Verbal episodic declarative memory can be assessed through word-list learning tasks or story recall. Hippocampus and surrounding regions play a fundamental rol in consolidation process [89, 90], especially in story recall tasks [91, 92].

Prefrontal regions are more implicated in the recall of non-structured information. Patients with frontal lesions do not show difficulties in contextualized, structured information recall, given they do not need to organize information. However, they do show difficulties in tasks like word-list learning tasks, in which the association of information must favor their performance [93, 94]. Binge drinkers perform lower than light drinkers in immediate and delayed story recall [95]. Except for a study with female college students, that identified inferior immediate recall score [84], other works have not confirmed immediate or delayed recall differences in word-list learning tasks among binge drinkers [80, 95].

Absence of differences in this task, mostly relying on executive processes, might inform about binge drinkers´ adoption of strategic alternatives of activation/processing (organizing information) in order to compensate possible retention limitations (observed on story recall). Also in visual declarative episodic memory, binge drinkers differences are not global. Binge drinkers perform less well than abstainers when recalling line drawings of common objects [80], but not when recalling visually presented scenes, compared to light drinkers [95]. This differential profile might be attributed to the second task easiness, with fewer elements to be memorized. Respect to non-declarative memory, BD do not present differences on procedimental learning performance, measured by Hanoi Tower [79, 84].

3.5. Executive Functions

Executive functions are the primordial function of prefrontal cortex and comprehend different processes of managing and organizing information in order to reach an objective, say it a behavior, language or reasoning [96].

3.5.1. Working Memory
Working memory is an ability highly used in everyday life. The most common example is when we have to hold on a telephone number that we will next use. It can be defined as the capacity to briefly retain and manipulate information, that can be verbal or visuo-spatial [97].

Binge drinkers are not affected in visuo-spatial working memory [84, 98, 99]. About verbal working memory, evidence is still not consolidated [84, 98].

3.5.2. Prospective Memory
Prospective memory refers to the action based on recall about expected future events/actions, more related to frontosubcortical circuits [100]. Although binge drinkers do not notice lapses on their prospective memory, they perform less well on time-based

prospective tasks (e. g., "Return a set of keys to the researcher when 7 min are remaining on the clock."), but no differences are observed on event-based prospective tasks (e.g., "When a cue word is encountered during the filler task, remember to return a book to the researcher.") [101]. Authors attribute this profile to differential implication of self-regulation in both kinds of tasks, suggesting more impact of binge drinking in the retrieval with higher degree of self-initiated control.

3.5.3. Categorization

Categorization is described as the ability to select different elements according to a specific criterion, like a phonetic cue (words that begin with the letter S). It has been associated to the activation of posterior regions of left frontal lobe [102, 103]. Phonetic fluency among binge drinkers is similar to light drinkers, without significant differences [98].

3.5.4. Concept Formation

The capacity to form a concept from a pattern of stimuli is commonly studied through rule learning tasks, like Wisconsin Card Sorting Test (WCST) or subtest Intra-Extra Dimensional Set Shift, from CANTAB. Its functioning has been related to dorsolateral prefrontal functioning [104] and seems not to suffer effect from binge drinking, due to similar scores presented by binge drinkers and light drinkers [98] or abstainers [80].

3.5.5. Cognitive Flexibility

Cognitive flexibility is a frontostriatal function [105] that can be described as the capacity to change a class of response according to changes in the situation. Binge drinkers present less cognitive flexibility in a complex task (perseverative errors in WCST-3) [98].

3.5.6. Planning

Planning is the capacity to previously organize multiple actions, in order to reach a specific objective, commonly associated to dorsolateral prefrontal activation [106]. Binge drinkers have no difficulties on planning accuracy [80, 98].

3.5.7. Self-Monitoring

Self-monitoring is the ability to supervise own response in order to guarantee a successful performance, related to medial frontal regions [107]. Perseveration, intromission and susceptibility to interference while performing a task might be a signal of difficulties on self-monitoring. Binge drinkers have showed these influences in a verbal learning task [79, 84, 95], in an inhibiton task (Stroop) [84], as well as in a self-ordering task [98].

3.5.8. Decision Making

Decision-making is the ability to select an advantageous choice out of different options, primordially attributed to ventromedial prefrontal activation [108]. Binge drinkers are less effective making decisions than abstainers. Those attend more to immediate positive consequences than to long-term consequences [109]. Among binge drinkers, intensive binge drinkers select less advantageous options than light binge drinkers [110]. Interestingly, less effective decision making has been associated to establishment or maintenance of binge drinking pattern one year later [111].

In conclusion, initial findings suggest that binge drinkers neuropsychological profile at late adolescence or early adulthood is marked by inferior: 1) focalized and sustained attention, as well as processing speed, respectively related to frontoparietal circuits and white matter integrity; 2) verbal and visual declarative episodic memory (with variations in function of task nature), associated mainly to medial temporal activation; 3) executive functioning that expresses self-regulation (cognitive flexibility, self-monitoring, time-based prospective memory) and engages medial frontal activation, but not the executive functions characterized by organization of information/objectives (planning, concept formation, categorization), associated to dorsolateral prefrontal activation; 4) decision making, dependent on ventromedial prefrontal regions.

4. BINGE DRINKING EFFECTS ON BRAIN STRUCTURE AND FUNCTIONING

4.1. Neurostructural Impact of Binge Drinking

Despite the multitude of studies along the last few decades indicating that adult alcoholic patients present serious changes at a neurostructural and neurofunctional level, the number of human studies on the impact of alcohol consumption on the adolescent brain is still relatively scarce. Most of the studies conducted with human samples have had adolescents and young adults with Alcohol Use Disorder (AUD) as participants; the studies that have used a non clinical sample – adolescents and young adults from general population who exhibit a BD pattern of alcohol consumption – are fewer and much more recent.

Studies with adolescents and young people with AUD using MRI technique are yet very scarce and inconclusive. Such studies seem to corroborate results from animal studies and have shown that these youngsters present significant reductions – up to 10% – of hippocampus volume [112], more characteristically in the left hemisphere [113, 114], and of the prefrontal cortex volume [115, 116]; brain regions which, as we have seen above, undergo a marked development in adolescence and early adulthood.

Regarding BD pattern of alcohol consumption, to our knowledge, there are few studies using neuroimaging techniques in the study of alterations in brain structure resulting from BD in adolescents and young people, and all of these correspond to Susan Tapert's group, from San Diego University (USA). Two of these studies have used DTI in order to evaluate the integrity of white matter, and the third one has used MRI to estimate the density of cortical grey matter.

The first two studies [117, 118] compared the integrity of white matter of a group of adolescents (from 16 to 19 years old) that showed a BD pattern with an age-matched control group. Results indicated that adolescents with a BD pattern showed less fractional anisotropy (index of structural complexity of myelinated axons) in several connection fibers, such as the superior and inferior longitudinal fasciculus, the fronto-occipital inferior fasciculus, or the pathways of limbic projection. Results from the first study [118] have also demonstrated a relationship between abstinence and withdrawal experiences and lower fractional anisotropy in the corpus callosum.

In the third, a very recent study conducted by Squeglia et al. in 2012 [119], MRI was used to compare cortical volume of a group of adolescents that showed a BD pattern of alcohol consumption with a control group also formed by adolescents. Besides the MRI, it has also been used a battery of neuropsychological evaluation tests, in order to estimate the executive functioning, attention and spatial planning ability, and also to estimate if the results in these trials were correlated to possible changes in the volume of the frontal cortex.

Results have only shown structural modifications in the frontal cortex density associated to the BD pattern when gender was considered. These modifications were selectively distinct for men and women: adolescent female binge drinkers showed larger cortical density in left frontal regions than demographically similar female non-drinkers, which was linked to worse visuospatial, inhibition, and attention performances. In contrast, adolescent binge drinking males showed lower cortical density in these areas than non-drinking males. Furthermore, thicker left frontal cortices correlated with poorer visuospatial planning, inhibition and attention performances in women and with worse attention in men with a BD pattern [119].

In summary, the few available structural neuroimaging studies definitely suggest that the BD pattern of alcohol consumption in adolescence is associated with structural differences in white matter (as indicated by the lower fractional anisotropy in fiber tracts that connect sensorial regions with the frontal lobe), as well as in grey matter (with changes in the frontal lobe structures, that correlate with cognitive deficits modulated by gender in attention and executive functioning tasks, such as planning and inhibition). Also, the involvement of grey matter seems to entail an inverse pattern between women and men, which would imply greater deficits in the former than in the latter. Nevertheless, more research is needed, especially longitudinal studies, in order to confirm these results and attain a precise knowledge of the neurostructural alterations associated to the BD pattern of alcohol consumption during adolescence and its possible implications.

4.2. Neurofunctional Changes in Adolescent Binge Drinkers

In addition to structural imaging studies, in the last years, functional magnetic resonance imaging (fMRI) technique has begun to be used to explore the effects of BD on the brain activity. Although scarce, these studies show that, even in absence of behavioral performance differences, intensive alcohol consumption has a significant impact on neural signaling in adolescents and young people.

The fMRI technique provides measures of brain activity by detecting changes in cerebral blood flow [120]. Through observation of changes in blood oxygen level-dependent (BOLD) signal, different estimations or inferences about neural activity can be made. As in the structural studies, major findings about the harmful effects of alcohol on young people and adolescents come from studies in subjects with AUD. In these studies, an abnormal pattern of brain activity has been recurrently observed in adolescents and young people with a history of alcohol abuse. Studies from Tapert and colleagues have shown that both adolescents (aged 14 to 17 years) and young people (aged 18 to 25 years) with AUD present differential neural activity compared to age-matched controls [121-123]. In particular, young women with alcohol dependence showed reduced BOLD response (i.e., reduced neural activity) during a spatial working memory task in parietal and frontal cortices [121]. Adolescents, meanwhile, had also decreased activity in certain regions of frontal and parietal cortices but it was accompanied by increased activation in posterior parietal, middle/inferior frontal and cerebellar cortices [122, 123]. According to the authors, these differences may be related to the greater cumulative lifetime of alcohol use in young people compared to adolescents. Initially, subtle neuronal disruptions can be compensated by reorganization (or additional neural recruitment) of some of the circuitries involving in task performance. However, if heavy drinking continues, the brain may not be able to compensate the damage and, consequently, it leads to reduced capacity in neural functioning.

Similar disruptions in neural activity appear to arise in the subclinical population of young binge drinkers. Thus, differences in brain activity during encoding of verbal items have been observed in bingers regard to controls [124, 125]. In particular, binge drinkers presented increased activation of frontoparietal systems along with hypoactivation of occipital cortex. The authors proposed that these findings were suggestive of the use by binge drinkers of alternative memory systems during verbal learning and also indicated greater "neural effort" performed by these subjects to resolve efficiently the task.

The other two studies that have used functional neuroimaging to explore BD effects in adolescents have also observed abnormal patterns of neural activity. Thus, adolescent binge drinkers showed enhanced activity in limbic brain regions while they performed an affective decision making task [126], as well as in frontal and anterior cingulate regions during a spatial working memory task [99].

Although the functional reason for these differences in brain activity is still unknown, the greater neural activity observed in binge drinkers compared to light or non-binge drinkers may reflect the employment of additional neural resources that would allow them to compensate emerging functional alterations in those regions involved in task performance. Likewise, the reduced activity of binge drinkers in some regions may suggest a limited capacity in neural functioning of these regions, which might no longer be able to counteract the harmful effects derived from this type of drinking.

Finally, these results appear to show that, in order to perform adequately on the task, a greater neural response and/or a greater neural recruitment from certain regions is used by binge drinkers to compensate the damage in these or in other regions.

4.3. Electrophysiological Correlates of Binge Drinking Pattern

In line with results from neuroimaging studies, anomalies in brain functioning in adolescents and young binge drinkers have been also observed by means of electrophysiological studies. Through this technique we can indirectly measure the neural (electrical) activity generated by the brain during resting states –electroencephalographic (EEG) recording- or during stimulus/events presentation – event-related potentials (ERP) recording.

Regarding ERPs, this technique has been commonly used in the study of brain functioning. Numerous studies have employed it to assess the neurofunctional effects of alcoholism, paying particular attention to the P3 component [for a review, see 127]. This positive wave, which peaks at around 300-600 ms after the stimulus onset and reaches its maximum amplitude at centroparietal sites, is elicited by visual or auditory "task-relevant" events and, although it can be related to different cognitive processes according to the task to perform, it has been functionally associated with attention and memory access [128]. In particular, while P3 latency is usually related to the time required to detect and evaluate a target stimulus/event (i.e., an index of classification speed), P3 amplitude has been linked to the amount of attentional resources involved in the processing of target stimuli/events, phenomena that appears to be related to memory processing [129].

Besides in chronic alcoholics, anomalies in latency and amplitude of this component have been also observed in binge drinkers. Adolescents with this pattern of consumption have showed delayed P3 latency in several studies [130-132], which has been interpreted as a slowed cerebral activity in these subjects. Similarly, differences between controls and binge drinkers in the P3 amplitude have been repeatedly observed in different paradigms such as emotional [130, 131], oddball [132, 133], working memory [134] or Go/NoGo tasks [135].

Although in some of these works lower P3 amplitude was observed in BDs than in non-BDs [130, 132], increased amplitude of this component in adolescents and young with a BD pattern was recorded in other studies [133, 135]. These discrepant findings probably reflect differences in the samples used (some of them with relevant factors such as family history of alcoholism or personal history of externalizing disorders), as well as differences in task demands resulting from the different paradigms used.

Special mention might be attributed to studies with the Go/NoGo paradigm given that it involves inhibitory control processes, a cognitive function widely related to addictive behaviors. In a recent study, a greater NoGo-P3 (a component that reflects inhibition-related activity [136, 137]) linked to a hyperactivation of right inferior frontal cortex (a region involved in inhibitory control process [138, 139]) was observed in young binge drinkers [135]. These results were interpreted as the activation of additional neural mechanisms needed to compensate emerging functional alterations in the regions engaged in inhibitory control, which would allow binge drinkers to perform efficient inhibitory control. In the same way, another recent study with heavy social drinkers showed a delayed NoGo-P3 component in these subjects compared to light drinkers, which was considered as an index of decreased neural processing speed related to inhibition [140]. All these anomalies might represent a neural antecedent of posterior difficulties in impulse control (and, therefore, in control of alcohol consumption) and might be considered as important vulnerability factors in developing alcohol misuse [135, 140]. Lastly, all the cerebral abnormalities observed in adolescents and young binge drinkers by both electrophysiological and blood flow measures appeared in the absence of behavioral impairments. In other words, they retained the ability to perform the tasks normally but responded abnormally at the neuronal level. This appears to be in contrast with the results observed in the neuropsychological tasks, where a poorer performance in several neurocognitive tests was showed in BD subjects. However, on the basis of the differences between both neurofunctional and neuropsychological studies, an explanation can be proposed. Probably, in the type of tasks used in neuroimaging and electrophysiological studies (in which a "ceiling effect" is common) less robust neural activation – as what is observed in BDs – may be enough to support the cognitive demands, leading to an absence of behavioral response differences. Neuropsychological paradigms, for their part, typically use more demanding tasks and, consequently, they are more sensitive to assess behavioral impairments. Together, it suggests that adolescents and young binge drinkers could have non-observable "latent" lesions which might be heralding future performance problems if BD continues and underlines the usefulness of neuroimaging as well as of electrophysiological studies to evaluate this kind of alterations that are still undetectable at the behavioral level.

5. FUTURE PERSPECTIVES

Although these findings are clarifying and highlight priority questions in youth health, diversified and replicated studies become necessary in order to reach consistence in the field. So, methodological differences might be overcome by the adoption of equivalent: criteria of BD and comparison drinking pattern (considering differences between countries on alcohol concentration and social habits), age range studied, and theoretically based tasks. Despite the initiative of some studies [80, 82, 83, 95, 98, 110], sex differences on neurocognitive impact of binge drinking are not sufficiently explored and might be more deeply investigated.

Likewise, it is still unclear whether these differences on neurocognitive functioning express a persistent profile or a malleable condition related to BD. Longitudinal studies are crucial for understanding the interaction between neurotoxic effects of BD and neurodevelopmental mechanisms.

As well as some questions have been answered, others have invariably emerged. What about emotional control? Analysis of the impact of BD on emotional processing and its regulation, controlling for premorbid emotional conditions, should clarify mechanisms engaged on BD maintenance and could enrich prevention polices. How is this neurocognitive profile expressed on social functioning? Ecological studies could relate laboratory performance to fulfillment of social demands, like college, work or home responsibilities.

Fortunately, BD phenomena is now better understood on its different dimensions, like epidemiologic, psychosocial, neurologic and neurocognitive domains. Nonetheless, what is unquestionable is the contribution of this field to the awakening about the complex and ongoing neurodevelopmental process during second and third decade of life, which demands more investment in youth health.

CONCLUSION

Alcohol is the most widely used drug among adolescents and young people. A singular form of alcohol consumption especially prevalent in this population is the binge drinking. This type of intensive and intermittent alcohol consumption turns out to be substantially detrimental to the adolescent brain, where cerebral and cognitive maturational processes are still ongoing.

The knowledge about the extent to which this form of alcohol consumption impacts on health of adolescents and young people is still an outstanding question. Even so, there is already a growing scientific evidence that shows that the BD pattern can have important consequences at neuropsychological, neurostructural and neurofunctional level in this population. However, the potential mid and long-term effects of BD remain unclear, so further studies should be conducted to elucidate the evolution of this neurocognitive profile, as well as to provide a more precise estimation of its reflection on the social functionality of binge drinkers. In that sense, although more research (especially of longitudinal type) is required to clarify the scope of the BD consequences, early prevention and treatment programs that attempt 1) to delay the onset of alcohol use, 2) to reduce BD habits in adolescents and young people, and 3) to help to identify any signs of BD-induced brain damage might be useful for a better and more efficient development of intervention strategies.

ACKNOWLEDGMENTS

The chapter has been partially supported by the FPU program (AP2008-03433) of the Spanish *Ministerio de Educación*.

REFERENCES

[1] Eurobarometer (2010). EU citizens' attitudes towards alcohol. Recovered from: http://www.ec.europa.eu/health/alcohol/docs /ebs_331_ en.pdf
[2] Hibell, B.; Guttormsson, U.; Ahlström, S.; Balakireva, O.; Bjarnason, T.; Kokkevi, A.; Kraus, L. (2009). The ESPAD report 2007. Alcohol and other drug use among students in 35 european countries. Stockholm: The Swedish concil for information on alcohol and other drugs (CAN) and the European Monitoring Centre for Drugs and Drug Addiction (EMCDDA).
[3] U.S. Departament of Health and Human Service (2012). Results from the 2011 National Survey on Drug Use and Health: National findings. Rockville, MD: Substance Abuse and Mental Health Services Administration (SAMHSA).
[4] Courtney, K. E.; Polich, J. (2009). Binge drinking in young adults: Data, definitions, and determinants. *Psychological Bulletin,* 135(1), 142-156.
[5] Parada, M.; Corral, M.; Caamano-Isorna, F.; Mota, N.; Crego, A.; Rodríguez Holguín, S.; Cadaveira, F. (2011). [Definition of adolescent binge drinking]. *Adicciones,* 23(1), 53-63.
[6] Bloomfield, K.; Stockwell, T.; Gmel, G.; Rehn, N. (2003). International comparisons of alcohol consumption. *Alcohol Research and Health,* 27(1), 95-109.
[7] Kuntsche, E.; Rehm, J.; Gmel, G. (2004). Characteristics of binge drinkers in Europe. *Social Science Medical,* 59(1), 113-127.
[8] Perkins, H. W. (2002). Surveying the damage: a review of research on consequences of alcohol misuse in college populations. *Journal of Studies on Alcohol,* Suppl(14), 91-100.
[9] Room, R.; Babor, T.; Rehm, J. (2005). Alcohol and public health. *Lancet,* 365(9458), 519-530.
[10] Grant, B. F.; Dawson, D. A.; Stinson, F. S.; Chou, S. P.; Dufour, M. C.; Pickering, R. P. (2004). The 12-month prevalence and trends in DSM-IV alcohol abuse and dependence: United States, 1991-1992 and 2001-2002. *Drug and Alcohol Dependence,* 74(3), 223-234.
[11] Grant, J. D.; Scherrer, J. F.; Lynskey, M. T.; Lyons, M. J.; Eisen, S. A.; Tsuang, M. T.; Bucholz, K. K. (2006). Adolescent alcohol use is a risk factor for adult alcohol and drug dependence: evidence from a twin design.. *Psychology Medical,* 36(1), 109-118.
[12] Jennison, K. M. (2004). The short-term effects and unintended long-term consequences of binge drinking in college: a 10-year follow-up study. *American Journal of Drug and Alcohol Abuse,* 30(3), 659-684.
[13] Gill, J. S. (2002). Reported levels of alcohol consumption and binge drinking within the UK undergraduate student population over the last 25 years. *Alcohol Alcohol,* 37(2), 109-120.

[14] Lange, J. E.; Clapp, J. D.; Turrisi, R.; Reavy, R.; Jaccard, J.; Johnson, M. B.; ... Larimer, M. (2002). College binge drinking: what is it? Who does it? *Alcoholism, Clinical and Experimental Research,* 26(5), 723-730.

[15] Christiansen, M.; Vik, P. W.; Jarchow, A. (2002). College student heavy drinking in social contexts versus alone. *Addictive Behaviors,* 27(3), 393-404.

[16] LaBrie, J. W.; Pedersen, E. R.; Tawalbeh, S. (2007). Classifying risky-drinking college students: another look at the two-week drinker-type categorization. *Journal of Studies on Alcoholand Drugs,* 68(1), 86-90.

[17] Sher, K. J.; Rutledge, P. C. (2007). Heavy drinking across the transition to college: predicting first-semester heavy drinking from precollege variables. *Addictive Behaviors,* 32(4), 819-835.

[18] Bendtsen, P.; Johansson, K.; Akerlind, I. (2006). Feasibility of an email-based electronic screening and brief intervention (e-SBI) to college students in Sweden. *Addictive Behaviour,* 31(5), 777-787.

[19] Caamaño-Isorna, F.; Corral, M.; Parada, M.; Cadaveira, F. (2008). Factors associated with risky consumption and heavy episodic drinking among Spanish university students. *Journal of Studies on Alcohol and Drugs,* 69, 308-312.

[20] Ham, L. S.; Hope, D. A. (2003). College students and problematic drinking: a review of the literature. *Clinical Psychology Review,* 23(5), 719-759.

[21] O´Malley, P. M.; Bachman, J. G.; Johnston, L. D. (1984). Period, age, and cohort effects on substance use among American youth 1976-1982. Michigan: Institute for Social Research.

[22] Wechsler, H.; Davenport, A.; Dowdall, G.; Moeykens, B.; Castillo, S. (1994). Health and behavioral consequences of binge drinking in college. A national survey of students at 140 campuses. *Journal of the American Medical Association,* 272(21), 1672-1677.

[23] Wechsler, H.; Dowdall, G. W.; Davenport, A.; Rimm, E. B. (1995). A gender-specific measure of binge drinking among college students. *American Journal of Public Health,* 85(7), 982-985.

[24] Jackson, K. M. (2008). Heavy episodic drinking: determining the predictive utility of five or more drinks. *Psychology of Addictive Behaviors,* 22(1), 68-77.

[25] Jackson, K. M.; Sher, K. J. (2008). Comparison of longitudinal phenotypes based on alternate heavy drinking cut scores: a systematic comparison of trajectory approaches III. *Psychology of Addictive Behaviors,* 22(2), 198-209.

[26] American Psychiatric Association (APA) (1994). Diagnostic and Statistical Manual of Mental Disorders, Fourth Edition (DSM-IV). Washington: American Psychiatric Association.

[27] Wechsler, H.; Nelson, T. F. (2006). Relationship between level of consumption and harms in assessing drink cut-points for alcohol research: Commentary on "Many college freshmen drink at levels far beyond the binge threshold". *Alcoholism, Clinical and Experimental Research,* 30(6), 922-927.

[28] Wechsler, H.; Lee, J. E.; Kuo, M.; Seibring, M.; Nelson, T. F.; Lee, H. (2002). Trends in college binge drinking during a period of increased prevention efforts. Findings from 4 Harvard School of Public Health College Alcohol Study surveys: 1993-2001. *Journal of American College Health,* 50(5), 203-217.

[29] Beirness, D. J.; Foss, R. D.; Vogel-Sprott, M. (2004). Drinking on campus: self-reports and breath tests. *Journal of Studies on Alcohol,* 65(5), 600-604.

[30] Naimi, T. S.; Brewer, R. D. (2005). "Binge" drinking and blood alcohol concentration. *Journal of Studies on Alcohol,* 66(3), 438-440.

[31] National Institute on Alcohol Abuse and Alcoholism (NIAAA) (2004). NIAAA council aapproves definition of Binge Drinking. Recovered from: http://pubs.niaaa.nih.gov/publications/Newsletter/winter2004 /Newsletter_Number3.pdf

[32] International Center for Alcohol Policies (ICAP) (2003). ICAP blue book. Practical guides for alcohol policy and prevention approaches. Recovered from: http://www.icap.org/LinkClick.aspx?fileticket=FZrP7 McTkLg%3d and tabid=161

[33] Herring, R.; Berridge, V.; Thom, B. (2008). Binge drinking: an exploration of a confused concept. *Journal of Epidemiology and Community Health,* 62(6), 476-479.

[34] McAlaney, J.; McMahon, J. (2006). Establishing rates of binge drinking in the UK: anomalies in the data. *Alcohol Alcohol,* 41(4), 355-357.

[35] National Institute on Alcohol Abuse and Alcoholism (NIAAA) (2002). A call to action: changing the culture of drinking at U.S. colleges. Recovered from: http://www.collegedrinkingprevention.gov/media /TaskForceReport.pdf

[36] Vik, P. W.; Tate, S. R.; Carrello, P. (2000). Detecting college binge drinkers using an extended time frame. *Addictive Behaviors,* 25(4), 607-612.

[37] LaBrie, J. W.; Pedersen, E. R.; Tawalbeh, S. (2007). Classifying risky-drinking college students: another look at the two-week drinker-type categorization. *Journal of Studies on Alcoholand Drugs,* 68(1), 86-90.

[38] Knight, J. R.; Wechsler, H.; Kuo, M.; Seibring, M.; Weitzman, E. R.; Schuckit, M. A. (2002). Alcohol abuse and dependence among U.S. college students. *Journal of Studies on Alcohol,* 63(3), 263-270.

[39] Core Alcohol and Drug Survey (CORE) (2009). The Core Alcohol and Drug Surveys. Recovered from: http://core.siu.edu/pdfs/report09.pdf

[40] Johnston, L. D.; O'Malley, P. M.; Bachman, J. G.; Schulenberg, J. E. (2012). Monitoring the Future National Results on Adolescent Drug Use: Overview of Key Findings, 2011. Ann Arbor: Institute for Social Research, University of Michigan.

[41] Spear, L. P. (2002). The adolescent brain and the college drinker: biological basis of propensity to use and misuse alcohol. *Journal of Studies on Alcohol,* Suppl, 71-81.

[42] Hermoye, L.; Saint-Martin, C.; Cosnard, G.; Lee, S. K.; Kim, J.; Nassogne, M. C.; Menten, R.; Clapuyt, P.; Donohue, P. K.; Hua, K.; Wakana, S.; Jiang, H.; van Zijl, P. C.; Mori, S. (2006). Pediatric diffusion tensor imaging: normal database and observation of the white matter maturation in early childhood. *Neuroimage,* 29, 493-504.

[43] Dubois, J.; Dehaene-Lambertz, G.; Perrin, M.; Mangin, J. F.; Cointepas, Y.; Duchesnay, E.; Le Bihan, D.; Hertz-Pannier, L. (2008). Asynchrony of the early maturation of white matter bundles in healthy infants: quantitative landmarks revealed noninvasively by diffusion tensor imaging. *Human Brain Mapping,* 29(1), 14-27.

[44] Faria, A. V.; Zhang, J.; Oishi, K.; Li, X.; Jiang, H.; Akhter, K.; Hermoye, L.; Lee, S. K.; Hoon, A.; Stashinko, E.; Miller, M. I.; van Zijl, P. C.; Mori, S. (2010). Atlas-based analysis of neurodevelopment from infancy to adulthood using diffusion tensor imaging and applications for automated abnormality detection. *Neuroimage,* 52(2), 415-428.

[45] Lebel, C.; Beaulieu, C. (2011). Longitudinal development of human brain wiring continues from childhood into adulthood. *The Journal of Neuroscience,* 31(30), 10937-10947.

[46] Yakovlev, P. A.; Lecours, I. R. (1967). The myelogenetic cycles of regional maturation of the brain. In A. Minkowski (Ed.), *Regional development of the brain in early life* (pp. 3–70). Oxford: Blackwell.

[47] Huttenlocher, P. R. (1979). Synaptic density in human frontal cortex - developmental changes and effects of aging. *Brain Research,* 163, 195-205.

[48] Huttenlocher, P. R.; De Courten, C.; Garey, L. J.; Van Der Loos, H. (1983). Synaptic development in human cerebral cortex. *International Journal of Neurology,* 16–17, 144–154.

[49] Giedd, J. N.; Snell, J. W.; Lange, N.; Rajapakse, J. C.; Casey, B. J.; Kozuch, P. L.; Vaituzis, A. C.; Vauss, Y. C.; Hamburger, S. D.; Kaysen, D.; Rapoport, J. L. (1996). Quantitative magnetic resonance imaging of human brain development: ages 4-18. *Cerebral Cortex,* 6(4), 551-560.

[50] Giedd, J. N.; Blumenthal, J.; Jeffries, N. O.; Castellanos, F. X.; Liu, H.; Zijdenbos, A.; Paus, T.; Evans, A. C.; Rapoport, J. L. (1999). Brain development during childhood and adolescence: a longitudinal MRI study. *Nature Neuroscience,* 2, 861-863.

[51] Gogtay, N.; Giedd, J. N.; Lusk, L.; Hayashi, K. M.; Greenstein, D.; Vaituzis, A. C.; Nugent, T. F.; Herman, D. H.; Clasen, L. S.; Toga, A. W.; Rapoport, J. L.; Thompson, P. M. (2004). Dynamic mapping of human cortical development during childhood through early adulthood. *Proceedings of the National Academy of Sciences of the United States of America,* 101(21), 8174-8179.

[52] Blakemore, S. J.; Choudhury, S. (2006). Development of the adolescent brain: implications for executive function and social cognition. *Journal of Child Psychology and Psychiatry,* 47(3-4), 296-312.

[53] Lebel, C.; Walker, L.; Leemans, A.; Phillips, L.; Beaulieu, C. (2008). Microstructural maturation of the human brain from childhood to adulthood. *Neuroimage,* 40(3), 1044-1055.

[54] Beaulieu, C. (2002). The basis of anisotropic water diffusion in the nervous system - a technical review. *NMR in Biomedicine,* 15(7-8), 435-455.

[55] Casey, B. J.; Giedd, J. N.; Thomas, K. M. (2000). Structural and functional brain development and its relation to cognitive development. *Biological Psychology,* 54, 241-257.

[56] Casey, B. J.; Tottenham, N.; Liston, C.; Durston, S. (2005). Imaging the developing brain: what have we learned about cognitive development? *Trends in Cognitive Sciences,* 9, 104-110.

[57] Hua, J. Y.; Smith, S. J. (2004). Neural activity and the dynamics of central nervous system development. *Nature Neuroscience,* 7, 327–332.

[58] Crews, F. T.; Braun, C. J.; Hoplight, B.; Switzer, R. C.; Knapp, D. J. (2000). Binge ethanol consumption causes differential brain damage in young adolescent rats compared with adult rats. *Alcoholism: Clinical and Experimental Research,* 24(11), 1712-1723.

[59] Silvers, J. M.; Tokunaga, S.; Mittleman, G.; Matthews, D. B. (2003). Chronic intermittent injections of high-dose ethanol during adolescence produce metabolic, hypnotic, and cognitive tolerance in rats. *Alcoholism: Clinical and Experimental Research*, 27(10), 1606-1612.

[60] Markwiese, B. J.; Acheson, S. K.; Levin, E. D.; Wilson, W. A.; Swartzwelder, H. S. (1998). Differential effects of ethanol on memory in adolescent and adult rats. *Alcoholism: Clinical and Experimental Research*, 22, 416-421.

[61] White, A. M.; Swartzwelder, H. S. (2005). Age-related effects of alcohol on memory and memory-related brain function in adolescents and adults. *Recent Developments in Alcoholism*, 17, 161-176.

[62] White, A. M.; Ghia, A. J.; Levin, E. D.; Swartzwelder, H. S. (2000). Binge pattern ethanol exposure in adolescent and adult rats: differential impact on subsequent responsiveness to ethanol. *Alcoholism: Clinical and Experimental Research*, 24, 1251-1256.

[63] Sircar, R.; Sircar, D. (2005). Adolescent rats exposed to repeated ethanol treatment show lingering behavioral impairments. *Alcoholism: Clinical and Experimental Research*, 29, 1402-1410.

[64] Coleman, L. G. Jr.; He, J.; Lee, J.; Styner, M.; Crews, F. T. (2011). Adolescent binge drinking alters adult brain neurotransmitter gene expression, behavior, brain regional volumes, and neurochemistry in mice. *Alcoholism: Clinical and Experimental Research*, 35, 671-688.

[65] Nixon, K.; Crews, F. T. (2002). Binge ethanol exposure decreases neurogenesis in adult rat hippocampus. *Journal of Neurochemistry*, 83(5), 1087-1093.

[66] Crews, F. T.; Mdzinarishvili, A.; Kim, D.; He, J.; Nixon, K. (2006). Neurogenesis in adolescent brain is potently inhibited by ethanol. *Neuroscience*, 137(2), 437-445.

[67] Becker, H. C. (1994). Positive relationship between the number of prior ethanol withdrawal episodes and the severity of subsequent withdrawal seizures. *Psychopharmacolgy* (Berl), 116(1), 26-32.

[68] Duka, T.; Gentry, J.; Malcolm, R.; Ripley, T. L.; Borlikova, G.; Stephens, D. N.; Veatch, L. M.; Becker, H. C.; Crews, F. T. (2004). Consequences of multiple withdrawals from alcohol. *Alcoholism: Clinical and Experimental Research*, 28(2), 233-246.

[69] Tamm, L.; Menon, V.; Reiss, A. L. (2002). Maturation of brain function associated with response inhibition. *Journal of the American Academy of Child and Adolescent Psychiatry*, 41(10), 1231-1238.

[70] Luna, B.; Sweeney, J.A. (2004). The emergence of collaborative brain function: FMRI studies of the development of response inhibition. *Annals of the New York Academy of Sciences*, 1021, 296-309.

[71] Anderson, P.; Baumberg, B. (2006). Alcohol in Europe. London: Institute of Alcohol Studies.

[72] Johnston, L. D.; O'Malley, P. M.; Bachman, J. G.; Schulenberg, J. E. (2009). The Monitoring the Future National Survey Results on Adolescent Drug Use: Overview of Key Findings. Bethesda, MD: National Institute on Drug Abuse.

[73] Hunt, W. A. (1993). Are binge drinkers more at risk of developing brain damage? *Alcohol*, 10, 559-561.

[74] Becker, H. C.; Hale, R. L. (1993). Repeated episodes of ethanol withdrawal potentiate the severity of subsequent withdrawal seizures: an animal model of alcohol withdrawal "kindling". *Alcoholism: Clinical and Experimental Research,* 17, 94-98.

[75] Becker, H. C. (1998). Kindling in alcohol withdrawal. *Alcohol Health and Research World,* 22, 25-33.

[76] Carrasco, M. (2011). Visual attention: The past 25 years. *Vision Research,* 51(13), 1484-1525.

[77] Corbetta, M.; Shulman, G. L. (2002). Control of Goal-Directed and Stimulus-Driven Attention in the Brain. *Nature Reviews Neuroscience,* 3, 201–216.

[78] Raz, A.; Buhle, J. (2006). Typologies of attentional networks. *Nature Reviews Neuroscience,* 7, 367–379.

[79] Sanhueza, C.; García-Moreno, L. M.; Expósito, J. (2011). Weekend alcoholism in youth and neurocognitive aging. *Psicothema,* 23(2), 209-214.

[80] Hartley, D. E.; Elsabagha, S.; File, S. E. (2004). Binge drinking and sex: effects on mood and cognitive function in healthy young volunteers. *Pharmacology, Biochemistry and Behavior,* 78, 611–619.

[81] Penke, L.; Maniega, S. M.; Murray, C.; Gow, A. J.; Hernández, M. C.V.; Clayden... Deary, I. J. (2010). A General Factor of Brain White Matter Integrity Predicts Information Processing Speed in Healthy Older People. *The Journal of Neuroscience,* 30(22), 7569 –7574.

[82] Scaife, J. C.; Duka, T. (2009). Behavioural measures of frontal lobe function in a population of young social drinkers with binge drinking pattern. *Pharmacology Biochemistry and Behavior,* 93, 354-62.

[83] Townshend, J. M.; Duka, T. (2005). Binge drinking, cognitive performance and mood in a population of young social drinkers. *Alcoholism: Clinical and Expermiental Research,* 29, 317-25.

[84] García-Moreno, L. M.; Expósito, J.; Sanhueza, C.; Gil, S. (2009). Rendimiento cognitivo y consumo de alcohol durante los fines de semana en mujeres adolescentes. *Revista Neuropsicología, Neuropsiquiatría y Neurociencias,* 9(1), 75-91.

[85] Kandel, E. R.; Wurtiz, R. H. (2000). Constructing the Visual Image. In: Kandel, E. R.; Schwartz, J. H.; Jessell, T. M. (Eds.). *Principles of Neural Science.* 4th Ed. New York: McGraw-Hill.

[86] Wurtiz, R. H.; Kandel, E. R. (2000). Perception of motion, depth, and form. In: Kandel, E. R.; Schwartz, J. H.; Jessell, T. M. (Eds.). *Principles of Neural Science.* 4th Ed. New York: McGraw-Hill.

[87] Fuster, J. M. (1995). Memory in the cerebral cortex: An empirical approach to neural networks in the human and nonhuman primate. Cambridge: *Mit Press.*

[88] Squire, L. R. (2009). Memory and Brain Systems: 1969-2009. *Journal of Neuroscience,* 29 (41), 12711-12716.

[89] Squire, L. R.; Zola, S. M. (1997). Amnesia, memory and brain systems. Philosophical Transactions of the Royal Society of London. Series B, *Biological Sciences,* 352(1362), 1663-1673.

[90] Tulving, E.; Markowitsch, H. J. (1998). Episodic and declarative memory: Role of the hippocampus. *Hippocampus,* 8(3), 198-204.

[91] Frisk, V.; Milner, B. (1990). The role of the left hippocampal region in the acquisition and retention of story content. *Neuropsychologia,* 28(4), 349-359.

[92] Vannest, J.; Szaflarski, J. P.; Privitera, M. D.; Schefft, B. K.; Holland, S. K. (2008). Medial temporal fMRI activation reflects memory lateralization and memory performance in patients with epilepsy. *Epilepsy and Behavior,* 12(3), 410-418.

[93] Alexander, M. P.; Stuss, D. T.; Fansabedian, N. (2003). California Verbal Learning Test: Performance by patients with focal frontal and non-frontal lesions. *Brain,* 126(6), 1493-1503.

[94] Baldo, J. V.; Shimamura, A. P. (2002). Frontal lobes and memory. In: A. D. Baddeley, M. D. Kopelman, B. A. Wilson (Eds.), The Handbook of Memory Disorders (2ª ed.). London: *Wiley and Sons.*

[95] Parada, M.; Corral, M.; Caamaño-Isorna, F.; Mota, N.; Crego, A.; Rodríguez Holguín, S.; Cadaveira, F. (2011). Binge Drinking and Declarative Memory in University Students. *Alcoholism: Clinical and Experimental Research,* 35(8), 1475-1484.

[96] Fuster, J. M. (2008). The prefrontal cortex. London: *Academic Press.*

[97] Baddeley, A. (2012). Working Memory: Theories, Models, and Controversies. *Annual Review of Psychology, 63,* 1–29.

[98] Parada, M.; Corral, M.; Mota, N.; Crego, A.; Rodríquez Holguín, S. R.; Cadaveira, F. (2012). Executive functioning and alcohol binge drinking in university students. *Addictive Behaviors,* 37, 167–172.

[99] Squeglia, L.M.; Schweinsburg, A. D.; Pulido, C.; Tapert, S. F. (2011). Adolescent Binge Drinking Linked to Abnormal Spatial Working Memory Brain Activation: Differential Gender Effects. *Alcoholism: Clinical and Experimental Research,* 35 (10), 1831–1841.

[100] Burgess, P. W.; Quayle, A.; Frith, C. D. (2001). Brain regions involved in prospective memory as determined by positron emission tomography. *Neuropsychologia,* 39, 545–55.

[101] Heffernan, T.; O´Neill, T. (2012). Time based prospective memory deficits associated with binge drinking: Evidence from the Cambridge Prospective Memory Test (CAMPROMPT). *Drug and Alcohol Dependence,* 123, 207–212.

[102] Birn, R. M.; Kenworthy, L.; Case, L.; Caravella, R.; Jones, T. B.; Bandettini, P. A.; Martin, A. (2010). Neural systems supporting lexical search guided by letter and semantic category cues: A self-paced overt response fMRI study of verbal fluency. *Neuroimage,* 49(1), 1099-1107.

[103] Sanjuán, A.; Bustamante, J. C.; Forn, C.; Ventura-Campos, N.; Barros-Loscertales, A.R.; Martínez, J. C.; Villanueva, V. (2010). Comparison of two fMRI tasks for the evaluation of the expressive language function. *Neuroradiology,* 52(5), 407-415.

[104] Strauss, E.; Sherman, E. M. S.; Spreen, O. (2006). A Compendium of Neuropsychological Tests: Administration, Norms, and Commentary (3a. ed.). New York: *Oxford University Press.*

[105] Kehagia, A. A.; Murray, G. K.; Robbins, T. W. (2010). Learning and cognitive flexibility: frontostriatal function and monoaminergic modulation. *Current Opinion in Neurobiology,* 20 (2), 199–204.

[106] Kaller, C. P.; Rahm, B.; Spreer, J.; Weiller, C.; Unterrainer, J. M. (2011). Dissociable contributions of left and right dorsolateral prefrontal cortex in planning. *Cerebral Cortex,* 21(2), 307-317.

[107] Ridderinkhof, K. R.; Ullsperger, M.; Crone, E. A.; Nieuwenhuis, S. (2004). The role of the Medial Frontal Cortex in Cognitive Control. *Science,* 306, 443–447.

[108] Damasio, A. R. (1998). Descartes' error: emotion, reason, and the human brain. New York: *Avon Books*.
[109] Johnson, C. A.; Xiao, L.; Palmer, P.; Sun, P.; Wang, Q.; Wei, Y., ... Bechara, A. (2008). Affective decision-making deficits, linked to a dysfunctional ventromedial prefrontal cortex, revealed in 10th grade Chinese adolescent binge drinkers. *Neuropsychologia,* 46(2), 714-726.
[110] Goudriaan, A. E.; Grekin, E. R.; Sher, K. J. (2007). Decision making and binge drinking: A longitudinal study. *Alcoholism, Clinical and Experimental Research,* 31(6), 928-938.
[111] Xiao, L.; Bechara, A.; Grenard, L. J.; Stacy, W. A.; Palmer, P.; Wei, Y.; ... Johnson, C. A. (2009). Affective decision-making predictive of Chinese adolescent drinking behaviors. *Journal of the international neuropsychological society,* 15(4), 547-557.
[112] De Bellis, M. D.; Clark, D. B.; Beers, S. R.; Soloff, P. H.; Boring, A. M.; Hall, J.; ... Keshavan, M. S. (2000). Hippocampal volume in adolescent-onset alcohol use disorders. *The American Journal on Psychiatry,* 157, 737-744.
[113] Nagel, B. J.; Schweinsburg, A. D.; Phan, V.; Tapert, S. F. (2005). Reduced hippocampal volume among adolescents with alcohol use disorders without psychiatric comorbidity. *Psychiatry Research,* 139(3), 181-190.
[114] Medina, K. L.; Schweinsburg, A. D.; Cohen-Zion, M.; Nagel, B. J.; Tapert, S. F. (2007). Effects of alcohol and combined marijuana and alcohol use during adolescence on hippocampal volume and asymmetry. *Neurotoxicology and Teratoogyl,* 29(1), 141-152.
[115] De Bellis, M. D.; Narasimhan, A.; Thatcher, D. L.; Keshavan, M. S.; Soloff, P.; Clark, D. B. (2005). Prefrontal cortex, thalamus, and cerebellar volumes in adolescents and young adults with adolescent-onset alcohol use disorders and comorbid mental disorders. *Alcoholism, Clinical and Experimental Research,* 29(9), 1590-1600.
[116] Medina, K. L.; McQueeny, T.; Nagel, B. J.; Hanson, K. L.; Schweinsburg, A. D.; Tapert, S. F. (2008). Prefrontal cortex volumes in adolescents with alcohol use disorders: unique gender effects. *Alcoholism, Clinical and Experimental Research,* 32(3), 386-394.
[117] Jacobus, J.; McQueeny, T.; Bava, S.; Schweinsburg, B. C.; Frank, L. R.; Yang, T. T.; Tapert, S. F. (2009). White matter integrity in adolescents with histories of marijuana use and binge drinking. *Neurotoxicology and Teratology,* 31(6), 349-355.
[118] McQueeny, T.; Schweinsburg, B. C.; Schweinsburg, A. D.; Jacobus, J.; Bava, S.; Frank, L. R.; Tapert, S. F. (2009). Altered white matter integrity in adolescent binge drinkers. *Alcoholism, Clinical and Experimental Research,* 33(7), 1278-1285.
[119] Squeglia, L. M.; Sorg, S. F.; Schweinsburg, A. D.; Wetherill, R. R.; Pulido, C.; Tapert, S. F. (2012). Binge drinking differentially affects adolescent male and female brain morphometry. *Psychopharmacology* (Berl), 220(3), 529-539.
[120] Logothetis, N. K. (2002). The neural basis of the blood-oxygen-level-dependent functional magnetic resonance imaging signal. Philosophical Transactions of the Royal Society B: *Biological Sciences,* 357(1424), 1003-1037.
[121] Tapert, S. F.; Brown, G. G.; Kindermann, S. S.; Cheung, E. H.; Frank, L. R.; Brown, S. A. (2001). fMRI measurement of brain dysfunction in alcohol-dependent young women. *Alcoholism: Clinical and Experimental Research,* 25(2), 236-245.

[122] Tapert, S. F.; Schweinsburg, A. D.; Barlett, V. C.; Brown, S.A.; Frank, L. R.; Brown, G. G.; Meloy, M. J. (2004). Blood oxygen level dependent response and spatial working memory in adolescents with alcohol use disorders. *Alcoholism: Clinical and Experimental Research*, 28(10), 1577-1586.

[123] Caldwell, L. C.; Schweinsburg, A. D.; Nagel, B. J.; Barlett, V. C.; Brown, S. A.; Tapert, S. F. (2005). Gender and adolescent alcohol use disorders on BOLD (blood oxygen level dependent) response to spatial working memory. *Alcohol Alcoholism*, 40(3), 194-200.

[124] Schweinsburg, A. D.; McQueeny, T.; Nagel, B. J.; Eyler, L. T.; Tapert, S. F. (2010). A preliminary study of functional magnetic resonance imaging response during verbal encoding among adolescent binge drinkers. *Alcohol*, 44(1), 111-117.

[125] Schweinsburg, A. D.; Schweinsburg, B. C.; Nagel, B. J.; Eyler, L. T.; Tapert, S. F. (2011). Neural correlates of verbal learning in adolescent alcohol and marijuana users. *Addiction*, 106(3), 564-573.

[126] Xiao, L.; Bechara, A.; Gong, Q.; Huang, X.; Li, X.; Xue, G.; Wong, S.; Lu, Z. L.; Palmer, P.; Wei, Y.; Jia, Y.; Johnson, C. A. (2012). Abnormal Affective Decision Making Revealed in Adolescent Binge Drinkers Using a Functional Magnetic Resonance Imaging Study. *Psychology of Addictive Behaviors*. [Epub ahead of print].

[127] Campanella, S.; Petit, G.; Maurage, P.; Kornreich, C.; Verbanck, P.; Noel, X. (2009). Chronic alcoholism: insights from neurophysiology. *Neurophysiologie Clinique/Clinical Neurophysiology*, 39(4-5), 191-207.

[128] Kok, A. (2001). On the utility of P3 amplitude as a measure of processing capacity. *Psychophysiology*, 38(3), 557-577.

[129] Polich, J. (2007). Updating P300: an integrative theory of P3a and P3b. *Clinical Neurophysiology*, 118(10), 2128-2148.

[130] Ehlers, C. L.; Phillips, E.; Finnerman, G.; Gilder, D.; Lau, P.; Criado, J. (2007). P3 components and adolescent binge drinking in Southwest California Indians. *Neurotoxicology and Teratology*, 29(1), 153-163.

[131] Maurage, P.; Pesenti, M., Philippot, P.; Joassin, F.; Campanella, S. (2009). Latent deleterious effects of binge drinking over a short period of time revealed only by electrophysiological measures. *Journal of Psychiatry and Neuroscience*, 34(2), 111-118.

[132] Maurage, P.; Joassin, F.; Speth, A.; Modave, J.; Philippot, P.; Campanella, S. (2012). Cerebral effects of binge drinking: respective influences of global alcohol intake and consumption pattern. *Clinical Neurophysiology*, 123(5), 892-901.

[133] Crego, A.; Cadaveira, F.; Parada, M.; Corral, M.; Caamaño-Isorna, F.; Rodríguez Holguín, S. (2012). Increased amplitude of P3 event-related potential in young binge drinkers. *Alcohol*, 46, 415-425.

[134] Crego, A.; Rodríguez Holguín, S.; Parada, M.; Mota, N.; Corral, M.; Cadaveira, F. (2009). Binge Drinking Affects Attentional and Visual Working Memory Processing in Young University Students. *Alcoholism, Clinical and Experimental Research*, 33, 1-10.

[135] López-Caneda, E.; Cadaveira, F.; Crego, A.; Gómez-Suárez, A.; Corral, M.; Parada, M.; Caamaño-Isorna, F.; Rodríguez Holguín, S. (2012). Hyperactivation of right inferior frontal cortex in young binge drinkers during response inhibition: a follow-up study. *Addiction*, 107, 1796–1808.

[136] Jonkman, L. M. (2006). The development of preparation, conflict monitoring and inhibition from early childhood to young adulthood: a Go/Nogo ERP study. *Brain Research,* 1097, 181-193.
[137] Smith, J. L.; Johnstone, S. J.; Barry, R. J. (2008). Movement-related potentials in the Go/NoGo task: the P3 reflects both cognitive and motor inhibition. *Clinical Neurophysiology,* 119, 704-714.
[138] Aron, A. R.; Robbins, T. W.; Poldrack, R. A. (2004). Inhibition and the right inferior frontal cortex. *Trends in Cognitive Sciences,* 8(4), 170-177.
[139] Chambers, C. D.; Garavan, H.; Bellgrove, M. A. (2009). Insights into the neural basis of response inhibition from cognitive and clinical neuroscience. *Neuroscience and Biobehavioral Reviews,* 33(5), 631-666.
[140] Petit, G.; Kornreich, C.; Noel, X.; Verbanck, P.; Campanella, S. Alcohol-related context modulates performance of social drinkers in a visual Go/No-Go task: a preliminary assessment of event-related potentials. PLoS ONE 7(5): e37466. [doi:10.1371/journal.pone. 0037466].

In: Binge Eating and Binge Drinking
Editor: Simon B. Harris

ISBN: 978-1-62618-580-7
© 2013 Nova Science Publishers, Inc.

Chapter 5

BINGE EATING DISORDER: AN OVERVIEW ON NEURAL, BIOLOGICAL AND GENETIC FACTORS

Deniz Atalayer[1,2,*], Nerys M. Astbury[1,2] and Christopher N. Ochner[3]

[1]Institute of Human Nutrition, Columbia University, New York, NY, US
[2]New York Obesity Nutrition Research Center,
St. Luke's-Roosevelt Hospital Center, New York, NY, US
[3]Adolescent Health Center, Mount Sinai School of Medicine,
New York, NY, US

ABSTRACT

Given the obesity epidemic and the comorbidity between obesity and binge eating disorder (BED), it is important to understand the pathophysiology of BED which causes significant distress for many overweight and obese individuals. BED has been traditionally viewed as a behavioral disorder and, as a result, its genetic and biological bases are not yet fully understood. As with most psychological disorders, both genetic and environmental factors are involved in the development of BED; however it is unclear how much they each contribute to its etiology. This chapter will review the current literature on the underlying genetic and biological factors of BED, as well as the neural mechanisms associate with the etiology of BED and binge-like eating by using evidence from both animal models and human studies. Evidence from heritability and its interaction with environment as well as hormonal and neural dysregulation involved in eating disorders will be presented to elucidate the possible predictors and diagnostic biomarkers that predispose an individual towards binge eating and BED.

INTRODUCTION

Binge Eating Disorder (BED) is characterized by: (a) recurrent episodes of binge eating larger than most people would eat with a sense of lack of control; (b) binge eating episodes (associated with three or more of the following: rapid eating, eating until uncomfortably full, eating large amounts of food when not physically hungry, eating alone because of embarrassment, and feeling guilty or depressed after overeating); (c) marked distress regarding binge eating; and (d) the absence of regular compensatory behaviors (e.g., vomiting) which are seen in patients with bulimia nervosa (BN) with a frequency of twice per week for 6 months. BED is listed in the Appendix of the Diagnostic and Statistical Manual of Mental Disorders, fourth edition, text revision (DSM IV-TR) of the American Psychiatric Association (APA) and is still considered a provisional diagnosis falling into the Eating Disorders Not Otherwise Specified (EDNOS) category (APA, 2000). Although initially described as a behavior that may be seen in obese persons (Stunkard, 1959), the high prevalence of BED (Franko et al., 2012) has led to its expected new status as a stand-alone clinical diagnostic entity in the upcoming DSM revision (DSM-V) due to be published in 2013 (Keel et al., 2011).

As with BN, diagnostic problems arise also with the diagnosis of BED because the definition of binge eating is ambiguous and the frequency and duration requirements for symptom presentation were established somewhat arbitrarily and lack empirical support. However, it has been consistently reported that contrary to BN, which typically occurs in normal weight individuals (Yanovski et al., 1993), BED presents in obese patients more frequently than BN (Yanovski, 2003). In contrast, a recent report of a community survey with 24,124 participants across 14 mostly upper-middle and high-income countries revealed no significant difference between BN versus BED in body weight status (i.e., underweight, normal weight, overweight, obese, or severely obese) (Kessler et al., 2013). The multi-site study also showed that for all countries in the survey, both lifetime and 12-month prevalence estimates were higher for BED than BN, which is consistent with the previous reports showing higher prevalence for BED within the overweight population (Spitzer et al., 1993). In another recent study, with a more unified population of 1383 Spanish women with eating disorders (ED), it has been found that the lifetime prevalence of obesity was 33% in BN, whereas it was 87% in BED (Villarejo et al., 2012). Although not all obese individuals have BED and vice versa, in persons who enroll in weight management treatments, the prevalence for BED is reported to be 30% (de Zwaan, 2001). Obese persons who exhibit binge eating behavior, compared to their non-binge or non-obese counterparts, are reported to have several different characteristics related to their eating habits. It has been shown that they are more likely to report an earlier onset of body shape and weight concern, more frequently diet to lose weight, and have greater weight fluctuation or repeated pattern of weight loss followed by weight regain compared with their non-binge or non-obese counterparts (de Zwaan, 2001). Moreover, obese individuals who exhibit binge eating behavior are more resistant to weight loss treatment, have higher dropout rates, and show greater recidivism after weight loss than non-BED obese persons (de Zwaan et al.,1994; Agras et al.,1997; Raymond et al., 2002: McGuire et al., 1999; de Zwaan, 2001). Based on these findings, investigators have inferred that BED may play a role in the development of obesity (Mussell et al., 1995; Yanovski, 2003). Several prospective longitudinal studies have shown that binge eating often precedes development of obesity (Stice et al.,1998; Stice, 1998; Leon et al., 1997; Mussell et al., 1995). Moreover, medical complications related to obesity can occur in patients with BED, including hypertension, adverse lipoprotein profiles, diabetes mellitus, atherosclerotic cerebrovascular disease, coronary heart disease, colorectal cancer, reduced lifespan, and death from all causes (Bulik et al., 2002). However one should caution interpreting results from these reports because binge eating is not the same as BED (Hudson et al., 2007). Thus comparing obese individuals with and without BED or the comparison between obese individuals who do and do not exhibit/report binge eating behavior should be analyzed separately.

Independent of body weight, binge eating is also related to psychiatric and medical risks such as insomnia, specific phobias, daily smoking, alcohol use, and physical pain independently of body weight. Unlike the classic eating disorders (anorexia nervosa (AN) and BN) which have a higher prevalence in women compared with men, BED is common amongst men, representing about 40% of BED patients (Spitzer et al., 1993). Current interventions for BED include combination treatments of psychological, psychological/nutritional (Wonderlich et al., 2003), behavioral (Wilfley et al., 2002), and psychopharmacological (Carter et al., 2003; Devlin et al., 2005) approaches, and without treatment, many patients with BED may not improve over time. Structured therapeutic treatments consist mainly of cognitive behavioral therapy (CBT), which is considered the gold standard treatment approach for BED, and interpersonal therapy (Wilfley et al., 2002). The treatments seek to reduce binge eating and body weight simultaneously through traditional "lifestyle change" dieting techniques, such as reducing the caloric density and portion sizes of meals as well as increasing physical activity are also being used. Pharmacological treatments may include tricyclic antidepressants, selective serotonin reuptake inhibitor (SSRI) antidepressants, or appetite suppressants (Hudson et al., 1998; McElroy et al., 2000). Tricyclic and SSRI antidepressants have the highest efficacy in reducing binge frequency; however, discontinuation of medication generally leads to a rapid return of binge episodes (Hudson et al., 1996).

Results from studies combining pharmacological and psychological treatments for BED show short-term reduction in binge eating and body weight (Carter et al., 2003) however, long-term improvements for BED are yet to be discovered (Reas and Grilo, 2008). Thus, severe medical consequences and concurrent rising epidemic of BED (Franko et al., 2012) along with obesity in both men and women highlight the importance and urgency to the study of its multifactorial pathogenesis.

FACTORS ASSOCIATED WITH BED

Dietary restraint has been implicated as a potential contributor to the development of binge eating behavior predisposing normal weight as well as overweight individuals to binge eating disorder and/or obesity (Marcus, 1993). It is defined as self-restriction of food intake due to concern over body shape or weight (Tuschl, 1990). According to restraint theory (Polivy and Herman, 1985), hunger that is induced by dieting establishes conditions that potentiate binge eating in the presence of specific disinhibitors, such as alcohol intake and dietary abstinence violations. Therefore, dieters were assumed to over-restrict their eating until they encounter some form of external disinhibiting stimulus, typically, an environmental stressor or ingestion of a "forbidden food," at which point they would become disinhibited and tend to overeat. It was presumed that this cycle of over-restriction and overeating would eventually lead to binge episodes and the development of BED and in some cases also obesity. However, there is considerable evidence suggesting that dieting does not predispose individuals to binge eating (Howard and Porzelius, 1999). Restraint theory states that dieting *leads to* binge eating; however, in studies specifically examining the temporal sequence of dieting and binging, only a small minority among the overweight persons who exhibit binge eating reported that their dieting preceded the onset of their binge eating (Mussell et al., 1995; Henderson and Huon, 2002). In addition, overweight persons who exhibit binge eating behavior have been shown to be no more likely than overweight individuals who do not exhibit binge eating to diet, which is the opposite of what the restraint theory would suggest (Wilson et al., 1993). Thus, there is disagreement (Howard and Porzelius, 1999) on the role and extent that dieting plays in the development of BED which led to the formation of other theories.

The most common explanation for the persistent binge eating behaviors is based on the influence of negative affect. There is considerable evidence that negative affect is a salient predictor of binge behaviors in overweight persons (Agras and Telch, 1998), and binge eating has been repeatedly shown to occur in response to negative affect (Henderson and Huon, 2002; Arnow et al., 1992; 1995; Heatherton and Baumeister, 1991; Lingswiler et al., 1989). One widely cited theory proposes that people who exhibit binge eating behavior learn to moderate negative emotions by binge eating (Heatherton and Bauumeister, 1991; Stice, 1994; McManus and Waller, 1995). In support of this theory, Arnow et al. (1992) examined the relationship between binge episodes and fluctuations in mood among obese persons with non-purging binge eating behavior and reported that typical binge episodes were precipitated by negative emotional states. More recently, a study by the same group showed that scores on all three subscales of the Emotional Eating Scale (anger/frustration, anxiety, and depression) correlated significantly with the occurrence of binge eating episodes across a one-week recall by overweight women (Arnow et al., 1995).

In addition, Eldredge and Agras (1996) found that, obese people with binge eating behavior were significantly more likely to report eating in response to negative affect compared with obese individuals who did not exhibit binge eating. Moreover, Yanovski and colleagues (Yanovski et al., 1993) found that overweight or obese men and women with BED are significantly more likely to have had major depression, panic disorder, bulimia nervosa, borderline personality disorder, and avoidant personality disorder (based on DSM III criteria). The relationship between binge eating and trait, depression, anxiety, and perceived stress has been also reported in several other studies (Cargill et al.,1999; Pinaquy et al., 2003) and these evidence support the model of emotionally-driven binge eating behavior. This is in line with research showing that overweight persons with binge eating behavior report more negative affect prior to binge episodes than prior to normal meals (Lingswiler et al., 1989). During binge episodes there is an increase in positive affect and/or a decrease in negative affect (Deaver et al., 2003; Stickney et al., 1999).

Thus, binge episodes temporarily improve mood, which then helps to reinforce the binge eating behavior. However, following the binge episode the person's mood reverts to a depressed state, often compounded by feelings of shame and guilt associated with the binge behavior (Wegner et al., 2002). Such negative mood states then increase the likelihood of a future binge episode (Henderson and Huon, 2002; Arnow, et al., 1992; 1995). In this way, the typical cycle of dietary restriction and binge eating is perpetuated by the recurrence of negative emotions.

Although aforementioned theories for the etiology of BED are widely accepted by the field, most scientists ascribe to a "diathesis-stress" model of eating disorders. This theory asserts that certain individuals will have a genetic predisposition (diathesis) towards developing BED. Thus, an individual with parents or close relatives suffering from BED will have an increased likelihood of developing BED themselves. However, according to the diatheses-stress model, these biological predisposition / diatheses is in itself not necessary or sufficient for the development of the disorder. While studies suggest that heritability of BED the actual development of the disorder depends upon environmental factors (Janaras et al., 2008). These factors include peer modeling, social influence, media messages, culture, and body image (Ochner and Geliebter, 2007). Furthermore, in a study including only women, Fairburn and colleagues (Fairburn et al., 1998) found that negative self-evaluation, parental depression, adverse childhood experiences, negative weight-related comments from family members, and pregnancy were associated with an increased risk for developing BED. Thus, a diathesis towards the development of BED would only be expressed when it interacts with sufficient environmental stress to express the predisposition. Likewise most but not all individuals who develop BED are presumed to have had a preexisting diathesis. However, although without the sufficient environment, a genotype may not be able to express its phenotype, it is still important to understand the underlying biological and genetic factors that may predispose certain individuals to BED.

Neurological Factors

Investigation of the role of the brain in eating disorders and BED is undeniably triggered by the knowledge of brain's role in energy homeostasis. Early pioneering studies showed that subcortical (e.g. hypothalamus) regions play an important role in food intake regulation (Bailey and Bremer, 1921; Hetherington 1939). Specifically, lesions in the ventromedial nucleus of hypothalamus (VMH) result in obesity in both humans and animals (Anand and Brobeck, 1951a), as also seen in Fröhlich's syndrome –a childhood disease caused by tumors in hypothalamus result in obesity, growth retardation (Morgan, 1959). Teitelbaum (1955) and others have shown, hyperphagic rats prefer certain foods over foods that they normally accept, which these investigators terms as "finickiness." Anand and Brobeck (1951a) also showed that rats and cats become obese as they become frantic eaters without any metabolic disturbance. In addition they also found that animals with lesions in lateral nucleus of hypothalamus (LH) stopped eating completely (Anand and Brobeck, 1951b). Thus, based on their experiments they named "hunger center" for LH and "satiety center" for VMH. Similarly, in 1954, another pioneer James Stellar suggested his dual center theory for hypothalamic regulation of energy homeostasis however, 40 years later he concluded that 'center' is a dangerous word to use, and stated that brain sites regulating food intake do not work in isolation (Stellar, 1994). We know now that not only there are multiple systems (e.g. behavioral, biological neurological etc.) involved in the regulation of eating behavior, but also the neural control of appetite and food intake comprise multiple neural systems (e.g. mesolimbic, mesocortical, hypothalamic) which collectively regulate eating behavior.

Animal models allowed the conduction of more invasive research techniques thus most of the early studies on neurochemical control of appetitive motivation and energy homeostasis use animal models of food intake. In animal studies, it has been shown that dopamine (DA) neurons in nucleus accumbens -a subcortical brain site implicated in neural processing of reward, pleasure, addiction, directly mediate the reinforcing properties of natural stimuli such as food (Salamone et al., 1997) and thus, increase appetite. Avena et al. (2008) also found that DA neurons in nucleus accumbens are highest during food foraging, whereas acetylcholine

(Ach) is shown to decrease as the feeing slows down thus, has an appetitive suppressing effect. Moreover, it has been shown that smoking or ingestion derived from the plant *Cannabis sativa* (i.e. marijuana) and also endogenous opiates (endorphin and enkephalin) increase craving for sweet or fatty foods (Cooper, 2004). Moreover, pharmaceuticals (e.g. naloxone) that decrease extracellular DA (Mucha and Iversen 1986), are also shown to increase Ach (Avena, 2007). Thus, taste preference release DA but the negative consequences release Ach. Based on these reports, although not a diagnostic addiction, the suggested term 'sugar addiction' has been speculated to work though the DA/Ach mechanism (Hoebel et al., 2009) that cause individuals to impulsively overeat sugar and became *"addicted"* eaters. The evidence from human studies also supports the view that BED represents a specific phenotype of obesity with increased food-related impulsivity (Schag et al., 2013). One may speculate that this may be one of the neural mechanisms that may lead binge eating behavior and obesity.

Following early studies with animal models of binge eating, new advances in technology has led to studying of human brain. Evidence from studies with non-invasive neuroimaging techniques elucidated the involvement of neural systems in binge eating in humans. Recent works employing these tools have implicated the frontal cortex, a brain region involved in decision making and regulating inhibitory-control, and the striatum, which is thought to be involved in food reward, satiety and pleasure, in mediating responses to food cues and feeding in normal-weight and obese individuals as well as persons with BED. Moreover, DA is selectively altered in striatum in obese relative to normal-weight individuals, and frontostriatal regions constitute a major component of DA circuitry. Similar to findings from the studies with the animal models of binging, using an positron emission tomography (PET) brain imaging technique, Wang et al. (2004) reported that decreased levels of DA receptors predisposed persons who are addicted to drugs to search for reinforcers –the drugs, obese individuals for food which temporarily compensated for a decreased sensitivity of DA regulated brains sites that process reward-related information. Moreover, using (single photon emission computed tomography) SPECT, a technique similar to, one study reported increased activation in frontal and prefrontal regions following exposure to a freshly cooked meal of their own selection, prior to consumption in obese women with BED compared to obese and normal-weight women with no binge eating behavior (Karhunen et al., 2000).

A later fMRI study reported greater activation to highly palatable visual and auditory food stimuli specifically in the frontal premotor area among obese binge-eating women, but not in obese non binge-eating, lean binge-eating or lean non binge-eating women (Geliebter et al., 2006).

The frontal activation demonstrated in these two studies may reflect either heightened reward or efforts at cognitive control in this population. More recently, Schienle et al. (2009) found that, when presented with high-caloric visual food stimuli, overweight BED women showed greater activation in the medial OFC than overweight or lean women without BED, and lean women with bulimia nervosa. These results provide further support for dysregulation in reward pathways in those with BED (Schienle et al., 2009).

Recent research has also demonstrated greater brain activation in obese individuals with binge eating behavior in response to binge-type food stimuli (Geliebter et al., 2006); all of which support a biological basis for BED.

Biological Basis

The association between BED and perturbations in normal patterns of food intake has led researchers to investigate the biological basis of BED by examining the role of various signals (e.g. gut hormones, neuropeptides) associated with the regulation of energy homeostasis. These signals can be broadly broken down into the signals that fluctuate in proportion to the magnitude of energy from stores, such as leptin, and those released by the gastrointestinal tract, which fluctuate in proportion to the quality and quantity of ingested foods and drinks such as cholecyctokinin (CCK), glucagon-like peptide-1 (GLP-1), peptide YY_{3-36} (PYY), and ghrelin. These signals are associated with a wide range of physiological responses including gastric emptying rate, gastrointestinal motility, subjective appetite sensations and subsequent voluntary food intake. Thus, abnormal secretion or reduced sensitivity for the actions of these signals could play an important role in the pathophysiology of BED.

Although several neuropeptides have been shown to stimulate appetite and food intake; some of these such as leptin, CCK, GLP-1 and PYY rise after meals and suppress food intake (Anubhuti, 2006; Stanley et al., 2004), whilst ghrelin is the only established orexigenic (hunger-inducing) hormone to date. Ghrelin is predominantly synthesized by the oxyntic cells in the stomach in response to a period of fasting (Kojima, et al., 1999). Unlike many of the other peptide hormones released by the gastrointestinal tract, plasma levels of ghrelin rise in response to a period of fasting (Erlanson-Albertsson 2005), and ghrelin concentrations are suppressed, rather than stimulated by nutrient exposure in the stomach, duodenum and jejunum (Cummings et al., 2002). When ghrelin is administered peripherally it causes increases in food intake (Wren et al., 2001), and the pre-prandial rise in plasma ghrelin concentrations is associated with subjective hunger ratings, suggesting that ghrelin is an important signal in meal initiation, opposed to within meal satiation (Cummings et al., 2004). Ghrelin also follows a diurnal pattern, increasing from the morning to the evening, and reaching a higher peak before dinner than before breakfast (Cummings, et al., 2002). This is consistent with the meal pattern in the United States, where dinner is usually the largest meal (Geliebter, 2002). Thus, higher ghrelin levels could help explain greater food intake, reduced metabolic rate, and subsequent weight gain in BED. Nevertheless, obese persons who exhibit binge eating behavior show dysregulation of ghrelin, produced by the stomach (Geliebter et al., 2004), which may be associated with the larger stomach capacity seen in people with binge eating behavior compared to obese persons with no binge eating (Geliebter et al., 2004). The majority of studies report that plasma ghrelin concentrations are decreased in obese BED, which is contrary to the expected higher levels (Geliebter et al., 2005; Monteleone et al., 2005; Troisi et al., 2005) which would suggest higher subjective hunger sensations. However, one study showed that fasting and postprandial ghrelin levels did not differ between overweight/obese individuals with BED and non-BED controls (BMI-matched) (Munsch et al., 2009). Despite decreased ghrelin levels, there does not appear to be a reduced propensity to gain weight in BED. The lower ghrelin, as also seen in the obese relative to lean individuals, may be due to down-regulation of ghrelin release in response to overeating or excess body weight. The initial smaller decline in ghrelin following a meal has been noted in obese BED patients (Geliebter et al., 2005), and conceivably this may act to maintain hunger. However, findings from studies in patients with BED suggest that binge eating may lead to reduced ghrelin levels irrespective of BMI (Atalayer et al., 2013).

Leptin is mainly released by adipose (fat) tissue in direct proportion to the size of the adipose stores (Campfield et al., 1996) but has also been shown to be secreted by the gastric chief cells in the stomach (Bado et al., 1998). Leptin decreases appetite and may have a role in short term satiety when released by the stomach (Anubhuti, 2006). Although serum leptin concentrations are higher in obese compared with lean individuals (Considine et al. 1996), one study reported that serum leptin concentrations in obese persons with BED were only weakly correlated with body mass. However concentrations of serum leptin were significantly higher in obese persons with BED compared with non-binging obese individuals matched for body mass and composition (Adami et al., 2002). These findings are somewhat contradictory, and suggest that in patients with BED, serum leptin concentrations are influenced not only by the size of body fat depots, but also by eating behaviors. Furthermore, binge behaviors are likely not to be triggered by low leptin concentrations, with further investigation warranted into leptin sensitivity in patients with BED.

CCK is secreted from the I cells of the duodenum and jejunum in response to the presence of nutrients in the intestinal lumen (Liddle et al., 1985, Parker et al., 2005; Lieverse et al., 1994). CCK acts as a satiation signal, with studies reporting that a peripheral CCK infusion during the course of a meal can reduce meal size as well as the duration of a meal (Kissileff et al., 1981; Ballinger et al., 1995). Furthermore CCK infusion increases the perception of fullness and decreases the perception of hunger experienced during the course of that meal (Liverese et al., 1994). Nutrient induced delay in gastric emptying rate is blocked when a CCK antagonist is administered (Lal et al., 2004), suggesting that nutrient induced delay in gastric emptying is mediated by CCK. To date no studies have investigated differences in CCK secretion patterns or sensitivity to CCK in patients with BED *per se*. However, one study compared the gastric emptying and gut hormone responses in patients with BN; a condition similar to BED in so far as patients demonstrate binge like episodes. The findings of this study demonstrate BN patients show that peak postprandial CCK response to a test meal was lower in BN patients compared with controls (Devlin et al., 2012).

GLP-1 is mainly released by the L cells of the distal small intestine in response to the presence of nutrients in the gastrointestinal tract (Hermann et al., 1995; Naslund et al., 1999). After a meal GLP-1 in secreted in two phases; the first short rapid release occurs 5-10 min postprandially (Ghatei et al., 1982; Hermann et al., 1995), followed by a second delayed and extended release occurring 30-60min postprandially (Adam and Westerterp-Plantenga 2005a; 2005b). Peripheral administration of GLP-11 suppresses subjective appetite sensations and reduces energy intake in some (Gutzwillwer et al., 1999; Naslund et al., 1999; Verdich et al., 2001; Stanley et al., 2004), but not all studies (Long et al., 1999; Brennan et al., 2005). There is consistent evidence that GLP-1 can inhibit gastric emptying, even at physiological concentrations (Naslund et al., 1998; Flint et al., et al. 2001; Meier et al., 2005). This delay in gastric emptying may enhance the effect of GLP-1 on food intake, in part due to greater gastric swelling. However there are no studies that have investigated the role of GLP-1 in the pathophysiology of BED.

PYY_{3-36}, is also released by the L cells of the distal gastrointestinal tract (Adrian et al., 1985), and is co-expressed in the cells that secrete GLP-1 (Stanley et al., 2004). PYY_{3-36} is secreted in response to the presence of nutrients, particularly fat in the gastrointestinal lumen (Essah et al., 2007; Helou et al., 2008). Plasma concentrations rise postprandially with peak plasma PYY_{3-36} concentrations are observed 1-2 hours following feeding. Peripheral infusion of PYY_{3-36} has been shown to suppress subjective appetite and reduce subsequent voluntary energy intake (Batterham et al., 2002). Before eating, lower PYY_{3-36} levels have been found in obese vs. lean participants and the postprandial increase in PYY_{3-36} has been found to be less in obese subjects compared with lean individuals (Batterham et al., 2003). Combining GLP-1 and PYY_{3-36} has shown to have an additive effect on food intake reduction (Neary et al., 2005). Nevertheless, a study comparing gut hormone responses in BED patients reported no difference in PYY responses to a standard liquid test meal compared with non-binge obese patients (Geliebter et al., 2008), suggesting that abnormal secretion of PYY_{3-36} was an unlikely contributing factor to binge eating in BED.

In summary, the major peripheral hormones which affect appetite can be separated into two categories; those which stimulate food intake (ghrelin) and decline following meals, and those that rise following meals and help decrease consumption (CCK, leptin, GLP-1, and PYY). To date there is a limited number of studies investigating the potential role of these hormones on the etiology of BED. Furthermore, there is inconsistency between the reported findings of these studies. Future studies should aim to differentiate gastric dysfunction and peptide hormone signaling mechanisms in BED may result in innovative therapeutic strategies to treat those affected by BED.

Genetic Factors

Binge eating disorder has been suggested to have a high heritability. In the Norwegian Twin Study with 1303 monozygotic (male = 526 and female = 777) and 1052 dizygotic (male = 397 and female = 655), and 979 opposite-sex dizygotic twin pairs were analyzed based on the binge-eating criteria over a period of six months. The result showed a 41% (ranging from 31% to 50%) of heritability for BED with environmental factors explaining for the remaining 59% (Reichborn-Kjennerud et al., 2004). Similar results were reported in a multi-center cross cultural analysis (US and Norway) by Janaras et al. (2008) showing that heritability of BED is approximately 30%, with the actual development of the disorder depending upon environmental factors which accounts for the remaining 80%. Familial studies also showed that children with one parent suffering from BED are more than twice as likely to develop BED and 2.5 times as likely to develop severe obesity (BMI ≥ 40 kg.m^2; Bulik et al., 2003).

Several genes that are shown to be involved in appetite regulation have been identified. The results from molecular genetics studies also supported the findings from familial and twin reports, suggesting a genetic component in the etiology of BED. Genes encoding for the hunger hormone ghrelin are shown to potentially contribute to the development of BED. Monteleone et al. (2006) assessed the 196G/A SNP of the human brain-derived neurotrophic factor (BDNF) gene in women with BN and BED; and found no differences in gene variant frequencies between groups, yet persons with the 196G/A SNP compared with 196A/G and 196G/G genotypes, had greater frequency of binge eating episodes. Monteleone et al. (2007) also found greater expression of the Leu72Met ghrelin gene variant in obese and normal-weight persons with BED relative to healthy, normal weight women. The Leu72Met ghrelin gene may therefore be associated with a genetic susceptibility for BED (Monteleone et al., 2007), whereas the AA variant of the 196G/A SNP of the human BDNF gene may predispose individuals to higher frequency of binge eating (Monteleone et al., 2006).

Moreover, several studies with both animal models and humans have indicated a genetic association between BED and mutations in the melanocortin-4 receptor (MC4R) of the hypothalamic nuclei of the brain (Branson et al., 2003; Farooqi et al., 2003). The hormone leptin secreted by adipose tissue regulates energy balance by binding to its receptors in the hypothalamus and excites proopiomelanocortin (POMC) neurons which trigger the production of α-melanocyte-stimulating hormone (Adan et al., 2006). Alpha-melanocyte-stimulating hormone binds to MC4Rs, and exerts its effects on food intake behavior by suppressing the appetite (Berthoud et al., 2006). Mice with mutations and deficiencies of MC4Rs display overeating and obesity (Atalayer et al., 2010). Human genetic studies showed that binge-eating disorder is a major phenotypic expression in individuals with a mutation in MC4Rs and suggest that *MC4R gene* is a candidate gene responsible for development of BED. Collectively, these reports from both familial and twin studies along with molecular genetics experiment indicate that relatives of those gene variants are at a much higher risk for BED than are relatives of healthy controls.

CONCLUSION

Contrary to conventional views, dieting is not necessary or sufficient to predict the development of BED. The negative affect theory proposes that individuals with BED have a tendency to binge eat in an attempt to attenuate negative emotions. Such attempts may be somewhat successful to attenuate the negative mood, but only during the binge eating episode; after which, there is usually further negative affect, priming the individual for the next binge eating episode. This common cycle of dietary restriction and binge eating behavior seen in individuals with BED is likely not *caused* by dietary restriction, but rather by an interaction between individuals' genetic makeup and their *food environment*. Food intake behavior is governed by complex interconnected systems and its disordered forms such as eating disorders (ED) and obesity cannot be reduced to single causality. Thus, taken together, current evidence suggests that a multifactorial approach is necessary to explain the factors that predispose an individual towards binge eating and development of BED. With the anticipated inclusion of BED as a stand-alone eating disorder in the upcoming DSM-V, we hope that further much-needed research on possible neural, biological and genetic factors associated with BED alongside the conventional theories will help elucidate the mechanisms responsible for this eating disorder and will potentially lead to more effective intervention methods.

REFERENCES

Adam, T.C., & Westerterp-Plantenga, M.S., (2005a). Nutrient-stimulated GLP-1 release in normal-weight men and women. *Hormone and Metabolic Research, 37,* 111-117.

Adam, T.C. & Westerterp-Plantenga, M.S., (2005b). Glucagon-like peptide-1 release and satiety after a nutrient challenge in normal-weight and obese subjects. *British Journal of Nutrition, 93,* 845-851.

Adan, R.A.H., Tiesjema, B., Hillebrand, J.J.G., la Fleur, S.E., Kas, M.J.H., de Krom, M. (2006). The MC4 receptor and control of appetite. *British Journal of Pharmacology 149:* 815–827.

Adami, G.F., Campostano, A., Cella, F., and Scopinaro, N., (2002). "Serum leptin concentration in obese patients with binge eating disorder." *International Journal of Obeity. and Related Metabolic Disorders 26(8):* 1125-1128.

Adrian, T.E., Ferri, G.L., Bacarese-Hamilton, A.J. Fuessl, H.S., Polak, J.M., and Bloom, S.R. (1985). "Human distribution and release of a putative new gut hormone, peptide YY." *Gastroenterology 89(5):* 1070-1077.

Agras, W.S., Telch, C.F., Arnow, B., Eldredge, K., and Marnell, M. (1997). One-year follow-up of cognitive behavioral therapy for obese individuals with binge eating disorder. *Journal of Consulting and Clinical Psychology, 65,* 343–347.

Agras, W.S., and Telch, C.F. (1998). The effects of caloric deprivation and negative affect on binge eating in obese binge-eating-disordered women. *Behavior Therapy, 29,* 491–503.

American Psychiatric Association. (2000). *Diagnostic and Statistical Manual of Mental Disorders, Fourth Edition, Text Revision.* American Psychiatric Association: Washington, DC.

Anand B.K., & Brobeck J.R. (1951a). Hypothalamic control of food intake in rats and cats. *Yale Journal of Biology and Medicine, 24(2),* 123–140.

Anand B.K., and Brobeck J.R. (1951b). Localization of a "feeding center" in the hypothalamus of the rat. *Experimental Biology and Medicine, 77(2),* 323-325.

Arnow, B., Kenardy, J., and Agras, W.S. (1992). Binge-eating among the obese: A descriptive study. *Journal of Behavioral Medicine, 15,* 155-170.

Arnow, B., Kenardy, J., and Agras, W.S. (1995). The Emotional Eating Scale: The development of a measure to assess coping with negative affect by eating. *International Journal of Eating Disorders, 18,* 79-90.

Anubhuti, A.S. (2006). Role of neuropeptides in appetite regulation and obesity- a review. *Neuropeptides, 40,* 375–401.

Atalayer, D., Robertson, K.R., Andreasen, A., Haskell-Luevano, C., Rowland, N.E. (2010). Food demand and meal size in mice with single or combined disruption of melanocortin type 3 and 4 receptor. *American Journal of Physiology-Regulatory, Comparative and Integrative Physiology, 298(6),* 1667-1674.

Atalayer, D., Gibson, C., Konopacka A., Geliebter, A. (2013). Ghrelin and eating disorders. *Progress in Neuropsychopharmacology: Biological Psychiatry, 40:* 70-82.

Avena, N.M. (2007). Examining the addictive-like properties of binge eating using an animal model of sugar dependence. *Experimental and Clinical Psychopharmacology. 15(5),* 481–491.

Avena, N.M., Rada, P., Hoebel, B.G. (2008). Evidence of sugar addiction: Behavioral and neurochemical effects of intermittent, excessive sugar intake. *Neuroscience and Biobehavioral Reviews. 32(1),* 20-39.

Bado, A., Levasseur, S., Attoub, S., Kermorgant, S., Laigneau, J.P., Bortoluzzi, M.N., Moizo, L., Lehy, T., Guerre-Millo, M., Le Marchand-Brustel Y., Lewin M. J. (1998). The stomach is a source of leptin. *Nature, 394(6695),* 790-793.

Bailey, P., Bremer, F. (1921). Experimental diabetes insipidus. *Archives of Internal Medicine* (Chic), *28(6),* 773-803.

Ballinger, A., McLoughlin, L., Medbak, S., Clark, M. (1995). Cholecystokinin is a satiety hormone in humans at physiological post-prandial plasma concentrations. *Clinical Science* (Lond), *89(4),* 375-381.

Batterham, R.L., Cowley, M.A., Small, C.J., Herzog, H., Cohen, M.A., Dakin, C.L., et al. (2002). "Gut hormone PYY(3-36) physiologically inhibits food intake." *Nature 418(6898),* 650-654.

Batterham R.L., Cohen M.A., Ellis S.M., et al. (2003). Inhibition of food intake in obese subjects by peptide YY3-36. *New England Journal of Medicine, 349(10),* 941-948.

Berthoud, H.R., Sutton-Townsend, L.G.M., Patterson, L.M., Zheng, H. (2006). Brainstem mechanisms integrating gut-derived satiety signals and descending forebrain information in the control of meal size. *Physiological Behavior, 89,* 517–524.

Branson, R., Potoczna, N., Kral, J.G., Lentes, K.U., Hoehe, M. R., Horber, F.F. (2003). Binge eating as a major phenotype of melanocortin 4 receptor gene mutations. *New England Journal of Medicine, 348,* 1096-1103.

Brennan, I. M., Feltrin, K.L., Horowitz, M., Smout, A.J., Meyer, J.H., Wishart J., and Feinle-Bisset, C. (2005). "Evaluation of interactions between CCK and GLP-1 in their effects on appetite, energy intake, and antropyloroduodenal motility in healthy men." *American Journal of Physiology- Regulatory, Integrative and Comparative Physiology 288(6),* R1477-1485.

Bulik, C.M., Sullivan, P.F., Kendler, K.S. (2002). Medical and psychiatric morbidity in obese women with and without binge eating. *International Journal of Eating Disorder, 32,(1),* 72–78.

Bulik, C.M., Sullivan, P.F., Kendler, K.S. (2003). Genetic and environmental contributions to obesity and binge eating. *International Journal of Eating Disorders, 33,* 293-298.

Campfield, L.A., Smith, F.J., Burn, P. (1996). The OB protein (leptin) pathway--a link between adipose tissue mass and central neural networks. *Hormone and Metabolic Research, 28(12),* 619-632.

Cargill, B., Clarck, M., Pera, V., Niaura, R. Abrams, D. (1999). Binge eating, body image, depression, and self-efficacy in an obese clinical population. *Obesity Research, 7,* 379-386.

Carter, W.P., Hudson, J.I., Lalonde, J.K., et al. (2003) Pharmacologic treatment of binge eating disorder. *International Journal of Eating Disorders, 34:,* S74–S88.(suppl).

Considine, R.V., Sinha, M.K., Heiman, M.L., Kriauciunas, A., Stephens, T.W., Nyce, M.R., et al. (1996). "Serum immunoreactive-leptin concentrations in normal-weight and obese humans." *New England Journal of Medicine, 334(5),* 292-295.

Cooper, S.J. (2004).Endocannabinoids and food consumption: Comparisons with benzodiazepine and opioid palatability-dependent appetite. *European Journal of Pharmacology, 500,* 37–49.

Cummings, D.E., Weigle, D.S., Frayo, R.S., Breen, P.A., Ma, M.K., Dellinger, E.P., and Purnell, J.Q. (2002). "Plasma ghrelin levels after diet-induced weight loss or gastric bypass surgery." *New England Journal of Medicine,* 346(21), 1623-1630.

Cummings, D.E., Frayo, R.S., Marmonier, C., Aubert, R., Chapelot, D. (2004). "Plasma ghrelin levels and hunger scores in humans initiating meals voluntarily without time- and food-related cues." *American Journal of Physiology - Endocrinology and Metabolism 287(2),* E297-304.

Davis, R., Freeman, R.J., Garner, D.M. (1988). A naturalistic investigation of eating behavior in bulimia nervosa. *Journal of consulting and Clinical Psychology, 56,* 273-279.

de Zwaan, M., Mitchell, J.E., Raymond, N.C., Spitzer, R.L. (1994). Binge eating disorder: clinical features and treatment of a new diagnosis. *Harvard Review of.Psychiatry. 1,* 310-1325.

de Zwaan, M. (2001). Binge eating disorder and obesity, *International Journal of Obesity, 25,* Suppl 1, S51–S55.

Deaver, C.M., Miltenberger, R.G., Smyth, J., Meidinger, A., Crosby, R. (2003). an evaluation of affect and binge eating. *Behavior Modification, 27,* 578-599.

Devlin, M.J., Goldfein, J.A., Petkova, E., Huiping, J., Raizman, P.S., Wolk, S., et al.(2005). Cognitive behavioral therapy and fluoxetine as adjuncts to group behavioral therapy for binge eating disorder. *Obesity Research, 13(6),* 1077–1088.

Devlin, M.J., Kissileff, H.R., Zimmerli, E.J., Samuels, F., Chen, B.E., Brown, A.J., Geliebter, A., and Walsh, B.T. (2012). "Gastric emptying and symptoms of bulimia nervosa: effect of a prokinetic agent." *Physiology and Behavior 106(2),* 238-242.

Eldredge, K.L., and Agras, W.S. (1996). Weight and shape overconcern and emotional eating in binge-eating disorder. *International Journal of Eating Disorders, 19,* 73-82.

Erlanson-Albertsson, C. (2005). "Appetite regulation and energy balance." *Acta Paediatrica Suppl. 94(448),* 40-41.

Essah, P.A., Levy, J.R., Sistrun, S.N., Kelly, S.M., and Nestler, J.E. (2007). "Effect of macronutrient composition on postprandial peptide YY levels." *Journal of Clinical Endocrinology & Metabolism, 92(10),* 4052-4055.

Fairburn, C.G., Doll, H.A., Welch, S.L., Hay, P.J., Davies, B.A., O'Connor, M.E. (1998). Risk factors for binge eating disorder: a community-based, case-control study. *Archives of General Psychiatry, 55,* 425 - 432.

Farooqi, I.S., Keogh, J.M., Yeo, G.S., Lank, E.J., Cheetham, T., and O'Rahilly, S. (2003). Clinical spectrum of obesity and mutations in the melanocortin 4 receptor gene. *New England Journal of Medicine, 348(20),* 1085-1095.

Flint, A., Raben, A., Ersboll, A.K., Holst J.J., Astrup, A. (2001). "The effect of physiological levels of glucagon-like peptide-1 on appetite, gastric emptying, energy and substrate metabolism in obesity." *International Journal of Obesity and Related Metabolic Disorders 25(6),* 781-792.

Franko, D.L., Thompson-Brenner, H., Thompson, D.R., Boisseau, C.L., Davis, A., Forbush, K.T., et al. (2012). Racial/ethnic differences in adults in randomized clinical trials of binge eating disorder. *Journal of Consulting and Clinical Psychology, 80(2),* 186-95.

Geliebter, A. (2002). Weight loss and plasma ghrelin levels. *New England Journal of Medicine, 347(17),* 1379-1381.

Geliebter, A., Yahav, E.K., Gluck, M.E., Hashim, S.A. (2004). Gastric capacity,test meal intake, and appetitive hormones in binge eating disorder. *Physiology and Behavior, 81,* 735-740.

Geliebter, A., Gluck M.E., and Hashim, S.A. (2005). "Plasma ghrelin concentrations are lower in binge-eating disorder." *Journal of Nutrition, 135(5),* 1326-1330.

Geliebter, A., Ladell, T., Logan, M., Schneider, T., Sharafi, M., and Hirsch, J. (2006). Responsivity to food stimuli in obese and lean binge eaters using functional MRI. *Appetite, 46,* 31-35.

Geliebter, A., Hashim S.A., Gluck, M.E. (2008). "Appetite-related gut peptides, ghrelin, PYY, and GLP-1 in obese women with and without binge eating disorder (BED)." *Physiology and Behavior, 94(5),* 696-699.

Gutzwiller, J.P., Goke, B., Drewe, J., Hildebrand, P., Ketterer, S., Handschin, D., Winterhalder, R., Conen D., Beglinger C. (1999). "Glucagon-like peptide-1: a potent regulator of food intake in humans." *Gut, 44(1),* 81-86.

Heatherton, T., and Baumeister, R. (1991). Binge eating as escape from selfawareness. *Psychological Bulletin, 110,* 86–108.

Helou, N., Obeid, O., Azar, S.T., and Hwalla, N. (2008). "Variation of postprandial PYY 3-36 response following ingestion of differing macronutrient meals in obese females." *Annals of Nutrition and Metabolism, 52(3),* 188-195.

Henderson, N.J. and Huon, G. F. (2002). Negative affect and binge eating in overweight women, *British Journal of Health Psychology, 7,* 77–87.

Herrmann, C., Goke, R., Richter, G., Fehmann, H.C., Arnold R., and Goke B. (1995). "Glucagon-like peptide-1 and glucose-dependent insulin-releasing polypeptide plasma levels in response to nutrients." *Digestion, 56(2),* 117-126.

Hetherington, A.W., and Ranson, S.W. (1942).The spontaneous activity and food intake of rats with hypothalamic lesions. *American Journal of Physiology, 136,* 609-617.

Hoebel, B.G., Avena, N.M., Bocarsly, M.E., Rada., P. (2009). Natural addiction: a behavioral and circuit model based on sugar addiction in rats. *Journal of Addiction Medicine, 3(1),* 33-41.

Howard, C.E., and Porzelius, L.K. (1999). The role of dieting in binge eating disorder: etiology and treatment implications. *Clinical Psychology Review, 19,* 25.

Hudson, J.I., Carter, W.P., Pope, H.G.Jr. (1996). Antidepressant treatment of binge eating disorder: research findings and clinical guidelines. *Journal of Clinical Psychiatry, 57*(suppl 8), 73–79.

Hudson, J.I., McElroy, S.L., Raymond, N.C., Crow, S., Keck, P.E. Jr., Carter, W.P., et al.,(1998). Fluvoxamine in the treatment of binge-eating disorder: a multicenter placebo-controlled, double-blind trial. *American Journal of Psychiatry, 155,* 1756–1762.

Hudson, J.I., Hiripi, E., Pope, H.G., Kessler, R.C. (2007).The prevalence and correlates of eating disorders in the national comorbidity survey replication, *Biological Psychiatry, 61(3),* 348–358.

Javaras, K.N., Laird, N.M., Reichborn-Kjennerud, T., Bulik, C.M., Pope, H.G., Hudson, J.I. (2008). Familiality and heritability of binge eating disorder: results of a case-control family study and a twin study. *International Journal of Eating Disorders, 41,* 174-179.

Karhunen, L.J., Vanninen, E.J., Kuikka, J.T., Lappalainen, R.I., Tiihonen, J., Uusitupa, M.I. (2000). Regional cerebral blood flow during exposure to food in obese binge eating women. *Psychiatry Research, 99,* 29-42.

Keel, P.K., Holm-Denoma, J.M., Crosby, R.D. (2011). Clinical significance and distinctiveness of purging disorder and binge eating disorder. *International Journal of Eating Disorders, 44(4),* 311-316.

Kessler, R.C., Berglund, P.A.., Chiu, W.T., Deitz, A.C., Hudson, J.I., Shahly, V., et al. (2013). The prevalence and correlates of binge eating disorder in the world health organization world mental health surveys. *Biological Psychiatry,* (In print).

Kissileff, H.R., Pi-Sunyer, F.X., Thornton, J., Smith, G.P. (1981). C-terminal octapeptide of cholecystokinin decreases food intake in man. *American Journal of Clinical Nutrition, 34(2),* 154-160.

Kojima, M., Hosoda, H., Date, Y., Nakazato, M., Matsuo, H., and Kangawa, K. (1999). Ghrelin is a growth-hormone-releasing acylated peptide from stomach. *Nature, 402(6762),* 656-660.

Lal, S., McLaughlin, J., Barlow, J., D'Amato, M., Giacovelli, G., Varro, A., et al. (2004). Cholecystokinin pathways modulate sensations induced by gastric distension in humans. *Am. J. Physiol. Gastrointestinal Liver Physiology,* 287(1), G72-79.

Leon, G.R., Keel, P.K., Klump, K.L., Fulkerson, J.A. (1997) The future of risk factor research in understanding the etiology of eating disorders. *Psychopharmacololy Bulletin, 33(3),* 405-11.

Liddle, R.A., Goldfine, I.D., Rosen, M.S., Taplitz, R.A., and Williams, J.A. (1985). Cholecystokinin bioactivity in human plasma. Molecular forms, responses to feeding, and relationship to gallbladder contraction. *Journal of Clinical Investigation, 75(4),* 1144-1152.

Lieverse, R.J., Jansen, J.B., Masclee, A.M., Lamers, C.B. (1994). Satiety effects of cholecystokinin in humans. *Gastroenterology, 106(6),* 1451-1454.

Lingswiler, V.M., Crowther, J.H., and Stephens, M.A. (1989). Affective and cognitive antecedents to eating episodes in bulimia and binge eating. *International Journal of Eating Disorders, 8,* 533–539.

Long, S.J., Sutton, J.A., Amaee, W.B., Giouvanoudi, A., Spyrou, N.M., Rogers, P.J., and Morgan, L.M. (1999). No effect of glucagon-like peptide-1 on short-term satiety and energy intake in man. *British Journal of Nutition,. 81(4),* 273-279.

Marcus, M. (1993). Binge-eating in obesity. In C. Fairburn and G. Wilson (Eds.). Binge-Eating: Nature, Assessment, and Treatment. New York: Guilford Press; 1993..

McElroy, S.L., Casuto, L.S., Nelson, E.B., Lake, K.A., Soutullo, C.A., Keck, P.E. et al., (2000). Placebo-controlled trial of sertraline in the treatment of binge eating disorder. *American Journal of Psychiatry, 157,* 1004-1006.

McGuire, M.T., Wing, R.R., Klem, M.L., Lang, W., Hill, J.O. (1999). What predicts weight regain in a group of successful weight losers? *Journal of Consulting and Clinical Psychology, 67(2),* 177-185.

McManus, F., and Waller, G. (1995). A functional analysis of binge-eating. *Clinical Psychology Review, 15,* 845–865.

Meier, J.J., Kemmeries, G., Holst, J.J., and Nauck, M.A. (2005). Erythromycin antagonizes the deceleration of gastric emptying by glucagon-like peptide 1 and unmasks its insulinotropic effect in healthy subjects. *Diabetes, 54(7),* 2212-2218.

Monteleone, P., Fabrazzo, M., Tortorella, A., Martiadis, V., Serritella, C., and Maj, M. (2005). Circulating ghrelin is decreased in non-obese and obese women with binge eating disorder as well as in obese non-binge eating women, but not in patients with bulimia nervosa. *Psychoneuroendocrinology 30(3):* 243-250.

Monteleone, P., Zanardini, R., Tortorella, A., Gennarelli, M., Castaldo, E., Canestrelli, B., et al. (2006). The 196G/A (val66met) polymorphism of the BDNF gene is significantly associated with binge eating behavior in women with bulimia nervosa or binge eating disorder. *Neuroscience Letters 406,* 133-7.

Monteleone, P., Tortorella, A., Castaldo, E., Di Filippo, C., Maj, M. (2007). The Leu72Met polymorphism of the ghrelin gene is significantly associated with binge eating disorder. *Psychiatric Genetics. 17,* 13-6.

Morgan, C.D. (1959). Fröhlich Syndrome. *Proceedings of the Royal Society of Medicine, 52(3)*, 180-181.

Mucha, R.F., Iversen, S.D. (1986). Increased food intake after opioid microinjections into nucleus accumbens and ventral tegmental area of rat. *Brain Research, 12, 397(2)*, 214-24.

Munsch, S., Biedert, E., Meyer, A.H., Herpertz, S. and Beglinger, C. (2009). CCK, ghrelin, and PYY responses in individuals with binge eating disorder before and after a cognitive behavioral treatment (CBT). *Physiology and Behavior, 97(1)*, 14-20.

Mussell, M. P., Mitchell, J., Weller, C., Raymond, N., Crow, S. Crosby, R. (1995). Onset of binge eating, dieting, obesity, and mood disorders among subjects seeking treatment for binge eating disorders. *International Journal of Eating Disorders, 17*, 395-401.

Naslund, E., Barkeling, B., King, N., Gutniak, M., Blundell, J.E., Holst, J.J., Rossner S., Hellstrom, P.M. (1999). Energy intake and appetite are suppressed by glucagon-like peptide-1 (GLP-1) in obese men. *International Journal of Obesity and Related Metabolic Disorders, 23(3)*, 304-311.

Naslund, E., Gutniak, M., Skogar, S., Rossner, S., Hellstrom, P.M. (1998). Glucagon-like peptide 1 increases the period of postprandial satiety and slows gastric emptying in obese men. *Americal Journal of Clinical Nutrition, 68(3)*, 525-530.

Neary, N.M., Small, C.J., Druce, M.R. et al. (2005). Peptide YY3-36 and glucagon-like peptide-17-36 inhibit food intake additively. *Endocrinology, 146(12)*, 5120-5127.

Ochner, C.N., and Geliebter, A. (2007). Binge eating disorder. *Obesity Management; 3(4)*, 161-164.

Parker, B.A., Doran, S., Wishart, J., Horowitz, M., Chapman, I.M. (2005). Effects of small intestinal and gastric glucose administration on the suppression of plasma ghrelin concentrations in healthy older men and women. *Clinical Endocrinology* (Oxf), *62(5)*, 539-546.

Pinaquy, S., Chabrol, H., Simon, C., Louvet, J., Barbe, P. (2003). Emotional eating, alexithymia, and binge-eating disorder in obese women. *Obesity Research, 11(2)*, 195-201.

Polivy, J., and Herman, C.P. (1985). Dieting and bingeing: a causal analysis. *American Psychologist, 40*, 193–201.

Raymond, N.C., de Zwaan, M., Mitchell, J.E., Ackard, D., and Thuras, P. (2002). Effect of a very low calorie diet on the diagnostic category of individuals with binge eating disorder. *International Journal of Eating Disorders*, 31, 49–56.

Reas, D.L., Grilo, C.M. (2008). Review and meta-analysis of pharmacotherapy for binge-eating disorder. *Obesity, 16*, 2024–2038.

Reichborn-Kjennerud, T., Bulik, C.M., Tambs, K., Harris, J.R. (2004). Genetic and environmental influences on binge eating in the absence of compensatory behaviors: A population-based twin study. *International Journal of Eating Disorders*,36, 307–314.

Salamone, J.D., Cousins, M.S., Snyder, B.J. (1997).Behavioral functions of nucleus accumbens dopamine: Empirical and conceptual problems with the anhedonia hypothesis. *Neuroscience and Biobehavioral Reviews, 21(3)*, 341–359.

Schienle, A., Schäfer, A., Hermann, A., Vaitl, D. (2009). Binge-eating disorder: reward sensitivity and brain activation to images of food. *Biological Psychiatry, 65(8)*, 654-61.

Spitzer, R.L., Yanovski, S., Wadden, T., Wing, R., Marcus, M., Stunkard, A., Devlin, M., Mitchell, J., Hasin, D., and Horne, R. (1993). Binge eating disorder: Its further validation in a multisite study. *International Journal of Eating Disorders, 13*, 137-153.

Stanley, S., Wynne, K., Bloom, S. (2004). Gastrointestinal satiety signals III. Glucagon-like peptide 1, oxyntomodulin, peptide YY, and pancreatic polypeptide. *American Journal of Physiology- Gastrointestinal and Liver Physiology, 286(5),* G693-G697.

Schag, K., Schönleber, J., Teufel, M., Zipfel, S., Giel, K.E. (2013). Food-related impulsivity in obesity and Binge Eating Disorder - a systematic review. *Obesity Rev*iews [Epub ahead of print].

Stellar, E., and Kratjse, N.P. (1954). A new streotaxic instrument for use with the rat. *Science, 120,* 664-666.

Stellar, E. (1994). The physiology of motivation. *Psychological Review, 61(1),* 5-22.

Stice, E. (1994). A review of the evidence for a sociocultural model of bulimia nervosa and an exploration of the mechanisms of action. *Clinical Psychology Review, 14,* 633–661.

Stice, E. (1998). Predicting onset and cessation bulimic behaviors during adolescence: A longitudinal grouping analysis. *Behavior Therapy, 29,* 276.

Stice, E., Killen, J.D., Hayward, C., Taylor, C.B. (1998). Age of onset for binge eating and purging during late adolescence: a 4-year survival analysis. *Journal of Abnormal Psychology, 107(4),* 671-675.

Stickney, M. I., Miltenberger, R.G., Wolff, G. (1999). A descriptive analysis of factors contributing to binge eating. *Journal of Behavior Therapy and Experimental Psychiatry, 30,* 177-189.

Stunkard, A.J. *(*1959). Eating patterns and obesity. *Psychiatr* Q.33*:* 284–295*.*

Teitelbaum, P. (1955). Sensory control of hypothalamic hyperphagia. *Journal of Comparative and Physiological Psychology, 48(3),* 156-163.

Troisi, A., Di Lorenzo, G., Lega, I., Tesauro, M., Bertoli, A., Leo, R. et al. (2005). Plasma ghrelin in anorexia, bulimia, and binge-eating disorder: relations with eating patterns and circulating concentrations of cortisol and thyroid hormones. *Neuroendocrinology, 81(4),* 259-266.

Tsao T.S., Lodish H.F., Fruebis J. (2002). ACRP30, a new hormone controlling fat and glucose metabolism. *European Journal of Pharmacology, 440(2-3),* 213-221.

Tuschl, R.J. (1990). From dietary restraint to binge eating: Some theoretical considerations. *Appetite, 14(2),*105–109.

Verdich, C., Flint, A., Gutzwiller, J.P., Naslund, E., Beglinger, C., Hellstrom, P.M., et al. (2001). A meta-analysis of the effect of glucagon-like peptide-1 (7-36) amide on ad libitum energy intake in humans. *J.ournal of Clinical Endocrinology and Metabolism 86(9),* 4382-4389.

Villarejo, C., Fernandez-Aranda, F., Jimenez-Murcia, S., Penas-Lledo, E., Granero, R., Penelo, E. et al. (2012). Lifetime obesity in patients with eating disorders: Increasing prevalence, clinical and personality correlates. *European Eating Disorders Reviews, 20,* 250–254.

Wang, G-J., Volkow, N.D., Thanos, P.K., Fowler, J.S. (2004). Similarity between obesity and drug addiction as assessed by neurofunctional imaging. *Journal of Addictive Diseases. 23(3),* 39-53.

Wegner, K.E., Smyth, J. M, Crosby, R.D., Wittrock, D., Wonderlich, S.A., and Mitchell, J.E. (2002). An evaluation of the relationship between mood and binge eating in the natural environment using ecological momentary assessment. *International Journal of Eating Disorders, 32,* 352-361.

Wilfley, D.E., Welch R.R., Stein, R.I., Spurrell E.B., Cohen L.R., Saelens B.E. et al. (2002) A randomized comparison of group cognitive-behavioral therapy and group interpersonal psychotherapy for the treatment of overweight individuals with binge eating disorder. *Archives of General Psychiatry, 59,* 713–721.

Wilson, G., Nonas, C., Rosenblum, G. (1993). Assessment of binge eating in obese patients. *International Journal of Eating Disorders, 13,* 25-33.

Wonderlich, S.A., de Zwaan, M., Mitchell, J.E., Peterson, C., Crow, S. *(*2003*).* Psychological and dietary treatments of binge eating disorder: conceptual implications. *International Journal of Eating Disorders, 34,* S58–S73. *(*suppl*).*

Wren A.M., Seal L.J., Cohen M.A., Byrnes A.E., Frost G.S., Murphy K.G. et al. (2001). Ghrelin enhances appetite and increases food intake in humans. *Journal of Clinical Endocrinology and Metabolism, 86,* 5992-5995.

Yanovski, S.Z. (2003). Binge eating disorder and obesity in 2003: could treating an eating disorder have a positive effect on the obesity epidemic? *International Journal of Eating Disorders, 34,* S117-S120.

Yanovski, S.Z., Nelson, J., Dubbert, B. and Sptitzer, R. (1993). Association of binge eating disorders and psychiatric comorbidity in obese subjects. *American Journal of Psychiatry, 150(10),* 1472-1479.

Yanovski, S.Z. (2003). Binge eating disorder and obesity in 2003: could treating an eating disorder have a positive effect on the obesity epidemic? *International Journal of Eating Disorders, 34,* S117–S120.

In: Binge Eating and Binge Drinking
Editor: Simon B. Harris

ISBN: 978-1-62618-580-7
© 2013 Nova Science Publishers, Inc.

Chapter 6

CULTURAL VARIATIONS IN THE PURSUIT OF ATTRACTIVENESS AND ASSOCIATED HARMS

Carolyn M. Pearson[1], Tamika C. B. Zapolski[1], Cheri A. Levinson[2], Amanda Woods[3] and Gregory T. Smith[4]
[1,4]University of Kentucky, US
[2]Washington University, US
[3]Georgia State University, US

ABSTRACT

The authors tested the following hypotheses concerning appearance standards in women from three different cultural groups (European American, African American, and Japanese): Women in each group (a) have appearance concerns related to their culture's specific standards of beauty; (b) invest more in pursuit of their culturally defined form of beauty; and (c) experience varying harms of different severity from pursuing culturally congruent forms of beauty. European American, African American, and Japanese women completed questionnaires measuring the importance, investment, and harms of pursuing thinness, straight hair, and tall appearance. Results from this study support the above hypotheses and suggest that women in different cultural groups tend to be exposed to different risks for harms as they pursue specific cultural markers of a positive appearance. These findings are important in the context of eating disorders and the growing influence of western culture.

Keywords: Eating disorders, ethnicity, culture, beauty, harm to women

INTRODUCTION

It is well known that eating disorders are associated with harms of considerable severity to women (American Psychiatric Association, 2000). It is equally well known that the diet-

---

[1] A table providing correlations among all the variables in the study is available from the authors.

binge-purge cycle characteristic of bulimia nervosa is largely a culturally specific disorder, experienced primarily by women in Western cultures (Keel and Klump, 2003). There is very good reason to think that Western standards of attractiveness for women, which emphasize thinness, contribute to this disorder (Polivy and Herman, 2002; Thompson, van den Berg, Roehrig, Guarda, and Heinberg, 2004). The intent of this paper is to shed further light on this process by comparing women of three different cultural backgrounds, and testing the hypotheses that (a) different cultures have different standards for female attractiveness, (b) women within a cultural group invest in behaviors consistent with the pursuit of their culture's standards, and (c) the different standards in different cultures vary in how harmful they are to pursue. We will test these hypotheses by comparing women with three different cultural backgrounds: European American women in the United States, African American women in the United States, and Japanese women in Japan.

CULTURALLY SPECIFIC STANDARDS FOR APPEARANCE

One set of attributes that appears to be associated with positive appearance for European American women in the United States is thinness (Miller and Pumariega, 2001), and numerous reports have shown that ideal female body types have become increasingly thinner in recent decades (Garner, Garfinkel, Schwartz, and Thompson, 1980; Owen and Laurel-Seller, 2000; Rubinstein and Caballero, 2000). There is evidence that European American women, in particular, perceive pressure to be thin (McKnight Investigators, 2003; Stice, 2001) and develop cognitive expectancies for overgeneralized reinforcement from dieting and thinness (Hohlstein, Smith, and Atlas, 1998; Smith, Simmons, Flory, Annus, and Hill, 2007).

Interestingly, evidence also suggests that Japanese women endorse an extremely thin body ideal as a result of cultural norms (Fukunaga and Kobayashi, 1993; Imai, Masuda, and Komiya, 1994; Matsura, Fujimura, Nozawa, Iida, and Hirayama, 1992). It seems as if thinness may be intrinsic to Japanese culture as it has historically been highly valued (e.g. Eskildsen, 1998; Wagatsuma, 1967). This cultural standard may have been maintained or intensified through influence of European American, Western culture (Darling-Wolf, 2004; Evans and McConnell, 2003; Iijima-Hall, 1995; Matsura et al., 1992). In contrast, the thin female figure appears to be less associated with beauty within African American culture (Powell and Kahn, 1995; Rucker and Cash, 1992) and African American women score lower than European American women on cognitive measures of dietary restraint, shape concern, weight concern, body dissatisfaction, and drive for thinness (Abrams, Allen, and Gray, 1993; Atlas, Smith, and Hohlstein, 2002; Bardone-Cone and Boyd, 2007).

For African American women, one physical characteristic that may currently be associated with beauty is straight hair (McMichael, 2003; Milkie, 1999). Though little research has been conducted on this topic, it seems that African American women have, during the course of their history in the United States, come to value European American-like hair that is straight and smooth in texture (Bond and Cash, 1992; Makkar and Strube, 1995; Neal and Wilson, 1989). In fact, it is estimated that over 60 percent of African American women today wear their hair chemically straightened (Byrd and Tharps, 2001). Interestingly, Japanese women also tend to relate beauty to straight hair (Kowner, 2004). Despite a dearth of research on the subject, it seems as though Japanese women desire even straighter hair than what they have (Kowner, 2004). In addition to these markers of beauty in Japanese culture, height is also strongly emphasized (Darling-Wolf, 2004; Iijima-Hall, 1995; Kowner, 2004; Mukai, Kambara, and Sasaki, 1998). It was found that Japanese women, on average, wished to be two and a half inches taller (Iijima-Hall, 1995), while also emphasizing *hattou shin,* or long-legged beauty (Mukai et al., 1998). With the significant influence of westernization, it is not surprising that Japanese women may express a growing desire to be like Western, European American women and have greater concerns related to height (Mukai, in press; Mukai et al., 1998; Yazaki, 1992). Currently there exist no empirical data on this topic; however, news reports suggest that it may be the case that Japanese women, perhaps partly to achieve *hattou shin,* place emphasis on wearing very high heels, with an accompanying emphasis on the beauty and style of their shoes (Sims, 1999).

Based on this set of considerations, we hypothesize that (a) European American and Japanese women will report greater appearance concerns related to thinness than will African American women; (b) African American and Japanese women will report greater appearance concerns related to straight hair than will European American women; and (c) Japanese women will report greater appearance concerns related to height and shoe quality than will European American and African American women.

CULTURAL VARIATION IN INVESTMENT IN DIFFERENT FORMS OF APPEARANCE

To the degree that women in different cultural groups tend to emphasize different standards of appearance, they are likely to invest varying amounts of time and resources in different appearance-related pursuits. Accordingly, we hypothesize that (a) European American and Japanese women will report more investment in activities designed to pursue thinness than will African American women; (b) African American and Japanese women will report greater investment in hair style, including hair straightening, than will European American women; and (c) Japanese women will report greater investment in shoes than will European American and African American women.

CULTURAL VARIATION IN HARMS FROM PURSUING DIFFERENT FORMS OF APPEARANCE

The pursuit of thinness, straightened hair, and height or *hattou shin* (through wearing extremely high heeled shoes) vary in the harms they are likely to bring to women. Many researchers identify cognitions and beliefs concerning thinness and the pursuit of extreme thinness as central components of risk for the eating disorder of bulimia nervosa, and considerable empirical evidence supports that view (Stice, 2002).

Even subclinical features of bulimia nervosa, including unhealthy thinness and restriction of food, can result in serious negative consequences such as dizziness, headaches, gastrointestinal discomfort, hair loss, anemia, fatigue, poor motor control, paresthesia, and an overall decrease in the body's physiological processes (Taylor and Keys, 1950; Berg, 1999).

Moreover, the pursuit of thinness often leads to an unhealthy cycle of binge eating and purging, which can result in numerous negative side effects such as enlarged salivary glands, significant and permanent loss of dental enamel, esophageal tears, gastric rupture, cardiac arrhythmias, and production of fluid and electrolyte abnormalities (American Psychiatric Association, 2000).

Hair straightening can also bring negative consequences, such as hair breakage or hair loss. Studies have shown that cicatricial hair loss and scarring of the frontal and vertex of the scalp may be due to continued use of chemical relaxers and other hair-care practices (McMichael, 2003). This form of harm is, of course, different from the harm of eating disorders, and, though important, is perhaps less serious in nature than the harm associated with bulimia nervosa. The frequent wearing of high-heeled shoes is, in fact, associated with increased risk for some types of harm. Wearing high-heeled shoes increase one's risk for falling as the height of the heels causes one's body mass to be in an elevated and forward position (Lee, Jeong, and Freivalds, 2001; Snow and Williams, 1994). According to several news reports, deaths have been reported from tripping or dangerous driving as a result of wearing very high-heeled shoes; in addition, women experience twisted ankles, broken bones, bruises, and cuts (Sims, 1999). In fact, an estimated 23% of women at one community college in Japan have fallen while wearing high heels, and nearly half of those falls resulted in fractures or other serious injuries (Sims, 1999). Furthermore, though perhaps less severe, wearing high heels increases the chances of chronic foot pain, bunions, calluses, and pinched nerves (Angier, 1991). Studies have also found that wearing high-heeled shoes are associated with negative side effects such as sprained ankles (Nieto and Nahigian, 1975), lower back pain and leg pain (Lee et al., 2001), and changes in gait pattern (Gastwirth, O'Brien, Nelson, Manger, and Kindig, 1991). Accordingly, we hypothesize that women in the three cultural groups we studied would report mean levels of harm that vary in their nature as a function of the pursuit of culturally congruent standards of appearance. Thus, (a) European American and Japanese women will report higher levels of restricting-based eating disorder symptoms than will African American women; (b) African American and Japanese women will report more hair damage than will European American women; and (c) Japanese women will report greater levels of foot pain and blisters than will European American and African American women.

We also considered the possibility that the anticipated effects vary as a function of the degree to which women identify with their cultural group. We therefore administered a measure of ethnic identity to test whether (a) variation in ethnic identity within each group was associated with appearance concerns, investment, and harms; and (b) variation in ethnic identity moderated between group differences on the same variables.

METHOD

Participants

The participants in this study consisted of 251 European American women, 188 African American women, and 58 Japanese women. The European American and African American women were sampled from the same Southeastern United States University and the Japanese women were sampled from a Japanese University and through a foreign exchange club in America, which placed them at the same university as the women in the other groups. Participants were excluded if they were not European American, African American, or Japanese women. All participants spoke fluent English. The mean age of each group was as follows: European American, 20 years old; African American, 21 years old; Japanese, 25 years old. All of the participants had been in college for between one and two years.

MEASURES

Measures of Culturally Specific Markers of Appearance

Physical Attitudinal Appearance Questionnaire (PAAQ). We developed this questionnaire to test the hypotheses of different concerns regarding culturally specific markers of female appearance. Following pilot data interviews with women of different ethnicities, we wrote items to assess multiple attitudinal and physical aspects of appearance for women on a 6-point Likert Scale, from (1) strongly agree to (6) strongly disagree. We constructed four scales on a rational basis.

Their names, coefficient alpha estimates of internal consistency from the current sample, and sample items are as follows: (1) Thinness Appearance Concerns (4 items, α = .87), "Thinness is an important aspect of attractiveness;" (2) Hair Appearance Concerns (7 items, α = .78), "I would not leave the house without styling my hair;" (3) Height Attractiveness Concerns (5 items, α = .72), "Height is an important aspect of attractiveness," and "I wear high heeled shoes to look taller than I am;" and (4) Shoes Attractiveness Concerns (7 items, α = .81), "Wearing high heeled shoes is a sign of beauty."

Measures of Investment in Pursing Culturally Specific Markers of Appearance

Investment Scale (IVS). Again following pilot data interviews, we formed three measures, on rational grounds, of investment in the different appearance dimensions of interest. The first was a single item measure to reflect investment in the pursuit of thinness: "How much money per month do you spend on weight loss (including gym membership) (in dollars)?"

There were 9 response options, from $0 - $20, $20 - $30, $30-$40, up to $100+. The second measured investment in hair (2 items, α = .63), "Over the past 6 months, how many times did you go to the salon for your hair?" The third measured investment in shoes (2 items, α = .74), "Over the past six months, how many times did you go shopping for shoes?"

Measures of Harms in Pursing Culturally Specific Markers of Appearance

Eating Disorder Inventory-2 (EDI-2; Garner, Olmsted, and Polivy, 1983). The EDI-2 is a 91-item self-report questionnaire designed to measure psychological features commonly associated with anorexia nervosa and bulimia nervosa. It has been shown to have good internal consistency and good convergent and discriminant validity (Garner et al., 1983), and it is frequently used by clinicians for the assessment of eating disorder symptoms (Brookings, 1994). Two of the eleven subscales were used for this study: the Drive for Thinness (DFT) and Body Dissatisfaction (BD) subscales. Items for these two subscales were rated on a 6-point Likert Scale from (1) never to (6) always. The DFT subscale includes 7 items which assess excessive concern with dieting, preoccupation with weight, and fear of gaining weight. The BD subscale includes 9 items which assess dissatisfaction with overall body shape as well as the size of specific regions of the body, such as hips, stomach, and thighs. In the current sample, drive for thinness ($\alpha = .86$) and body dissatisfaction ($\alpha = .88$) were both internally consistent.

Eating Disorder Examination-Q(EDE-Q: Fairburn and Beglin, 1994). The EDE-Q is a questionnaire version of the Eating Disorders Examination semi-structured interview (Cooper and Fairburn, 1993) designed to assess cognitive and behavioral features of eating disorders. The EDE-Q has been shown to have good reliability and validity (Cooper and Fairburn, 1993; Luce and Crowther, 1999; Mond, Hay, Rodgers, Owen, andBeumont, 2004). It includes 41 items that are scored on a 7-point, forced-choice, rating scheme that focuses on behaviors exhibited in the past 28 days. The four subscales of the EDE-Q and estimates of their internal consistency in the current sample are as follows: Restraint ($\alpha = .77$), Eating Concern ($\alpha = .75$), Weight Concern ($\alpha = .87$), and Shape Concern ($\alpha = .92$) (Mond, Hay, Rogers, and Owen, 2006). It also includes items that, though not contributing to subscale scores, assess the frequency of eating disorder behaviors (e.g. binge eating and compensatory behaviors) as well as objective and subjective episodes of overeating.

Harms Scale Measure (HSM). We created this measure on rational grounds (using a 1 to 6 Likert Scale) to assess harms associated with the pursuit of beauty with respect to hair and height/shoes. We measured harm from chemical hair treatments with a rationally constructed 2 item scale ($\alpha = .79$), "Have you had any hair breakage occur as a result of chemically treating your hair?" We measured harm from height/shoes with a 3 item scale ($\alpha = .61$), "Have you injured yourself because of the shoes that you wore?"

Moderator Measure

Multigroup Ethnic Identity Measure (MEIM; Phinney, 1992). The MEIM used for this study is a revised version of the original 24-item self-administered questionnaire. The revised MEIM is a 12-item self-report questionnaire developed to assess the degree to which an individual identifies with her ethnic group.

The original construction of the MEIM consisted of 4 subscales: Affirmation and belonging, ethnic identity achievement, ethnic behavior practices, and other group orientation. The other-group orientation scale was considered by the measurement developers to be a separate construct (Phinney, 1992); for that reason, it is not included in the revised MEIM. The scale has shown good reliability and validity across a wide range of ethnic groups and ages (Phinney, 1992).

Responses to the MEIM are on a 4-point, Likert scale. An example question is, "I have a clear sense of ethnic background and what it means for me." In the current sample, the measure was internally consistent ($\alpha = .89$).

Procedure

The questionnaires were administered online and took about 45 minutes to complete. The European American and African American women completed the surveys as part of a large Southeastern University Psychology 100 subject participation requirement; therefore, they received class credit for completing the survey. The Japanese participants were from a university in Japan and from a student exchange program at a Southeastern University. They received five dollars, or five hundred yen, compensation. Questionnaires distributed to Japanese participants were written and answered in English.

Data Analysis

Because the PAAQ, IVS, and HSM were constructed for the purposes of this study, we began by investigating their factor structure. We used confirmatory factor analysis (CFA) to test whether each measure's factor structure conformed to our rationally developed structure. Responses to each measure were on a six point Likert-type scale, so we considered item responses to be ordered categorical for the purpose of the factor analysis. We therefore used the robust weighted least squares estimator (referred to as WLSMV in Mplus), implementedin the Mplus program (version 5, Muthén and Muthén, 1998-2009). This estimator is appropriate for categorical data and does not require multivariate normality. In determining factor structure, global model fit was evaluated using the: (a) Tucker-Lewis incremental fit index (TLI; Tucker and Lewis, 1973), (b) comparative fit index (CFI: Bentler, 1990), and the (c) root mean square error of approximation (RMSEA; Steiger and Lind, 1980). The magnitudes of these indices were evaluated with the aid of recommendations by Hu and Bentler (1999).

Essentially, for (a) and (b), values of .90 and above were considered adequate, whereas values of .95 or above were considered very good; for (c) values of .08 and below were considered adequate and .05 or less very good. One evaluates model fit by reviewing the values of each of the three fit indices. Then, to test each set of hypotheses described above, we used analysis of variance (ANOVA) and planned contrasts designed to provide the comparisons indicated by our hypotheses.

RESULTS

Factor Structure of Newly Constructed Measures

Table 1 presents the standardized factor loadings for the CFA for each of the three measures and correlations among them. The factor model for the PAAQ included four factors, consisting of concerns related to thinness, hair, height, and shoes. The fit was just adequate: CFI = .94; TLIU = .87; RMSEA = .11. Our test of the investment measure factor structure was a test of a two-factor model: We could not represent investment in the pursuit of thinness, because that construct was measured by a single item.

Table 1. Confirmatory Factor Analysis Item Loadings on Measures

	PAAQ				IVS			HSM	
	Hair	Thinness	Height	Shoes	Hair	Height/Shoes	Hair	Height/Shoes
Item 1	.62	.93	.47	.69	.89	.90	.85	.61
Item 2	.57	.63	.69	.60	.76	.76	.92	.85
Item 3	.70	.89	.78	.62				.62
Item 4	.61	.88	.68	.67				
Item 5	.55		.79	.77				
Item 6	.81			.81				
Item 7	.58			.64				

Note: In this confirmatory factor analysis model, each item was constrained to load on only one factor: all other loadings were constrained to zero. Thus, the item labels in this table refer to different items for the different factors; they are presented together to conserve space.

Table 2. Correlations among Appearance, Investment, and Harms Measures

		PAAQ				IVS			HSM	
		Hair	Thinness	Height	Shoes	Hair	Height/Shoes	Thinness	Hair	Height/Shoes
PAAQ	Hair	--	.16**	.28**	.34**	.27**	.21**	.10*	.21**	.12**
	Thin-ness		--	.23**	.20**	-.07	-.01	.25**	.03	.22**
	Height			--	.52**	.07	.16**	.22**	.11*	.28**
	Shoes				--	.17**	.39**	.09*	.10*	.29**
IVS	Hair					--	.39**	.13**	.13**	.01
	Height/Shoes						--	.24**	.07	.26**
	Thin-ness							--	-.07	.19**
HSM	Hair								--	.20**
	Height/Shoes									--

Note: Values in table are correlation coefficients. *$p < .05$; ** $p < .001$.
African Americans $n = 189$.
European Americans $n = 251$.
Japanese $n = 54$.

The two factor model measuring investment in straightened hair and high heeled shoes fit the data well: CFI = 1.0; TLI = .99; RMSEA = .05. Our test of the harms measure factor structure was also a two factor test: It involved measuring harm from the pursuit of chemically straightened hair and harm from high heeled shoes (other measures were used to assess harm from the pursuit of thinness, as noted above). The two factor structure fit well: CFI = 1.0; TLI = 1.0; RMSEA = .03. As shown in Table 2, the scales tend to be moderately correlated with each other, indicating that each scale has reliable variance that is not shared with the other scales.[1]

Hypotheses Concerning Appearance Concerns

Table 3 presents the results for each appearance-related hypothesis. Our first hypothesis was that European American and Japanese women would report greater appearance concerns about thinness than would African American women. Using Analysis of Variance (ANOVA), we tested this hypothesis with a planned contrast comparing the first two groups to the third. The hypothesis was supported by a significant contrast, such that European American and Japanese women reported significantly more thinness-based appearance concerns than African Americans. Our second hypothesis, that African American and Japanese women would report more appearance concerns regarding straight hair than European Americans was also supported: A planned contrast comparing the first two groups to the latter group was statistically significant.

Table 3. Culturally Specific Appearance Concerns

	African Americans	European Americans	Japanese	t-test
Thinness	2.99 (1.28)[b]	4.23 (1.10)[a]	4.04 (1.30)[a]	9.54**
Hair	3.22 (.94)[a]	2.65 (.91)[b]	3.27 (.78)[a]	6.19**
Height	2.34 (.90)[b]	2.35 (.87)[b]	2.81 (.99)[a]	3.65**
Shoes	2.94 (.95)[b]	2.75 (.94)[b]	3.33 (.85)[a]	3.70**

Note: Values in table are means, with standard deviations in parentheses. t-test is for the planned comparison hypothesis test; * $p < .05$; ** $p < .001$. Within a row, groups with common superscripts do not differ. African Americans $n = 189$; European Americans $n = 251$; Japanese $n = 54$.

Our third hypothesis was that Japanese women would endorse more appearance-related concerns with respect to height and to shoes than would women in the other two groups. As Table 3 shows, contrasts comparing Japanese women to the other women were significant for both comparisons: In each case, Japanese women reported stronger concerns than did African American or European American women.

Hypotheses Concerning Investment in the Pursuit of Culturally Defined Appearance

Our first hypothesis was that European American and Japanese women would report more investment in activities designed to pursue thinness than would African American women. As indicated in Table 4, this hypothesis was supported by a significant planned contrast comparing the former two groups of women to the latter group. Our second hypothesis, that African American and Japanese women would invest more time and money in hair style, including hair straightening, than would European American women, was also supported by a significant planned contrast (see Table 4).

Table 4. Investment (Cost and Time) in Pursuing Culturally Specific Standards of Attractiveness

	African Americans	European Americans	Japanese	t-test
Money on Weight Loss	.55 (1.46)	.71 (1.60)	1.07 (2.10)	2.04*
Hair	1.95 (2.06)	.70 (1.34)	1.19 (1.44)	5.26**
Shoes	1.26 (1.24)[a]	.83 (1.00)[b]	1.22 (1.32)[a]	1.15

Note: Values in table are means, with standard deviations in parentheses. t-test is for the planned comparison hypothesis test, * $p < .05$; ** $p < .001$. Within a row, groups with common superscripts do not differ. African Americans $n = 189$; European Americans $n = 251$; Japanese $n = 54$.

Our third hypothesis concerned investment in shoes. We did not find that Japanese women invested more in shoes than did the composite of the African American and European American women: That hypothesis was not supported. Instead, it appears from Table 4 that African American women reported investing in shoes to a similar degree as did Japanese women. A contrast test comparing those two groups to European American women was significant: $t(491) = 3.56$, $p < .001$; those two groups invested more than did European American women.

Hypotheses Concerning Cultural Variation in Harms from Pursuing Different Forms of Appearance

Our first hypothesis was that European American and Japanese women would report higher levels of restricting-based eating disorder symptoms than would African American women. As Table 5 shows, this hypothesis was supported. Again using planned contrasts comparing the former two groups to the latter group, European American and Japanese women reported significantly higher levels of body dissatisfaction, drive for thinness, EDE restraint, shape concerns, weight concerns; and eating concerns, binge eating behavior, purging behavior, and excessive exercise behavior. They did not report higher levels of laxative use: In our sample, the rates of laxative use were quite low for all groups.

Second, we hypothesized that African American and Japanese women would report more hair damage than would European American women. That hypothesis was also supported by a significant planned contrast test. Women in those two groups reported similar levels of hair damage and significantly more than did European American women. Third, we hypothesized that Japanese women would report more foot damage than would either African American or European American women. We tested that hypothesis with a planned contrast, comparing Japanese women to the average of the other two groups. The contrast test was significant and indicated that Japanese women reported more foot harm than did women in the other groups.

Table 5. Harms Associated with Pursuing Culturally Specific Standards of Attractiveness

	African American	European American	Japanese	t-test
EDE Restraint	.865 (1.12)[b]	1.75 (1.61)[a]	1.38 (1.26)[a]	4.75**
EDE Shape	1.61 (1.59)[b]	2.67 (1.71)[a]	2.83 (1.27)[a]	6.71**
EDE Weight	1.48 (1.62)[b]	2.46 (1.69)[a]	2.64 (1.37)[a]	6.25**
EDE Eating	.60 (.97)[b]	1.07 (1.18)[a]	1.19 (1.12)[a]	4.64**
EDE Binge	.48 (1.32)[b]	.80 (1.26)[a]	.69 (.81)[a]	2.00*
EDE Purge	.03 (.17)	.16 (.96)	.71 (.78)	1.74*
EDE Exercise	.83 (2.04)	2.41 (3.97)	1.30 (3.18)	2.94**
EDE Laxatives	.14 (.68)	.20 (.83)	.06 (.21)	-.11
Drive for Thinness	3.26 (1.23)[b]	3.83 (1.25)[a]	3.93 (.98)[a]	3.11**
Body Dissatisfaction	2.77 (1.11)	3.55 (1.05)	4.27 (1.17)	9.99**
Hair Loss and Hair Breakage due to Chemical Treatments	1.66 (1.67)[a]	.92 (1.32)[b]	1.69 (1.65)[a]	5.03**
Foot Pain, Blisters, Injuries, or Falls due to Shoes	.58 (.47)[b]	.78 (.48)[b]	1.04 (.51)[a]	5.09**

Note: Values in table are means, with standard deviations in parentheses. t-test is for the planned comparison hypothesis test, * $p < .05$; ** $p < .001$. Within a row, groups with common superscripts do not differ. African Americans $n = 189$; European Americans $n = 251$; Japanese $n = 54$.

Ethnic Identity

We tested the possible role of ethnic identity in two ways. First, we tested whether variation in ethnic identity was associated with culturally specific concerns, investments, and harms within each group.

It was not: No correlations relating the MEIM to any of the target variables were significant within groups. Second, we tested whether ethnic identity moderated any of the observed group differences. It did not.

DISCUSSION

The research described in this report was driven by the following hypotheses. Women are likely to form concerns about meeting culturally prescribed standards of appearance. They are thus likely to invest resources to meet those standards. Depending on the nature of a culture's appearance standards, pursuit of a positive appearance can result in harms to women. Thus, the risk for harm from pursuing beauty varies across cultures, as a function of the nature of a culture's standards of appearance.

The results of this study supported this set of hypotheses. Women in three different cultural groups (European American women in the United States, African American women, and Japanese women) had different patterns of concerns regarding their appearance. Women in each group tended to invest more in the pursuit of their culture's specific markers of appearance, and they reported harms specific to their pursuit of their culture's appearance markers.

As hypothesized, European American and Japanese women reported stronger concerns over appearing thin than did African American women and they invested more resources in the pursuit of thinness. Consistent with their concerns and investment, they reported significantly higher levels of cognitive and behavioral eating disorder symptoms (e.g., shape concerns, weight concerns, drive for thinness, body dissatisfaction, binge eating, purging) than did African American women. Thus, the presence of thinness as a cultural marker of appearance, and women's pursuit of thinness, are associated with higher levels of restraint-based eating disorder symptoms.

African American and Japanese women emphasized straight hair as a marker of beauty more than did European American women, and they invested more resources into their hair, particularly in efforts to straighten their hair. Again consistent with their concerns and investment, they reported higher levels of harm to their hair than did European American women (harms included hair loss and hair breakage). Their pursuit of straightened hair had negative, harmful consequences.

As hypothesized, Japanese women reported higher levels of appearance concerns regarding their height and the quality of their shoes. They did report investing more resources in their shoes than did European American women, but not more than did African American women. Perhaps as a result of their high level of concern and investment, Japanese women reported higher levels of foot pain, injuries, and falls due to their shoes than did women in the other two groups. Their concern related to height and *hattou shin*, and of attractive high-heeled shoes, resulted in harm.

Taken together, these findings suggest that women in different cultural groups tend to be exposed to different risks for harm as they pursue culturally defined markers of positive appearance. The theory that eating disorder risk is, at least in part, a function of cultural standards of appearance that emphasize thinness is quite well-known (Polivy and Herman, 2002; Thompson et al., 2004). What has received very little attention, though, has been the risk for harm from the pursuit of other, different markers of appearance by women from non-European American cultural groups. Japanese women are at increased risk for harm to their feet, and both Japanese and African American women are at increased risk for harm to their hair as a result of pursuing markers of appearance that are important to them. Within our current sample, none of these effects were moderated by women's level of ethnic identification.

This research did not investigate why the three cultural groups we studied have their particular standards. Nevertheless, it appears that the growing influence of western cultural norms plays a role in each form of risk that we have studied. For example, western influences appear to have augmented the emphasis in Japanese culture on thinness as attractive in women, and the same may be true for straight hair and height (Chisuwa and O'Dea, 2009; Darling-Wolf, 2004; Pike and Borovoy, 2004). It may also be true that for African American women the desire for straight hair originated in an effort to resemble the dominant, European American culture (Durham, 1991; Richerson and Boyd, 2005). An interesting, new line of inquiry could focus on whether harms attendant to the pursuit of beauty are present for women in cultural groups whose norms are influenced by other forces, such as cultural groups quite removed from western influence.

Although we did not measure the magnitude of the harms experienced by the women in the three groups, it certainly appears to be the case that the magnitude differs for women in different groups. Eating disorders, with their mortality rate of 5% per decade (Birmingham, Su, Hlynsky, Goldner, and Gao, 2005) and their other negative consequences, likely result in more harm to women than does hair damage or foot problems, as serious as those latter problems can be. It thus seemed that African American women were experiencing the least harm from the pursuit of attractiveness, European American women tended to experience much greater harm, and Japanese women were experiencing harms associated with each domain: Thinness, hair, and height/shoes. Though our sample of African American women seemed to be at least risk for developing eating disorders, it is of course true that some African American women are indeed at risk for eating disorders (e.g., Henrickson, Crowther, and Harrington, 2010). Furthermore, this study did not examine other damaging beauty practices, such as skin bleaching, which has been shown to increase harm for African American women (Charles, 2003).

The findings of this study should be understood in the context of its limitations. Of course, the most basic limitation concerns the limited range of groups studied. We sampled from only three cultural groups, each of which is influenced by western cultural norms. It should be noted that although our group of Japanese women were sampled from two locations (U.S. and Japan), there were no significant differences between the women on any of the variables. Nonetheless, we cannot know the degree to which the findings described here apply to other women.

Other limitations were as follows. First, we created many of the key measures for the study on rational grounds. Because those new measures thus do not have a history of construct validation on which to rely, it is possible that errors in measurement contributed to the findings reported here. However, the findings were generally quite consistent with prior theory and the study hypotheses, which supports the validity of the measures used (Landy, 1986; Strauss and Smith, 2009), and confirmatory factor analyses supported our rational structure to the scales. Second, we relied on self-report questionnaires. Interview assessments may have provided the opportunity to clarify questions, and thus more precision in participant responses.

Third, there could certainly be cultural differences in how women responded to the questionnaires. Although there are reports that Japanese respondents tend to produce lower scores than Americans on questionnaires requiring self-description (Lincoln, 1989), it also appears to be true that Japanese students do not seem to engage in socially desirable responding when completing anonymous questionnaires (Heineand Lehman, 1995). Indeed, some previous research has found no cross cultural differences in self-report format questionnaires (Okazaki, 2000). Fourth, these results are based on reports by college women. We do not know whether less educated, non-college women from each group emphasize different markers of attractiveness or experience either more or less harms than do college women. We also do not know the degree to which higher estimates of disordered behavior, such as binge eating and purging, which might come from use of a clinical sample, would alter any of the findings reported here.

Despite these limitations, the results reported here were internally consistent (women's appearance-related concerns, their investments in the pursuit of beauty, and the harms they experienced were consistently based on the same dimensions of appearance) and, for the most part, consistent with a priori predictions. Accordingly, it may be the case that women in different cultural groups seek to meet the standards of appearance of their groups and are at risk to experience harms as a result. This knowledge can lead to important future investigations, including (a) exploration of women in different cultures, their standards of a positive appearance, and whether they experience harms as they pursue those standards; (b) examination of cultural variables that may mediate ethnic differences; and (c) the development of culturally specific, culturally informed risk models and culturally informed interventions. Although eating disorders are a very serious harm some women face, it may be the case that the pursuit of beauty leads to very different harms that require different tools for intervention in different cultural contexts.

REFERENCES

Abrams, K., Allen, L., and Gray, J. (1993). Disordered eating attitudes and behaviors, psychology adjustment, and ethnic identity: A comparison of Black and White female college students. *International Journal of Eating Disorders, 14*, 49-57.

American Psychiatric Association.(2000). *Diagnostic and statistical manual of mental disorders – text revision* (4th edition). Washington, DC: APA.

Angier, N. (1991). Many Women Buy Foot Trouble With Fashionable High Heels. New York Times.

Atlas, J. G., Smith, G. T., Hohlstein, L. A., McCarthy, D. M., and Kroll, L. (2002). Similarities and differences between European American and African American women on eating disorder risk factors and symptoms.*The International Journal of Eating Disorders, 32*(3), 326-334.

Bardone-Cone, A. M., and Boyd, C. A. (2007). Psychometric properties of eating disorder instruments in black and white young women: Internal consistency, temporal stability, and validity. *Psychological Assessment, 19,* 356-362.

Bentler, P. M. (1990). Comparative fit indexes in structural models. *Psychological Bulletin, 107*, 238-246.

Berg, F. M. (1999). Health risks associated with weight loss and obesity treatment programs. *Journal of Social Issues, 55,* 277-297.

Birmingham, C. L., Su, J., Hlynsky, J. A., Goldner, E. M., and Gao, M. (2005). The mortality rate from anorexia nervosa.*International Journal of Eating Disorders, 38*, 143-146.

Bond, S., and Cash, T. F. (1992). Black beauty: Skin color and body images among African American college women. *Journal of Applied Social Psychology, 22*, 874-888.

Brookings, J. B., and Wilson, J. F. (1994). Personality and family-environment predictors of self-reported eating attitudes and behaviors.*Journal of Personality Assessment, 63*, 313-326.

Buss, D. M. (2006). Debating sexual selection and mating strategies. *Science, 312*, 690-691.

Buss, D. M., and Schmitt, D. P. (1993).Sexual strategies theory – An evolutionary perspective on human mating.*Psychological Review, 100*, 204-232.

Byrd, A. and Tharps, L. (2001). *Hair story: Untangling the roots of Black hair in America.* New York: St. Martin's Press.

Charles, C. (2003). Skin bleaching, self-hate, and black identity in Jamaica.*Journal of Black Studies, 33*, 711-728.

Chisuwa, N., and O'Dea, J. A. (2010). Body image and eating disorders amongst Japanese adolescents: A review of the literature. *Appetite, 54*, 5-15.

Cooper, M. J., Fairburn, C. G. (1993). Demographic and clinical correlates of selective information-processing in patients with bulimia-nervosa. *International Journal of Eating Disorders, 13*, 109-116.

Darling-Wolf, F. (2004). Sites of attractiveness: Japanese women and westernized representations of feminine beauty. *Critical Studies in Media Communications, 21*, 325-345.

Durham, W. (1991). *Coevolution: Genes, Culture, and Human Diversity*. Stanford, CA: Stanford University Press.

Eskildsen, S. (1998).*Asceticism in early Taoist religion.*New York: State University of New York Press.

Evans, P. and McConnell, A. (2003). Do racial minorities respond in the same way to mainstream beauty standards? Social comparison processes in Asia, Black, and White women. *Self and Identity, 2*, 153-167.

Fairburn, C.G. and Beglin, S.J. (1994). Assessment of eating disorders: Interview or self-report questionnaire? *International Journal of Eating Disorders, 16*, 363-370.

Fukunaga, S., and Kobayashi, E. (1993).The recognition of body weight in female students.*Japanese Journal of School Health, 35*, 396-404.

Garner, D. M., Garfinkel, P. E., Schwartz, D., and Thompson, M. (1980). Cultural expectations of thinness in women.*Psychological Reports, 47*, 483-491.

Garner, D. M., Olmsted, M. P., and Polivy, J. (1983) Development and validation of a multidimensional eating disorder inventory for anorexia nervosa and bulimia. *International Journal of Eating Disorders, 2*, 15–19.

Gastwirth, B. W., O'Brien, T. D., Nelson, R. M., Manger, D. C., and Kindig, S. A. (1991).An electrodynographic study of foot function in shoes of varying heel heights.*Journal of the American Pediatric Medical Association, 81*, 463-472.

Heine, S. J., and Lehman, D. R. (1995). Social desirability among Canadian and Japanese students. *Journal of Social Psychology, 135*, 777-779.

Henrickson, H. C., Crowther, J. H., and Harrington, E. F. (2010). Ethnic identity and maladaptive eating: Expectancies about eating and thinness in African American women. *Cultural Diversity and Ethnic Minority Psychology, 16*, 87-93.

Hohlstein, L. A., Smith, G. T., and Atlas, J. G. (1998). An application of expectancy theory to eating disorders: Development and validation of measures of eating and dieting expectancies. *Psychological Assessment, 10,* 49-58.

Hu, L., and Bentler, P. M. (1999). Cutoff criteria for fit indices in covariance structure analysis: Conventional criteria versus new alternatives. *Structural Equation Modeling, 6,* 1-55.

Iijima-Hall, C. C. (1995) Asian eyes: Body image and eating disorders of Asian and Asian American women. *Eating Disorders; The Journal of Treatment and Prevention, 3,* 8-19.

Imai, K., Masuda, T., and Komiya, S. (1994).Actual state of misconception regarding physique and desire for slenderness in female adolescents.*Japanese Journal of Nutrition, 52,* 75-82.

Kowner, R. (2004). When ideals are too "far off": Physical self-ideal discrepancy and body dissatisfaction in Japan. *Genetic, Social, and General Psychology Monographs, 130,* 333-361.

Landy, F. J. (1986). Stamp collecting versus science – validation as hypothesis-testing. *American Psychologist, 41,* 1183-1192.

Lee, C., J, E., and Freivalds, A. (2001). Biomechanical effects of wearing high-heeled shoes.*International Journal of Industrial Ergonomics, 28,* 321-326.

Lincoln, J. R. (1989). Employee work attitudes and management practice in the United States and Japan: Evidence from a large comparative survey. *California Management Review, Fall,* 89-106.

Lovejoy, M. (2001). Disturbances in the social body: Differences in body image and eating problems among African American and White women. *Gender and Society, 15,* 239-261.

Luce, K. H., and Crowther, J. H. (1999). The reliability of the eating disorder examination-self-report questionnaire version (EDE-Q). *International Journal of Eating Disorders, 25,* 349-351.

Makkar, J. K., and Strube, M. J. (1995). Black women's self-perceptions of attractiveness following exposure to White versus Black beauty standards: The moderating role of racial identity and self-esteem. *Journal of Applied Social Psychology, 25,* 1547-1566.

Matsura, K., Fujimura, M., Nozawa, Y., Iida, Y., and Hirayama, M (1992). The body shape preferences of Japanese female students. *International Journal of Obesity, 16,* 87-93.

McKnight Investigators. (2003). Risk factors for the onset of eating disorders in adolescent girls: results of the McKnight longitudinal risk factor study. *American Journal of psychiatry, 160,* 248-254.

McMichael, A. (2003). Ethnic hair update: Past and present. *Journal of American Academy of Dermatology, 48,* S127-133.

Milkie, M. A. (1999). Social comparisons, reflected appraisals, and mass media: The impact of pervasive beauty images on black and white girls' self-concepts. *Social Psychology Quarterly, 62,* 190-210.

Miller, M. N., and Pumariega, A. J. (2001). Culture and eating disorders: A historical and cross-cultural review. *Psychiatry-Interpersonal and Biological Processes, 64,* 93-110.

Mond, J. M., Hay, P. J., Rodgers, B., and Owen, C. (2006). Eating Disorder Examination Questionnaire (EDE-Q): Norms for young adult women. *Behaviour Research and Therapy, 44,* 53-62.

Mond, J. M., Hay, P. J., Rodgers, B., Owen, C., and Beumont, P. J. V. (2004). Temporal stability of the eating disorder examination questionnaire. *International Journal of Eating Disorders, 36*, 195-203.

Mukai, T. (in press). Body image and the Westernization of Japanese women. In S. A. O'Neale and C. Thompkins (Eds.), *Keepers of the flame: Power, myth, and cultural consciousness in ethnic female identity.* Detroit, MI: Wayne State University Press.

Mukai, T. (1996). Body dissatisfaction, depressive affect and eating problems among Japanese adolescent girls: A prospective study. *Japanese Journal of Counseling Science, 29,* 37-43.

Muthén, L. K., and Muthén, B. O. (1998-2009). *Mplus user's guide.* (Fourth Edition ed.). Los Angeles, CA: Muthén and Muthén.

Neal, A. M., and Wilson, M. L. (1989). The role of skin color and features in the black community: Implications for black women and therapy. *Clinical Psychology Review, 9,* 323-333.

Nieto, E., and Nahigian, S. H. (1975). Severe ankle injuries while wearing elevated platform shoes. *Ohio Medicine, 71,* 137-141.

Okazaki, S. (2000). Asian American and white American differences on affective distress symptoms: Do symptom reports differ across reporting methods. *Journal of Cross-Cultural Psychology, 31,* 603-625.

Owen, P. R., and Laurel-Seller, E. (2000). Weight and shape ideals: Thin is dangerously in. *Journal of Applied Social Psychology, 30,* 979-990.

Phinney, J. (1992). The multigroup ethnic identity measure: A new scale for use with adolescents and young adults from diverse groups. *Journal of Adolescent Research, 7,* 156-176.

Pike, K.M. and Borovoy, A. (2004) The rise of eating disorders in Japan: Issues of culture and limitations of the model of "westernization." *Culture, Medicine and Psychiatry, 28,* 493-531.

Polivy, J., and Herman, C. P. (2002). Causes of eating disorders.*Annual Review of Psychology, 53,* 187-213.

Powell, A. D., and Kahn, A. S. (1995). Racial-differences in women's desires to be thin.*International Journal of Eating Disorders, 17,* 191-195.

Richerson, P. J., and Boyd, R. (2005). *Not by Genes Alone: How Culture Transformed Human Evolution.* Chicago: University of Chicago Press.

Rubinstein, S., and Caballero, B. (2000). Is Miss America an undernourished role model.*Journal of the American Medical Association, 283,* 1569.

Rucker, C.E. III, and Cash, T.F. (1992). Body images, body-size perceptions and eating behaviors among African-American and white college women. International Journal of Eating Disorders, 12, 291-300.

Shackelford, T. K., Schmitt, D. P., and Buss, D. M. (2005). Universal dimensions of human mate preferences.*Personality and Individual Differences, 39,* 447-458.

Sims, C. (1999) Be tall and chic as you wobble to the orthopedist. *Tokyo Journal.*

Smith, G. T., Simmons, J. R., Flory, K., Annus, A. M., and Hill, K. K. (2007). Thinness and eating expectancies predict subsequent binge eating and purging behavior among adolescent girls. *Journal of Abnormal Psychology, 116,* 188-197.

Snow, R. E., and Williams, K. R. (1994). High heeled shoes: Their effect on center of mass position, posture, three-dimensional kinematics, rearfoot motion, and ground reaction forces. *Archives of Physical Medicine and Rehabilitation, 75,* 568-576.

Steiger, J. H., and Lind, J. C. (1980).Statistically-based tests for the number of factors.*Annual Spring Meeting of the Psychometric Society.* Iowa City, Iowa.

Stice, E. (2001). A prospective test of the dual-pathway model of bulimic pathology: Mediating effects of dieting and negative affect. *Journal of Abnormal Psychology, 110,* 124-135.

Stice, E. (2002). Risk and maintenance factors for eating pathology: A meta-analytic review. *Psychological Bulletin, 128,* 825-848.

Strauss, M. E., and Smith, G. T. (2009). Construct validity: Advances in theory and methodology. *Annual Review of Clinical Psychology, 5,* 1-25.

Taylor, H. L., and Keys, A. (1950). Adaptation to caloric restriction.*Science, 112,* 215-218.

Thompson, J. K., van der Berg, P., Roehrig, M. Guarda, A. S., and Heinberg, L. J. (2004). The sociocultural attitudes towards appearance scale-3 (SATAQ-3): Development and validation. *International Journal of Eating Disorders, 35,* 293-304.

Tucker, L. R., and Lewis, C. (1973). A reliability coefficient for maximum likelihood factor analysis.*Psychometrika, 38,*1-10.

Wagatsuma, H. (1967). The social perception of skin color in Japan.*Daedalus, 96,* 407-443.

Yazaki, Y. (1992). *Dare ga daietto wo hajim etaka?* [Who started dieting?] Tokyo Ota Shuppan.

In: Binge Eating and Binge Drinking
Editor: Simon B. Harris
ISBN: 978-1-62618-580-7
© 2013 Nova Science Publishers, Inc.

Chapter 7

REVISION OF THE MEASURES TO DETECT CHILDHOOD BINGE EATING DISORDER AND OTHER RELATED DISORDERED EATING

Ausiàs Cebolla,[1,2,*] *Conxa Perpiñá*[2,3,†]
and Cristina Botella[1,2,‡]

[1]Department of Basic Psychology, Clinical and Psychobiology Universitat Jaume I, Castellón, Spain
[2]CIBEROBN Fisiopatologia de la Obesidad y la Nutrición, Spain
[3]Universitat de Valencia, Valencia, Spain

ABSTRACT

Binge eating disorder (BED) is characterized by the presence of recurrent overeating episodes, accompanied by loss of control in a short period of time. BED may manifest itself differently in children than in adults. Recently, researchers have proposed provisional criteria for measuring BED in children, the most frequent of all eating disorders in obese children. Research has shown that children who report episodes of loss of control have more severe obesity and increased symptoms of depression and anxiety. Furthermore, these children have been found to have greater difficulties and need longer weight loss treatments than children who only have overeating episodes. In order to make a differential diagnosis and detect the early signs of binge eating disorder, and thus improve treatment, it is essential to have sensitive and psychometrically valid instruments. The aim of this chapter is to review the most useful psychological instruments for the detection of BED and its associated symptoms. The present review will include instruments that directly measure the presence of binge eating, such as the Questionnaire of eating and weight patterns, adolescent and parent version (Johnson, Kirk and Reed, 2001) or the Children's binge eating disorder scale (Shapiro, et al., 2007). It will also describe other instruments that measure traits or styles directly related to

---

[*] Ausiàs Cebolla: Department of Basic Psychology, Clinical and Psychobiology. University Jaume I, Castelló de la Plana, Avd/ Sos Banyat s/n, Telf: 964387643, E-mail: Ausiàs Cebolla: acebolla@uji.es.
[†] Conxa Perpiñá. E-mail: Conxa Perpiñá: perpinya@uv.es.
[‡] Cristina Botella. E-mail: Cristina Botella mail: botella@uji.es.

BED, such as emotional eating, restraint or diet, weight preoccupation, compensatory behaviors or risk factors. Finally, the latest research developed to treat BED will be reviewed, and future directions will be suggested.

INTRODUCTION

It may seem that humans instinctively and automatically acquire the ability to feed and nourish themselves in a healthy and autonomous way. However, the fact that there are medical and mental problems such as obesity (considered an epidemic in the 21st century) and eating disorders suggests that these capabilities depend on several factors and complex processes. Children depend on their caregivers for their nutritional requirements; thus, eating meets biological functions, but also psychological and social ones. Feeding and nurturance are of fundamental significance to the child's experience of the world and his/her place in it (Cooper and Stein, 2006).

Eating problems or disordered eating can occur at any point across the developmental course, and they typically first appear during childhood and adolescence (Le Grange, 2011). They are often developmentally appropriate "phases" that, in most cases, resolve themselves without requiring any treatment (Bryant-Waugh, and Lask, 1995).

However, if these problems are not overcome, the children can go on to develop more serious difficulties for a longer time, causing medical complications (Cooper and Stein, 2006). Disordered eating or feeding problems could be defined as eating patterns or behaviors that result in disruptions in expected growth, development and/or functioning.

In practice, issues that cause concern and lead to clinical presentation usually include impairments in physical functioning, causes of childhood distress, and situations in which the child's eating significantly interferes with family life (Bryant-Waugh and Nicholls, 2011).

Although childhood and early adolescence is a period of heightened vulnerability to these disorders, the official classification systems, such as the Diagnostic and Statistical Manual of Mental Disorders, fourth edition, text revision (DSM-IV-TR; American Psychiatric Association [APA], 2000), describe them poorly and lack a developmental perspective. On the one hand, in "Feeding and Eating Disorders of Infancy and Early Childhood" under the category of "Disorders usually first diagnosed in infancy, childhood, or adolescence", the Feeding disorder of early childhood, Pica, and the Rumination disorder are all included.

On the other hand, the category of Eating Disorders is defined by severe disturbances in eating behavior that intrude upon preoccupations with food, eating, body shape and weight (Eddy, Herzog and Zucker, 2011), and includes two main diagnoses: Anorexia Nervosa and Bulimia Nervosa, which have somewhat different presentations in children compared to young adults or adults (Bryant-Waugh, Markham, Kreipe, and Walsh, 2010).

Binge eating disorder (BED) was included as a diagnostic category subsumed under Eating Disorders Not Otherwise Specified (EDNOS) in the fourth edition of the DSM (APA, 1994). The central feature of BED is the presence of recurrent binge eating episodes consisting both of consuming large quantities of food and experiencing a sense of loss of control over eating, in the absence of the regular use of inappropriate compensatory behaviors (vomiting, purging, fasting or excessive excising).

The binge eating episode must also be associated with at least three of the following: eating much more rapidly than normal; eating until one feels uncomfortably full; eating large amounts of food without being hungry; eating alone because it is an embarrassing situation; or feeling disgusted with oneself, depressed or guilty after overeating. Symptoms must occur twice a week for six months. Binge eating is often triggered by emotional cues, especially negative ones, and may serve affect-regulation purposes (Binford, Pederson, Peterson, Crow, and Mitchell, 2004; Wolff, Crosby, Roberts and Wittrock, 2000).

Binge eating without regular compensatory behavior can occur in children and adolescents, although the available data suggest that dieting behavior may not be prominent in early-onset BED (Marcus and Kalarchian, 2003). These authors proposed modified diagnostic criteria for BED that are appropriate for children younger than 14 years of age.

A diagnosis of BED should be made if recurrent binge eating occurs (during at least a 3-month period), includes both food seeking when not hungry and loss of control over eating, and is characterized by food seeking in response to negative affect, food seeking as a reward, or sneaking or hiding food.

Moreover, there is no use of regular compensatory behaviors, and the symptoms do not occur exclusively within the context of an episode of anorexia or bulimia nervosa (Marcus and Kalarchian, 2003).

Similar to BED in adults, a sense of loss of control, but not the amount of food intake, seems to influence the subjective experience of BE (Tanofsky-Kraff, Yanovski; Schevey, Olsen, Gustafson and Yanovski, 2009). Loss of control rather than mere overeating or dieting is further associated with a greater eating disorder, disturbed eating cognitions and general psychopathology, a higher BMI, and higher body fat percentages (Roehrig, Sperry, Lock and Thompson, 2008; Tanofsky-Kraff, et al., 2009).

Recently, new preliminary diagnostic criteria have been developed by Tannofsky-Kraff et al. (2008), called the Loss of Control Eating Disorder (LOC-ED), to be used with children aged 12 years and younger. These preliminary diagnoses describe consuming food while experiencing a lack of control over eating, regardless of the amount of food consumed, which is more sensitive to children's characteristics.

It is not known whether binge eating in childhood progresses into BED in adulthood (Marcus and Kalarchian, 2003). Retrospective studies of adults with BED suggest that binge eating symptoms began between the ages of 11 and 13 in those who reported binge eating symptoms before dieting, whereas binge-eating symptoms developed in late adolescence in those who reported that dieting preceded the binge-eating behavior (Marcus and Kalarchian, 2003; Munsch and Hilbert, 2005).

Childhood obesity, adverse childhood experiences such as teasing about shape and weight, a predisposition to depressive mood and obesity, and the transmission of dysfunctional eating behavior related to a thin–ideal internalization are considered risk factors contributing to its development (Munsch Berlinger, 20005; Wertheim, Paxton, and Blaney, 2004).

Little is known about the prevalence and course of binge eating episodes and BED in children and adolescents. In fact, the data are very different depending on the assessment instruments used and the characteristics of the sample studied. The prevalence of binge eating episodes in children and adolescents ranges from 7-28% (Munsch and Hilbert, 2005), and these episodes appear to be more common in overweight or obese children than in their normal-weight peers (Tanofsky–Kraff, et al., 2004). These results are usually obtained with self-reports. The full syndrome of BED in children, according to the DSM-IV criteria, ranges from 1 to 3% (Munsch and Hilbert, 2005).

Approximately 1% of overweight and obese children seeking weight loss treatment met full diagnostic criteria for BED, whereas 9% admitted to overeating with a loss of control, but did not meet other diagnostic criteria for BED (Decaluwe and Braet, 2003). These data are most often assessed with interviews.

Detecting eating problems in children may be complicated. First, a complaint is made by the caregiver, leading to its evaluation and appraisal. Second, upon referral, the description of the problem may be very vague, and the symptoms may broadly fall within the domains of problems related to eating, weight, compensatory behaviors, and concerns related to body image. Furthermore, the DSM criteria for ED in children and adolescents receive criticism for not capturing its different aspects and for being too focused on adult behavior (for example, the freedom to decide which foods to buy or have available).

All these controversies mean that the issue of assessment instruments is a key factor in making further progress in understanding disordered eating and, especially, in its early detection. Therefore, it is important to have a good battery of tests, self-reports and interviews for both parents and children.

ASSESSMENT OF BINGE EATING DISORDER AND LOSS OF CONTROL IN CHILDREN

Children have difficulty responding to BED adult diagnostic questions because of the length of time required to administer the SCID (2007) interview and the open ended questions. Therefore, it is essential to have instruments specifically designed to measure and diagnose BED in children.

In the past ten years, specific instruments have been designed to measure binge eating and loss of control over eating in children. The instruments to assess BED can be divided into interviews and self-reports.

It is important to combine both methods due to the ambiguity of terms such as "a large amount of food" and "loss of control", which are the most important behaviors to be measured when assessing BED in children.

However, parents should also be considered in the evaluation; research has found that there is poor concordance in observed rates of binge eating when child self-reports are compared to parent-reports of children's behavior, as parents may be misinformed about their children's behaviors (Tanofsky-Kraff, Yanofski, and Yanofski, 2005).

Finally, there are other relevant measures, such as eating styles or eating without hunger, that must be measured, due to their relationship with BED as risk factors, or even as a severity continuum measure, as in the case of emotional eating (Davis et al., 2012).

Next, the most relevant instruments designed to measure BED will be presented. The first group of instruments will be the specific measures for binge eating episodes and loss of control to be answered by parents and children. Then, other relevant measures related to eating and general psychopathology will be presented, also to be answered by both children and parents.

SPECIFIC MEASURES FOR BINGE EATING EPISODES AND LOSS OF CONTROL

Children

Interview

Children's binge eating disorder scale (C-BEDS; Shapiro, et al., 2007). This interview-administered scale is designed to measure BED in children, taking into account the adapted provisional criteria (Marcus and Kalarchian, 2003). It is composed of 7 questions based on the seven critical behaviors proposed by Marcus and Kalarchian (2003). It requires a "yes" or "no" answer.

In comparing methods to detect BED in children, this scale was more sensitive to detecting BED than the SCID adult criteria, increasing the percentage from 6-9% to 12.9-22% (Cebolla, Perpiñá, Botella, Alvarez and Lurbe, 2012; Shapiro et al., 2007). 40% of those diagnosed with BED using the SCID were also diagnosed with the C-BEDS (Shapiro et al., 2007). This interview is a simple, easily understood, and quick way to ask about or assess binge eating in children. It can be used as an initial screening tool to detect BED in children, and it is more adapted to the specific characteristics of children's behavior.

The Child Eating Disorder Examination (ChEDE, Bryan-Waugh, Cooper, Taylor and Lask, 1994). This is a semi-structured interview that assesses behavioral and attitudinal correlates of EDs in children aged 8–14 years. It is an adaptation of the Eating Disorders Examination (Cooper and Fairburn, 1987) and generates four subscales: restraint, eating concern, weight concern and shape concern. It also has a global score of ED severity in children. It identifies three types of eating episodes: objective binge eating (overeating with loss of control), subjective binge eating (loss of control without overeating), and objective overeating (without loss of control) (Tanofsky-Kraff, Yanofski and Yanofski, 2005). This scale has demonstrated excellent inter-rater reliability (Spearman rank correlations from 0.91-1.0).

Self-Report

Questionnaire of eating and weight patterns-adolescent version (QEWP-A; Johnson, Grieve, Adams, and Sandy, 1999) This self-report questionnaire is designed to measure eating disorders. Adapted from the Questionnaire on eating and weight pattern-revised (QEWP; Spitzer et al., 1993), it simply modifies various words and adapts the language to children. This questionnaire is composed of 16 items and assesses the presence or absence of binge eating and compensatory methods for weight control; it also provides decision rules for the differential diagnosis of BED (Cebolla et al., 2012). It differentiates between three different populations: those who report overeating episodes (OE); overeating with loss of control or binge eating episodes (BE); and no episodes of disordered eating (NE).

The questionnaire has adequate stability, predictive ability, and concurrent validity in the adult version (Antony, Johnson, Carr-Nangle, and Abel, 1994; Spitzer et al., 1992, Johnson, Kirk and Reed, 2001).

Youth Eating Disorder Examination-Questionnaire (YEDE-Q; Goldschmidt, Doyle, Wilfley; 2007) This self-report questionnaire measures ED psychopathology, including BED, and is to be used in children 12–17 years old.

It is an adaptation of the Eating Disorder Examination-Questionnaire (Luce and Crowther, 1999), and assesses the full spectrum of ED psychopathology, but adapted to children by including examples, pictures and vignettes exemplifying a child experiencing loss of control. It is composed of 41 items and four factors: Restraint, Eating Concern, Weight Concern and Shape Concern. The answers range from "not at all" to "a little bit", "a lot", and "very, very much". It shows good subscale internal consistency; Cronbach's alpha (0.78–0.95). YEDE-Q and ChEDE were significantly correlated, with correlations ranging from .58 to .84 (Goldschmidt, Doyle, Wilfley; 2007).

Parents

Questionnaire of eating and weight patterns-parents' version (QEWP-P; Johnson et al., 1999). This version of the QEWP, to be answered by the parents, is identical to the children's version. The QEWP-P had reasonably high specificity, but low sensitivity for the presence of binge episodes (sensitivity 50%, specificity 83%) or objective overeating (sensitivity 30%, specificity 79%) during the past month (Johnson et al., 1999). Compared to children, the parents are better at reporting (or do it more often) that their children engage in binge eating than their children are. However, children reported more compensatory behaviors than parents did (Steinberg et al., 2003).

OTHER RELEVANT MEASURES RELATED TO EATING AND GENERAL PSYCHOPATHOLOGY

Other relevant measures refer to scales that measure different behaviors or attitudes that have been shown to be related to BED. Eating in the absence of hunger, emotional eating, and loss of control eating may each play a role in promoting excessive weight gain and disordered eating pathology in youth (Vannucci et al., 2012). Another interesting measure refers to Eating Attitudes. These eating attitudes are a risk factor for developing any ED, but they are useful for measuring vulnerability to developing BED.

Children

Children's Eating Attitudes Test (ChEAT; Maloney et al., 1988). This self-report questionnaire is designed to measure maladaptive attitudes toward their eating and dieting behavior in children under 15 years old. It is an adaptation of the Eating Attitudes Test (EAT; Garner, Olmsted, Bohr and Garfinkel, 1982), which was developed and tested on adolescents and adults. Composed of 26 items, it is rated on a Likert scale from 1 (always) to 6 (never). It is composed of four subscales: 'body/weight concern' (I am scared of being overweight), 'food preoccupation' (I think about food a lot of the time), 'dieting' (I eat diet foods), and 'eating concern' (I stay away from eating when I am hungry) (Ranzenhofer et al., 2008). The ChEAT has shown adequate to good internal reliability (Smolak and Levine, 1994) and good test-retest reliability (Maloney et al., 1989). The authors agree that it is a screening and research instrument, rather than a diagnostic tool (Smolak and Levine, 1994).

Dutch Eating Behavior Questionnaire for Children (DEBQ-C; original Dutch version) (Van Strien and Oosterveld, 2008). This questionnaire measures the three main eating styles in children from 7 to 10 years old: restraint (cognitive suppression of internal hunger signals in order to lose or maintain a particular weight), external (eating in response to external food-related cues (e.g., sight and smell of attractive food), and emotional (eating in response to negative emotions (e.g., anxiety or irritability) in order to relieve stress while disregarding internal physiological signals of hunger and satiety). It is an adaptation of the adult version of the questionnaire (Van strien, et al., 1986). It is composed of 20 items with 3 possible answers (1="no", 2="sometimes", 3="yes"), 7 items in the restrained factor, 7 items in the emotional factor, and 6 items in the external factor. This structure was invariant for sex, body mass index (BMI) and age. Moreover, Cronbach's alphas ranging from 0.73 to 0.82 were obtained. Emotional eating showed a positive correlation with "bulimia and food preoccupation". "Restrained eating" correlated positively with "diet" and "bulimia and food preoccupation"; it also showed a relationship with "oral control". Emotional eating has been used as a risk factor and continuum variable in BED, and it has also been related to loss of control episodes (Goossens et al., 2007). In children, results for "Emotional eating" showed that this kind of eating is more frequent in clinical overweight children than non-clinical ones.

Emotional eating scale for children (EES-C; Tanofsky-Kraft et al., 2007). The Emotional Eating Scale is a self-report measure used to assess the urge to cope with negative affect by eating. It is an adaptation of the Emotional Eating Scale for adults (Arnow, Kenardy, and Agras, 1995), and was designed for use with 8- to 17-year-old children. It is a 25-item self-report questionnaire scored on a 5-point Likert scale (no desire to eat to very strong desire to eat). It is composed of three subscales: depression, anger/anxiety/frustration and feeling unsettled. In a later validation (Perpiñá, Cebolla, Botella, Lurbe and Torró, 2011), a 5-factor structure appeared: Anger, Anxiety, Depression, Restlessness and Helplessness. The EES-C subscales have demonstrated good internal consistency (alphas: 0.83 to 0.95), convergent and discriminant validity, and adequate temporal stability (Tanofsky-Kraff et al., 2007; Perpiñá et al., 2010) for eating psychopathology. Furthermore, children with binge eating episodes report a significantly higher level of desire to eat when feeling anger (Perpiñá et al., 2010).

Eating in the Absence of Hunger Questionnaire for Children and Adolescents (EAHC; Tanofsky-Kraff et al., 2008) The EAH-C is a self-report questionnaire designed to assess the frequency of eating without hunger in youth (8–19 years old). It consists of 14 items and has a three-factor structure: Negative Affect (feeling angry or frustrated), External Eating (food looks, tastes or smells so good), and Fatigue/Boredom (feeling tired). All questions were rated on a 5-point Likert scale from 1 = never to 5 = always, and they measure the frequency with which children eat past satiation and in the absence of hunger. The questionnaire's instructions refer to the number of times the children eat after experiencing satiation. The main instructions state: "Imagine that you are eating a meal or snack at home, school or in a restaurant. Imagine that you eat enough of your meal so that you are no longer hungry". The sentence for each of the seven items begins, "In this situation, how often do you keep eating because…". The questionnaire shows good psychometric properties, with Cronbach's alphas ranging from 0.80 to 0.83 (Tanofsky-Kraff et al., 2008). Overweight and obese youth ate more in the absence of hunger than non-overweight youth and those with loss of control (Tanofsky-Kraff et al., 2008; Shomaker et al., 2010).

Parents

The Child Behavior Checklist (CBCL; Achenbach, 1991). This is a self-report measure to be answered by the parent about the child's functioning across a range of behavioral domains (e.g., depression, anxiety, social problems). This scale was designed to be used as an objective tool for screening symptoms of psychopathology in children. It is composed of a 138-item rating scale (0= not true to 2=very true or often true) that yields scores for total behavior problems, internalizing and externalizing behaviors, and three scores for competence (activity, social competence and school competence). The CBCL generates eight clinical subscales grouped in two scales, the Internalizing scale (Withdrawn, Somatic Complaints, and Anxious/Depressed Mood) and the Externalizing scale (Disruptive and Aggressive Behavior). It has good reliability and validity (Achenbach, 1991; Achenbach and Elderbrock, 1991).

Child feeding questionnaire (Birch et al., 2001) This is a self-report measure to assess parental beliefs, attitudes, and practices regarding child feeding, with a focus on obesity proneness in children. It is composed of 31 items with a 5-point Likert-type scale and a seven factor structure: Perceived responsibility (How often are you responsible for deciding what your child's portion sizes are?); Parent's perceived weight (the weight in childhood, adolescence, etc.); Perceived child weight (The weight of the child as a toddler); Parent's concern about child's weight (How concerned are you about your child eating too much when you are not around her?); and three additional factors that assess parents' attitudes and practices regarding their use of controlling child feeding strategies, such as monitoring (How much do you keep track of the high-fat foods that your child eats?), restriction (I have to be sure that my child does not eat too many high-fat foods), and pressure to eat (If my child says, "I'm not hungry", I try to get her to eat anyway).

It is based on Costanzo and Woody's (1985) model, which proposes that parental control has adverse effects on eating behaviors and weight in children, because it does not allow them to develop self-control skills, but this imposition of control in feeding is currently due to a concern about the child's risk of obesity. The questionnaire has good psychometric properties and test-retest reliability (Birch et al., 2001).

TREATMENT PERSPECTIVES

Most of the research on the treatment of eating disorders such as Bulimia Nervosa (BN) and BED has been conducted in adults, and the results point out that cognitive-behavioral Therapy (CBT) is the treatment of choice (National Institute of Clinical Excellence, NICE, 2004). Regarding children and adolescents, it remains unclear whether these approaches are also successful in reducing symptoms of disordered eating and helping to lose weight in those cases where obesity and overweight are present. However, several authors agree in pointing out some strategies: 1) the need for the problem to be addressed by a multidisciplinary team; 2) treatment of the disordered eating before weight regulation (which seems to be a precondition for stable weight reduction in adults); or 3) the need to make adjustments to the CBT for age, circumstances and level of development, as well as including family members in treatment, as appropriate.

Regarding the first issue, from several points of view it is essential to take a multidisciplinary approach in order to manage changes in habits related to food, nurturance, physical activity, social competence, emotional management and interpersonal relationships. Regarding the second point, following Munsch and Hilbert (2005) or Goldfield and Epstein (2002), children should learn to identify and change the triggering and maintaining cues of binge eating; that is, they are taught to analyze target behavior by applying behavioral techniques such as self-monitoring, stimulus control and response prevention. For weight management purposes, the children are advised to follow a balanced nutritional style and encouraged to engage in regular physical activity. Regarding point 3, based on their previous experiences with ED, Campbell and Schmidt (2011) claimed that adolescents are strongly reliant on their families, and results of research studies have shown good outcomes using family approaches in the treatment of adolescents, specifically for AN, BN or BED. Moreover, parents must be trained in their role to support, promote and supervise children's efforts. Therefore, they must be an important pillar in training the child in social competences such as self-assertiveness and coping techniques. Finally, children and parents, in order to work on the maintenance of the improvements in weight and eating behavior, are taught to identify lapses and relapses in the early stage, and accept them as a natural step in the change (Munsch and Hilbert, 2005).

In a recent study, Moens, Braet and Van Winckel (2010) presented results of an 8-year evolution of overweight children treated in an outpatient program. Although the study is focused on the treatment of overweight, it is clear that disordered eating was present as well. The authors concluded with the recommendation of taking into account the child's age, degree of overweight and global self-worth, as well as the occurrence of maternal psychopathology. Pre-treatment factors related to later weight stabilization have the greatest informative value for recommendations about treatment assignments.

FURTHER RESEARCH AND QUESTIONS

DSM criteria for ED have often been criticized for not sufficiently capturing the breadth of eating problems seen in children and adolescents. Bryant-Waugh and Lask (1995) claimed that ED often presents differently in children than in adults. These investigators proposed an alternate classification scheme for the diagnosis of eating disorders and disordered eating in children that includes this developmental perspective. These criteria, known as the Great Ormond Street Criteria, have better reliability in young children than the criteria in the DSM-IV (APA, 1994).

In the DSM-5, the first and most evident change is the name of the global diagnostic category "Feeding and Eating Disorders", which includes not only AN, BN or BED, but also Pica, Rumination Disorder and Avoidant/Restrictive Food Intake Disorder, formerly included in a separate cluster (Disorders Usually First Diagnosed in Infancy, Childhood or adolescence) in previous editions of the DSM. This renaming could be merely testimonial, or it could give rise to a developmental perspective of feeding and disordered eating. Further research will end up deciding this conceptual issue regarding ED.

In the same sense, BED may be conceptualized as a mental disorder, a psychiatric syndrome, or a behavioral symptom associated with obesity. It has important consequences from a developmental perspective, taking into account that successful treatment of BED in children and adolescents may stabilize weight or at least prevent further weight gain. Considering the increasing prevalence of childhood obesity, which seems related to BED in adults, prevention and treatment in these early years are crucial issues (Musch and Hilbert, 2005).

However, the study of BED in children remains problematic for several reasons. The diagnostic validity of BED criteria has not yet been established in children and adolescents. Epidemiological studies addressing the course of childhood BED and considering possible fluctuations in its presentation are needed, and there is a lack of suitable assessment methods that are comparable across languages. All these issues point to the need for good and efficient measurement and assessment instruments. They are essential for the early detection of new cases, and not only in the context of mental health, but also in the context of primary care and pediatric attention. Only in this way will we be able to make precise differential diagnoses and achieve early detection of patients or at-risk populations.

REFERENCES

American Psychiatric Association. Available at: http://www.dsm5.org/ProposedRevisions/Pages/EatingDisorders.aspx. Acceded November 21, 2011.

American Psychiatric Association (1994). Diagnostic and statistical manual of mental disorders. 4th Ed. Washington DC: American Psychiatric. Association.

American Psychiatric Association (2000). *Diagnostic and statistical manual of mental disorders : DSM-IV-TR*. Washington, DC: American Psychiatric Association.

Achenbach, T. M. (1991) *Integrative Guide to the 1991 CBCL/4-18, YSR, and TRF Profiles.* Burlington, VT: University of Vermont, Department of Psychology

Achenbach, T. M. and Edelbrock, C. (1991). *The child behavior checklist and revised child behavior profile.* Burlington, VT: University Associates in Psychiatry

Antony, M. M., Johnson, W. G., Carr-Nangle, R. E., and Abel, J. L. (1994). Psychopathology correlates of binge eating and binge eating disorder. *Comprehensive psychiatry*, 35(5), 386-392.

Arnow, B., Kenardy, J. and Agras, W. S. (1995). The Emotional Eating Scale: the development of a measure to assess coping with negative affect by eating. *The International journal of eating disorders*, 18(1), 79-90.

Birch, L. L., Fisher, J. O., Grimm-Thomas, K., Markey, C. N., Sawyer, R., and Johnson, S. L. (2001). Confirmatory factor analysis of the Child Feeding Questionnaire: a measure of parental attitudes, beliefs and practices about child feeding and obesity proneness. *Appetite*, 36(3), 201-210.

Bryant-Waugh, R. J., Cooper, P. J., Taylor, C. L., and Lask, B. D. (1996). The use of the eating disorder examination with children: a pilot study. *The International journal of eating disorders*, 19(4), 391-397.

Binford, R. B., Pederson, M., Peterson, C. B., Crow, S. J., and Mitchell, J. E. (2004). Relation of binge eating age of onset to functional aspects of binge eating in binge eating disorders. *International Journal of Eating Disorders*, 35, 286-292.

Bryant-Waugh, R. and Lask, B. (1995). Eating disorders in children. *Journal of Child Psychology and Psychiatry and Allied Disciplines*, 36, 191–202.

Bryant-Waugh, R. and Nicholls, D. (2011). *Diagnosis and classification of disordered eating in childhood*. In: D. Le Grange and J. Lock. Eating Disorders in children and adolescents. A clinical Handbook. New York: The Guilford press. pp.107-125

Bryant-Waugh, R., Markham, L., Kreipe, R. E., and Walsh, B. T. (2010). Feeding and Eating Disorders in Childhood. *International Journal of Eating Disorders*; 43, 98-111.

Campbell, M. and Schmidt, U. (2011). Cognitive-behavioral therapy for adolescent bulimia nervosa and binge eating disorder. In: D. Le Grange and J. Lock. *Eating Disorders in children and adolescents. A clinical Handbook.* New York: The Guilford press. pp. 305-334.

Cebolla, A., Perpiñá, C., Ferrer, E. L., Pitti, J. Á., and Botella, C. (2012). Prevalencia del trastorno por atracón en una muestra clínica de obesos. *Anales de Pediatría*, 77(2), 98-102.

Celio, A. A., Wilfley, D. E., Crow, S. J., Mitchell, J., and Walsh, B. T. (2004). A comparison of the binge eating scale, questionnaire for eating and weight patterns-revised, and eating disorder examination questionnaire with instructions with the eating disorder examination in the assessment of binge eating disorder and its symptoms. *The International journal of eating disorders*, 36(4), 434-444.

Costanzo, P. R. and Woody, E. Z. (1985). Domain-Specific Parenting Styles and Their Impact on the Child's Development of Particular Deviance: The Example of Obesity Proneness. *Journal of Social and Clinical Psychology*, 3(4), 425-445.

Cooper, P. J. and Stein, A. (2006). *Introduction*. In: P. J. Cooper and A. Stein (Eds.,). *Childhood Feeding Problems and Adolescent Eating Disorders*. East Sussex: Routledge. pp. 1-6.

Decaluwe, V. and Braet, C. (2003). Prevalence of binge-eating disorder in obese children and adolescents seeking weight loss treatment. *International Journal of Obesity*, 27, 404-409.

Decaluwé, V. and Braet, C. (2004). Assessment of eating disorder psychopathology in obese children and adolescents: interview versus self-report questionnaire. *Behaviour research and therapy*, 42(7), 799-811.

D' Emden, H., Holden, L., McDermott, B., Harris, M., Gibbons, K., Gledhill, A., and Cotterill, A. (2012). Concurrent validity of self-report measures of eating disorders in adolescents with type 1 diabetes. *Acta paediatrica* 101(9), 973-978.

Eddy, K. T., Herzog, D. B. and Zucker, N. L. (2011). Diagnosis and classification of eating disorders in adolescence. In: D. Le Grange and J. Lock. Eating Disorders in children and adolescents. *A clinical Handnbook*. New York: The Guilford press. pp.126-136.

Elder, K. A., Grilo, C. M., Masheb, R. M., Rothschild, B. S., Burke-Martindale, C. H., and Brody, M. L. (2006). Comparison of two self-report instruments for assessing binge eating in bariatric surgery candidates. *Behaviour research and therapy*, 44(4), 545-560.

First, Michael B., Williams, Janet B. W., Spitzer, Robert L., and Gibbon, Miriam: *Structured Clinical Interview for DSM-IV-TR Axis I Disorders, Clinical Trials Version (SCID-CT)*. New York: Biometrics Research, New York State Psychiatric Institute, 2007.

Fisher, J. O. and Birch, L. L. (2002). Eating in the absence of hunger and overweight in girls from 5 to 7 y of age. *The American journal of clinical nutrition*, 76(1), 226-231.

Garner, D. M., Olmsted, M. P., Bohr, Y., and Garfinkel, P. E. (1982). The eating attitudes test: psychometric features and clinical correlates. *Psychological medicine*, 12(4), 871-878.

Glasofer, D. R., Tanofsky-Kraff, M., Eddy, K. T., Yanovski, S. Z., Theim, K. R., Mirch, M. C., ... Yanovski, J. A. (2007). Binge Eating in Overweight Treatment-Seeking Adolescents. *Journal of pediatric psychology*, 32(1), 95-105.

Goldschmidt, A. B., Doyle, A. C. and Wilfley, D. E. (2007). Assessment of binge eating in overweight youth using a questionnaire version of the Child Eating Disorder Examination with Instructions. *The International journal of eating disorders*, 40(5), 460-467.

Goldfield, G. S., Epstein, L. H. (2002) Management of obesity in children. Fairburn, C. G., Brownell, K. D. eds. *Eating Disorders and Obesity: A Comprehensive Handbook.* 2nd ed. New York, NY Guilford Press; 573- 577.

Goossens, L., Braet, C. and Decaluwé, V. (2007). Loss of control over eating in obese youngsters. *Behaviour Research and Therapy*, 45(1), 1-9.

Johnson, W. G., Grieve, F. G., Adams, C. D., and Sandy, J. (1999). Measuring binge eating in adolescents: adolescent and parent versions of the questionnaire of eating and weight patterns. *The International journal of eating disorders*, 26(3), 301-314.

Johnson, W. G., Kirk, A. A. and Reed, A. E. (2001). Adolescent version of the questionnaire of eating and weight patterns: reliability and gender differences. *The International journal of eating disorders*, 29(1), 94-96.

Le Grange, D. (2011). Childhood and Adolescence: Looking at Eating Disorders When They Start. In: D. Le Grange and J. Lock. *Eating Disorders in children and adolescents. A clinical Handnbook*. New York: The Guilford press. pp.3-10.

Luce, K. H. and Crowther, J. H. (1999). The reliability of the Eating Disorder Examination-Self-Report Questionnaire Version (EDE-Q). *The International journal of eating disorders*, 25(3), 349-351.

Maloney, M. J., McGuire, J. B. and Daniels, S. R. (1988). Reliability testing of a children's version of the Eating Attitude Test. *Journal of the American Academy of Child and Adolescent Psychiatry*, 27(5), 541-543.

Marcus, M. D. and Kalarchian, M. A. (2003). Binge eating in children and adolescents. *The International journal of eating disorders*, 34 Suppl., S47-57.

Moens, E., Braet, C. and Van Winckel, M. (2010). An 8-year follow-up of treated obese children: children's, process and parental predictors of successful outcome. *Behaviour research and therapy*, 48(7), 626-633.

Munsch, S. and Hilbert, A. (2005). Binge eating disorder in childhood. What do we know about it?. In: S. Munsch and C. Berlinger. *Obesity and Binge Eating Disorder*. Basel: Karger. Pp. 180-196.

National Institute of Clinical Excellence (2004) *Eating Disorders: Core Interventions in the Treatment and Management of Anorexia Nervosa, Bulimia Nervosa and Related Eating Disorders.* London: The British Psychological Society.

Perpiñá, C., Cebolla, A., Botella, C., Lurbe, E., and Torró, M.-I. (2011). Emotional Eating Scale for children and adolescents: psychometric characteristics in a Spanish sample. *Journal of clinical child and adolescent psychology,* 53, 40(3), 424-433.

Ranzenhofer, L. M., Tanofsky-Kraff, M., Menzie, C. M., Gustafson, J. K., Rutledge, M. S., Keil, M. F., Yanovski, J. A. (2008). Structure analysis of the Children's Eating Attitudes Test in overweight and at-risk-for-overweight children and adolescents. *Eating behaviors*, 9(2), 218-227.

Roehrig, M., Sperry, S., Lock, J. and Thompson, J. K. (2008). Eating Problems. In: A. R. Eisen (Ed.,). *Treating Childhood Behavioral and Emotional Problems*. New York: Guilford Press, pp.309-364.

Sancho, C., Asorey, O., Arija, V., and Canals, J. (2005). Psychometric characteristics of the Children's Eating Attitudes Test in a Spanish sample. *European Eating Disorders Review*, 13(5), 338–343.

Shapiro, J. R., Woolson, S. L., Hamer, R. M., Kalarchian, M. A., Marcus, M. D., and Bulik, C. M. (2007). Evaluating binge eating disorder in children: development of the children's binge eating disorder scale (C-BEDS). *The International journal of eating disorders*, 40(1), 82-89.

Shomaker, L. B., Tanofsky-Kraff, M., Zocca, J. M., Courville, A., Kozlosky, M., Columbo, K. M., Yanovski, J. A. (2010). Eating in the absence of hunger in adolescents: intake after a large-array meal compared with that after a standardized meal123. *The American Journal of Clinical Nutrition*, 92(4), 697-703.

Smolak, L. and Levine, M. P. (1994). Psychometric properties of the Children's Eating Attitudes Test. *The International journal of eating disorders*, 16(3), 275-282.

Steinberg, E., Tanofsky-Kraff, M., Cohen, M. L., Elberg, J., Freedman, R. J., Semega-Janneh, M., Yanovski, J. A. (2004). Comparison of the child and parent forms of the Questionnaire on Eating and Weight Patterns in the assessment of children's eating-disordered behaviors. *The International journal of eating disorders*, 36(2), 183-194.

Spitzer, R. L., Devlin, M., Walsh, B. T., Hasin, D., Wing, R., Marcus, M., ... Nonas, C. (1992). Binge eating disorder: A multisite field trial of the diagnostic criteria. *International Journal of Eating Disorders*, 11(3), 191–203.

Tanofsky-Kraff, M., Marcus, M. D., Yanovski, S. Z., and Yanovski, J. A. (2008). Loss of control eating disorder in children age 12 years and younger: proposed research criteria. *Eating behaviors*, 9(3), 360-365.

Tanofsky-Kraff, M., Ranzenhofer, L. M., Yanovski, S. Z., Schvey, N. A., Faith, M., Gustafson, J., and Yanovski, J. A. (2008). Psychometric properties of a new questionnaire to assess eating in the absence of hunger in children and adolescents. *Appetite*, 51(1), 148-155.

Tanofsky-Kraff, M., Theim, K. R., Yanovski, S. Z., Bassett, A. M., Burns, N. P., Ranzenhofer, L. M., ... Yanovski, J. A. (2007). Validation of the emotional eating scale adapted for use in children and adolescents (EES-C). *The International journal of eating disorders*, 40(3), 232-240.

Tanofsky-Kraff, M., Yanovski, S. Z., Wilfley, D. E., Marmarosh, C., Morgan, C. M., and Yanovski, J. A. (2004). Eating-Disordered Behaviors, Body Fat, and Psychopathology in Overweight and Normal-Weight Children. *Journal of consulting and clinical psychology*, 72(1), 53-61.

Tanofsky-Kraff, M., Yanovski, S. Z. and Yanovski, J. A. (2005). Comparison of child interview and parent reports of children's eating disordered behaviors. *Eating behaviors*, 6(1), 95-99.

Van Strien, T., Frijters, J. E. R., Bergers, G. P. A., and Defares, P. B. (1986). The Dutch Eating Behavior Questionnaire (DEBQ) for assessment of restrained, emotional, and external eating behavior. *International Journal of Eating Disorders*, 5(2), 295–315.

Van Strien, T. and Oosterveld, P. (2008). The children's DEBQ for assessment of restrained, emotional, and external eating in 7- to 12-year-old children. *The International journal of eating disorders*, 41(1), 72-81.

Vannucci, A., Tanofsky-Kraff, M., Shomaker, L. B., Ranzenhofer, L. M., Matheson, B. E., Cassidy, O. L., Yanovski, J. A. (2012). Construct validity of the emotional eating scale adapted for children and adolescents. *International journal of obesity (2005)*, 36(7), 938-943.

Wertheim, E., Paxton, S. and Blaney, S.(2004). Risk factors in the development of body image disturbances. In: J. K. Thompson (Ed.), *Handbook of eating disorders and obesity* (pp.565-589). Hoboken, NJ: Wiley.

Wilfley, D. E., Schwartz, M. B., Spurrell, E. B., and Fairburn, C. G. (1997). Assessing the specific psychopathology of binge eating disorder patients: Interview or self-report? *Behaviour Research and Therapy*, 35(12), 1151-1159.

Wolff, G. E., Crosby, R. D., Roberts, J. A., and Wittrock, D. A. (2000). Differences in daily stress, mood, coping, and eating behavior in binge eating and non-binge eating college women. *Addictive Behavior*, 25, 205-216.

In: Binge Eating and Binge Drinking
Editor: Simon B. Harris

ISBN: 978-1-62618-580-7
© 2013 Nova Science Publishers, Inc.

Chapter 8

BINGE DRINKING: PATHOPHYSIOLOGICAL AND PSYCHOLOGICAL ASPECTS

Tatjana Radosavljević and Danijela Vučević*
Institute of Pathophysiology, Faculty of Medicine,
University of Belgrade, Belgrade, Serbia

> The drunk is unlovely to look at. Nevertheless his refusal to accept the realities of this world, babyish as it may be, compels us to take another look at this world and reflect upon our motives for accepting it.
> *Wystan Hugh Auden (From "The Dyer's hand and other essays")*

ABSTRACT

Binging is a behavior with undesirable outcomes for drinkers and those around them. A debate over recent years has focused on how this harmful and potentially life threatening pattern of drinking should be defined and how many drinks make up a binge. From a clinician's stand-point, a binge refers to a pattern of drinking to intoxication, usually a solitary activity lasting up to several days and involving loss of control over consumption.

The National Institute of Alcohol Abuse and Alcoholism (Bethesda, Maryland, US) defines binge drinking episodes as consumption of five or more drinks (male) or four or more drinks (female) in the space of about 2 hours. However, this definition does not consider the amount of alcohol intake in one binge episode, nor the possibility that some individuals may go on several binges during the same day. Generally speaking, binge drinking implies "drinking too much too fast." Periods of binge drinking (several consecutive days, weeks or months) are typically followed by periods of abstinence or, in some cases, significantly lower levels of consumption.

Thus, the nature and severity of the problems that binge drinking causes depends on how frequently it occurs and over how long a period it is maintained. This pattern of drinking is extremely common, especially among young adults, and remains the leading

---

* Corresponding author: TatjanaRadosavljević, MD, PhD. Institute of Pathophysiology, Faculty of Medicine, University of Belgrade, DrSubotića 9, 11000 Belgrade, Serbia. E-mail: tanjamm@med.bg.ac.rs.

cause of death among college-aged students in the US, with similar worldwide rates of problematic alcohol use across Europe, South America and Australia. Due to the physiological and psychological changes occurring in adolescence and youth, binge drinking may have lasting harmful consequences, including greater risk for the development of alcohol dependence. It is known that alcohol affects virtually every organ system in the body, and in high doses, can cause coma and death. Namely, in the brain it affects several neurotransmitter systems, including opiates, γ-aminobutyric acid (GABA), glutamate, serotonin and dopamine. Increased opiate levels help explain the euphoric effect of alcohol, while its effects on GABA cause anxiolytic and sedative effects. Additionally, binge drinking increases the risk of acute hemorrhagic and ischemic strokes by up to ten-fold.

It also leads to cardiovascular problems (atrial fibrillation, known as "holiday heart", sudden cardiac death, etc.). Repeated binge drinking can cause damage to the esophagus resulting in acute hemorrhage, gastritis, pancreatitis and myopathy. For pregnant women, binge drinking has been correlated with harm to the developing fetus, especially during the early stages of pregnancy. This pattern of drinking combined with smoking is responsible for a rise in oral cancer in men and women in their twenties and thirties.

Additionally, it is feared that the increase in binge drinking among young women will lead to a significant increase in breast cancer in the next half century. It is well established that binge drinking causes a higher level of psychological morbidity, particularly anxiety and neurosis, than the same amount of alcohol consumed more steadily over a longer period. Interestingly, young binge drinkers are substantially more likely than non-binge drinkers to take illegal drugs.

INTRODUCTION

Alcohol, primarily in the form of ethyl alcohol (ethanol) has occupied an important place in the history of humankind for at least 8000 years. In Western society, beer and wine were a main staple of daily life until the 19th century. These relatively dilute alcoholic beverages were preferred over water, which was known to be associated with acute and chronic illness (Masters, 2001).

Today, alcohol is widely consumed. Like other sedative-hypnotic drugs, alcohol in low to moderate amounts relieves anxiety and fosters a feeling of well-being or even euphoria (Masters, 2001). However, alcohol is also the most commonly abused drug in the world, an occasion for vast medical and societal costs (Masters, 2001; Kuntsche et al., 2005; Pignone and Salazar, 2011; Koob, 2013).

Binging is a behavior with undesirable outcomes for drinkers and those around them. A debate over recent years has focused on how this harmful and potentially life threatening pattern of drinking should be defined and how many drinks make up a binge. From a clinician's stand-point, a binge refers to a pattern of drinking to intoxication, usually a solitary activity lasting up to several days and involving loss control over consumption. The National Institute of Alcohol Abuse and Alcoholism (Bethesda, Maryland, US) defines binge drinking episodes as consumption of five or more drinks (male) or four or more drinks (female) in the space of about 2 hours. However, this definition does not consider the amount of alcohol intake in one binge episode, nor the possibility that some individuals may go on several binges during the same day. Generally speaking, binge drinking implies "drinking too much too fast." Periods of binge drinking (several consecutive days, weeks or months) are typically followed by periods of abstinence or, in some cases, significantly lower levels of consumption.

Thus, the nature and severity of the problems that binge drinking causes depends on how frequently it occurs and over how long a period it is maintained (Bobak et al., 2004; Tolstrup et al., 2004; The National Institute of Alcohol Abuse and Alcoholism, 2004; Institute on Alcohol Studies, 2007;Mathurin and Deltenre, 2009; International Center for Alcohol Policies). Despite the investment of many resources and much basic researches, this dangerous pattern of alcohol consumption is difficult to treat.

METABOLIC PATHWAYS OF ETHANOL

Ethanol is a small water-soluble molecule that is absorbed rapidly from the gastrointestinal tract. After ingestion of alcohol in the fasting state, peak blood alcohol concentrations are reached within 30 minutes. The presence of food in the gut delays absorption by slowing gastric emptying. Distribution is rapid, with tissue levels approximating the concentration in blood. The volume of distribution for ethanol approximates total body water (0.5-0.7 L/kg). For an equivalent oral dose of alcohol, women have a higher peak concentration than men, in part because women have a lower total body water content.In the central nervous system, the concentration of ethanol rises quickly since the brain receives a large proportion of blood flow and ethanol readily crosses biologic membranes (Masters, 2001). Over 90% of alcohol consumed is oxidized in the liver: much of the remainder is excreted through the lungs and in the urine. The excretion of a small but consistent proportion of alcohol by the lungs is exploited by breath alcohol tests that serve as a basis for a legal definition of "driving under the influence" in many countries. The typical adult can metabolize 7-10g (150-220 mmol) of alcohol per hour, the equivalent of approximately 10 oz of beer, 3.5 oz of wine, or 1 oz of distilled 80 proof spirits(Masters, 2001; Caballeria, 2003).Two major pathways of alcohol metabolism to acetaldehyde have been identified. The third minor metabolic pathway refers to catalase activity. Acetaldehyde is then oxidized by a third metabolic process (Figure 1).

Alcohol Dehydrogenase Pathway

The primary pathway for alcohol metabolism involves alcohol dehydrogenase (ADH), a cytosolic enzyme that catalyzes the conversion of alcohol to acetaldehyde (Figure 1).

This enzyme is located mainly in the liver, but it is also found in other organs such as the brain and stomach. A significant amount of ethanol metabolism by gastric ADH occurs in the stomach in men, but a smaller amount occurs in women, who appear to have lower levels of the gastric enzyme (Masters, 2001).

During the conversion of ethanol to acetaldehyde, a hydrogen ion is transferred from alcohol to the cofactor nicotinamide adenine dinucleotide (NAD$^+$) to form NADH. As a net result, alcohol oxidation generates an excess of reducing equivalents in the liver, chiefly as NADH. The excess NADH production appears to underlie a number of metabolic disorders that accompany chronic alcoholism(Masters, 2001; Caballeria, 2003).

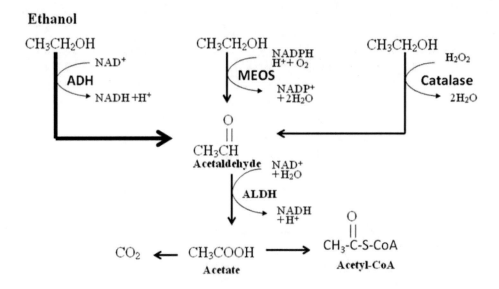

Abbreviations: ADH, alcohol dehydrogenase; MEOS, Microsomal Ethanol Oxidizing System; ALDH, aldehyde dehydrogenase.

Figure 1. Metabolism of ethanol.

Microsomal Ethanol Oxidizing System (MEOS)

This enzyme system uses NADPH as a cofactor in the metabolism of ethanol (Figure 1). At blood concentrations below 100 mg/dL (22 mmol/L), the MEOS system contributes little to the metabolism of ethanol. However, when large amounts of ethanol are consumed, the ADH system becomes saturated owing to depletion of the required cofactor NAD^+. As the concentration of ethanol increases above 100 mg/dL, there is increased contribution from the MEOS system, which does not rely upon NAD^+ as a cofactor (Masters, 2001; Lieber, 2004). During chronic alcohol consumption, MEOS activity increases. This enzyme induction is associated with an increase in various constituents of the smooth endoplasmic reticulum in the liver. As a result, chronic alcohol consumption results in significant increases not only in ethanol metabolism, but also in the clearance of other drugs eliminated by hepatic microsomal enzyme systems. Similarly, other "inducing" drugs, such as barbiturates, may also enhance the rate of blood alcohol clearance slightly. However, the effect of other enzyme-inducing drugs on ethanol clearance is less important because the MEOS is not the primary pathway for ethanol metabolism (Masters, 2001).

Acetaldehyde Metabolism

Much of the acetaldehyde formed from alcohol appears to be oxidized in the liver. While several enzyme systems may be responsible for this reaction, mitochondrial NAD^+-dependent ADH appears to be in the main pathway for acetaldehyde oxidation. The product of this reaction is acetate, which can be further metabolized to carbon dioxide (CO_2) and water.

Chronic alcohol consumption results in a decreased rate of acetaldehyde oxidation in intact mitochondria(Masters, 2001; Caballeria, 2003). Some people, primarily of Asian descent, have a genetic deficiency in the activity of the mitochondrial form of ADH. When these individuals drink alcohol, they develop high blood acetaldehyde concentrations (Masters, 2001).

BINGE DRINKING AND ACUTE INTOXICATION

For a 70-kg person, an ounce of whiskey, a 4-to 6-oz glass of wine, or a 12-oz bottleof beer (roughly 15, 11 and 13 grams of alcohol, respectively) may raise the level of alcohol in the blood by 25 mg/dL. For a 50-kg person, the blood alcohol level would rise even higher (35 mg/dL) with the same consumption. Blood alcohol levels below 50 mg/dL rarely cause significant motor dysfunction (the legal limit for driving under the influence is commonly 80 mg/dL). Intoxication as manifested by ataxia, dysarthria and nausea and vomiting indicates a blood level above 150 mg/dL and lethal blood levels range from 350 to 900 mg/dL. Serious overdoses are frequently due to a combination of alcohol with other sedatives and lead to death (Eisendrath and Lichtmacher, 2011).

Central Nervous System

The central nervous system (CNS) is markedly affected by acute alcohol consumption. Alcohol causes sedation and relief of anxiety and, at higher concentrations, slurred speech, ataxia, impaired judgement and disinhibited behavior, a condition usually called drunkenness. These CNS effects are most marked as the blood level is rising, because acute tolerance to the effects of alcohol occurs after a few hours of drinking. For chronic drinkers who are tolerant to the effects of alcohol, much higher concentrations are needed to elicit these CNS effects.

For example, a chronic alcoholic may appear sober or only slightly intoxicated with a blood alcohol concentration of 300-400 mg/dL, whereas this level is associated with marked intoxication or even coma in a nontolerant individual. The propensity of moderate doses of alcohol to inhibit the attention and information processing skills, as well as the motor skills required for operation of motor vehicles has profound effects (Masters, 2001). Like other sedative-hypnotic drugs, alcohol is a CNS depressant. At high blood concentrations, it induces respiratory depression, stupor, seizures, shock syndrome, coma and death (Eisendrath and Lichtmacher, 2011).

Recent results obtained from animal models have suggested that ethanol exerts dose-dependent anticonvulsive effects (Mladenović et al., 2007; Mladenović et al., 2008; Rašić-Marković et al., 2009).

No specific receptor for ethanol has been identified. Instead, ethanol has been shown to affect a large number of membrane proteins that participate in signaling pathways (neurotransmitter receptors for amines, aminoacids and opioids), enzymes (Na^+/K^+ATPase, adenylyl cyclase, phosphoinositide-specific phospholipase C, etc.) and ion channels, such as those for calcium (Ca^{2+}) (Ferreira and Willoughby 2008; Kaur et al., 2012; Lowery-Gionta et al., 2012; Changhai et al., 2013). Much attention has focused on alcohol's effects upon neurotransmission by glutamate and γ-aminobutyric acid (GABA), the main excitatory and inhibitory neurotransmitters in the CNS (Masters, 2001). Acute ethanol exposure enhances the action of GABA at $GABA_A$ receptors. Ethanol also inhibits the ability of glutamate to open the cation channel associated with the N-methyl-D-aspartate (NMDA) subtype of glutamate receptors. The NMDA receptor is implicated in many aspects of cognitive function, including learning and memory. "Blackouts", periods of memory loss that occur with high levels of alcohol, may result from inhibition of NMDA receptor activation (Criswell et al., 2003; Carpenter-Hyland and Chandler 2007; Bajo et al., 2008).

Additionally, increased opiate levels help explain the euphoric effect of alcohol, while its effects on GABA cause anxiolytic and sedative effects (Eisendrath and Lichtmacher, 2011).

Heart

Significant depression of myocardial contractility has been observed in individuals who acutely consume moderate amounts of alcohol (blood ethanol concentration above 100 mg/dL). Myocardial biopsies in humans before and after infusion of small amounts of alcohol have shown ultrastructural changes that may be associated with impaired myocardial function. Acetaldehyde is implicated as a cause of heart abnormalities by altering myocardial stores of catecholamines (Masters, 2001).

Smooth Muscle

Ethanol is a vasodilator, probably as a result of both central nervous system effects (depression of the vasomotor center) and direct smooth muscle relaxation caused by acetaldehyde (Masters, 2001). Binge drinking can cause acute myopathy, typical symptoms being muscle pain, usually around the lip and shoulder girdles and in the calves. It can also cause muscle swelling and progressive weakness, particularly in the legs (Institute on Alcohol Studies, 2007).In cases of severe overdose, hypothermia caused by vasodilation may be marked in cold environments (Masters, 2001).

EFFECTS OF BINGE DRINKING IN THE LONGER TERM (CONSEQUENCES OF CHRONIC ALCOHOL CONSUMPTION)

Binge drinking over the longer time is extremely common, especially among young adults, and remains the leading cause of death among college-aged students in the US, with similar worldwide rates of problematic alcohol use across Europe, South America and Australia (Karam et al., 2007; Miller et al., 2007; Dietz, 2008). Due to the physiological and psychological changes occurring in adolescence and youth, binge drinking may have lasting harmful consequences, including greater risk for the development of alcohol dependence, that often coexists with other substance disorders as well as with mood, anxiety and personality disorders (Institute on Alcohol Studies, 2007; Pignone and Salazar, 2011). Furthermore, alcohol and other drug abuse patients have a much higher prevalence of lifetime psychiatric disorders. Namely, depression is often present and should be evaluated carefully. Besides, the majority of suicides and intrafamily homicides involve alcohol. Alcohol is a major factor in rapes and other assaults, too (Eisendrath and Lichtmacher, 2011; Newberry et al., 2013).

Chronic alcohol consumption profoundly affects the function of several vital organs, particularly the liver and the nervous, gastrointestinal and cardiovascular systems (Table 1).

Table 1. Consequences of chronic alcohol consumption

Psychoneurologic syndromes
Acute alcoholism (intoxication, excitement, coma)
Withdrawal syndromes (hallucinosis, convulsions, delirium tremens)
Nutritional syndromes (Wernicke-Korsakoff syndrome, pellagra)
Gastrointestinal disorders
Acute and chronic gastritis
Malabsorption syndrome
Fatty liver
Cirrhosis
Acute and chronic pancreatitis
Hematologic disorders
Anemia due to acute or chronic blood loss
Cytoplasmic vacuolization of erythroid precursors
Megaloblastic marrow alterations (inhibition of folate metabolism) with anemia
Sideroblastic bone marrow abnormalities
Stomatocytic erythrocyte changes
Hemolytic anemia
Thrombocytopenia
Defective granulocyte mobilization
Neuromuscular disorders
Peripheral polyneuropathy
Acute and chronic alcoholic myopathy
Cardiovascular disorders
Alcoholic cardiomyopathy
Metabolic disorders
Lactic acidosis
Hypoglycemia
Hypomagnesemia
Hypouricemia
Hyperlipidemia
Pulmonary disorders
Pulmonary aspiration
Respiratory infections
Lung volumes, airway resistance, diffusion and gas exchange are adversely affected
Conditions aggravated by alcohol traumatic encephalopathy
Epilepsy
Hodgkin's disease
Porphyria
Peptic ulcer

Ethanol has direct toxicity. In addition, since it is a very weak drug that requires concentrations thousands of times higher than other misused drugs (cocaine, opiates, amphetamines, etc.) to produce its intoxicating effects, it is often consumed in quantities large enough to qualify it as a food. The disruption in metabolism caused by chronic consumption of such large quantities of this energy-rich drug contributes to the organ toxicity seen during chronic use, as do also the malnutrition and vitamin deficiencies(Masters, 2001).

Liver and Gastrointestinal Tract

Liver disease is the most common medical complication of alcohol abuse. It is estimated that about 15-30% of chronic heavy drinkers eventually develop severe liver disease. Clinically significant alcoholic liver disease may be insidious in onset and progress without evidence of overt nutritional abnormalities (Devanshi et al., 2011). Alcoholic fatty liver, a reversible condition, may progress to alcoholic hepatitis and finally to cirrhosis and liver failure (Nagata et al., 2007).

In the United States, chronic alcohol abuse is the leading cause of liver cirrhosis and of the need for liver transplantation (Masters, 2001). The risk of developing liver disease is related both to the average amount of daily consumption and to the duration of alcohol abuse (Oekonomaki et al., 2004). Women appear to be more susceptible to alcohol hepatotoxicity than men(Masters, 2001). Metabolism of 70g or more of alcohol (about a six-pack of beer, an amount that alcoholics will often consume daily) places a large load upon the liver and leads to a number of metabolic abnormalities. The increased $NADH/NAD^+$ ratio, that results from oxidation of ethanol results in reduced gluconeogenesis, hypoglycemia and ketoacidosis.

It also promotes triglyceride synthesis from free fatty acids, which contributes to accumulation of fat in the liver parenchyma (Aparajita and Cederbaum, 2006; Rocha et al., 2011).The excess of acetaldehyde also adversely affects liver function.

Since metabolism of acetaldehyde via aldehyde dehydrogenase results in the generation of NADH, some of the acetaldehyde effects may be attributable to NADH excess. Acetaldehyde is itself a very reactive compound that has many toxic effects. Formation of acetaldehydeprotein adducts promotes collagen production and stimulates hepatic inflammation and oxidative stress (Masters, 2001). Cold-induced stress and acute cadmium intoxication can contribute to oxidative liver injury during binge drinking, too (Nešović-Ostojić et al., 2012; Radosavljević et al., 2012).

In some cases, nutritional factors are critical in alcohol-induced liver disease. It has been suggested that essential factors, such as glutathione may be decreased in a malnourished alcoholic. Thus removing a valuable scavenger of toxic free radicals that otherwise will injure the liver (Das and Vasudevan, 2007). Hormonal factors may also contribute to this disease, because female alcoholics are at greater risk for alcohol-induced liver dysfunction than males(Masters, 2001).

Other portions of the gastrointestinal tract may also be injured. Binge drinking increases gastric and pancreatic secretion and alters mucosal barriers, so that the risk of acute gastritis and pancreatitis is enhanced (Pronko et al., 2002; Institute on Alcohol Studies, 2007; Clemens and Mahan, 2010; Kim et al., 2010; Pandol et al., 2010; Rakesh et al., 2011; Laniewska-Dunaj, et al., 2012).Repeated binge drinking can cause damage to the esophagus resulting in acute hemorrhage (Institute on Alcohol Studies, 2007).Additionally, chronic alcoholics are prone to develop increased susceptibility to blood and plasma protein loss during drinking, which may contribute to anemia and protein malnutrition. Alcohol also reversibly injures the small intestine, leading to diarrhea, weight loss and multiple vitamin deficiencies (Masters, 2001).

Nervous System - Tolerance and Physical Dependence

The consumption of alcohol in high doses over a long period results in tolerance and in physical and psychologic dependence. Tolerance to the intoxicating effects of alcohol is a complex process involving poorly understood changes in the nervous system. Although minor degrees of metabolic tolerance after chronic alcohol use have been demonstrated in which the subject's capacity to metabolize the drug increases, the maximal increase in alcohol metabolism is insufficient to account for the magnitude of the observed clinical tolerance.

As with other sedative-hypnotic drugs, there is a limit to tolerance, so that only a relatively small increase in the lethal dose occurs with increasing alcohol use (Masters, 2001).Chronic alcohol drinkers, when forced to reduce or discontinue alcohol, experience a withdrawal sundrome, which indicates the existence of physical dependence. Alcohol withdrawal symptoms classically consist of hyperexcitability in mild cases and convulsions, toxic psychosis and delirium tremens in severe ones. The dose, rate and duration of alcohol consumption determines the intensity of the withdrawal syndrome. When consumption has been very high, merely reducing the rate of consumption may lead to signs of withdrawal(De Witte et al., 2003; Kozan et al., 2007). Psychologic dependence upon alcohol is characterized by a compulsive desire to experience the rewarding effects of alcohol and, for current drinkers, a desire to avoid the negative consequences of withdrawal. Detoxified, abstinent alcoholics experience periods of intense craving for alcohol that can be set off by environmental cues associated with drinking in the past, such as familiar places, groups of people, or events(Masters, 2001).The molecular basis of alcohol tolerance and dependence is not known. Chronic exposure of animals or cultured cells to alcohol elicits a multitude of adaptive responses involving neurotransmitters and their receptors, ion channels and enzymes that participate in signal transduction pathways. Up-regulation of the NMDA subtype of glutamate receptors and voltage-sensitive Ca^{2+} channels has been implicated in the seizures that accompany the alcohol withdrawal syndrome (Hillbom et al., 2003).

Based on the ability of sedative-hypnotic drugs that enhance GABAergic neurotransmission to substitute for alcohol during alcohol withdrawal and evidence of down-regulation of $GABA_A$-mediated responses with chronic alcohol exposure, GABA neurotransmission appears to play a central role in the development of tolerance and withdrawal(Masters, 2001).Neurotransmission events involved in the sensation of reward are also important. Alcohol causes an acute increase in the local concentrations of neurotransmitters involved in brain reward circuits (serotonin, opioids and dopamine), whereas chronic use lowers the basal levels of these chemicals.

A strong desire for alcohol may represent the brain's effort to bring these neurotransmitters back to normal (Gilpin and Roberto, 2012).

Neurotoxicity

Consumption of large amounts of alcohol over extended periods (usually years) can also lead to neurologic deficits. There is evidence to suggest that adolescent brains are particularly vulnerable to alcohol neurotoxic effects. American studies that compared brain scans and cognitive tests in underage binge drinkers and nondrinkers found that the drinkers had impaired memory and reasoning skills, and their hippocampi (brain area that hendles memory and learning) were about 10 percent smaller than the nondrinkers. It is not known if these effects are reversible (Institute on Alcohol Studies, 2007). Additionally, the most frequent neurologic abnormality in chronic alcohol consumption is a generalized symmetric peripheral nerve injury that begins with distal paresthesias of the hands and feet. Chronic alcoholic patients may also exhibit gait disturbances and ataxia that are due to degenerative changes in the CNS. Other neurologic disturbances include dementia, and rarely demyelinating disease(Masters, 2001).

Wernicke-Korsakoff syndrome is a relatively uncommon but important entity characterized by paralysis of the external eye muscles, ataxia and a confused state that can progress to coma and death. It is apparently associated with thiamin deficiency, but is rarely seen in the absence of alcoholism. Wernicke's encephalopathy represents the acute phase of this disease. It may be difficult to distinguish from the acute confusional state created by acute alcohol intoxication, which later blends in with the perceptual and behavioral problems associated with alcohol withdrawal. A distinguishing feature of Wernicke's encephalopathy is the longer duration of the confusional state and the relative absence of the agitation that would be expected during withdrawal. Because of the importance of thiamine in this pathologic condition, all patients suspected of having Wernicke-Korsakoff syndrome should receive thiamine therapy. Often, the ocular signs, ataxia and confusion improve upon prompt administration of thiamine. However, most patients are left with a chronic disabling memory disorder known as Korsakoff's psychosis (Eisendrath and Lichtmacher, 2011).

Alcohol may also impair visual acuity, with painless blurring that occurs over several weeks of heavy alcohol consumption. Changes are usually bilateral and symmetric and may be followed by optic nerve degeneration (Masters, 2001).

Cardiovascular System

Binge drinking increase the risk of ischemic strokes by up to ten fold. It also leads to cardiovascular problems (atrial fibrillation, known as "holiday heart", sudden cardiac death, etc.) (Institute on Alcohol Studies, 2007).

Heavy alcohol consumption of long duration is associated with a dilated cardiomyopathy with ventricular hypertrophy and fibrosis (Piano, 2012). Direct injury to the myocardium resulting from alcohol abuse was originally thought to be caused by thiamine deficiency or by contaminants in alcoholic beverages (Masters, 2001). More recent studies indicate that the cardiomyopathy occurs even in the absence of vitamin or other dietary deficiencies. In animals and humans, alcohol induces a number of changes in heart cells that may contribute to cardiomyopathy. They include membrane disruption, depressed function of mitochondria and sarcoplasmic reticulum, intracellular accumulation of phospholipids and fatty acids and up-regulation of voltage-dependent calcium channels (Ren and Wold, 2008; Ferreira Seiva et al., 2009; Kalaz et al., 2012). In many cases of alcohol-induced cardiomyopathy, cessation of drinking is associated with a reduction in cardiac size and improved function (Piano, 2012).

Heavy drinking and especially binge drinking are associated with both atrial and ventricular arrhythmias. Patients undergoing alcohol withdrawal syndrome can develop severe arrhythmias, that may reflect abnormalities of potassium or magnesium metabolism, as well as enhanced release of catecholamines (Piano, 2012). Seizures, syncope and sudden death during alcohol withdrawal may be due to these arrhythmias(Institute on Alcohol Studies, 2007).

A link between heavier alcohol consumption (more than three drinks per day) and hypertension has been firmly established in epidemiologic studies. Alcohol is estimated to be responsible for approximately 5% of cases of hypertension, making it one of the most common causes of reversible hypertension. This association is independent of obesity, salt intake, coffee drinking or cigarette smoking. The mechanisms responsible for the sustained increase in blood pressure have not been identified. A reduction in alcohol intake appears to be effective in lowering blood pressure in hypertensives who are also heavy drinkers. The hypertension seen in this population is also responsive to standard blood pressure medications(Masters, 2001).

Blood

Alcohol indirectly effects hematopoiesis through metabolic and nutritional effects and may also directly inhibit the proliferation of all cellular elements in bone marrow. The most common hematologic disorder seen in chronic drinkers is mild anemia resulting from alcohol-related folic acid deficiency. Iron deficiency anemia may result from gastrointestinal bleeding.

Alcohol has been implicated as a cause of several hemolytic syndromes, some of which are associated with hyperlipidemia and severe liver disease (Masters, 2001). Besides, it is of importance in maintainance of enzymes concentration and fatty acids in serum of rats treated with lindane (Radosavljević et al., 2008). Furthermore, abnormalities in platelets and leukocytes have been described in alcoholics. These effects may account for some of the hemostatic impairment and increased frequency of infection in these individuals (Masters, 2001).

Endocrine System and Electrolyte Balance

Chronic alcohol use has important effects on the endocrine system and on fluid and electrolyte balance. Clinical reports of gynecomastia and testicular atrophy in alcoholics with cirrhosis suggest a derangement in steroid hormone balance. Gynecomastia and testicular atrophy have also been noted in alcoholics who have little evidence of liver disease (Masters, 2001).

Alcoholics with chronic liver disease may have disorders of fluid and electrolyte balance, including ascites, edema and effusions. These factors may be related to decreased protein synthesis and portal hypertension.

Alterations of whole body potassium induced by vomiting and diarrhea, as well as severe secondary aldosteronism, may contribute to muscle weakness and can be worsened by diuretic therapy. Some alcoholic patients develop hypoglycemia, probably as a result of impaired hepatic gluconeogenesis. Some alcoholics also develop ketosis, caused by excessive lipolytic factors, especially increased cortisol and growth hormone(Devanshi et al., 2011).

Immune System

Alcoholics have a higher than normal rate of infection and are especially prone to respiratory infections, such as pneumonia and tuberculosis. While secondary effects of alcohol dependence, including nutritional deficiencies and social conditions such as homelessness, contribute to the high rate of infection, a number of studies have indicated that chronic ethanol consumption can directly impair immune function (Thiele et al., 2004). This could also be a major factor underlying the increased incidence of certain forms of cancer in alcoholics. The types of immunologic changes reported include alterations in chemotaxis of granulocytes, lymphocyte response to mitogens, T cell numbers, natural killer cell (NK) activity and levels of tumor necrosis factor. Even a single dose of ethanol may alter some of these variables (Masters, 2001; Thiele et al., 2004).

Increased Risk of Cancer

Chronic alcohol use increases the risk for cancer of the mouth, pharynx, larynx, esophagus and liver. It is feared that the increase in binge drinking among young women will lead to a significant increase in breast cancer in the next half century (Institute on Alcohol Studies, 2007). Alcohol itself does not appear to be a carcinogen in most test systems. However, alcoholic beverages may carry potential carcinogens produced in fermentation or processing and may alter liver function, so that the activity of potential carcinogens is increased(Masters, 2001).

Fetal Alcohol Syndrome

For pregnant women, binge drinking has been correlated with harm to the developing fetus, especially during the early stages of pregnancy (Institute on Alcohol Studies, 2007). Fetal alcohol syndrome includes one or more of the following developmental defects in the offspring of alcoholic women: 1. low birth weight and small size with failure to catch up in size or weight; 2. mental retardation with an average IQ in the 60s; and 3. a variety of birth defects, with a large percentage of facial and cardiac abnormalities. The fetuses are very quiet *in utero*, and there is an increased frequency of breech presentations. There is a higher incidence of delayed postnatal growth and behavior development. The risk is appreciably higher the more alcohol ingested by the mother each day (Eisendrath and Lichtmacher, 2011).

The mechanisms that underlie ethanol's teratogenic effects are unknown. Ethanol rapidly crosses the placenta and reaches concentrations in the fetus that are similar to those in maternal blood. The fetal liver has little or no ADH activity, so the fetus must rely upon maternal and placental enzymes for elimination of alcohol. The poorly defined neuroadaptive changes that are responsible for development of tolerance and dependence in adults probably also occur in the fetus and may lead to permanent neurologic changes in the vulnerable developing brain. The neuropathologic abnormalities seen in humans and in animal models of fetal alcohol syndrome indicate that ethanol causes aberant neuronal and glial migration in the developing nervous system. In tissue culture systems, ethanol causes a striking reduction in neurite outgrowth. Alcohol's toxicity to the developing brain may be due to selective interference with the synthesis or function of molecules that are critical for cell recognition and migration, such as cell adhesion molecules, as well as gangliosides, which are major structural components of neuronal plasma membranes (Masters, 2001).

CONCLUSION

Binge drinking is associated with increased health risk. It also has wide range of adverse personal and social effects. However, precise mechanisms responsible for this pattern of alcohol consumption should be further investigated.

FUNDING

This work was supported by the Ministry of Education and Science of Republic of Serbia, Grant No. 175015.

REFERENCES

Aparajita, D., Cederbaum, A. I. Alcohol and oxidative liver injury. *Hepatology* 2006;43:S63-S74.

Bajo, M., Cruz, M. T., Siggins, G. R., et al. Protein kinase C epsilon mediation of CRF- and ethanol-induced GABA release in central amygdala. *Proc. Natl. Acad. Sci. US* 2008;105;8410-8415.

Bobak, M., Room, R., Pikhart, H., et al. Contribution of drinking patterns to differences in rates of alcohol related problems between three urban populations. *J. Epidemiol. Commun. Health* 2004;58:238-242.

Caballeria, J. Current concepts in alcohol metabolism.*Ann. Hepatol.* 2003;2:60-8.

Carpenter-Hyland, E. P., Chandler, L. J. Adaptive plasticity of NMDA receptors and dendritic spines: implications for enhanced vulnerability of the adolescent brain to alcohol addiction. *Pharmacol. Biochem. Behav.* 2007; 86:200-208.

Changhai, C., Noronha, A., Morikawa, H., et al. New insights on neurobiological mechanisms underlying alcohol addiction. *Neuropharmacology* 2013;67:223-232.

Clemens, D. L., Mahan, K. J. Alcoholic pancreatitis: lessons from the liver. *World J. Gastroenterol.* 2010;16:1314-1320.

Criswell, H. E., Ming, Z., Griffit, B. L., et al. Comparison of effect of ethanol on N-methyl-D-aspartate and GABA-gated currents from acutely dissociated neurons: absence of regional differences in sensitivity to ethanol. *J. Pharmacol. Exp.* 2003;304:192-199.

Das, S. K., Vasudevan, D. M. Alcohol-induced oxidative stress. *Life Sci.* 2007;81:177-187.

Devanshi, S., Haber, P. S., Syn, W. K., et al. Pathogenesis of alcohol-induced liver disease: classical concepts and recent advances. *J. Gastroenterol. Hepatol.* 2011;26:1089-1105.

De Witte, P., Pinto, E., Ansseau, M., et al.Alcohol and withdrawal: from animal research to clinical issues. *Neurosci. Bio Behav. Rev.* 2003;27:189–197.

Dietz, C. M. Development of binge drinking behavior in college students: a developmental analysis. *Graduate J. Counsel. Psychol.* 2008;1:86-96.

Eisendrath, S. J., Lichtmacher, J. E. Psychiatricdisorders. In: McPhee, S. J., Papadakis, M. A., eds. *Current medical diagnosis and treatment.* McGraw Hill New York, 2011. p 995-1049.

Ferreira, M. P., Willoughby, D. Alcohol consumption: the good, the bad and the indifferent. *Appl. Physiol. Nutr. Metab.*2008; 33: 12-20.

Ferreira Seiva, F. R., Amauchi, J. F., Ribeiro Rocha, K. K., et al. Alcoholism and alcohol abstinence: N-acetylcysteine to improve energy expenditure, myocardial oxidative stress, and energy metabolism in alcoholic heart disease. *Alcohol* 2009;43:649-656.

Gilpin, N. W., Roberto, M. Neuropeptide modulation of central amygdala neuroplasticity is a key mediator of alcohol dependence. *Neurosci. Bio Behav. Rev.* 2012;36:873-888.

Hillbom, M., Pieninkeroinen, I., Leone, M. Seizures in alcohol-dependent patients. *CNS Drugs* 2003;17:1013-1030.

Institute on Alcohol Studies. Binge drinking and Europe. July 2007.

International Center for Alcohol Policies. Binge drinking. Blue Book, Module 6. See: http://icap.org/Publication/ICAPBlueBook/tabid/148/Default.aspx.

Kalaz, E. B., Evran, B., Develi, S., et al.Effect of binge ethanol treatment on prooxidant-antioxidant balance in rat heart tissue. *Pathophysiology* 2012;19:49-53.

Karam, E., Kypri, K., Salamoun, M. Alcohol use among college students: an international perspective. *Curr. Opin. Psychiatry* 2007;20(3):213-221.

Kaur, S., Li,J., Stenzel-Poore, M. P., et al. Corticotropin-releasing factor acting on corticotropin-releasing factor receptor type 1 is critical for binge alcohol drinking in mice. *Alcohol Clin. Exp. Res.* 2012;36:369-376.

Kim, J. Y., Song, E. H., Lee, H. J. Chronic ethanol consumption induced pancreatic beta-cell dysfunction and apoptosis through glucokinase nitration and its down regulation. *J. Biol. Chem.* 2010;285:37251-37262.

Koob, G. F. Theoretical frameworks and mechanistic aspects of alcohol addiction: alcohol addiction as a reward deficit disorder. *Curr. Top Behav. Neurosci.* 2013;13:3-30.

Kozan, R., Ayyildiz, M., Yildirim, M., et al. The influence of ethanol intake and its withdrawal on the anticonvulsant effect of α-tocopherol in the penicillin-induced epileptiform activity in rats. *Neurotoxicology* 2007;28:463-470.

Kuntsche, E., Knibbe, R., Gmel, G., Engels,R. Why do young people drink? A review of drinking motives. *Clin. Psychol. Rev.* 2005;25:841-861.

Laniewska-Dunaj, M., Jelski, W., Szmitkowski, M. The effect of ethanol on the stomach. *Pol. Merkur Lekarski* 2012;32:194-197.

Lieber, C. S. The discovery of the microsomal ethanol oxidizing system and its physiologic and pathologic role.*Drug Metabol. Rev.* 2004;36(3-4):511-529.

Lowery-Gionta, E. G., Navarro, M., Li, C., et al. Corticotropin releasing factor signaling in the central amygdala is recruited during binge-like ethanol consumption in C57BL/6J mice. *J. Neurosci.* 2012;32:3405-3413.

Masters, B. S. The alcohols. In: Katzung, B. G., eds. *Basic and clinical pharmacology.* McGraw Hill New York, 2001. p 382-394.

Mathurin, P., Deltenre, P. Effect of binge drinking on the liver: an alarming public health issue? *GUT* 2009;58:613-617.

Miller, J. W., Naimi, T. S., Brewer, R. D., et al. Binge drinking and associated health risk behaviors among high school students. *Pediatrics* 2007;119:76-85.

Mladenović, D., Hrnčić, D., Vučević, D., et al. Ethanol suppressed seizures in lindane-treated rats. Electroencephalographic and behavioral studies. *J. Physiol. Pharmacol.* 2007;58(4):641-656.

Mladenović, D., Hrnčić, D., Radosavljević, T., et al. Dose-dependent anticonvulsive effect of ethanol on lindane-induced seizures in rats. *Can. J. Physiol. Pharmacol.* 2008;86:148-152.

Nagata, K., Suzuki, H., Sakaguchi, S. Common pathogenic mechanism in development progression of liver injury caused by non-alcoholic or alcoholic steatohepatitis. *J. Toxicol. Sci.* 2007;32:453-468.

National Institute on Alcohol Abuse and Alcoholism. (2004, Winter). NIAAA Council approves definition of binge drinking. NIAAA Newsletter, p. 3.

Nešović Ostojić, J., Mladenović, D., Ninković, M., et al. The effects of cold-induced stress on liver oxidative injury during binge drinking. *Hum. Exp. Toxicol.* 2012;31:387-396.

Newberry, M., Williams, N., Caulfield, L. Female alcohol consumption motivations for aggression and aggressive incidents in licensed premises. *Addictive Behaviors* 2013;38:1844-1851.

Oekonomaki, E., Notas, G., Mouzas, I. A., et al. Binge drinking and nitric oxide metabolites in chronic liver disease. 2004;*Alcohol Alcohol* 39:106-109.

Pandol, S. J., Gorelick, F. S., Gerloff, A., et al. Alcohol abuse, endoplasmic reticulum stress and pancreatitis. *Digestiv Dis.* 2010;28:776-782.

Piano, M. R. Alcoholic cardiomyopathy: Incidence, clinical characteristics and pathophysiology *Chest* 2012;121:1638-1650.

Pignone, M., Salazar, R. Disease prevention and health promotion. In: McPhee, S. J., Papadakis, M. A., eds. *Current medical diagnosis and treatment.* McGraw Hill New York, 2011. p 1-21.

Pronko, P., Bardina, L., Satanovskaya, V., et al. Effect of chronic alcohol consumption on the ethanol-and acetaldehyde-metabolizing systems in the rat gastrointestinal tract. *Alcohol* 2002;37:229-235.

Radosavljević, T., Mladenović, D., Vučević, D., et al. Effect of acute lindane and alcohol intoxication on serum concentration of enzymes and fatty acids in rats.*Food Chem. Toxicol.* 2008;46:1739–1743.

Radosavljević, T., Mladenović, D., Ninković, M., et al. Oxidative stress in rat liver during acute cadmium and ethanol intoxication. *J. Serb. Chem. Soc.* 2012;77(2):159-176.

Rakesh, K., Kumar, T., Garg, P. Oxidative stress in chronic pancreatitis: pathophysiological relevance and management. *Antioxid. Red Signal* 2011;15:2757-2766.

Rašić-Marković, A., Djurić, D., Hrnčić, D., et al. High dose of ethanol decreases total spectral power density in seizures induced by D,L-homocysteine thiolactone in adult rats. *Gen. Physiol. Biophys.* 2009;Special Issue 28:25-32.

Ren, J., Wold, L. E. Mechanisms of alcoholic heart disease. *Ther. Adv. Cardiovasc. Dis.* 2008;2:497-506.

Rocha, K. K. H. R., Souza, G. A., Seiva, F. R. F., et al.Weekend ethanol consumption and high-sucrose diet: resveratrol effects on energy expenditure, substrate oxidation, lipid profile, oxidative stress and hepatic energy metabolism. *Alcohol Alcohol* 2011;46(1):10-16.

Thiele, G. M., Freeman, T. K., Klassen, L. W. Immunological mechanisms of alcoholic liver disease. *Semin. Liver Dis.* 2004;24:273-287.

Tolstrup, J. S., Jensen, M. K., Tjonneland, A., et al. Drinking pattern and mortality in middle-aged men and women. *Addiction* 2004;99:323-330.

In: Binge Eating and Binge Drinking
Editor: Simon B. Harris

ISBN: 978-1-62618-580-7
© 2013 Nova Science Publishers, Inc.

Chapter 9

BORDERLINE PERSONALITY DISORDER MEDIATES THE EFFECT OF CHILDHOOD ABUSE ON SUBSTANCE DEPENDENCE

Jessica L. Combs[1], Leila Guller[1], Stacey B. Daughters[2], Gregory T. Smith[1] and Carl Lejuez[2]
[1]University of Kentucky, US
[2]University of Maryland, US

ABSTRACT

To better understand the sequelae of childhood emotional, physical and sexual abuse, the authors provided the first test of a risk model in which borderline personality disorder (BPD) is differentiated from post-traumatic stress disorder (PTSD) in the mediation of the influence of childhood abuse on substance dependence. Among 311 adults in a substance abuse rehabilitation center, childhood abuse was associated with alcohol and cocaine dependence in adulthood and that relationship was significantly mediated by BPD but not PTSD. The additive influence of sexual abuse above physical and emotional abuse on alcohol and cocaine dependence was also mediated by BPD, and this relationship was significantly stronger than for experiencing non-sexual forms of abuse alone. Individuals with histories that include sexual abuse appear to be at increased risk for BPD and alcohol and cocaine dependence, even in a substance abuse population. Substance use dependence, including binge drinking is related to sexual trauma exposure in women.

INTRODUCTION

The experience of emotional, sexual, and physical abuse in childhood has been linked to numerous negative outcomes, including anxiety, fear, depression, aggression, and substance dependence (Johnson, Cohen, Brown, Smailes, and Bernstein, 1999; Neumann, Houskamp, Pollock, and Briere, 1996). Perhaps the most well-known consequence of abuse is later posttraumatic stress disorder (PTSD), though only a small subset of trauma victims develops PTSD (less than 10%; Breslau, 2009).

A childhood history of abuse can also, and perhaps more fundamentally, lead to ongoing disturbances in one's characteristic ways of viewing the world and acting in it; that is, childhood abuse is associated with later personality disorders (Trull, Sher, Minks-Brown, Durbin, and Burr, 2000). Though prototypical PTSD has commonly been assumed to be the primary outcome of traumatic events such as childhood abuse, there is growing evidence that fundamental disruptions in ongoing personality functioning following abuse may play a bigger role in understanding some other adult disorders (Vanderlinden, Van Dyck, Vandereycken, Vertommen, and Jan Verkes, 1993; Waller, 1994). It is therefore important to develop and test models relating childhood abuse history and disordered behavior while understanding the differential impact of PTSD and personality disorders on those relationships.

In this paper, we propose and provide a first test of one such model, as follows. Early emotional, physical and sexual abuse influence the emergence of borderline personality disorder (BPD) symptomatology, which in turn influences the likelihood of substance use and dependence as an adult. In this model, traditional PTSD is not thought to mediate the relationship between early abuse and adult substance dependence.

Childhood Abuse, Borderline Personality Disorder, and PTSD

BPD is a collection of symptoms that lead to emotional, cognitive, and interpersonal distress. Some researchers have found substantial evidence for childhood abuse, particularly sexual abuse, in the history of women with BPD, with abuse predicting BPD above and beyond other factors like negative affectivity and disinhibition (Herman, Perry, and Van der Kolk, 1989; Sabo, 1997; Trull, 2001; Yen et al., 2002). Reports of childhood sexual abuse in inpatients and outpatients with BPD range from 40-82%; this relationship is particularly strong for those who engage in substance abuse (Herman et al., 1989; Paris et al., 1994a, 1994b; Silk et al., 1995; Shearer, Peters, Quaytman, and Ogden, 1990; Van Den Bosch, Verheul, Langeland, and Van Den Brink, 2003; Zanarini et al., 2002).

Post-traumatic stress disorder (PTSD) includes several components of dysfunction: re-experiencing of the trauma, avoidance, hyperarousal and dysphoria/emotional numbing (Simms, Watson and Doebbelling, 2002; King, Leskin, King and Weathers, 1998). However, the literature has recently begun to support the idea of a more complex symptom picture than the typical DSM-IV-TR PTSD diagnosis (American Psychiatric Association, 2000; Cloitre et al., 2009; Zink et al., 2009).

As childhood abuse tends to be continuous and sustained, developmental researchers propose that a complex PTSD is more likely to develop, which includes other symptoms such as identity problems, anxious arousal, dissociative symptoms, unstable relationships and self-injurious behaviors (Cloitre et al., 2009; Herman, 1992, Lewis and Grenyer, 2009). This "complex PTSD" is very similar in nature to BPD, and, in fact, some research has questioned whether they are in fact distinct disorders (Bryant, 2010; Lewis and Grenyer, 2009). This research indicates that it is perhaps more likely for a BPD-like symptom picture to occur than a typical simple PTSD symptom picture after childhood abuse.

Childhood Abuse Predicts Future Substance Use Disorders

There is also substantial research suggesting that childhood abuse predicts future substance use disorders. Patients with substance dependence problems report histories of child abuse at high rates, from 29%-90% in women and from 16%-77% in men (Cohen and Densen-Gerber, 1982; MacMillan et al., 2001; Ouimette, Kimmerling, Shaw and Moos, 2000; Schaefer, Sobieraj, and Hollyfiled, 1988; Triffleman, Marmar, Delucci and Ronfeldt, 1995). There is some evidence of predictive relationships between childhood abuse and substance abuse, though the results are inconsistent (Bailey and McCloskey, 2005; Brady, Killeen, Saladin, Dansky, and Becker, 2010; Gordon, 2002; Najavits, Weiss, and Shaw, 1999; Wu et al., 2010). It is at least plausible that childhood abuse increases the likelihood of future substance use problems. Nonetheless, because substance abuse is a complex behavior in its own right, characterized by traits associated with affective instability, traits predictive of impulsive actions (Cyders, Flory, Rainer, and Smith, 2009; Sher and Trull, 1994; Whiteside and Lynam, 2003) and other factors, it does not seem likely that the pathway from childhood abuse to substance dependence is direct. Because much of the research linking the two suggests that there are co-occurring issues such as self-harm, attempted suicide, emotion dysregulation, and impulsivity (Corrigan, Fisher, and Nutt, 2011; Cuomo, Sarchiapone, Giannantonio, Mancini, and Roy, 2008; Darke, Torok, Kaye, and Ross, 2010; Gratz and Tull, 2010), BPD (which is often characterized by these behaviors) is indeed a good candidate for a potential mediator in the relationship between childhood abuse and substance dependence. Within the literature on BPD, there is substantial research linking the disorder and its traits to substance abuse (James and Taylor, 2008; McGlashan et al., 2000; Oldham, Skodol, Kellman, and Hyler, 1995; Trull, Sher, Minks-Brown, Durbin, and Burr, 2000; Zanarini, Frankenburg, Hennen, Reich, and Silk, 2004; Zimmerman and Mattia, 1999).

Most of these data are cross-sectional, and it should be noted that the research suggesting a prospective relationship between BPD and substance dependence is mixed (Cohen, Chen, Crawford, Brook and Gordon, 2007; Walter et al., 2009).

The Current Study

The model driving this study is that childhood emotional, sexual and physical abuse increase the likelihood of BPD and, perhaps, PTSD traits; BPD, but not PTSD, in turn increases the likelihood of adult substance dependence. Our specific hypotheses are as follows. First, we hypothesize that (a) all types of childhood abuse will be associated with adult substance dependence and (b) those associations will be mediated by BPD, but not PTSD. Second, we hypothesize that (a) childhood sexual abuse will provide incremental prediction of future substance dependence above and beyond other types of abuse and (b) that relationship will be mediated by BPD and not PTSD.

We test these pathways in a sample of individuals in treatment for cocaine and/or heroin addiction, thus testing whether childhood abuse history predicts variation in substance dependence in a sample already at very high risk for this diagnosis. Thus, this test is a stringent one that speaks to the potential etiological importance of childhood abuse. Because this initial test is cross-sectional, it is not a test of the causal processes implied by the model; rather, it is a test of whether our model is plausible. A negative finding would cast serious doubt on the model. A positive finding would speak to the value of testing the model with more rigorous longitudinal designs.

METHOD

Subjects

Subjects were recruited from a residential substance abuse treatment facility in Washington DC (n = 311, mean age= 43.7, S.D.= 9.7; 74.4% male, 87.4% African American, 80.1% single, 80.5% unemployed, 68.6% high school education or less, mean annual income < $25,000, with 55.7% making less than $10,000 past year, and 55.2% court-mandated to attend treatment). All patients admitted to the treatment facility completed assessments with doctoral level graduate students and senior level research staff. These assessments provided health and psychiatric information to counselors at the treatment facility. Furthermore, if patients provided consent, assessment information was entered into a research database.

Measures

Subjects were administered the Structured Clinical Interview for the DSM-IV (SCID-IV, First, Spitzer, Williams, and Gibbon, 1997) to assess for Axis I disorders and the Diagnostic Interview for Personality Disorders (DIPD; Zanarini, Frankenburg, Chauncey, Gunderson, 1987) to assess for BPD, as it has been argued to be a more comprehensive and precise measure of this disorder than the SCID-IV (Zanarini et al., 1987). Demographic information was collected using a brief questionnaire that assessed age, sex, race/ethnicity, marital status, income, education, occupation and employment status.

Patients who endorsed three or more SCID-IV substance dependence symptoms in the year prior to the assessment were diagnosed with current substance dependence, while those reporting three or more symptoms before this time period were diagnosed with past substance dependence per the DSM-IV-TR diagnostic criteria. BPD, PTSD and substance dependence diagnoses could take on three values: no diagnosis, subthreshold diagnosis (as defined in the SCID-IV), and full diagnosis. Childhood sexual, physical and emotional abuse was assessed using the short form of the Childhood Trauma Questionnaire (CTQ-SF; Bernstein et al., 2003). The CTQ-SF in a self-report questionnaire, with each question beginning with the phrase "while you were growing up." Each subscale has five items employing a 5-point scale ranging from 1 (never true) to 5 (very often true). The subscales of the CTQ-SF have been shown to preserve the meaning of the parent form subscales in substance abusing populations, have good internal consistency, and good criterion-related validity (Bernstein et al., 2003).

Procedure

Assessment procedures were typically completed within four to seven days of entering the treatment facility (the four-day waiting period was to minimize the potential presence of withdrawal symptoms). Participants were administered the SCID and DIPD as part of their treatment, and data was used in further research analysis only when consent was obtained.

Participants who provided consent to take part in a larger study were administered the CTQ-SF in addition to a battery of additional assessments, and were paid $25 in the form of a grocery store gift card upon discharge from treatment.

Data Analytic Method

To test our hypotheses concerning the mediation of BPD and PTSD on the influence of childhood abuse on adult substance dependence diagnosis, we first created a combination variable which included alcohol, cocaine, and opioid dependence disorders over the patient's lifetime, so as to understand whether the effect was best understood when looking at all three disorders separately or together. We then tested each mediation using the Preacher and Hayes (2004) bootstrapping method.

This method is based on the product of the coefficients from the independent variable to the mediator, and from the mediator to the dependent variable. Because products of coefficients are often not normally distributed, we used a bootstrapping approach (1,000 iterations) to obtain accurate estimates of standard errors, and hence confidence intervals. When using confidence intervals, significance is considered present when the confidence interval does not include zero (Preacher and Hayes, 2004).

RESULTS

Descriptive Statistics

Out of 311 participants, 47 (9.2%) reported no emotional, physical, or sexual abuse. There were 221 (71%) who reported experiencing emotional abuse; of these, 24 (10.9%) reported *only* experiencing emotional abuse. There were 224 (72%) who reported experiencing physical abuse; of these, 36 (16.1% of the overall sample) reported *only* experiencing physical abuse. There were 99 (31.8%) who reported experiencing sexual abuse; of these, 4 (4%) reported *only* experiencing sexual abuse.

Also, 39.4% of the participants reported meeting the threshold for an alcohol dependence diagnosis at some point in time in their life, 55.8% participants met criteria for cocaine use disorder, and 19.2% participants met criteria for an opioid use disorder. Of the sample, 24.6% reported meeting criteria for BPD while 13.2% reported meeting criteria for PTSD.

Besides substance use disorders and borderline personality disorder, the sample displayed a range of other current disorder diagnoses. The most common diagnosis (besides those for substance use disorders) was major depressive disorder (24.1% met criteria). Other common diagnoses include generalized anxiety disorder (9.4%), specific phobia (6.9%), and social phobia (6.1%). A breakdown of study diagnoses by sex can be found in Table 1.

Table 1. Percentage of participants given diagnosis by sex

	Male	Female
Childhood Emotional Abuse	67.4%	80.1%
Childhood Physical Abuse	74.8%	64.3%
Childhood Sexual Abuse	24.2%	52.3%
Borderline Personality Disorder	24.7%	36.2%
Post-Traumatic Stress Disorder	12.2%	19.0%
Major Depressive Disorder	21.0%	37.6%
Panic Disorder	2.7%	3.2%
Social Phobia	9.1%	10.7%
Generalized Anxiety Disorder	7.9%	11.5%
Obsessive-Compulsive Disorder	2.7%	3.1%
Lifetime Alcohol Dependence	43.6%	34.1%
Lifetime Cocaine Dependence	62.8%	69.7%
Lifetime Opioid Dependence	29.3%	22.0%

Note. N = 311.

Correlations among Childhood Abuse, Borderline Personality Disorder, and Substance Use Disorder Lifetime Diagnosis

Table 2 presents correlations among the study variables. As seen in the table, childhood sexual, physical and emotional abuse are related to BPD, though only emotional abuse is related to PTSD. The three types of abuse are also all related to alcohol, cocaine, and the combination of all three major substance dependence diagnoses during the lifetime of the participant, though they are not related to opioid lifetime diagnoses. Also, BPD diagnoses are related to higher levels of lifetime alcohol and cocaine dependence diagnoses, as well as to the combination dependence variable, while PTSD diagnoses were only related to cocaine dependence diagnoses, as well as to the combination dependence variable.

Preliminary Analyses

In order to test whether there was an effect of sex, we created a regression model to predict alcohol, cocaine, opioid and combination dependence from each type of abuse. We entered sex at step 1, the type of abuse at step 2, and BPD and PTSD at step 3. The effect of sex was nonsignificant.

Prediction of Lifetime Substance Dependence from Childhood Abuse

We first created several standard linear regression models to separately predict alcohol, cocaine, opioid and combination dependence from each type of abuse. The results of this set of regression models can be found in Table 3. All forms of childhood abuse consistently significantly predicted alcohol dependence and, to a lesser extent, cocaine dependence. They did not significantly predict opioid dependence, but they significantly predicted the combination variable.

Table 2. Correlations between childhood abuse, borderline personality disorder, post-traumatic stress disorder and lifetime substance use disorder diagnoses

	CEA	CSA	CPA	BPD	PTSD	ALC	COC	OPD	COM
CEA	--	.55**	.70**	.38**	.19**	.34**	.23**	-.06	.30**
CSA		--	.46**	.21**	.09	.21**	.15*	-.02	.20**
CPA			--	.23**	.11	.27**	.14*	-.02	.23**
BPD				--	.24**	.26**	.19**	.04	.27**
PTSD					--	.07	.11*	.02	.11*
ALC						--	.17	.03	.66**
COC							--	.07	.67*
OPD								--	.55**
COM									--

Note. N = 311. *p<.05; **p<.01. CEA = Childhood emotional abuse, CSA = Childhood sexual abuse, CPA = Childhood physical abuse, BPD = Borderline personality disorder, PTSD = Post-traumatic stress disorder, ALC = Presence of alcohol SUD diagnosis in lifetime, COC = Presence of cocaine SUD diagnosis in lifetime, OPD = Presence of alcohol SUD diagnosis in lifetime, COM = Presence of alcohol, cocaine or opioid SUD diagnosis in lifetime.

Table 3. Linear regression results for the prediction of substance dependence from childhood abuse

	Prediction of Substance Dependence							
	ALC		OPD		COC		COM	
	R^2	ß	R^2	ß	R^2	ß	R^2	ß
Childhood Emotional Abuse	.03	.18**	.00	.05	.03	.16**	.05	.22**
Childhood Sexual Abuse	.05	.22**	.00	-.04	.01	.10*	.03	.17**
Childhood Physical Abuse	.02	.13**	.00	-.02	.02	.12*	.02	.13*

NOTE. N = 311. The results of four linear regressions are presented in each row of the table. ALC = Lifetime presence of alcohol dependence disorder. OPD = Lifetime presence of opioid dependence disorder. COC= Lifetime presence of cocaine dependence disorder. COM = Lifetime presence of alcohol, opioid, and/or cocaine dependence disorder. *significant at p<.05, ** significant at p<.01.

Indirect Effect of BPD and PTSD on Lifetime Substance Dependence

We then performed several mediations using bootstrapping to test the indirect effect of BPD and PTSD on the prediction of substance dependence from childhood abuse.

The results of these mediations can be found in Table 4. The mediation analyses were consistent with BPD mediating the influence of childhood sexual, emotional, and physical abuse on adult alcohol dependence and cocaine dependence, but not opioid dependence. The test of BPD mediating the influence of each form of childhood abuse on the composite dependence variable was also significant. PTSD did not significantly mediate any of the relationships. We repeated these analyses after removing the component of our borderline personality variable that included substance use (participating in impulsive behaviors like binge drinking or using illicit substances) and our results were unchanged.

Table 4. Results from bootstrapping test of indirect effect of BPD and PTSD on the relationship between childhood abuse and substance dependence

	Indirect Effect of BPD			
	ALC	OPD	COC	COM
Childhood Emotional Abuse	.02 - .07**	-.02 - .01	.01 - .05**	.01 - .04**
Childhood Sexual Abuse	.03 - .20**	-.05 - .04	.02 - .16**	.02 - .11**
Childhood Physical Abuse	.01 - .04**	-.01 - .01	.01 - .03*	.01 - .02*
Childhood Emotional Abuse	-.01 - .03	-.01 - .02	-.01 - .02	-.01 - .01
Childhood Sexual Abuse	-.01 - .07	-.02 - .05	-.01 - .08	-.01 - .06
Childhood Physical Abuse	-.01 - .01	-.01 - .01	-.01 - .01	-.00 - .01

NOTE. N = 311. Information presented is a series of confidence intervals. ALC = Lifetime presence of alcohol dependence disorder. OPD = Lifetime presence of opioid dependence disorder. COC= Lifetime presence of cocaine dependence disorder. COM = Lifetime presence of alcohol, opioid, and/or cocaine dependence disorder. *significant at p<.05, ** significant at p<.01.

Impact of Different Types of Abuse on Alcohol and Cocaine Dependence

To test our hypothesis about the incremental impact of sexual abuse on the prediction of substance dependence through BPD, we created a variable which attached a value of 0 to having experienced only emotional abuse, only physical abuse, or both and a value of 1 to having experienced emotional and sexual abuse, physical and sexual abuse, or all three. Thus, this analysis included only individuals who reported some history of childhood abuse.

We performed a test of mediation using bootstrapping for alcohol dependence, and we found evidence for a significant partial mediation (CI: .02 - .19, p <.01). We did the same for cocaine and opioid dependence and did not find significance, suggesting that sexual abuse does not provide incremental impact in the prediction of future cocaine or opioid use through BPD.

DISCUSSION

As expected, we found that our variables of interest were significantly related to each other, with the exception of opioid dependence diagnosis. Notable are the high relationships between the three types of abuse in childhood, as well as cocaine and alcohol's relationship with all types of abuse and BPD, but not PTSD. Our hypothesis that childhood abuse would predict all types of substance dependence was supported, as was our hypothesis that BPD would partially mediate the relationship between childhood abuse and future substance dependence. We did not expect PTSD to mediate the relationship between childhood abuse and adult dependence; consistent with our expectation, we found no evidence that it did.

As stated before, there is significant research suggesting that BPD is similar to what is called complex PTSD: Both include such dysfunction as identity problems, interpersonal relationship issues, and behavioral problems like self-harm or suicidal behavior (Lewis and Grenyer, 2009). It is possible that in victims of childhood abuse, the more prevalent manifestation of post-abuse distress is not traditional PTSD, but rather pervasive disruption in personality, as described by the diagnosis of BPD (used in the current study) or complex PTSD. Perhaps one way that abuse history leads to substance dependence is through its influence on the development of such BPD-like or complex PTSD-like characteristics as emotional dysregulation and affect-driven impulsivity, which can then plausibly increase the likelihood of developing substance dependence. The possibility that a childhood history of abuse increases the likelihood of the development of these characteristics, which in turn increases the likelihood of alcohol or cocaine dependence, is supported by these cross-sectional data and merits further investigation with more rigorous longitudinal designs.

There is reason to believe that perhaps the different effects that are experienced from different types of substances may have an impact on the differential predictive abilities of abuse for each substance tested. Alcohol could be consistently predicted from childhood abuse of all types, whereas cocaine was less reliably predictable from abuse and opioid dependence was not predictable at all from abuse.

In addition, our hypothesis regarding the significant additive effect of childhood sexual abuse above and beyond the experience of other types of abuse was supported. Having experienced childhood sexual abuse in addition to childhood physical and emotional abuse is highly predictive of future alcohol and cocaine issues, above and beyond having experienced emotional abuse alone, physical abuse alone, or physical and emotional abuse together, and this relationship appeared to be mediated by BPD. One important implication of these findings, should they be confirmed using longitudinal designs, is that researchers and clinicians should consider not just abuse history, but the specific forms of past abuse. Individuals with abuse histories that include sexual abuse appear to be at increased risk for BPD and substance dependence: Treatments based on the specific contours of past abuse may facilitate recovery.

In an important way, these tests were quite stringent. The sample was made up of individuals undergoing inpatient treatment for cocaine and/or heroin abuse, and so constituted a sample high on risk factors and high on the target diagnoses of BPD, PTSD and substance dependence. To find that abuse history, and also that sexual abuse in particular, predicted yet higher BPD and substance dependence scores is striking. This finding may well speak to the profound effects of childhood abuse, although additional research comparing groups like the present one to less-disordered or non-disordered community samples is necessary before drawing such a conclusion.

This paper has some limitations that must be remembered when interpreting the results. First, the design was cross-sectional. We have therefore provided no test of the temporal sequence of effects: Longitudinal designs are necessary for that purpose. Another feature of this design is that the childhood abuse data were collected retrospectively and without reference to a specific time period in which abuse occurred. Participant reports of childhood abuse were provided following BPD diagnosis and substance use history. Of course, this limitation characterizes this type of research; there will always be reason to question the accuracy of retrospective reports of childhood abuse, perhaps more so when those reports come from inpatients at substance use treatment centers. However, in the absence of long-term longitudinal studies that begin early in childhood and follow individuals through admission to substance use treatment facilities, retrospective reports will remain one source of this important information. This study used an inpatient substance abuse treatment sample. Although the nature of this sample is a strength of this study, it is also a weakness, in that we do not yet know to which populations these results can be generalized. Finally, we do not have information regarding family history of substance dependence, which would provide valuable information regarding the heritability of such disorders.

Despite these limitations, the current findings highlight the importance of integrating information on environmental and personality factors to best understand the risk process for substance use disorders. Childhood abuse has long been understood as a possible risk factor for future substance dependence; a major contributor to this process may well be impairment in basic personality functioning, as represented by the diagnosis of BPD. We found no evidence that traditional PTSD mediated the relationship between childhood abuse and adult substance dependence. Childhood sexual abuse appears to have a deleterious impact above and beyond other forms of abuse. These findings speak to the ongoing life consequences of childhood abuse, particularly sexual abuse, and may prove important for the diagnosis and treatment process.

REFERENCES

American Psychiatric Association.(2000). Diagnostic and statistical manual of mental disorders (4th ed., text rev.). Washington, DC: Author.

Bailey, J.A., and McCloskey, L.A. (2005). Pathways to adolescent substance use among sexually abused girls. *Journal of Abnormal Child Psychology, 33,* 39-53.Doi: 10.1007/s10802-005-0933-0.

Bernstein, D. P., Stein, J. A., Newcomb, M. D., Walker, E., Pogge, D., Ahluvalia, T., and ... Zule, W. (2003). Development and validation of a brief screening version of the Childhood Trauma Questionnaire. *Child Abuse and Neglect, 27*(2), 169-190.Doi: 10.1016/S0145-2134(02)00541-0.

Brady, K.T, Killeen, T., Saladin, M.E., Dansky, B. and Becker, S. (2010). Comorbid substance abuse and posttraumatic stress disorder: Characteristics of women in treatment. *The American Journal on Addictions, 3,* 160-164.Doi: 10.3109/10550499409117249.

Breslau, N. (2009). The epidemiology of trauma, PTSD, and other posttrauma disorders. *Trauma Violence Abuse, 10,* 198-210.

Bryant, R.A. (2010). The complexity of complex PTSD. *American Journal of Psychiatry, 167,* 879-881.Doi: 10.1176/appi.ajp.2010.10040606.

Cloitre, M., Stolbach, B.C., Herman, J.L., van der Kolk, B., Pynoos, R., Wang, J., and Petkova, E. (2009). A developmental approach to complex PTSD: childhood and adult cumulative trauma as predictors of symptom complexity. *Journal of Traumatic Stress, 22,* 399-408.

Cohen, F. S., and Densen-Gerber, J. (1982). A study of the relationship between child abuse and drug addiction in 178 patients: Preliminary results. *Child Abuse and Neglect, 6, 4,* 383-387.Doi: 10.1016/0145-2134(82)90081-3.

Cohen, P., Chen, H., Crawford, T. N., Brook, J. S., and Gordon, K. (2007). Personality disorders in early adolescence and the development of later substance use disorders in the general population. *Drug and Alcohol Dependence*, 88S71-S84.

Corrigan, F. M., Fisher, J. J., and Nutt, D. J. (2011). Autonomic dysregulation and the window of tolerance model of the effects of complex emotional trauma. *Journal of Psychopharmacology, 25, 1*, 17-25.Doi: 10.1177/0269881109354930.

Cuomo, C., Sarchiapone, M., Giannantonio, M., Mancini, M., and Roy, A. (2008). Aggression, impulsivity, personality traits, and childhood trauma of prisoners with substance abuse and addiction. *The American Journal of Drug and Alcohol Abuse, 34,3*, 339-345.

Cyders, M. A., Flory, K., Rainer, S., and Smith, G. T. (2009). The role of personality dispositions to risky behavior in predicting first-year college drinking. *Addiction, 104, 2*, 193-202.

Darke, S., Torok, M., Kaye, S., and Ross, J. (2010). Attempted suicide, self-harm, and violent victimization among regular illicit drug users. *Suicide and Life-Threatening Behavior, 40,6*, 587-596.Doi: 10.1521/suli.2010.40.6.587.

First, M. B., Spitzer, R. L., Williams, J. B. W., and Gibbon, M. (1997). *Structured Clinical Interview of DSM-IV Disorders (SCID).*Washington, DC; American Psychiatric Association.

Gordon, H.W. (2002). Early environmental stress and biological vulnerability to drug abuse. *Psychoneuroendocrinology, 27*, 115-126.

Gratz, K. L., and Tull, M. T. (2010). The relationship between emotion dysregulation and deliberate self-harm among inpatients with substance use disorders. *Cognitive Therapy and Research, 34*(6), 544-553.Doi: 10.1007/s10608-009-9268-4

Herman, J.L. (1992). Complex PTSD: A syndrome in survivors of prolonged and repeated trauma. *Journal of Traumatic Stress, 5*, 377-391.Doi: 10.1002/jts.2490050305.

Herman, J. L., Perry, J., and Van der Kolk, B. A. (1989). Childhood trauma in borderline personality disorder. *The American Journal of Psychiatry, 146*(4), 490-495.

James, L. M., and Taylor, J. (2008). Associations between symptoms of borderline personality disorder, externalizing disorders, and suicide-related behaviors. *Journal of Psychopathology and Behavioral Assessment, 30*(1), 1-9.Doi: 10.1007/s10862-007-9074-9.

Johnson, J. G., Cohen, P., Brown, J., Smailes, E., and Bernstein, D. P. (1999). Childhood maltreatment increases risk for personality disorders during early adulthood. *Archives of General Psychiatry, 56*(7), 600-606.

King, D.W., Leskin, G.A., King, L.A. and Weathers, F.W. (1998). Confirmatory factor analysis of the clinician-administered PTSD Scale: evidence for the dimensionality of posttraumatic stress disorder. *Psychological Assessment, 10*, 90–96.

Lewis, K.L, and Grenyer, B.F.S. (2009). Borderline personality disorder or complex posttraumatic stress disorder? An update on the controversy. *Harvard Review of Psychiatry, 17*, 322-328.Doi: 10.3109/10673220903271848.

MacMillan, H. L., Fleming, J. E., Streiner, D. L., Lin, E., Boyle, M. H., Jamieson, E., and ... Beardslee, W. R. (2001). Childhood abuse and lifetime psychopathology in a community sample. *The American Journal of Psychiatry, 158*(11), 1878-1883.Doi: 10.1176/appi.ajp.158.11.1878.

McGlashan, T. H., Grilo, C. M., Skodol, A. E., Gunderson, J. G., Shea, M. T., Morey, L. C., and ... Stout, R. L. (2000). The Collaborative Longitudinal Personality Disorders Study: Baseline Axis I/II and II/II diagnostic co-occurrence. *Acta Psychiatrica Scandinavica, 102, 4,* 256-264.Doi: 10.1034/j.1600-0447.2000.102004256.x.

Najavits, L., Weiss, R., and Shaw, S. (1997) The link between substance abuse and posttraumatic stress disorder in women: A research review. *American Journal on Addictions, 6, 4,* 273-283.Doi: 10.1111/j.1521-0391.1997.tb00408.x

Neumann, D. A., Houskamp, B. M., Pollock, V. E., and Briere, J. (1996). The long-term sequelae of childhood sexual abuse in women: A meta-analytic review. *Child Maltreatment, 1*(1), 6-16.Doi: 10.1177/1077559596001001002.

Oldham, J. M., Skodol, A. E., Kellman, H., Hyler, S. E., Doidge, N., Rosnick, L., and Gallaher (1995). Comorbidity of axis I and axis II disorders. *The American Journal of Psychiatry, 152,* 4, 571-578.Doi: 10.1176/appi.ajp.160.8.1494.

Ouimette, P.C., Kimerling, R., Shaw, J., and Moos, R.H. (2000). Physical and sexual abuse among women and men with substance use disorders. *Alcoholism Treatment Quarterly, 18,* 3, 7-17.Doi: 10.1300/J020v18n03_02.

Paris, J., Zweig-Frank, H., and Guzder, J. (1994a). Psychological risk factors for borderline personality disorder in female patients. *Comprehensive Psychiatry, 35*(4), 301-305.Doi: 10.1016/0010-440X(94)90023-X

Paris, J., Zweig-Frank, H., and Guzder, J. (1994b). Risk factors for borderline personality in male outpatients. *Journal of Nervous and Mental Disease, 182*(7), 375-380.

Preacher, K. J., and Hayes, A. F. (2004). SPSS and SAS procedures for estimating indirect effects in simple mediation models. *Behavior Research Methods, Instruments and Computers, 36*(4), 717-731.

Sabo, A. N. (1997). Etiological significance of associations between childhood trauma and borderline personality disorder: Conceptual and clinical implications. *Journal of Personality Disorders, 11*(1), 50-70.Doi: 10.1521/pedi.1997.11.1.50.

Schaefer, M. R., Sobieraj, K., and Hollyfield, R. L. (1988). Prevalence of childhood physical abuse in adult male veteran alcoholics. *Child Abuse and Neglect,* 12(2), 141-149.Doi: 10.1016/0145-2134(88)90022-1.

Shearer, S. L., Peters, C. P., Quaytman, M. S., and Ogden, R. L. (1990). Frequency and correlates of childhood sexual and physical abuse histories in adult female borderline inpatients. *The American Journal of Psychiatry, 147*(2), 214-216.

Sher, K. J., and Trull, T. J. (1994). Personality and disinhibitory psychopathology: Alcoholism and antisocial personality disorder. *Journal of Abnormal Psychology, 103,* 92-102.

Silk, K. R., Lee, S., Hill, E. M., and Lohr, N. E. (1995). Borderline personality disorder symptoms and severity of sexual abuse. *The American Journal of Psychiatry,* 152(7), 1059-1064.

Simms, L.J., Watson, D., and Doebbelling, B.N. (2002). Confirmatory factor analyses of posttraumatic stress symptoms in deployed and nondeployed veterans of the Gulf War. *Journal of Abnormal Psychology, 111,* 637-647.

Trifflemann, E. G., Marmar, C. R., Delucchi, K. L., and Ronfeldt, H. (1995). Childhood trauma and posttraumatic stress disorder in substance abuse inpatients. *Journal of Nervous and Mental Disease, 183*(3), 172-176.Doi: 10.1097/00005053-199503000-00008.

Trull, T. J. (2001). Structural relations between borderline personality disorder features and putative etiological correlates. *Journal of Abnormal Psychology, 110*(3), 471-481.

Trull, T. J., Sher, K. J., Minks-Brown, C., Durbin, J., and Burr, R. (2000). Borderline personality disorder and substance use disorders: A review and integration. *Clinical Psychology Review, 20*(2), 235-253.

Van Den Bosch, L. C., Verheul, R., Langeland, W., and Van Den Brink, W. (2003). Trauma, dissociation, and posttraumatic stress disorder in female borderline patients with and without substance abuse problems. *Australian and New Zealand Journal of Psychiatry, 37*(5), 549-555.Doi: 10.1046/j.1440-1614.2003.01199.x.

Vanderlinden, J., Van Dyck, R., Vandereycken, W., Vertommen, H., Jan Verkes, R. (1993). The dissociation questionnaire (DIS-Q): Development and characteristics of a new self-report questionnaire. *Clinical Psychology and Psychotherapy, 1, 1*, 21-27. Doi:10.1002/cpp.5640010105.

Waller, G. (1994). Childhood sexual abuse and borderline personality disorder in the eating disorders. *Child Abuse and Neglect, 18,* 97-101. Doi:10.1016/0145-2134(94)90099-X.

Walter, M., Gunderson, J. G., Zanarini, M. C., Sanislow, C. A., Grilo, C. M., McGlashan, T. H., and … Skodol, A. E. (2009). New onsets of substance use disorders in borderline personality disorder over 7 years of follow-ups: Findings from the Collaborative Longitudinal Personality Disorders Study. *Addiction, 104*(1), 97-103.Doi: 10.1111/j.1360-0443.2008.02413.x.

Whiteside, S. P., and Lynam, D. R. (2003). Understanding the role of impulsivity and externalizing psychopathology in alcohol abuse: Application of the UPPS Impulsive Behavior Scale. *Experimental and Clinical Psychopharmacology, 11*(3), 210-217.Doi: 10.1037/1064-1297.11.3.210.

Widom, C.S. (1999). Posttraumatic stress disorder in abused and neglected children grown up. *American Journal of Psychiatry, 156,* 1223-1229.Doi: 10.1176/appi.ajp.160.3.580.

Wu, N.S., Schairer, L.C., Dellor, E., and Grella, C. (2010). Childhood trauma and health outcomes in adults with comorbid substance abuse and mental health disorders. *Addictive Behaviors, 35,* 68-71.Doi: 10.1016/j.addbeh.2009.09.003.

Yen, S.R., Shea, M., Battle, C. L., Johnson, D. M., Zlotnick, C., Dolan-Sewell, R., and … McGlashan, T. H. (2002). Traumatic exposure and posttraumatic stress disorder in borderline, schizotypal, avoidant and obsessive-compulsive personality disorders: *Nervous and Mental Disease, 190*(8), 510-518.

Zanarini, M. C., Frankenburg, F. R., Hennen, J., Reich, D., and Silk, K. R. (2004). Axis I comorbidity in patients with borderline personality disorder: 6-year follow-up and prediction of time to remission. *The American Journal of Psychiatry, 161*(11), 2108-2114.doi: 10.1176/appi.ajp.161.11.2108.

Zanarini, M. C., Yong, L., Frankenburg, F. R., Hennen, J., Reich, D., Marino, M. F., and Vujanovic, A. (2002). Severity of reported childhood sexual abuse and its relationship to severity of borderline psychopathology and psychosocial impairment among borderline inpatients. *Journal of Nervous and Mental Disease, 190*(6), 381-387.

Zanarini, M. C., Frankenburg, F. R., Chauncey, D. L., and Gunderson, J. G. (1987). The Diagnostic Interview for Personality Disorders: Interrater and test-retest reliability. *Comprehensive Psychiatry, 28*(6), 467-480.doi:10.1016/0010-440X(87)90012-5.

Zimmerman, M., and Mattia, J. I. (1999). Axis I diagnostic comorbidity and borderline personality disorder. *Comprehensive Psychiatry, 40*(4), 245-252.doi:10.1016/S0010-440X(99)90123-2.

Zink, T., Klesges, L., Stevens, S., and Decker, P. (2008). The development of a sexual abuse severity score: Characteristics of childhood sexual abuse associated with trauma symptomatology, somatization, and alcohol abuse. *Journal of Interpersonal Violence, 24,* 537-546.doi:10.1177/0886260508317198.

INDEX

A

abstinence, vii, x, 1, 3, 14, 19, 23, 25, 27, 28, 31, 49, 81, 86, 87, 104, 107, 109, 116, 128, 136, 153, 201, 203, 214
abuse, vii, x, 2, 3, 6, 7, 8, 9, 10, 12, 14, 17, 18, 19, 23, 31, 32, 37, 47, 58, 79, 119, 122, 124, 143, 208, 215, 217, 218, 219, 220, 221, 222, 223, 224, 225, 226, 227
access, 13, 16, 18, 22, 23, 24, 25, 26, 27, 28, 29, 30, 32, 34, 35, 49, 53, 54, 56, 79, 81, 84, 102, 138
accounting, 64
acetaldehyde, 38, 203, 204, 206, 208, 215
acetylcholine, vii, 2, 10, 14, 15, 18, 32, 33, 35, 40, 43, 45, 48, 59, 81
acid, x, 8, 106, 108, 120, 202, 206
acidosis, 207
ACTH, 17
action potential, 131
acute confusional state, 210
adaptation(s), 10, 57, 79, 129, 130, 191, 192, 193
addictive behavior, viii, 12, 13, 18, 56, 60, 61, 79, 80, 139
adenine, 203
ADH, 203, 204, 212
ADHD, 74, 75
adhesion, 213
adipose, 158, 160, 162
adipose tissue, 160, 162
adiposity, 93
adjustment, 132, 182
adolescent boys, 3
adolescent development, 8
adolescent drinking, 39, 148
adolescent female, 65, 137
adolescents, vii, viii, 1, 3, 6, 23, 48, 49, 53, 59, 67, 85, 86, 89, 91, 111, 118, 119, 123, 127, 128, 130, 131, 132, 136, 137, 138, 139, 140, 145, 148, 149, 183, 184, 185, 189, 190, 192, 194, 195, 196, 197, 198, 199, 200
adulthood, x, 8, 23, 31, 34, 41, 43, 50, 52, 55, 131, 136, 143, 144, 149, 189, 217, 227
adults, ix, x, 2, 6, 9, 67, 71, 74, 75, 80, 84, 85, 86, 119, 132, 136, 145, 163, 187, 188, 189, 192, 193, 194, 195, 196, 212, 217, 229
advancement(s), 80, 117
adverse effects, 194
affective experience, 125
African American women, 71, 72, 170, 171, 172, 175, 177, 178, 180, 181, 182, 183
African American(s), 71, 72, 73, 176, 177, 178, 179, 185
age, 2, 3, 6, 7, 9, 39, 43, 52, 56, 64, 65, 67, 70, 72, 76, 91, 130, 131, 136, 137, 140, 142, 173, 189, 193, 194, 195, 196, 197, 199, 220
aggression, 129, 215, 217
agonist, 11, 15, 16, 19, 54
alcohol abuse, viii, 3, 4, 6, 7, 9, 10, 12, 13, 14, 15, 18, 22, 23, 30, 31, 32, 34, 35, 38, 42, 44, 46, 50, 52, 53, 58, 59, 61, 64, 77, 78, 98, 105, 119, 121, 128, 129, 130, 137, 141, 208, 210, 229
alcohol concentrations, vii, 1, 5, 27, 39, 203
alcohol cravings, viii, 97, 99, 103, 104, 107, 108, 110, 115, 116
alcohol dependence, vii, x, 1, 2, 3, 4, 9, 10, 12, 14, 17, 21, 25, 31, 34, 38, 39, 41, 43, 44, 50, 57, 58, 98, 120, 137, 202, 206, 212, 214, 221, 222, 223, 224
alcohol problems, 6, 49, 60, 91, 112, 124, 125
alcohol research, 16, 35, 59, 142
alcohol use, vii, viii, 1, 2, 18, 23, 31, 36, 38, 40, 42, 43, 51, 56, 60, 78, 83, 97, 98, 99, 100, 101, 102, 103, 104, 105, 106, 107, 108, 109, 110, 111, 112, 114, 116, 117, 119, 120, 121, 122, 128, 130, 132, 138, 140, 141, 148, 149, 153, 209, 211, 212
alcohol withdrawal, 4, 41, 107, 109, 115, 116, 145, 146, 209, 210

alcoholic liver disease, 208, 216
alcoholics, 3, 4, 11, 13, 32, 33, 40, 51, 52, 55, 58, 60, 93, 118, 123, 129, 139, 208, 209, 211, 212, 228
alcoholism, 2, 3, 4, 5, 7, 12, 14, 15, 16, 21, 22, 23, 32, 33, 37, 41, 43, 44, 45, 46, 47, 48, 49, 50, 51, 52, 53, 56, 57, 59, 60, 74, 83, 122, 138, 139, 146, 149, 203, 207, 210
alcohols, 214
aldosteronism, 211
alexithymia, 166
allele, 22, 91
alters, 10, 11, 31, 41, 47, 48, 56, 83, 145, 208
American culture, 170, 181
American Psychiatric Association, 7, 33, 62, 63, 65, 69, 80, 81, 142, 152, 161, 169, 172, 182, 188, 196, 218, 226, 227
American Psychological Association, 92
amines, 205
amino, 8
amino acid(s), 10, 12, 16, 17, 38, 44
amphetamines, 207
amplitude, 138, 139, 149
amygdala, 11, 16, 17, 18, 32, 34, 40, 41, 42, 43, 44, 47, 48, 49, 51, 55, 57, 60, 213, 214
anemia, 171, 207, 208, 211
anger, 71, 125, 154, 193
anisotropy, 136, 137
ankles, 172
anorexia, 83, 97, 122, 153, 167, 174, 183, 189
anorexia nervosa, 83, 97, 122, 183
ANOVA, 175, 177
antagonism, 19, 20, 44, 45
anterior cingulate cortex, 133
antibiotic, 55
anticonvulsant, 214
antidepressants, 13, 153
antioxidant, 214
anxiety, ix, x, 3, 11, 16, 31, 39, 46, 52, 56, 57, 60, 70, 74, 76, 80, 81, 89, 101, 111, 122, 154, 187, 193, 194, 202, 205, 206, 217
anxiety disorder, 74, 112, 122
APA, 7, 62, 63, 65, 66, 68, 69, 78, 79, 80, 81, 120, 142, 152, 182, 188, 195
apoptosis, 30, 214
appetite, 13, 33, 78, 106, 119, 121, 153, 155, 157, 158, 159, 160, 161, 162, 163, 166, 168
appraisals, 184
ARC, 30
arginine, 47
arousal, 218
ascites, 211
Asia, 183
aspartate, 8, 27, 41, 44, 206, 213

aspiration, 207
assault, 128, 129
assertiveness, 195
assessment, 118, 124, 150, 167, 174, 189, 190, 196, 197, 199, 200, 220
astrocytes, 56
asymmetry, 148
ataxia, 7, 205, 210
atrial fibrillation, x, 202, 210
at-risk populations, 196
atrophy, 211
Attention Deficit Hyperactivity Disorder, 74
attentional bias, 105, 106, 109, 119, 122
attitudes, 64, 95, 122, 141, 182, 183, 184, 186, 192, 194, 198
authority, 128
automatic processes, 125
aversion, 7
avoidance, 113, 218
awareness, 62, 64, 101, 102, 121
axon terminals, 44
axons, 131, 136

B

BAC, 5, 6, 7, 14, 29, 129
back pain, 172
barbiturates, 204
barriers, 208
basic research, 203
beer, 23, 202, 203, 205, 208
behavioral approach system, 73
behavioral change, 75
behavioral disorders, 83
behavioral inhibition system, 101
behavioral manifestations, 56
behavioral problems, 210, 225
benchmarks, 29
benefits, 103
benzodiazepine, 162
beverages, 129, 202, 210, 212
bias, 85, 105, 119, 124
binge alcohol drinking, vii, 1, 4, 6, 7, 10, 11, 13, 14, 15, 16, 31, 32, 214
binge drinkers, vii, viii, x, 1, 4, 5, 6, 7, 32, 47, 58, 127, 133, 134, 135, 136, 137, 138, 139, 140, 141, 143, 145, 148, 149, 202, 209
binge eating (BE), viii, 61
Binge Eating Disorder (BED), vii, viii, viiii, ix, 61, 62, 63, 64, 65, 66, 67, 68, 69, 70, 71, 72, 73, 74, 75, 76, 77, 78, 79, 80, 81, 82, 83, 84, 85, 86, 87, 88, 89, 90, 91, 92, 93, 94, 95, 97, 111, 120, 125, 151, 152, 153, 154, 155, 156, 157, 158, 159, 160,

Index

161, 162, 163, 164, 165, 166, 168, 187, 188, 189, 190, 191, 192, 193, 194, 195, 196, 197, 199, 200
bingeing, 78, 81, 124, 166
biomarkers, ix, 151
bipolar disorder, 74, 87, 88
birth weight, 212
black women, 92, 185
Blacks, 93
bleaching, 181, 183
blends, 210
blood, vii, 1, 5, 14, 21, 36, 38, 39, 45, 106, 108, 124, 129, 137, 139, 143, 148, 149, 203, 204, 205, 206, 207, 208, 211, 212
blood flow, 139, 203
blood pressure, 106, 108, 211
body dissatisfaction, 85, 87, 170, 174, 178, 180, 184
body fat, 158, 189
body image, viii, 61, 64, 68, 72, 80, 85, 88, 89, 155, 162, 183, 184, 190, 200
body mass index (BMI), 68, 69, 72, 75, 76, 77, 84, 90, 122, 157, 159, 189, 193
body shape, 65, 68, 71, 72, 152, 153, 174, 184, 188
body size, 72
body weight, 22, 29, 30, 57, 65, 76, 77, 78, 86, 89, 152, 153, 183
bonding, 123
bone(s), 172, 207, 211
bone marrow, 207, 211
borderline personality disorder, vii, x, 75, 76, 154, 217, 218, 221, 223, 227, 228, 229
brain activity, viii, 127, 137, 138
brain damage, 10, 58, 140, 144
brain functioning, 138
brain structure, 19, 21, 31, 66, 131, 132, 136
Brazil, 127
breakdown, 221
breast cancer, x, 2, 202, 212
breathing, 76
breeding, 22, 43
Britain, 4, 52
bulimia, 81, 83, 84, 85, 86, 88, 90, 92, 94, 97, 100, 103, 119, 121, 122, 124, 152, 154, 156, 162, 163, 165, 167, 170, 171, 172, 174, 183, 189, 193, 197
bulimia nervosa, 81, 83, 84, 85, 94, 97, 100, 103, 119, 121, 122, 124, 154, 156, 162, 163, 165, 171, 172, 174

C

Ca^{2+}, 205, 209
cadmium, 208, 215
calcium, 205, 210
caloric intake, 74, 78, 89
caloric restriction, 186
calorie, 42, 90, 166
cancer, x, 75, 202, 212
candidates, 197
carbon, 10, 204
carbon dioxide, 204
carcinogen, 212
cardiac arrhythmia, 172
cardiomyopathy, 207, 210, 215
cardiovascular system, 207
caregivers, 188
cascades, 10
catecholamines, 206, 210
categorization, 136, 142, 143
cation, 206
Caucasians, 71, 73
causal relationship, 2, 102
causality, 160
CDC, 2
cell culture, 23
cell line, 22
central nervous system (CNS), 10, 11, 12, 13, 14, 15, 33, 34, 40, 45, 49, 53, 205, 206, 210, 214, 144, 203, 205, 206
cerebral blood flow, 87, 137, 164
cerebral cortex, 146
cerebrovascular disease, 152
CFI, 175, 177
challenges, 92
chaperones, 30
chemical(s), 172, 174, 209
chemotaxis, 212
Chicago, 185
child abuse, 219, 226
Child Behavior Checklist, 194
childhood, vii, x, 131, 143, 144, 149, 155, 188, 189, 194, 196, 197, 198, 217, 218, 219, 221, 222, 223, 224, 225, 226, 227, 228, 229
childhood history, 218, 225
childhood sexual abuse, 218, 219, 225, 228, 229
children, ix, 60, 86, 159, 187, 188, 189, 190, 191, 192, 193, 194, 195, 196, 197, 198, 199, 200, 229
chromosome, 57
chronic illness, 202
cigarette smokers, 86
cigarette smoking, 55, 78, 211
cingulate region, 138
cirrhosis, 208, 211
City, 186
classes, 15
classical conditioning, 103, 104, 105, 107, 109, 115, 116, 117, 121

classification, 5, 40, 68, 69, 82, 84, 92, 95, 130, 139, 188, 195, 197
clients, 93, 94
clinical presentation, 188
clinical psychology, 199
clinical trials, 85, 163
CO_2, 204
cocaine, x, 19, 35, 37, 40, 44, 46, 52, 53, 80, 82, 88, 207, 217, 219, 221, 222, 223, 224, 225
cocaine dependence, x, 88, 217, 222, 223, 224, 225
coffee, 211
cognition, 11
cognitive abilities, 132
cognitive biases, 120
cognitive deficit(s), 3, 12, 137
cognitive development, 36, 132, 144
cognitive flexibility, 135, 136, 147
cognitive function, 13, 39, 59, 139, 146, 206
cognitive impairment, 41, 132
cognitive load, 125
cognitive performance, 47, 58, 146
cognitive process, viii, 127, 132, 138
cognitive-behavioral therapy, 94, 168
collagen, 208
college campuses, 90
college students, 2, 7, 37, 45, 47, 48, 72, 90, 95, 100, 111, 121, 122, 124, 128, 130, 134, 142, 143, 182, 214
colleges, 143
color, 133, 183, 185, 186
colorectal cancer, 152
coma, x, 202, 205, 207, 210
communication, 30
community, 6, 64, 65, 72, 77, 79, 84, 86, 91, 92, 93, 152, 163, 172, 185, 225, 227
comorbidity, viii, ix, 38, 65, 71, 74, 75, 77, 86, 93, 94, 95, 97, 98, 110, 112, 114, 119, 121, 148, 151, 164, 168, 229
compensation, 175
compilation, vii
complexity, 38, 133, 136, 226
complications, viii, 61, 77, 152, 188
composition, 158, 163
compounds, 16, 19
comprehension, viii, ix, 127
compulsion, 89
compulsive behavior, 82
compulsive personality disorder, 75, 85, 229
computed tomography, 156
concept map, 86
conception, 23
conceptualization, viii, 4, 31, 61
concordance, 190

conditioned response, 103, 104, 105
conditioned stimulus, 103
conditioning, 36, 49, 103, 107, 110, 124
conduct disorder, 2
conductance, 106, 108
conduction, 131, 155
conflict, 149
Congress, 55
consciousness, 185
consensus, 62, 78
consent, 129, 220, 221
consolidation, 134
constituents, 204
construction, 174
consulting, 162, 199
consumption habits, 129
consumption rates, 105
control group, 25, 28, 30, 136, 137
controversies, 190
coping strategies, 123
coronary heart disease, 75, 152
corpus callosum, 136
correlation, 38, 176
correlation coefficient, 176
correlations, 169, 175, 179, 191, 192, 222
cortex, 9, 16, 58, 66, 131, 132, 148
cortical neurons, 36, 48, 58
corticotropin, 21, 45, 214
cortisol, 167, 211
cost, viii, 2, 103, 127
craving, 13, 30, 33, 34, 38, 39, 46, 48, 54, 56, 78, 86, 89, 106, 107, 108, 119, 123, 156, 209
CRF, 10, 17, 21, 30, 43, 60, 213
critical period, 36
criticism, 190
CSA, 223
cues, viii, 66, 73, 86, 97, 99, 103, 105, 106, 117, 120, 121, 122, 123, 125, 147, 156, 162, 189, 193, 195, 209
cultural differences, 181
cultural norms, 170, 181
culture, ix, 48, 143, 155, 169, 170, 171, 180, 181, 185, 212
cycles, vii, 1, 4, 17, 19, 23, 24, 26, 28, 31, 54, 144
cycling, 70
cytoskeleton, 30

D

database, 81, 90, 143, 220
deaths, 75, 84, 98, 172
declarative memory, 134, 146
defects, 212

deficiency(ies), 13, 59, 75, 82, 83, 160, 205, 208, 210, 211
deficit, 47, 83, 88, 89, 124, 214
degradation, 42
delirium, 207, 209
delirium tremens, 207, 209
Delta, 48, 51
dementia, 210
demographic characteristics, 69
demographic factors, 71
demyelinating disease, 210
dendritic spines, 213
dependent variable, 221
depression, ix, 58, 62, 64, 67, 70, 72, 74, 76, 78, 81, 88, 89, 90, 122, 124, 154, 155, 162, 187, 193, 194, 205, 206, 207, 217
deprivation, 16, 23, 24, 25, 26, 27, 28, 29, 30, 34, 35, 39, 49, 54, 56, 57, 58, 81, 118, 161
depth, 146
desensitization, 14
detection, ix, 143, 187, 190, 196
detoxification(s), vii, 1, 3, 25, 26, 30, 32, 39, 48
developing brain, 56, 58, 131, 144, 145, 212
developmental change, 144
developmental process, 131, 132
DFT, 174
diabetes, 62, 152, 161
diabetes insipidus, 161
Diagnostic and Statistical Manual of Mental Disorders, viii, 7, 33, 61, 62, 129, 142, 152, 161, 188
diagnostic criteria, 2, 6, 38, 62, 67, 68, 71, 72, 80, 88, 93, 95, 189, 190, 199, 220
diarrhea, 208, 211
diet(ing), x, 22, 23, 65, 70, 71, 76, 78, 79, 80, 88, 90, 100, 101, 102, 115, 122, 152, 153, 154, 160, 162, 164, 166, 169, 170, 174, 184, 186, 188, 189, 192, 193, 215
differential diagnosis, ix, 187, 191
differential treatment, 72
diffusion, 131, 143, 207
dilated cardiomyopathy, 210
dimensionality, 227
directionality, 74
disability, 121
discomfort, 112, 171
discrimination, 72, 133
diseases, 95
dissatisfaction, 72, 85, 174, 185
dissociation, 43, 229
distress, viii, ix, 62, 63, 64, 67, 68, 69, 70, 85, 97, 99, 110, 111, 112, 113, 114, 115, 116, 117, 121, 151, 152, 185, 188, 218, 225

distribution, 16, 42, 43, 60, 84, 161, 203
diuretic, 211
diversity, 80, 110
dizygotic, 159
dizziness, 171
dogs, 103
dopamine, vii, x, 2, 10, 12, 18, 26, 27, 33, 34, 35, 36, 37, 39, 40, 41, 42, 44, 45, 49, 51, 52, 53, 54, 55, 56, 57, 59, 60, 75, 79, 81, 82, 83, 84, 86, 87, 88, 91, 93, 94, 155, 166, 202, 209
dopaminergic, 9, 34, 38, 41, 42, 44, 48, 52, 57
dorsolateral prefrontal cortex, 147
double-blind trial, 164
down-regulation, 25, 157, 209
drawing, viii, 61, 225
drinking pattern(s), 40, 131, 133, 140, 213
drug abuse, 7, 8, 10, 15, 40, 43, 206, 227
drug addiction, 41, 93, 167, 226
drug consumption, 132
drug dependence, 21, 119, 124, 141
drug withdrawal, 60
drugs, x, 8, 9, 12, 17, 18, 19, 21, 36, 55, 77, 78, 79, 125, 131, 141, 156, 202, 204, 205, 207, 209
DSM, 68, 152, 154, 188, 190, 195
DSM-IV-TR, 7, 62, 63, 64, 65, 68, 69, 79, 188, 196, 197, 218, 220
duodenum, 157, 158
dysarthria, 205
dyslipidemia, 62
dysphoria, 3, 218

E

EAE, 18, 33
eating behavior, viii, 61, 67, 71, 77, 86, 90, 97, 98, 99, 100, 101, 102, 103, 107, 109, 110, 111, 112, 113, 114, 115, 116, 122, 123, 152, 154, 155, 156, 157, 158, 160, 162, 185, 188, 189, 194, 195, 199, 200
eating disturbances, 76
ecology, 41
edema, 211
EDI-2, 173
EDNOS, 63, 69, 84, 93, 152, 188
education, 220
EEG, 46, 138
electrolyte, 172, 211
electrophoresis, 32
EMCDDA, 141
emergency, 36
emission, 36, 59, 156
emotion, 73, 85, 112, 121, 147, 219, 227
emotional deficits, vii, 1

emotional distress, 112, 113
emotional experience, 119
emotional state, 21, 154
emotional stimuli, 6
emotionality, 119
empirical studies, 101
employment, 138, 220
employment status, 220
enamel, 172
encephalopathy, 207, 210
encoding, 42, 47, 134, 138, 149, 159
endocrine system, 211
endorphins, 15
enemas, 65
energy, 30, 155, 157, 158, 159, 160, 162, 163, 165, 167, 208, 214, 215
energy expenditure, 214, 215
England, 53
enkephalins, 15
environment(s), ix, 21, 104, 121, 151, 155, 160, 167, 183, 206
environmental factors, ix, 151, 155, 159
environmental influences, 166
environmental stress, 153, 155, 227
enzyme induction, 204
enzyme(s), 203, 204, 205, 209, 211, 212, 215
epidemic, ix, 75, 88, 89, 117, 151, 153, 168, 188
epidemiologic, 128, 130, 140, 211
epidemiologic studies, 211
epidemiology, 226
epilepsy, 146
episodic memory, 134, 136
epistasis, 51
ERPs, 138
esophagus, x, 202, 208, 212
ethanol, 2, 10, 22, 23, 24, 29, 33, 34, 35, 36, 37, 38, 39, 40, 41, 42, 43, 44, 45, 46, 47, 48, 49, 50, 51, 52, 53, 54, 55, 56, 57, 58, 81, 83, 144, 145, 202, 203, 204, 205, 206, 208, 212, 213, 214, 215
ethanol metabolism, 203, 204
ethnic background, 174
ethnic groups, 174
ethnicity, viii, 61, 64, 67, 71, 72, 78, 90, 92, 169, 220
ethyl alcohol, 202
etiology, ix, 151, 154, 159, 164, 165
EU, 141
euphoria, 3, 105, 106, 202
Europe, x, 3, 47, 141, 145, 202, 206, 214
European, 141
event-related potential, 138, 149, 150
everyday life, 134
evidence, vii, viii, ix, 1, 4, 6, 7, 10, 11, 12, 13, 15, 16, 19, 25, 26, 27, 32, 33, 40, 52, 53, 54, 57, 60, 65, 67, 69, 77, 83, 92, 97, 109, 123, 127, 134, 140, 141, 151, 153, 154, 156, 158, 160, 167, 170, 171, 208, 209, 211, 218, 219, 224, 226, 227
evolution, viii, ix, 127, 128, 140, 195
excess body weight, 157
excitability, 46
excitation, 7, 17, 36
excitotoxicity, 36
exclusion, 68
excretion, 203
executive function(s), viii, 4, 127, 136, 137, 144
executive functioning, 136, 137
executive processes, 13, 134
exercise, 63, 64, 65, 69, 77, 178
exposure, xi, 7, 8, 9, 10, 12, 13, 14, 16, 19, 21, 22, 23, 24, 26, 27, 28, 31, 32, 34, 35, 36, 39, 40, 41, 48, 49, 52, 54, 56, 79, 80, 87, 104, 106, 107, 108, 109, 120, 122, 123, 124, 125, 131, 132, 145, 156, 157, 164, 184, 206, 209, 217, 229
externalizing behavior, 194
externalizing disorders, 139, 227
extraction, 27
eye-tracking, 117

F

face validity, viii, 2, 23
facial expression, 3, 58
factor analysis, 175, 176, 186, 196, 227
families, 13, 195
family history, 2, 4, 7, 33, 139, 226
family life, 188
family members, 155, 194
famine, 66
fasting, 63, 65, 157, 188, 203
fat, 86, 106, 119, 158, 167, 194, 208
fatty acids, 208, 210, 211, 215
FDA, 15
fear, 101, 174, 217
feelings, 7, 110, 114, 154
female rat, 8, 32, 39
fermentation, 212
fetal alcohol syndrome, 212
fetus, x, 202, 212
fiber(s), 60, 131, 136, 137
fibrosis, 210
fights, 128
financial, viii, 127
flame, 185
flexibility, 120, 135
fluctuations, 154, 196
fluid, 25, 26, 172, 211
fluoxetine, 47, 163

folate, 207
folic acid, 211
food cravings, viii, 97, 99, 103, 108, 109, 115, 116
food intake, viii, 43, 65, 86, 91, 95, 97, 99, 100, 101, 102, 105, 106, 108, 109, 114, 119, 121, 123, 126, 153, 155, 157, 158, 159, 160, 161, 162, 164, 166, 168, 189
football, 50
Ford, 57
forebrain, 19, 44, 50, 162
foreign exchange, 173
formation, 131, 136, 154
foundations, 88
fractures, 172
fragments, 17
free radicals, 208
freedom, 190
frontal cortex, 9, 36, 43, 93, 137, 139, 144, 149, 150, 156
frontal lobe, 135, 137, 146
functional analysis, 165
Functional Magnetic Resonance Imaging (fMRI), 6, 73, 82, 137, 146, 147, 148, 149, 156, 163

G

GABA, vii, x, 2, 8, 10, 11, 19, 21, 32, 41, 43, 44, 47, 51, 53, 57, 60, 202, 206, 209, 213
gait, 172, 210
gallbladder, 165
gambling, 9, 121, 123
gastrin, 106, 108
gastritis, x, 202, 207, 208
gastrointestinal bleeding, 211
gastrointestinal tract, 157, 158, 203, 208, 215
gay men, 72
gel, 32
gender differences, 128, 198
gender effects, 148
gender gap, 2
gene expression, 10, 11, 15, 17, 30, 40, 49, 50, 80, 91, 145
generalized anxiety disorder, 221, 222
genes, 22, 30, 38, 50, 55, 159
genetic background, 21, 34
genetic components, 55
genetic factors, vii, 155, 160
genetic marker, 9
genetic predisposition, 23, 52, 154
genetics, 2, 22, 39, 76, 159, 160
genome, 22
genotype, 12, 155
globus, 21

glucagon, 157, 163, 165, 166, 167
glucocorticoids, 17
gluconeogenesis, 208, 211
glucose, 164, 166, 167
glutamate, vii, x, 2, 10, 11, 14, 18, 19, 21, 26, 28, 30, 32, 35, 39, 46, 47, 49, 51, 54, 56, 57, 202, 206, 209
glutamate receptor antagonists, 10
glutamine, 57
glutathione, 208
glycine, 17
goal-directed behavior, 42
grading, 68
graduate students, 220
grants, 33
grazing, 66
grouping, 167
growth, 9, 17, 36, 42, 155, 165, 188, 211, 212
growth hormone, 17, 42, 211
growth spurt, 9
guidelines, 164
guilt, 154
guilty, 63, 69, 152, 189
gynecomastia, 211

H

hair, ix, 169, 170, 171, 172, 173, 174, 175, 177, 178, 180, 181, 183, 184
hair loss, 171, 172, 180
harmful effects, 132, 137, 138
health, viii, 49, 51, 70, 75, 77, 90, 92, 95, 124, 127, 140, 141, 164, 213, 215, 220, 229
Health and Human Services, 60
health care, 90
health problems, 70, 95
health promotion, 215
health services, 70, 124
heart disease, 214, 215
heart rate, 36, 105, 106, 107, 108
heavy drinking, 25, 37, 41, 55, 91, 112, 118, 124, 125, 128, 138, 142
height, 171, 172, 174, 175, 177, 180, 181
hemisphere, 47
hemorrhage, x, 202, 208
hepatitis, 208
hepatitis a, 208
hepatotoxicity, 208
heritability, ix, 151, 155, 159, 164, 226
heroin, 55, 58, 219, 225
heterogeneity, 54
high fat, 106
high school, 2, 6, 45, 49, 215, 220

hippocampus, 11, 16, 17, 21, 39, 40, 44, 132, 136, 145, 146
Hispanics, 73
history, viii, 4, 7, 17, 34, 56, 61, 64, 65, 71, 76, 78, 89, 91, 94, 137, 170, 181, 202, 218, 219, 224, 225
homelessness, 212
homeostasis, 10, 46, 155, 157
homocysteine, 215
hormone(s), 9, 17, 30, 41, 46, 47, 57, 157, 158, 159, 160, 161, 162, 163, 167, 211
host, viii, 61
human, ix, 8, 13, 16, 22, 31, 36, 37, 47, 89, 91, 99, 108, 118, 119, 121, 131, 136, 144, 146, 147, 151, 156, 159, 165, 183, 185
human behavior, 119
human brain, 16, 36, 144, 147, 156, 159
human cerebral cortex, 144
human subjects, 31, 108
Hunter, 125
hydrogen, 203
hyperactivity, 9, 83, 88, 89, 124
hyperarousal, 218
hyperlipidemia, 211
hypertension, 62, 152, 211
hypertrophy, 210
hypoglycemia, 208, 211
hypothalamus, 16, 17, 21, 155, 160, 161
hypothermia, 206
hypothesis, 4, 10, 12, 15, 16, 22, 46, 75, 77, 102, 124, 125, 166, 177, 178, 179, 184, 224, 225
hypothesis test, 177, 178, 179

I

ICS, 26
ideal(s), 72, 170, 184, 185, 189
identification, 181
identity, 172, 174, 179, 182, 183, 184, 185, 218, 224
identity achievement, 174
illicit drug use, 227
illicit substances, 224
image(s), 72, 80, 84, 86, 90, 91, 106, 119, 166, 183, 184, 185
immune function, 212
immunoreactivity, 60
impairments, viii, 58, 75, 101, 102, 125, 127, 139, 145, 188
improvements, 153, 195
impulsive, vii, 1, 4, 16, 31, 75, 82, 100, 115, 219, 224
impulsiveness, 100

impulsivity, 4, 33, 73, 74, 80, 83, 84, 100, 102, 117, 118, 119, 120, 121, 124, 125, 156, 167, 219, 225, 227, 229
in utero, 212
in vitro, 22, 23, 36, 51, 52
in vivo, 49, 117, 120
incidence, 13, 86, 89, 91, 121, 212
income, 152, 220
independence, 41
independent variable, 221
Indians, 149
indirect effect, 223, 224, 228
individual development, 131
individual differences, 8
industry, 79
ineffectiveness, 64
infancy, 143, 188
infants, 143
infection, 211, 212
inferences, 137
inflammation, 208
information processing, 205
ingestion, 9, 12, 17, 41, 113, 114, 153, 156, 164, 203
inhibition, 3, 13, 16, 41, 58, 88, 101, 102, 120, 125, 137, 139, 145, 149, 150, 206, 207
inhibitor, 40
initiation, 29, 43, 93, 125, 157
injections, 48, 123, 144
injure, 208
injury(ies), 172, 180, 185, 208, 210, 213, 215
insomnia, 153
institutions, 130
insulin, 105, 106, 164
integration, viii, 127, 133, 228
integrity, 136, 148
interaction effect, 27
interface, 55
interference, 135, 213
internal consistency, 173, 174, 192, 193, 220
internalization, 189
internalizing, 74, 194
interneurons, 9
interpersonal relationships, 195
intervention, 140, 142, 160, 182
intervention strategies, 140
intoxication, x, 4, 5, 6, 7, 29, 31, 32, 36, 38, 53, 100, 101, 103, 105, 107, 108, 119, 123, 128, 201, 202, 205, 207, 208, 210, 215
investment(s), ix, 140, 169, 171, 172, 173, 175, 177, 178, 179, 180, 182, 203
ion channels, 14, 205, 209
Iowa, 186
irritability, 193

isolation, 155
Israel, 53, 119
issues, 80, 92, 188, 196, 213, 219, 225
Ivan Pavlov, 103

J

Jamaica, 183
Japan, 170, 172, 175, 181, 184, 185, 186
Japanese women, ix, 169, 170, 171, 172, 177, 178, 180, 181, 183, 185
jejunum, 157, 158
juveniles, 8

K

K^+, 205
ketoacidosis, 208
kicks, 50
kinase activity, 30

L

labeling, 71
laboratory studies, 76, 88
lack of control, 62, 63, 65, 68, 69, 71, 151, 189
languages, 196
larynx, 212
latency, 139
Latin America, 89
Latinos, 71, 72
laxatives, 65
lead, x, 11, 14, 22, 67, 75, 77, 79, 99, 101, 102, 110, 111, 112, 113, 114, 115, 116, 128, 153, 156, 157, 160, 182, 188, 202, 205, 209, 212, 218
learning, viii, 12, 82, 103, 116, 117, 122, 125, 127, 132, 134, 135, 138, 149, 206, 210
learning process, 116, 117
learning task, 134, 135
left hemisphere, 136
legs, 206
leptin, 17, 157, 158, 159, 160, 161, 162
lesions, 134, 139, 147, 155, 164
leukocytes, 211
life course, 131
life expectancy, 76
lifetime, viii, 36, 60, 61, 64, 69, 71, 74, 76, 98, 138, 152, 206, 221, 222, 223, 227
light, 6, 7, 41, 44, 47, 62, 120, 133, 134, 135, 138, 139, 170
Likert scale, 174, 192, 193
limbic system, 132

liver, 203, 204, 207, 208, 211, 212, 213, 214, 215
liver cirrhosis, 208
liver disease, 208, 211, 213, 215
liver failure, 208
liver transplantation, 208
localization, 35, 133
loci, 40, 50
locomotor, 44, 45, 51
locus, 16, 21, 57
longitudinal study, 91, 148
long-term memory, 101, 102, 123
low risk, 128
lumen, 158

M

magnesium, 210
magnetic resonance imaging, 33, 73, 91, 131, 137, 144, 148, 149
magnetic resonance spectroscopy, 52
magnitude, 6, 24, 157, 181, 209
major depression, 154
major depressive disorder, 74, 221
majority, 22, 23, 31, 62, 63, 70, 72, 79, 128, 157, 207
malnutrition, 208
maltreatment, 85, 227
mammals, 41
man, 164, 165
management, 184, 195, 215
mapping, 58, 144
marijuana, 41, 46, 148, 149, 156
marital status, 220
marrow, 207
Maryland, 201, 202, 217
mass, 68, 86, 158, 162, 172, 184, 186, 193
mass media, 184
matrix, 58
matter, 22, 31, 66, 68, 90, 131, 132, 136, 137, 148
measurement, 55, 148, 174, 181, 196
media, 143, 155
media messages, 155
median, 33
mediation, x, 17, 43, 213, 217, 221, 223, 224, 228
medical, vii, viii, 2, 21, 58, 61, 77, 80, 87, 90, 152, 153, 188, 202, 208, 214, 215
medication, 13, 53, 77, 125, 153
medicine, 198
melanocyte stimulating hormone, 17
membership, 173
membranes, 203
memory, viii, 12, 47, 52, 78, 93, 101, 102, 127, 132, 134, 136, 138, 145, 146, 147, 206, 209, 210
memory loss, 206

memory performance, 146
menarche, 77
mental disorder, 80, 81, 82, 148, 182, 195, 196, 226
mental health, 70, 71, 84, 164, 196, 229
mental illness, 38
mental retardation, 212
meta-analysis, 122, 166, 167
Metabolic, 84, 126, 160, 161, 162, 163, 166, 203, 207
metabolic disorder(s), 203
metabolism, 30, 41, 163, 167, 203, 204, 207, 208, 209, 210, 213, 214, 215
metabolites, 215
metabolized, 204
metabolizing, 215
methodology, 22, 186
mice, 11, 15, 29, 31, 35, 36, 38, 42, 43, 44, 45, 46, 49, 50, 53, 55, 56, 145, 161, 214
microdialysis, 25, 26, 32, 40, 44
microinjection, 50, 55
microstructure, 131
midbrain, 33, 44
migration, 212
Ministry of Education, 213
minorities, 71
misuse, 43, 65, 111, 118, 139, 141, 143
mitochondria, 205, 210
mitogens, 212
model system, 22, 32
models, vii, ix, 2, 6, 7, 8, 10, 16, 21, 23, 29, 31, 32, 34, 35, 38, 40, 42, 49, 50, 54, 56, 57, 59, 81, 151, 155, 156, 159, 182, 205, 212, 218, 222, 228
moderates, 122
modifications, 132, 137
molecular biology, 22
molecules, 213
momentum, 118
mood disorder, 74, 80, 88, 166
morbidity, x, 81, 82, 85, 121, 202
mortality, viii, 2, 61, 91, 98, 121, 181, 183, 216
mortality rate, 91, 181, 183
mortality risk, viii, 61, 98
motivation, 12, 19, 36, 46, 48, 52, 78, 85, 155, 167
motor control, 171
motor skills, 205
MRI, 131, 136, 137, 144
mRNA, 15, 32, 42, 44, 57, 60
multidimensional, 183
multiple regression analysis, 27
muscarinic receptor, 46
muscles, 210
mutations, 51, 159, 160, 162, 163
myocardium, 210

myopathy, x, 202, 206, 207

N

Na^+, 205
NAD, 203, 204, 208
NADH, 203, 208
National Academy of Sciences, 144
National Survey, 45, 130, 141, 145
Native Americans, 72, 73
natural killer cell, 212
nausea, 205
negative affectivity, 218
negative consequences, 100, 115, 121, 130, 156, 171, 172, 181, 209
negative emotions, 71, 73, 111, 112, 113, 119, 154, 160, 193
negative experiences, 101
negative mood, 110, 111, 122, 154, 160
negative outcomes, 128, 217
negative reinforcement, 4, 10, 11, 12, 111, 112, 113, 114
nerve, 50, 210
nervous system, 10, 42, 59, 144, 205, 209, 212
Netherlands, 81
neural function, 138
neural network(s), 132, 146, 162
neural system(s), 155, 156
neurobiology, vii, 1, 8, 18, 32, 45, 57
neurodegeneration, 41
neurogenesis, 9, 41, 51, 132, 145
neuroimaging, 136, 137, 138, 139, 156
neuronal circuits, 47, 93
neurons, 12, 13, 15, 17, 19, 33, 36, 39, 41, 42, 44, 46, 48, 49, 51, 52, 53, 54, 57, 155, 160, 213
neuropeptides, 157, 161
neurophysiology, 149
neuroscience, 150
neurotransmission, 10, 11, 12, 13, 14, 17, 20, 25, 30, 32, 51, 56, 206, 209
neurotransmitter(s), x, 9, 10, 11, 13, 14, 17, 18, 21, 30, 31, 32, 34, 58, 145, 202, 205, 206, 209
neutral, 103, 104, 105
neutral stimulus, 103
New England, 162, 163
New Zealand, 123, 229
nicotinamide, 203
nicotine, 14, 15, 35, 37, 39, 43, 45, 46, 47, 48, 51, 52, 55, 77
nitric oxide, 215
NMDA receptors, 213
NMR, 144
non-clinical population, 129

non-smokers, 82
norepinephrine, 10
North America, 3, 125
Norway, 123, 159
nuclei, 17, 21, 26, 28, 33, 44, 160
nucleus, 4, 11, 13, 18, 19, 21, 28, 30, 34, 35, 36, 40, 41, 42, 43, 44, 45, 46, 47, 48, 49, 51, 53, 55, 57, 60, 66, 80, 155, 166
nurturance, 188, 195
nutrient(s), 157, 158, 160, 164
nutrition, 197
nutritional deficiencies, 212
nutritional status, 33

O

obesity, viii, ix, 55, 61, 62, 64, 70, 74, 75, 76, 77, 78, 80, 81, 82, 83, 84, 85, 86, 87, 88, 89, 90, 91, 92, 93, 94, 117, 151, 152, 153, 155, 156, 159, 160, 161, 162, 163, 165, 166, 167, 168, 182, 187, 188, 189, 194, 195, 196, 198, 200, 211
occipital cortex, 138
oil, 87
oncogenes, 30
opiates, x, 125, 156, 202, 207
opioids, 10, 15, 32, 79, 89, 205, 209
opportunities, 59
optic nerve, 210
organ(s), x, 53, 202, 203, 207, 208
organize, 134, 135
outpatient, 95, 195
outpatients, 90, 91, 218, 228
overlap, 76, 120
oversight, 68
overtime, 31
overweight, viii, ix, 61, 62, 68, 70, 72, 73, 74, 75, 76, 78, 84, 85, 86, 88, 89, 90, 92, 94, 100, 107, 121, 151, 152, 153, 154, 156, 157, 164, 168, 189, 190, 192, 193, 194, 195, 197, 198, 199
oxidation, 203, 204, 208, 215
oxidative stress, 208, 213, 214, 215
oxygen, 137, 148, 149

P

Pacific, 73, 78
Pacific Islanders, 73, 78
pain, 70, 77, 153, 172, 180, 206
pairing, 103, 109
pancreatitis, x, 202, 207, 208, 213, 215
panic disorder, 74, 154
parallel, vii, 1, 6, 8, 31
paralysis, 210
parenchyma, 208
parental attitudes, 196
parental control, 194
parents, 53, 154, 190, 192, 194, 195
paresthesias, 210
parietal cortex, 132
participants, 68, 100, 103, 107, 130, 136, 152, 159, 172, 175, 221, 222
patents, 34
pathogenesis, 153
pathology, 35, 42, 46, 71, 72, 84, 93, 186, 192
pathophysiological, vii, 215
pathophysiology, ix, 151, 157, 158, 215
pathways, viii, 9, 97, 99, 103, 113, 114, 115, 117, 118, 136, 156, 165, 203, 209, 219
PCR, 32
pellagra, 207
penicillin, 214
peptide(s), vii, 2, 10, 15, 17, 18, 27, 157, 159, 160, 161, 162, 163, 164, 165, 166, 167
perfectionism, 64
periodicity, 5
personal history, 139
personality, 36, 37, 64, 75, 76, 85, 91, 118, 120, 123, 124, 154, 167, 206, 218, 223, 224, 225, 226, 227, 228
personality disorder(s), 75, 76, 85, 91, 154, 206, 218, 223, 226, 227, 228
personality factors, 226
personality measures, 64
personality traits, 118, 227
pharmaceuticals, 156
pharmacological treatment, 10, 15, 31
pharmacology, 59, 214
pharmacotherapy, 39, 40, 166
pharynx, 212
phencyclidine, 36
phenotype(s), 11, 12, 16, 22, 41, 40, 50, 80, 83, 87, 142, 155, 156, 162
phobia, 221
phospholipids, 210
physical abuse, 217, 221, 223, 224, 225, 228
physical activity, 153, 195
physical health, viii, 61, 77
physical inactivity, 76
Physiological, 46, 162, 167
physiology, 56, 167
pilot study, 196
placebo, 105, 122, 123, 124, 164
placenta, 212
plasma levels, 157, 164
plasma membrane, 213

plasticity, 30, 35, 46, 49, 58, 213
platelets, 211
platform, 185
plausibility, 81
pleasure, 75, 155, 156
pneumonia, 212
Poland, 36
policy, 143
polymerase chain reaction, 32
polymorphism, 7, 13, 48, 57, 165
polypeptide, 30, 37, 106, 164, 167
population, xi, 7, 37, 46, 50, 58, 70, 74, 76, 81, 82, 84, 85, 86, 89, 90, 108, 109, 123, 128, 129, 136, 138, 140, 141, 146, 152, 156, 162, 166, 211, 217, 226
portal hypertension, 211
Portugal, 127, 129
positive correlation, 193
positive mood, 120
positive reinforcement, 4, 12
positron emission tomography (PEY), 55, 147, 156
posttraumatic stress, 226, 227, 228, 229
post-traumatic stress disorder (PTSD), x, 217, 218, 218, 219, 220, 221, 222, 223, 224, 225, 226, 227
potassium, 210, 211
praxis, 133
predictive validity, 3
prefrontal cortex, 8, 18, 35, 38, 39, 40, 41, 44, 52, 55, 57, 58, 59, 131, 134, 136, 147, 148
pregnancy, x, 155, 202, 212
preparation, 149
preparedness, 124
prevalence rate, 130
prevention, 49, 56, 114, 115, 116, 117, 122, 124, 140, 142, 143, 195, 196, 215
primate, 146
priming, 48, 123, 160
prisoners, 227
probability, 14, 31, 38
probands, 41, 124
problem drinking, 59, 121, 122
problematic alcohol use, x, 77, 98, 99, 104, 202, 206
problem-solving task, 102
procurement, 9, 18
prolactin, 39
proliferation, 18, 132, 211
protein synthesis, 211
proteins, 28, 30, 205
proteomics, 30
pruning, 9, 18, 132
psychiatric disorders, 21, 76, 207
psychiatric morbidity, 162
psychiatry, 49, 184, 196

psychological distress, 67, 68, 84, 87
psychological instruments, ix, 187
psychological problems, 77, 98
psychological stress, 111
psychology, 92, 182, 198
psychometric properties, 193, 194
psychopathology, 33, 35, 64, 67, 68, 75, 84, 86, 88, 93, 94, 123, 124, 189, 190, 191, 192, 193, 194, 195, 197, 200, 227, 228, 229
psychosis, 209, 210
psychosocial cofactors, viii, 61
psychosocial transition, 131
psychotherapy, 168
puberty, 132
public health, vii, viii, 1, 22, 31, 61, 70, 141, 214
punishment, 101
pyramidal cells, 58

Q

quality of life, 51, 76, 87, 90
questionnaire, 58, 90, 123, 173, 174, 183, 184, 185, 191, 192, 193, 194, 197, 198, 199, 220, 229

R

race, 90, 91, 220
racial minorities, 183
rash, 120
rating scale, 194
reactivity, 114, 117, 119, 122
reading, 133
reality, 51, 84
reasoning, 11, 134, 209
reasoning skills, 11, 209
recall(ing), 101, 102, 103, 134, 154
receptors, 10, 11, 13, 14, 15, 16, 17, 18, 19, 21, 33, 34, 37, 39, 40, 41, 42, 43, 44, 45, 48, 49, 50, 51, 52, 53, 54, 56, 60, 83, 86, 93, 156, 160, 205, 209
recidivism, 152
recognition, 58, 133, 183, 213
recommendations, 68, 175, 195
recovery, 225
recurrence, 154
regression, 27, 222, 223
regression line, 27
regression model, 222
rehabilitation, x, 217
reinforcement, 3, 4, 9, 12, 15, 49, 73, 113, 121, 170
reinforcers, 32, 66, 156
relapses, 195
relatives, 154, 160

relaxation, 104, 105, 206
relevance, viii, 127, 215
reliability, 93, 174, 184, 186, 191, 192, 194, 195, 198
relief, 111, 112, 113, 114, 205
religion, 183
remission, 57, 229
replication, 122, 164
requirements, 69, 152, 188
researchers, ix, 62, 64, 68, 117, 118, 157, 171, 187, 218, 225
resistance, 207
resolution, 32
resources, 75, 100, 115, 138, 139, 171, 180, 203
respiration, 58
response, 3, 7, 14, 36, 38, 47, 52, 53, 56, 60, 66, 67, 68, 82, 88, 91, 103, 104, 105, 107, 111, 120, 122, 123, 133, 135, 137, 138, 139, 145, 147, 148, 149, 150, 154, 156, 157, 158, 164, 173, 189, 193, 195, 212
responsiveness, 145
restrictions, 100
resveratrol, 215
retardation, 155
reticulum, 204, 210, 215
rewards, 9, 18, 19, 32, 73, 75
ribonucleic acid, 32
risk factors, x, 5, 36, 37, 43, 76, 83, 108, 110, 118, 182, 188, 189, 190, 225, 228
risks, ix, 18, 153, 169, 180, 182
RMSEA, 175, 177
rodents, 13, 16, 41, 49
root(s), 175, 183
Royal Society, 93, 146, 148, 166
rules, 100, 191

S

saccharin, 45, 51, 58, 82
salivary gland(s), 172
SAS, 228
Scandinavia, 85
school, 2, 45, 193, 194
science, 118, 184
scientific theory, 118
scope, 8, 29, 140
secrete, 158
secretion, 106, 108, 120, 157, 158, 159, 208
sedative(s), x, 46, 202, 205, 206, 209
seizure, 46
selective attention, 66, 121
selective serotonin reuptake inhibitor, 153
selectivity, 27
self-awareness, 72, 102, 121

self-concept, 184
self-control, 194
self-efficacy, 76, 82, 88, 162
self-esteem, 72, 85, 184
self-monitoring, 135, 136, 195
self-ordering, 135
self-perceptions, 184
self-regulation, 118, 119, 135, 136
self-report data, 77
self-reports, 143, 189, 190
self-worth, 195
seminiferous tubules, 37
sensation(s), 157, 158, 165, 209
senses, 65
sensitivity, 6, 33, 39, 40, 41, 43, 54, 56, 57, 73, 90, 101, 125, 156, 157, 158, 166, 192, 213
sensitization, 51
Serbia, 201, 213
serotonin, vii, x, 2, 9, 10, 13, 32, 39, 50, 52, 53, 57, 60, 202, 209
sertraline, 165
serum, 39, 106, 108, 158, 211, 215
services, 36
sex, viii, 9, 18, 32, 61, 64, 67, 70, 71, 72, 140, 146, 159, 193, 220, 221, 222
sex differences, 67, 71, 140
sex hormones, 9
sexual abuse, x, 217, 218, 219, 221, 223, 224, 225, 226, 228, 229
sexual assaults, 98
sexual orientation, 71, 72
shame, 154
shape, 64, 68, 73, 85, 86, 132, 163, 170, 178, 180, 185, 189, 191
shock, 205
showing, 152, 154, 159
siblings, 53
side effects, 172
signal transduction, 209
signaling pathway, 205
signals, 73, 157, 162, 167, 193
signs, ix, 4, 25, 79, 140, 187, 209, 210
Sinai, 151
skin, 105, 106, 107, 108, 181, 185, 186
small intestine, 158, 208
smoking, x, 53, 77, 78, 83, 87, 89, 90, 93, 94, 109, 120, 153, 156, 202
smoking cessation, 78, 89, 94
smooth muscle, 206
snacking, 66
SNP, 159
social cognition, 144
social competence, 194, 195

social context, 142
social desirability, 103
social environment, 71
social influence, 155
social learning, 119, 121
social perception, 186
social phobia, 221
social problems, 194
social support, 72
societal cost, 202
society, 148, 202
socioeconomic status, 90
solution, 22, 81
somatization, 229
South America, x, 202, 206
Spain, 127, 187
species, 8
speech, 205
Spring, 186
stability, 182, 185, 191, 193
stabilization, 195
standard deviation, 177, 178, 179
standard error, 221
state(s), 10, 11, 13, 14, 59, 82, 83, 90, 92, 100, 104, 107, 109, 115, 117, 118, 123, 138, 153, 154, 184, 193, 203, 210
stem cells, 51
steroids, 39
stimulant, 46
stimulation, 6, 7, 12, 41, 44, 45, 51, 57
stimulus, 44, 79, 103, 104, 105, 121, 133, 138, 153, 195
stock, 22
stomach, 17, 157, 158, 161, 165, 174, 203, 214
stress, 21, 35, 43, 48, 55, 56, 58, 72, 104, 121, 123, 154, 193, 200, 208, 215, 218, 223, 229
stress response, 43
stressors, 111
striatum, 4, 21, 50, 51, 66, 86, 91, 101, 156
structural modifications, 137
structure, 33, 42, 44, 47, 132, 175, 177, 181, 184, 193, 194
stupor, 205
style(s), 171, 178, 195, 197
subgroups, 91
subjective experience, 189
substance abuse, x, 36, 37, 56, 71, 217, 218, 219, 220, 226, 227, 228, 229
Substance Abuse and Mental Health Services Administration (SAMHSA), 2, 6, 55, 141
substance use, 2, 37, 59, 74, 75, 77, 78, 80, 83, 87, 92, 118, 123, 126, 142, 218, 219, 221, 223, 224, 225, 226, 227, 228, 229

substrate(s), 41, 80, 163, 215
sucrose, 15, 37, 44, 81, 215
SUD, 223
suicidal behavior, 225
suicide, 219, 227
Sun, 10, 57, 148
suppression, 45, 166, 193
survival, 9, 167
survivors, 227
susceptibility, 10, 135, 159, 208
Sweden, 142
swelling, 158, 206
symptomology, 11
symptoms, ix, 4, 43, 46, 50, 67, 68, 69, 70, 74, 79, 81, 83, 87, 89, 90, 116, 120, 121, 123, 163, 172, 174, 178, 180, 182, 185, 187, 189, 190, 194, 197, 206, 218, 220, 227, 228
synapse, 49, 58
synaptic plasticity, 30
synaptic strength, 39
synaptic transmission, 8, 46, 51, 59
syndrome, 75, 82, 83, 87, 124, 155, 189, 195, 205, 207, 209, 210, 212, 227
synthesis, 208, 213

T

T cell, 212
target, 12, 13, 14, 15, 17, 40, 43, 52, 53, 139, 179, 195, 225
target behavior, 195
target stimuli, 139
target variables, 179
task demands, 139
Task Force, 64
task performance, 101, 138
techniques, 136, 153, 155, 156, 195
technology(ies), 117, 156
teenage girls, 83
teeth, 79
telephone, 134
temperature, 105, 107
tension, 107
teratology, 38
terminals, 14, 50
testing, 117, 170, 184, 198, 219
test-retest reliability, 193, 194, 229
textbook, 119
texture, 170
thalamus, 21, 148
therapeutics, 46
therapy, 14, 48, 94, 153, 161, 163, 185, 197, 198, 210, 211

thiamin, 210
thiamin deficiency, 210
thoughts, 36
thyroid, 167
time frame, 58, 129, 143
tissue, 12, 131, 158, 203, 212, 214
TLR4, 48
tobacco, viii, 61, 74, 77, 86
tonic, 11, 41
top-down, 52
toxic effect, 208
toxicity, 207, 212
trafficking, 57
training, 195
traits, x, 22, 82, 121, 125, 187, 219
trajectory, 3, 56, 142
transcription, 15, 30, 32
transcription factors, 30
transition to adulthood, 132
translation, vii, 2
transmission, 40, 43, 46, 131, 189
transport, 19, 30
trauma, xi, 217, 218, 226, 227, 228, 229
traumatic events, 218
trial, 64, 86, 165, 199
tricyclic antidepressant(s), 153
tuberculosis, 212
tumor(s), 155, 212
tumor necrosis factor, 212
type 1 diabetes, 197
type 2 diabetes, 75

U

UK, 50, 53, 129, 141, 143
ulcer, 207
unconditioned response, 103, 104, 105
unconditioned, 103, 104, 105, 107, 109, 121, 125
underlying mechanisms, 98
United States (US), 1, 2, 7, 31, 39, 41, 43, 48, 50, 88, 89, 92, 97, 117, 121, 129, 130, 136, 141, 144, 157, 170, 172, 180, 184, 208
urban population, 213
urban, 213
urine, 203

V

vaccine, 42
Valencia, 187
validation, 29, 68, 80, 85, 91, 119, 120, 122, 124, 166, 181, 183, 184, 186, 193, 226

valuation, 32
variables, viii, 6, 61, 90, 95, 128, 130, 142, 169, 172, 181, 182, 212, 222, 224
variations, vii, 132, 136
vasodilation, 206
vasodilator, 206
vasomotor, 206
vehicles, 205
ventricular arrhythmias, 210
verbal fluency, 147
victimization, 227
victims, 218, 225
visual acuity, 210
visual attention, 119
vomiting, 65, 124, 152, 188, 205, 211
vulnerability, 9, 33, 36, 40, 73, 76, 139, 188, 192, 213, 227

W

Washington, 33, 45, 46, 80, 81, 92, 120, 142, 161, 182, 196, 220, 226, 227
water, 9, 22, 23, 24, 25, 26, 27, 28, 29, 46, 144, 202, 203, 204
water diffusion, 144
weakness, 206, 211, 226
wear, 170, 173
weight control, 64, 66, 78, 88, 90, 93, 191
weight gain, 65, 78, 89, 94, 157, 192, 196
weight loss, ix, 70, 76, 91, 95, 152, 162, 173, 182, 187, 190, 197, 208
weight management, 86, 152, 195
weight reduction, 194
weight status, 77
well-being, 3, 202
Western blot, 32
western culture, ix, 169
white matter, 131, 132, 133, 136, 137, 143, 148
windows, 8, 33
Wisconsin, 135
withdrawal, 3, 4, 10, 11, 14, 21, 22, 28, 30, 39, 51, 59, 78, 79, 94, 104, 105, 107, 109, 115, 116, 132, 136, 145, 209, 210, 211, 213, 214, 221
withdrawal symptoms, 22, 209, 221
working memory, 11, 38, 101, 102, 124, 132, 134, 137, 138, 139, 149
World Health Organization, 79, 95
worldwide, vii, x, 1, 89, 202, 206

Y

young adults, vii, x, 1, 6, 23, 31, 37, 41, 45, 49, 87, 91, 122, 130, 136, 141, 148, 185, 188, 201, 206

young people, viii, 42, 127, 128, 131, 132, 136, 137, 140, 214

young women, x, 84, 91, 137, 148, 182, 202, 212